Disney Channel T

ALSO EDITED BY CHRISTOPHER E. BELL

Transmedia Harry Potter:
Essays on Storytelling Across Platforms (2019)

Inside the World of Harry Potter:
Critical Essays on the Books and Films (2018)

Wizards vs. Muggles: Essays on Identity
and the Harry Potter Universe (2016)

From Here to Hogwarts:
Essays on Harry Potter Fandom and Fiction (2016)

Hermione Granger Saves the World:
Essays on the Feminist Heroine of Hogwarts (2012)

American Idolatry: Celebrity, Commodity
and Reality Television (2010)

Disney Channel Tween Programming

Essays on Shows from
Lizzie McGuire *to* Andi Mack

Edited by CHRISTOPHER E. BELL

McFarland & Company, Inc., Publishers
Jefferson, North Carolina

LIBRARY OF CONGRESS CATALOGUING-IN-PUBLICATION DATA

Names: Bell, Christopher E., 1974– editor.
Title: Disney Channel tween programming : essays on shows from Lizzie McGuire
    to Andi Mack / edited by Christopher E. Bell.
Description: Jefferson : McFarland & Company, Inc.,
    Publishers, 2020. | Includes bibliographical references and index.
Identifiers: LCCN 2020032651 | ISBN 9781476681948 (paperback : acid free
    paper ♾)
    ISBN 9781476639635 (ebook)
Subjects: LCSH: Preteens on television. | Disney Channel (Firm)
Classification: LCC PN1992.8.P74 D57 2020 | DDC 791.45/3522—dc23
LC record available at https://lccn.loc.gov/2020032651

BRITISH LIBRARY CATALOGUING DATA ARE AVAILABLE

ISBN (print) 978-1-4766-8194-8
ISBN (ebook) 978-1-4766-3963-5

Front cover images © 2020 Shutterstock

Printed in the United States of America

*McFarland & Company, Inc., Publishers
  Box 611, Jefferson, North Carolina 28640
  www.mcfarlandpub.com*

For Liv and Megan:
Like *Liv and Maddie*, only different.

Table of Contents

Introduction

A Road Map to the Disney Channel Universe

CHRISTOPHER E. BELL, MARISSA LAMMON,
ANGELA M. GUIDO *and* JULIE ESTLICK

The Walt Disney Company occupies a powerful position in the realm of American popular culture, particularly in terms of its content for children. Academic studies of Disney content tend to focus more on films (Padilla-Walker, Coyne, Fraser, & Stockdale, 2013; Holcomb, Lathan, & Fernandez-Baca, 2015; Nielsen, Patel, & Rosner, 2013; Van Wormer & Juby, 2016; Garlen & Sandlin, 2017), with more particular attention paid to the Disney princesses (Azmi, Ab Rashid, Rahman, & Safawati, 2016; Coyne, Linder, Rasmussen, Nelson & Birkbeck, 2016; Dale, Higgins, Pinkerton, Couto, Mansolillo, Weisinger, & Flores, 2016) than most other character types.

While Disney films are more well known to audiences, Disney's television programs have been growing in popularity. In 2015, the Disney Channel edged out Nickelodeon to become the most popular cable TV network, especially with children ages 6–11 (Kissell, 2015). With a large variety of shows, Disney has created another separate universe from that of the big screen. This "television universe" has not been analyzed in the same way Disney's films have been. By examining Disney television shows and understanding their messages, parents can learn more about what their children are really watching.

While many works exist on the nature of the Walt Disney Company, particularly its animated films, few works hone in explicitly on the relationship between the Disney Channel and its specific audience. By the turn of the millennium, the Disney Channel had identified and explicitly began to program toward an audience of 9- to 12-year-olds, particularly girls. This volume is intended to not only provide a history of the Disney Channel's

1

tween programming, but also to provide a series of essays demonstrating how one might critique the individual programs and enter into discussion about the audience impact of each show. It is both historical and critical in nature, highlighting both the positive and negative impacts the Disney Channel's programming may have had on its intellectually developing audience. The collection begins with a top-down view of the Disney Channel using quantitative data culled from nearly 600 hours of viewing and coding of the Disney Channel's signature programs. The collection then rolls chronologically through 15 of the Disney Channel's most major programmatic offerings, offering an example of critique for each. Coupling textual analysis with the empirical data taken from viewing, this collection draws together critique and the numbers into a coherent and cohesive examination of the universe the Disney Channel has created for its tween audience.

The Walt Disney Company

Disney is not just a brand; it is a universe. The Walt Disney Company has created a universe filled with products, films, television shows, theme parks and resorts. In 1936, the company granted over 70 licenses to produce clothing, food, toys, books, phonograph records, and sheet music (Wasko, 2013), and this ability to replicate its products intertextually has been a hallmark of its commercial success. As a transnational media corporation, the ultimate goal of Disney is to make money. This is a practical mission for any company; Disney's own mission statement reads:

> The mission of The Walt Disney Company is to be one of the world's leading producers and providers of entertainment and information. Using our portfolio of brands to differentiate our content, services and consumer products, we seek to develop the most creative, innovative and profitable entertainment experiences and related products in the world ["The Walt Disney Company," n.d.].

Since its very first feature-length film, this profitability has been, in large part, due to Disney's success in selling products to girls. Disney's first animated feature film, *Snow White and the Seven Dwarfs* (1938), was a box office hit, grossing $8.5 million within the first three months of its premiere (Wasko, 2013). In the context of the film, Snow White is supposed to be 14 years old; the first Disney princess is also the youngest Disney princess. This film was the progenitor of a phenomenon; the Walt Disney Company quickly realized they could make a significant amount of money selling fairy tale princesses to very young girls. As of 2016, there are twelve "official" Disney princesses, as featured on princess.disney.com: Ariel, Aurora, Belle, Cinderella, Elena of Avalor, Jasmine, Merida, Mulan, Pocahontas, Rapunzel, Snow White, and

Tiana (princess.disney.com). When adjusted for inflation, the 12 official Disney princess films have grossed a combined $8,360,469,327 at the box office (which does not include the additional $414 million "unofficial princess" monster hit *Frozen)* ("BoxOfficeMojo" n.d.). Seven of the twelve princesses are white, four of the twelve are age sixteen or younger, eight of the twelve are age eighteen or younger.

In 2016, linguists Carmen Fought and Karen Eisenhauer found that, in Disney princess films, women tend to speak far less than men, particularly in the "renaissance" Disney films (*The Little Mermaid, Beauty and the Beast, Aladdin, Pocahontas,* and *Mulan)* (Guo, 2016). Quantity of speech is not the only problem, though; as Fought points out: "We don't believe that little girls naturally play a certain way or speak a certain way…. They're not born liking a pink dress. At some point we teach them. So a big question is where girls get their ideas about being girls" (Guo, 2016). Clearly, one of those places where girls get their ideas about being girls is from the Walt Disney Company (Baker-Sperry, 2007; Craven, 2002; DoRozario, 2004).

Disney's Live Action Tween Programming

With a substantial amount of revenue originating from their success in the creation and marketing of the Disney princess, the Walt Disney Company continued its reign in the entertainment industry through their unique animation techniques. As a successful contender in the media outlet, the Walt Disney Company received an ample amount of scrutiny for their realism pursuits and deviations from the monotonous approaches to animation uncontrolled by convention (Jenkins, 2013). Unlike their competitors, Disney animators were particularly driven by a set of realistic principles (Telotte, 2007) and aimed to produce animation that reflected characters with pragmatic movements and motivations (Pallant, 2010).

These realistic approaches Disney employed in animation soon transitioned to a transient stage of the hybrid approach to theatre, including a distinguishable combination of animation and live-action. Over a four-year timespan in the late 1920s, Disney produced over 50 short films that exemplified the hybrid technique, featuring a young girl navigating through quixotic, cartoon adventures (Telotte, 2007). Disney's incorporation of live-action allowed for fewer staff and rapid production and produced a new approach, espousing live-action cinema while retaining its unique characteristics of animation (Jenkins, 2013). The company underwent several transitions in which it abandoned live-action programming only to reuse it again during times of economic and stylistic opportunity (Telotte, 2007), including contemporary media.

A large portion of Disney's success today stems from live-action programming, primarily due to the engagement and connection of their young audiences with the talent portrayed in each series (DeBenedittis as cited in Graser, 2013). Arguably, the eruption of Disney's live-action programming over the past ten years derives from marketing toward the tween audience (Northup & Liebler, 2010). As the top network for adolescents ages 9 through 14 (Northup & Liebler, 2010), the Disney Channel has been exploiting the commercial value of the tween audience through program production aimed at the demographic most influenced by cultural values and social trends (Bakir, Palan, & Kolbe, 2013).

Although "tween" is widely used today to describe children who are not kids and yet not quite adults, the term first appeared in the 1940s and has since occupied a variety of different definitions both culturally and academically (Cook & Kaiser, 2004). According to *Collins English Dictionary* (2012), the term "tween" or, more specifically, "tweenager," is the marriage of the word "between" and "teenager." It is commonly used to refer to a child 9 to 14 years of age and has replaced the word "preadolescent" to describe children in this age bracket. With disparity in age ranges as well as changes in marketing practices shifting content to younger audiences, the "tween" also embodies a particular state of mind and behaviors (Prince & Martin, 2011). The definitions continue to grow in complexity with the rise of the Kids Grow Old Younger (KGOY) phenomenon that suggests media influences a younger group of audiences into maturation at a faster rate than previous generations (Cook & Kaiser, 2004; Prince & Martin, 2011). Despite such claims, to dismiss this stage of youth as "children who are growing up too fast" is to miss an opportunity to understand the ever-changing phenomenon of the tween. This group adheres to social and cultural practices that allow them to define new ways of being, all while staying young in the world (Tomaz, 2014). The nature of tweens must be examined in order to understand how they are being targeted by media, as well as what social conceptions tweens are developing from media consumption.

Early advertisers realized tweens had an enormous influence on the spending habits of the family. Children 9 to 14 represented a unique variant of individuals that were vulnerable to the messages in advertisements and able to convince their parents to purchase the items that they saw in commercials. As early as the 1940s and '50s, car and cosmetic companies began to capitalize on this new market of the tween consumer (Cook & Kaiser, 2004). Disney's Tinkerbell dominated the part of the cosmetic industry in the 1950s that marketed products to girls between the ages of four to ten. They sold fun props that allowed little girls to play dress up instead of raiding Mommy's make-up drawer, but as the tween evolved, so did Tinkerbell. The modern Tinkerbell caters to tweens in SOHO, New York, that are cosmopolitan and educated, discerning consumers (Hymowitz, 2000). Just as products marketed under the Tinkerbell brand would suggest, the consumption of tween products and merchandise varies across the globe.

While the tween market can be identified globally, there are distinct differences in consumption patterns and purchase decisions for tweens across the United States, Denmark, and Japan (Andersen, Tufte, Rasmussen, & Chan, 2007; Giges, 1991; Prince & Martin, 2011). Yet, regardless of the differences among tween spending habits, the tween cohort occupies immense cultural and economic influence. Tweens spend over $1.5 billion annually, much to the delight of companies who are hoping to create brand loyalty in a generation of children that are more brand conscious than ever (Prince & Martin, 2011). The reason for this, according to Martin Lindstrom and Patricia B. Seybold (2003), is that this generation of consumers has more of an understanding of today's economic world. They are more connected and more informed, which is why companies are increasingly interested in the tween market. Companies can gain more insight into the world of tweens by thinking of them less as children of a specific age, and more of a state of mind and behaviors (Prince & Martin, 2011). Media companies in particular have begun marketing toward the tween demographic by taking into consideration the tween appeal and constructions of what it means to be a girl.

The tween generation demands unlimited choices, speed, and convenience. They expect instant gratification, since their concept of time differs dramatically from that of past generations (Osborn). According to a study by the Center for Disease Control and Prevention (2000), today's tweens still look to their parents to guide them through what is right and wrong, and at the same time, are still encouraged to make their own choices. Tweens are very good at multi-tasking, which is why they can easily divide their attention between cellphones, TV, the Internet and music ("Center for Disease Control," 2000). They also consume more media than their parents, and even more than their older teenage counterparts. Tweens spend, on average, 2.21 hours a day watching TV, 2.09 hours playing video games and 1.54 hours a day listening to music ("Common Sense Media," 2015). An often-overlooked contributor to this extensive media use is the availability of content specifically designed for this group; several media outlets are available to tween audiences without parental supervision. Their voracious consumption makes them the perfect target for marketing agencies, but tweens are also susceptible to media messages and advertising because of their stage of development (Linstrom & Seybold, 2003).

In part due to their cognitive developmental state, tweens are attracted to things they can emulate. They are drawn to specific characters that embody their internal selves; *Pokémon*, for example, remains popular among the tween demographic because audiences see the characters as young, friendly and mischievous, which is how tweens see themselves (whether or not their parents agree with that perception). A huge developmental characteristic of this age group involves a lack of confidence and individual identity, often resulting in the attempt to define themselves through products and media culture (Hulan, 2007). The tween years are largely focused on developing identity, and media inevitably play a role in eliminating uncertainty while simultaneously contributing to an identity structure that revolves around physical presentation and emotional expression (Hulan, 2007; Blue, 2017). Where narrative analyses may reveal problematic portrayals regarding racial identity and diversity, Disney attempts to maintain its appeal to the tween audience through failures in familial settings that are common among adolescent experiences. These can manifest as struggles tweens and teens have with failing to meet parental expectations—a theme noted across several adolescent programs (Patrikakou, 2016). These appeals largely relate back to questions regarding self-discovery and belonging, and the ways in which characters respond to inner conflict contributes to character identification within media texts.

Given the characteristics of this demographic, character identifications play a unique role in development and can manifest as parasocial relationships that result from perception of characters as "similar and real" (Cole & Leets, 1999, p. 496). Considering the presumptions in social learning, perceived similarity is a construct often used to measure character identification (Greenwood, 2007). Reaching this demographic, therefore, necessarily involves the construction of specific characters that exemplify a relatable persona while maintaining a marketable product line. These characters and products have, for decades, largely been distinguished between boys and girls based on cultural teachings that create very different developmental experiences for both groups. With newfound challenges in reaching a specific age group while also taking into consideration the differences in gendered content, Disney attempted to reach the largest possible demographic by producing content on the Disney XD Network that was gender-neutral and could feature product lines that would appeal to both boys and girls (Prince & Martin, 2011). This attempt did not appear until 2009, however, and an examination of both early and current Disney tween programming reveals specific attempts made by Disney to reach a young female audience and simultaneously perpetuate representations of girlhood (Blue, 2017).

Disney's live-action programming to the tween cohort is marketed directly to a primarily female audience (Northup & Liebler, 2010). While it could be argued that *Kids, Incorporated* was the Disney Channel's first live-action program for tweens way back in 1984, in the modern era, it is recognized that the company first offered programming specifically for tweens in 2000 with the creation of *Even Stevens*, followed by *Lizzie McGuire* in 2001.

The latter continued onto a successful feature film in 2003 that drew in a larger tween audience and sparked extensive synergistic attempts by Disney to cross promote content through television, music, film, concerts, and consumer products (Blue, 2017). A large portion of the success must also be attributed to the strategical shift in lifestyle marketing, during which the company sought more targeted ways to reach the tween girl audience, specifically through casting. Disney participates in the construction of "tween" as feminine and produces discourses related to girlhood not only through narratives and appeals to girls, but also the copromotion of product and marketing of girl celebrities (Blue, 2017).

With this in mind, Disney has strategically produced celebrities with whom girls strongly identify and who dominate their relationship with media culture (McGladrey, 2014). From its early production days in the 1950s and 1960s, Disney has relied heavily on tween actors and actresses in order to develop and produce narrative franchise for tween audiences (Blue, 2017). The talent in most Disney Channel programs have been identified as the most prominent celebrities influential to girls' engagement with media (McGladrey, 2014) and are older in age than the girls they reach (Northup & Liebler, 2010). Disney's *Wizards of Waverly Place*, featuring actress Selena Gomez, was identified as the most frequently watched program among adolescent females; at the time, Gomez was eighteen years old, and the show was marketed to an audience of girls aged nine to eleven (McGladrey, 2014). The purposeful integration of teen actresses in tween programming originates— and remains successful—from the desire tweens have to be viewed and treated as older and more sophisticated, much like their teenage counterparts (Prince & Martin, 2011). The enculturation of the teenage lifestyle before it actually begins is a phenomenon that several advertisers, including the Disney Channel, have adopted through the use of older teen actors (McGladrey, 2014; Northup & Liebler, 2010) in order to reach the tween market. Where the incorporation of older teen actors as the primary identification factor has proven valuable, the age of characters plays an important role in how many seasons of a particular show can be produced. Although the actors in tween programming are identified as "young stars," they inevitably grow and change in their development; noticeable physical or emotional changes in actors or actresses can then create disparities among younger audience members who no longer identify with the character (Blue, 2017).

Beyond the age of talent Disney recruits, the company makes attempts to produce narratives that audiences will identify with, both internally and externally. The construction of *Hannah Montana* derives from a translation that mimics the narrative of Miley Cyrus' rise to fame (Blue, 2017). The publicly recognizable parallel of both actress Miley Cyrus and character Miley Stewart as talented, hardworking girls that achieve success—coupled with a live-action platform—exemplifies Disney's attempt to reach the tween girl while still marketing the classic princess trope. Through live-action content that involves purposeful talent casting and narrative construction, Disney manages to present its princess culture in a more practical, realistic way that appeals to the older, more sophisticated adolescent demographic.

Disney's contemporary live-action programming adheres to the strategic business-oriented decisions of a major corporation by selecting actors that aid in captivation of their tween audience members; however, the company furthers its appeal to viewers by creating and presenting a culture of which children are made members (McGladrey, 2014). The validity of this presentation has been questioned through Disney's targeting of female audience members (Northup & Liebler, 2010) and the superficially visible portrayal of racial identity that renders race amendable with ease in commercial settings (McGladrey, 2014).

shows.disney.com

The Disney Channel's main website, shows.disney.com, features the ability to watch select Disney programming on demand as well as in-depth information about each of its major television programs. At the time of this writing, the shows featured on shows.disney.com include *A.N.T. Farm, Austin & Ally, Best Friends Whenever, Bunk'd, Dog with a Blog, Fish Hooks, Girl Meets World, Good Luck Charlie, I Didn't Do It, Jessie, K.C. Undercover, Lab Rats, Liv and Maddie, Mighty Med, Phineas and Ferb, Shake It Up, Win, Lose or Draw,* and *Wizards of Waverly Place.* Of these, many programs have been canceled and are shown on the site as reruns, much like syndicated programs. Only *Bunk'd, Girl Meets World, K.C. Undercover, Lab Rats* and *Liv and Maddie* are still producing current episodes.

These programs make up the contemporary Disney Channel tween universe. Given these programs, and the extant literature on the pedagogical nature of Disney media (particularly directed at girls, and especially in the tween demographic), the Fought and Eisenhauer (2016) study would seem a salient starting point for this study. If Disney princesses (aimed at a younger female demographic) speak less than their male contemporaries, girls are being taught the value of their voices in comparison to boys. Would this hold true if the study were extended to the Disney tween universe? What type of people make up the Disney tween universe—who is considered important within that universe? Does it exhibit racial and gender diversity? In order to determine the nature of the universe Disney presents to the tween demographic, the following research questions are proposed:

RQ$_1$: In Disney Channel live action tween programming, what is the distribution of speaking roles between male and female characters?

RQ$_2$: In Disney Channel live action tween programming, what is the distribution of lines between male and female characters?

RQ$_3$: In Disney Channel live action tween programming, what is the distribution of speaking roles between whites and people of color?

RQ$_4$: In Disney Channel live action tween programming, what is the distribution of lines between whites and people of color?

RQ$_5$: In Disney Channel live action tween programming, what is the distribution of storylines between whites and people of color?

Method

In order to collect data about the Disney Channel tween universe, a wide range of Disney Channel programming was necessary for study. To this end, every program listed on shows.disney.com was included in the sample. Then, *Fish Hooks* and *Phineas and Ferb* were excluded since they are animated programs and the study focused only on live action programming. *Win, Lose or Draw* was also excluded from the sample, as it is a game show, rather than a narrative, fictional, episodic program. The remaining eligible sample included *A.N.T. Farm, Austin & Ally, Best Friends Whenever, Bunk'd, Dog with a Blog, Girl Meets World, Good Luck Charlie, I Didn't Do It, Jessie, K.C. Undercover, Lab Rats, Liv and Maddie, Mighty Med, Shake It Up*, and *Wizards of Waverly Place.* Due to availability of episodes, not every season of every program was analyzed; what was readily available at the time of writing is what was used, with the understanding that programs on the Disney Channel generally do not change substantially over the course of their run, and in most cases, the full run is not necessary to make a determination as to the nature of the program's dialogue tendencies.

Once the programs were determined, it was decided that there would be no sampling—every single episode of each of the programs would be coded in order to maximize the accuracy of the results. Each episode would be coded as follows: number of lines spoken by white males, number of lines spoken by white females; number of lines spoken by males of color; number of lines spoken by females of color; number of white male speaking roles; number of white female speaking roles; number of males of color speaking roles; number of females of color speaking roles; number of white males integral to the main episode storyline; number of white females integral to the main episode storyline; number of males of color integral to the main episode storyline; number of females of color integral to the main episode storyline; number of white males integral to secondary episode storylines; number of white females integral to secondary episode storylines; number of males of color integral to secondary episode storylines; and number of females of color integral to secondary episode storylines.

Given the enormity of the sample (632 episodes in all), numerous research assistants were necessary to complete the coding. Seven research assistants were trained by the four researchers to code episodes. Definitions were agreed upon as to what constituted a line, how to determine the difference between main storyline and any secondary storylines, and how to identify a person of color. For this study, people of color were only identified visually (as this is the primary way a likely tween viewer would determine race); if a character's actor identifies as a person of color "in real life," but is presented within the text as white, the character was coded as white. This was particularly important for an actress like Rowan Blanchard; while the actress herself is Middle Eastern, on *Girl Meets World*, she is presented with two clearly white parents and a clearly white brother—contextually, she is coded as white.

Each researcher and research assistant was initially given a single episode of a program to code: for example, *Girl Meets World,* season one, episode three. Intercoder reliability was reached, with a Cronbach's alpha of 0.839. Programs were then distributed to the research team. Each researcher or research assistant was responsible for every episode in a single season of their assigned program; most coders were assigned multiple seasons, but only three coders were assigned multiple shows.

Results

Across 632 episodes of programming broadcast on the Disney Channel and/or featured on shows.disney.com, there are definite trends that emerge. Across all programs and all years as a whole, white characters speak 2.3 more lines than characters of color (Table 1). Among those lines, male and female white characters are nearly at parity, with female characters speaking slightly more than male characters (Table 1). Female characters of color speak significantly more lines than male characters of color (Table 1). This is reflective of casting in general, as shows across all programs and all years average three white male characters, three white female characters, and two characters of color (one male and one female) per program (Table 2). Storylines also reflect this focus, as white males garner the majority of both primary and secondary storylines (Tables 3 and 4).

Table 1. Average number of lines per episode (*n* = 632)

White Male Lines	105.26
White Female Lines	109.21
Person of Color Male Lines	39.58
Person of Color Female Lines	52.75

Table 2. Average number of speaking roles per episode (*n* = 632)

White Male Roles	3.33
White Female Roles	2.63
Person of Color Male Roles	1.29
Person of Color Female Roles	1.37

Table 3. Average number of main ("A") storylines per episode (*n* = 632)

White Male Storylines	1.84
White Female Storylines	1.60
Person of Color Male Storylines	0.64
Person of Color Female Storylines	0.80

Table 4. Average number of secondary ("B") storylines per episode (*n* = 632)

White Male Storylines	1.45
White Female Storylines	1.03
Person of Color Male Storylines	0.67
Person of Color Female Storylines	0.54

Individual programs, however, tell a slightly different story. It is clear that older programs (those that ended before 2016) contained more male characters and more male lines than newer programs (those that aired after 2016). For example, *Good Luck Charlie* (Table 6) aired from 2010 to 2014, and white male characters were featured more, received the most lines, the most primary storylines, and the most secondary storylines. *Bunk'd*, which aired from 2016 to 2019 (Table 17) is the opposite; white female characters are featured the most, with the most lines, the most primary storylines, and the most secondary storylines. In fact, in every program airing after 2016, female characters speak more than male characters. The only program, across all years and all programs, in which characters of color speak more than white characters, is *K.C. Undercover* (Table 16), which features a mostly Black cast.

Table 5. *Wizards of Waverly Place* (2007–2012) averages per episode by season (*n* = 104)

	Season 1	Season 2	Season 3	Season 4	Overall
White Male Lines	55.43	51.7	69.96	103.8	69.89
White Female Lines	26.10	40.97	49.07	53.92	43.26
Person of Color Male Lines	63.10	69.20	90.14	88.96	78.36
Person of Color Female Lines	84.67	76.97	105.79	94.64	90.53
White Male Roles	3.43	3.13	2.64	3.44	3.13
White Female Roles	2.05	2.27	1.39	1.8	1.88
Person of Color Male Roles	2.38	2.17	2.14	2.04	2.17
Person of Color Female Roles	2.29	1.77	2.11	2.08	2.04
White Male A Storylines	1.19	1	1.75	2.36	1.57
White Female A Storylines	0.48	.80	1.21	1.24	0.95
Person of Color Male A Storylines	1.29	1.47	1.75	1.48	1.51
Person of Color Female A Storylines	1.33	1.1	1.71	1.48	1.40
White Male B Storylines	2.29	2.13	0.71	0.84	1.47
White Female B Storylines	1.57	1.47	0.32	0.4	0.92
Person of Color Male B Storylines	1.14	0.7	0.75	0.6	0.78
Person of Color Female B Storylines	1.0	0.73	0.64	0.68	0.75

Table 6. *Good Luck Charlie* (2010–2014) averages per episode by season (*n* = 55)

	Season 1	Season 2	Overall
White Male Lines	111.08	123.33	119.44
White Female Lines	105.52	105.27	106.96
Person of Color Male Lines	9.16	8.67	8.89
Person of Color Female Lines	15	19.1	17.5
White Male Roles	4.32	4.67	4.56
White Female Roles	3.04	3.13	3.15
Person of Color Male Roles	0.84	0.7	0.76
Person of Color Female Roles	1.04	1.23	1.16
White Male A Storylines	2.96	3.03	3.05
White Female A Storylines	2	2.33	2.02
Person of Color Male A Storylines	0.04	0	0.02
Person of Color Female A Storylines	0.12	0.23	0.18
White Male B Storylines	1.4	1.83	1.65
White Female B Storylines	1.04	0.8	0.93
Person of Color Male B Storylines	0.8	0.7	0.75
Person of Color Female B Storylines	0.96	1.0	1.0

Table 7. *Shake It Up* (2010–2013) averages per episode by season (*n* = 44)

	Season 1	Season 2	Overall
White Male Lines	47.33	66.70	57.45
White Female Lines	68.14	75.43	71.95
Person of Color Male Lines	29.19	38.17	33.89
Person of Color Female Lines	47.48	65.70	57
White Male Roles	2.95	3	2.98
White Female Roles	2.43	2.3	2.36
Person of Color Male Roles	1.76	1.74	1.75
Person of Color Female Roles	1.67	1.60	1.64
White Male A Storylines	0.67	0.48	0.57
White Female A Storylines	1.14	1.26	1.20
Person of Color Male A Storylines	0.29	0.09	0.18
Person of Color Female A Storylines	1.10	1	1.04
White Male B Storylines	2.29	2.52	2.41
White Female B Storylines	1.29	1.04	1.16
Person of Color Male B Storylines	1.48	1.65	1.57
Person of Color Female B Storylines	0.52	0.61	0.57

Table 8. *A.N.T. Farm* (2011–2014) averages per episode by season (*n* = 44)

	Season 1	Season 2	Overall
White Male Lines	66.84	59.57	63.52
White Female Lines	90.96	86.19	88.78
Person of Color Male Lines	48.72	30.43	40.37
Person of Color Female Lines	76.8	90.24	82.93
White Male Roles	2.96	2.52	2.76
White Female Roles	3.44	3.19	3.33
Person of Color Male Roles	1.44	1.29	1.37
Person of Color Female Roles	1.28	1.57	1.41
White Male A Storylines	1.52	1.33	1.43
White Female A Storylines	1.56	1.67	1.61
Person of Color Male A Storylines	0.4	0.38	0.39
Person of Color Female A Storylines	1.04	1.43	1.22
White Male B Storylines	1.48	1.29	1.39
White Female B Storylines	1.88	1.52	1.72
Person of Color Male B Storylines	1.04	0.90	0.98
Person of Color Female B Storylines	0.24	0.14	0.20

Table 9. *Austin & Ally* (2011–2016) averages per episode by season (*n* = 45)

	Season 1	Season 2	Overall
White Male Lines	155.47	143.46	148.53
White Female Lines	101.31	87.04	93.07
Person of Color Male Lines	8.79	14.85	12.29
Person of Color Female Lines	56.68	65.0	61.49

continued on page 14

Table 9. *Austin & Ally* (2011–2016) averages per episode by season (*n* = 45) (continued)

	Season 1	Season 2	Overall
White Male Roles	3.68	3.38	3.51
White Female Roles	1.63	2.04	1.87
Person of Color Male Roles	0.58	0.69	0.64
Person of Color Female Roles	1.21	1.50	1.38
White Male A Storylines	1.8	1.81	1.82
White Female A Storylines	1.21	1.12	1.16
Person of Color Male A Storylines	0.26	0.23	0.24
Person of Color Female A Storylines	0.84	0.65	0.73
White Male B Storylines	1.32	1.58	1.47
White Female B Storylines	1.0	0.92	0.96
Person of Color Male B Storylines	0.11	0.27	0.2
Person of Color Female B Storylines	0.47	0.77	0.64

Table 10. *Dog with a Blog* (2012–2015) averages per episode by season (*n* = 46)

	Season 1	Season 2	Overall
White Male Lines	131.4	115.33	123.17
White Female Lines	178.7	179.67	179.19
Person of Color Male Lines	1.6	4.10	2.88
Person of Color Female Lines	9.8	7.76	8.76
White Male Roles	2.7	2.86	2.78
White Female Roles	3.85	3.86	3.85
Person of Color Male Roles	0.25	0.14	0.19
Person of Color Female Roles	0.3	0.24	0.27
White Male A Storylines	1.9	1.81	1.85
White Female A Storylines	2.95	2.57	2.76
Person of Color Male A Storylines	0.2	0.14	0.17
Person of Color Female A Storylines	0.2	0.19	0.19
White Male B Storylines	0.9	1.0	0.95
White Female B Storylines	0.95	1.33	1.15
Person of Color Male B Storylines	0.05	0.0	0.24
Person of Color Female B Storylines	0.1	0.05	0.07

Table 11. *I Didn't Do It* (2014–2015) averages per episode by season (*n* = 37)

	Season 1	Season 2	Overall
White Male Lines	188.3	159.47	174.26
White Female Lines	178.8	169.68	174.36
Person of Color Male Lines	13.9	10.74	12.36
Person of Color Female Lines	59.4	94.58	76.54
White Male Roles	3.9	3.53	3.72
White Female Roles	3.15	2.89	3.03
Person of Color Male Roles	0.8	0.53	0.67
Person of Color Female Roles	1.4	2.21	1.79
White Male A Storylines	1.2	1.26	1.23

	Season 1	Season 2	Overall
White Female A Storylines	1.25	1.11	1.18
Person of Color Male A Storylines	0.15	0.11	0.13
Person of Color Female A Storylines	0.25	0.58	0.41
White Male B Storylines	1.35	1.63	1.49
White Female B Storylines	1.3	1.42	1.36
Person of Color Male B Storylines	0.15	0.26	0.21
Person of Color Female B Storylines	0.5	1.26	0.87

Table 12. *Jessie* (2011–2015) averages per episode by season (*n* = 78)

	Season 1	Season 2	Season 3	Overall
White Male Lines	89.38	82.08	53.37	74.67
White Female Lines	151.27	148.27	115.63	138.10
Person of Color Male Lines	38.08	41.77	61.04	47.14
Person of Color Female Lines	37.85	35.42	32.37	35.18
White Male Roles	3.15	2.97	2.15	2.75
White Female Roles	2.96	2.92	2.81	2.89
Person of Color Male Roles	1.08	1.08	2.22	1.47
Person of Color Female Roles	1.0	1.0	1.26	1.09
White Male A Storylines	2.38	2.31	0.81	1.82
White Female A Storylines	2.46	2.38	1.89	2.24
Person of Color Male A Storylines	0.69	0.69	1.33	0.91
Person of Color Female A Storylines	0.69	0.69	0.63	0.67
White Male B Storylines	0.77	0.77	1.37	0.97
White Female B Storylines	0.46	0.46	0.93	0.62
Person of Color Male B Storylines	0.38	0.38	0.93	0.57
Person of Color Female B Storylines	0.27	0.27	0.63	0.39

Table 13. *Lab Rats* (2012–2016) averages per episode by season (*n* = 44)

	Season 1	Season 2	Overall
White Male Lines	163.4	171.5	167.45
White Female Lines	53.55	57.65	55.6
Person of Color Male Lines	68.35	70.12	69.24
Person of Color Female Lines	23.7	26.6	25.15
White Male Roles	3.75	3.6	3.68
White Female Roles	1.5	1.7	1.6
Person of Color Male Roles	1.05	1.6	1.33
Person of Color Female Roles	0.8	0.9	0.85
White Male A Storylines	3.4	3.5	3.45
White Female A Storylines	0.95	0.87	0.91
Person of Color Male A Storylines	1.0	1.0	1.0
Person of Color Female A Storylines	0.6	0.5	0.55
White Male B Storylines	1.45	1.66	1.56
White Female B Storylines	0.85	1.0	0.93
Person of Color Male B Storylines	0.55	0.51	0.53
Person of Color Female B Storylines	0.35	0.2	0.28

Table 14. *Liv and Maddie* (2013–2017) averages per episode by season ($n = 45$)

	Season 1	Season 2	Overall
White Male Lines	109.81	131.96	121.62
White Female Lines	178.81	157.67	167.53
Person of Color Male Lines	33.86	25.88	29.6
Person of Color Female Lines	20.24	19.38	19.78
White Male Roles	3.33	3.92	3.64
White Female Roles	2.48	3.54	3.04
Person of Color Male Roles	2.29	1.04	1.16
Person of Color Female Roles	1.0	0.96	0.98
White Male A Storylines	1.80	2.29	2.07
White Female A Storylines	1.71	2.38	2.07
Person of Color Male A Storylines	0.58	0.54	0.56
Person of Color Female A Storylines	0.76	0.75	0.76
White Male B Storylines	1.57	1.63	1.6
White Female B Storylines	1.48	1.25	1.36
Person of Color Male B Storylines	0.90	0.58	0.73
Person of Color Female B Storylines	0.24	0.17	0.2

Table 15. *Girl Meets World* (2014–2017) averages per episode by season ($n = 50$)

	Season 1	Season 2	Overall
White Male Lines	160.05	158.4	159.36
White Female Lines	189	201.53	194.22
Person of Color Male Lines	7.10	16.13	10.86
Person of Color Female Lines	7.67	12.67	9.75
White Male Roles	4.71	4.6	4.67
White Female Roles	4.14	4.6	4.33
Person of Color Male Roles	0.24	0.53	0.36
Person of Color Female Roles	0.38	0.47	0.42
White Male A Storylines	2.95	3.93	3.36
White Female A Storylines	2.71	2.93	2.81
Person of Color Male A Storylines	0.19	0.4	0.28
Person of Color Female A Storylines	0.05	0.33	0.17
White Male B Storylines	1.19	0.8	1.03
White Female B Storylines	1.33	1.13	1.25
Person of Color Male B Storylines	0.05	0.07	0.06
Person of Color Female B Storylines	0.09	0.07	0.08

Table 16. *K.C. Undercover* (2015–2018) averages per episode by season ($n = 51$)

	Season 1	Season 2	Overall
White Male Lines	12.48	10.35	11.42
White Female Lines	36.79	40.12	38.46
Person of Color Male Lines	84.31	88.26	86.28
Person of Color Female Lines	143.17	161.34	152.26
White Male Roles	1.45	1.56	1.50

	Season 1	Season 2	Overall
White Female Roles	1.55	1.77	1.66
Person of Color Male Roles	2.48	2.61	2.55
Person of Color Female Roles	3.14	3.16	3.15
White Male A Storylines	0.07	0.04	0.05
White Female A Storylines	0.38	0.46	0.42
Person of Color Male A Storylines	1.79	1.75	1.77
Person of Color Female A Storylines	2.17	2.15	2.16
White Male B Storylines	1.38	0.95	1.17
White Female B Storylines	1.14	1.42	1.28
Person of Color Male B Storylines	0.72	0.94	0.83
Person of Color Female B Storylines	0.97	1.14	1.05

Table 17. *Bunk'd* (2016–2019) averages per episode by season ($n = 42$)

	Season 1	Season 2	Overall
White Male Lines	45.91	46.42	46.16
White Female Lines	159.91	164.43	162.17
Person of Color Male Lines	91.73	96.23	93.98
Person of Color Female Lines	73.27	70.35	71.81
White Male Roles	1.0	1.0	1.0
White Female Roles	3.0	3.0	3.0
Person of Color Male Roles	2.09	2.34	2.22
Person of Color Female Roles	1.82	1.92	1.87
White Male A Storylines	0.82	0.77	0.79
White Female A Storylines	1.82	1.76	1.79
Person of Color Male A Storylines	0.91	0.91	0.91
Person of Color Female A Storylines	0.91	0.91	0.91
White Male B Storylines	0.91	0.91	0.91
White Female B Storylines	1.18	1.34	1.26
Person of Color Male B Storylines	1.09	1.27	1.18
Person of Color Female B Storylines	0.91	0.91	0.91

Table 18. *Best Friends Whenever* (2018) averages per episode by season ($n = 30$)

	Season 1	Season 2	Overall
White Male Lines	219	212	215.5
White Female Lines	276.75	255.68	266.22
Person of Color Male Lines	3.75	2.12	2.94
Person of Color Female Lines	16.83	14.74	15.79
White Male Roles	4.42	4.61	4.51
White Female Roles	2.67	2.55	2.61
Person of Color Male Roles	0.17	0.18	0.17
Person of Color Female Roles	0.5	0.39	0.45
White Male A Storylines	4.0	5.0	4.5
White Female A Storylines	2.58	3.1	2.84
Person of Color Male A Storylines	0.08	0.06	0.07

continued on page 18

Table 18. *Best Friends Whenever* (2018) averages per episode by season (*n* = 30) (continued)

	Season 1	Season 2	Overall
Person of Color Female A Storylines	0.42	0.52	0.47
White Male B Storylines	0.42	0.36	0.39
White Female B Storylines	0.08	0.08	0.08
Person of Color Male B Storylines	0.08	0.08	0.08
Person of Color Female B Storylines	0.08	0.08	0.08

Looking more longitudinally across the programs reveals a trend over time in the way in which characters are cast, given story prominence, and given lines. In the earliest programs, those which aired from 2007 to 2013 (*Witches of Waverly Place, Good Luck Charlie, Shake It Up,* and *A.N.T. Farm*), white male characters average the most lines (Table 19); however, overall, female characters actually speak more than male characters. This can largely be attributed to female characters of color having a prominent role in those programs (Selena Gomez on *Wizards of Waverly Place*; Zendaya Coleman on *Shake It Up*; China Anne McClain on *A.N.T. Farm*). Female characters of color nearly equal the number of lines as white female characters, while male characters of color lag significantly behind white male characters. That said, white male characters do still appear, on average, more than white female characters, or characters of color of any gender, and still receive more main and secondary storylines (Tables 20, 21, and 22).

Table 19. Average number of lines per episode (Early Shows)

White Male Lines	75.57
White Female Lines	70.15
Person of Color Male Lines	47.57
Person of Color Female Lines	67.63

Table 20. Average number of speaking roles per episode (Early Shows)

White Male Roles	3.30
White Female Roles	2.50
Person of Color Male Roles	1.65
Person of Color Female Roles	1.66

Table 21. Average number of main ("A") storylines per episode (Early Shows)

White Male Storylines	1.62
White Female Storylines	1.36
Person of Color Male Storylines	0.71
Person of Color Female Storylines	1.05

Table 22. Average number of secondary ("B") storylines per episode (Early Shows)

White Male Storylines	1.67
White Female Storylines	1.13
Person of Color Male Storylines	0.97
Person of Color Female Storylines	0.65

The programs in the middle range, those airing between 2014 and 2016 (*Austin & Ally, Dog with a Blog, I Didn't Do It, Jessie, Lab Rats, Liv and Maddie,* and *Girl Meets World*), shift meaningfully, primarily due to the precipitous drop in characters of color. White female characters take over as the main deliverers of lines (Table 23); however, white male characters still receive the most roles, and the most main and secondary storylines (Tables 24, 25, and 26). Characters of color speak roughly half the time they did in the early shows, appear nearly half as often, and receive fewer than half of the main and secondary storylines. Three programs (*Dog with a Blog, Liv and Maddie,* and *Girl Meets World*) essentially feature all-white casts (or, in the case of *Girl Meets World*, casts that are all coded as white within the context of the show).

Table 23. Average number of lines per episode (Mid Shows)

White Male Lines	134.22
White Female Lines	143.23
Person of Color Male Lines	27.75
Person of Color Female Lines	33.94

Table 24. Average number of speaking roles per episode (Mid Shows)

White Male Roles	3.48
White Female Roles	2.93
Person of Color Male Roles	0.94
Person of Color Female Roles	0.97

Table 25. Average number of main ("A") storylines per episode (Mid Shows)

White Male Storylines	2.21
White Female Storylines	1.89
Person of Color Male Storylines	0.50
Person of Color Female Storylines	0.51

Table 26. Average number of secondary ("B") storylines per episode (Mid Shows)

White Male Storylines	1.26
White Female Storylines	1.05
Person of Color Male Storylines	0.34
Person of Color Female Storylines	0.36

The programs in the most recent grouping (*Bunk'd*, *K.C. Undercover*, and *Best Friends Whenever*), airing from 2017 to 2019, evidence numbers that are slightly skewed due to the sheer volume of lines spoken on *Best Friends Whenever* (Table 18). However, even taking that into account, female characters on the whole speak vastly more than male characters (Table 27). Characters of color speak twice as much as they did in the mid programs, and more than they did even in the early programs (Table 27). This can largely be attributed to casting; nearly twice as many characters of color appear on the recent programs than did in the mid programs (Table 28). Some of these characters of color clearly are represented by *K.C. Undercover*'s nearly all Black cast, but the racially diverse *Bunk'd* is also a significant contributor that helps to offset the all white cast of *Best Friends Whenever*. For the first time, white female characters outnumber white male characters, and female characters in general outnumber male characters, on average (Table 28). That said, even on these three female-heavy programs, white male characters receive the majority of main storylines (*Best Friends Whenever*'s wide discrepancy is offset by *K.C. Undercover*'s equally wide discrepancy), although white female characters occupy more of the secondary storylines (Tables 29 and 30).

Table 27. Average number of lines per episode (Recent Shows)

White Male Lines	91.02
White Female Lines	155.61
Person of Color Male Lines	61.06
Person of Color Female Lines	79.95

Table 28. Average number of speaking roles per episode (Recent Shows)

White Male Roles	2.34
White Female Roles	2.42
Person of Color Male Roles	1.64
Person of Color Female Roles	1.82

Table 29. Average number of main ("A") storylines per episode (Recent Shows)

White Male Storylines	1.78
White Female Storylines	1.68
Person of Color Male Storylines	0.91
Person of Color Female Storylines	1.18

Table 30. Average number of secondary ("B") storylines per episode (Recent Shows)

White Male Storylines	0.82
White Female Storylines	0.87
Person of Color Male Storylines	0.69
Person of Color Female Storylines	0.68

Discussion

What, then, does the Disney Channel universe look like, between 2007 and 2019? Largely, and perhaps unsurprisingly, the universe is very white. However, surprisingly, the universe is also more male than expected. While that trend has shifted slightly over time, for the programs featured on shows.disney.com at the time of this writing, white males are the driving narrative force on the Disney Channel. This revelation contrasts sharply to the current lineup on the Disney Channel, which features programs like *Bizaardvark*, *Stuck in the Middle*, and *Andi Mack*, all of which present female characters of color in the main roles and many of the supporting roles as well. It would appear as though the Disney Channel is making a conscious effort to shift the focus from its programming of the past, which empirically centered on white male characters. In the most recent programs, white female characters took over (to some extent) from white male characters in terms of whose voices are heard the most; however, even in these supposedly "female-centric" programs, white male characters still monopolize the major storylines and are the most frequently appearing characters. This echoes Fought and Eisenhauer's 2016 study that found, in animated Disney films, that male characters speak more than female characters in most Disney animated films since 1989, and male characters outnumber female characters in nearly every Disney animated film ever made (Guo, 2016). What appears to be centered on girls is often an illusion, as the numbers in this study prove.

For decades, the Disney live-action platform has presented a universe in which one's physical appearance directly correlates with his/her societal role and comprehensive value. Tween girls have been witnesses to a variety of different scenarios, families, encounters, and lifestyles that—though distinct in several ways—are nearly identical in their presentation of male versus female characters as well as whites versus people of color. Extremely skewed casting choices coupled with a developing audience eager to satisfy identification crises have the potential to vastly alter a tween viewer's reality and subsequent interactions with others in the real world. This potential is essentially magnified when taking into consideration *what* presentations are disproportionate; Disney makes specific choices in representation that directly correlate with identification facets and are centered around physical appearance—an overwhelmingly valued feature in Western culture and social status.

Shades of White

Clearly, from 2002 to 2018, whiteness was tremendously overrepresented in the Disney Channel's programming. Across all 632 episodes, white characters dominate each category, and characters of color are consistently less represented in regard to storylines, speaking roles, and number of lines. In fact, the taken averages of all collective shows as well as averages for shows in the oldest program, middle program, and most recent program categories indicate that people of color *never* occupy a higher average than whites for speaking roles, lines, and storylines (Tables 1–4 and 19–30). Where there may be instances in which specific episodes or series produce a higher total for people of color, the vast majority as reflected in the averages suggests that the visual scenario an audience member will most likely encounter involves white characters interacting with and talking to other white characters. This would certainly fail any sort of "Bechdel Test for People of Color," in which two characters of color talk to each other about something other than a white character. These purposeful production choices present a uniform society in which minorities are not only grossly underrepresented, but diversity as a whole is entirely overlooked. Even shows such as *Girl Meets World* that attempt to touch on social issues do so from a linear casting perspective, where white male characters occupy over four times the number of storyline roles (4.71, 4.60, 4.67) than male characters of color (0.24, 0.53, 0.36) and the same is observed for white female characters (4.14, 4.60, 4.33) versus female characters of color (0.38, 0.47, 0.42) across all three seasons (Table 15).

In other series such as *Wizards of Waverly Place* or *A.N.T. Farm*, where the main character is a person of color—and, in both these instances, a female person of color—the number of lines for female characters of color is significantly higher than other shows, consistently producing the highest number of lines for almost all of their respective seasons (Table 5 and 8). Yet, even in these series, people of color still occupy less storyline roles compared to whites—because despite the main characters being a Latinx or Black family, the group exists in a world of white families. Creating a show about people of color living in a world for whites is not a progressive attempt to display diversity, but rather a clear demonstration of tokenism. There are noticeable attempts to include white characters in both main and secondary storyline roles in these programs to an even higher degree than the primary characters; in more recent shows such as *K.C. Undercover*, where people of color have more lines and storyline roles than white characters, the differences in number of storyline roles do not reflect the sizable gap in the opposite direction noticed for the majority of other shows (Table 16).

This has destructive implications in regard to tween development, specifically identification with characters that correlates with real-world formation of one's own identity and persona. From an ecological perspective, media serve as environmental contexts in which viewers—particularly those who are in the identity development stages—make decisions regarding core structures and values including appearance and behavior (Lloyd, 2002). These decisions are largely based on social interaction including that observed on screen, where fictional characters interact with one another in similar contexts as tween viewers experience in their daily lives. When taking into consideration the purposeful features in plot, producers include typical tween dilemmas—disapproving parents, strict teachers, deception—that create a strong commonality between the alternate reality on screen and the viewer's own experiences. These similarities in tween struggles coupled with the lack of representation for people of color isolate a vast number of viewers, resulting in the potential of a decrease in self-esteem and disruption of racial identity (Martin, 2014). In a negatively defined culture, discovering oneself involves discovering what one is not—for racially diverse viewers engaging with Disney tween programing, the typical young, attractive, popular tween is *not* female or a person of color and exists in a world dominated by white men and women. Those that appear visibly different than viewers of color are presented in ways that suggest they hold more valuable roles in society and have their voices heard more often—allowing the presentation of others different from oneself to integrate into the formation of identity. Tweens of color watching shows on the Disney Channel quickly learn that they largely occupy secondary sidekick spaces in relation to their white friends, but are rarely the focus of anything. Of course, the presentation of characters that are visibly relatable and visibly dissimilar includes a value judgment on those characters based on their appearances. These representations in media are directly constitutive of culture and construct a reality that reinforces dominant ideologies regarding the value of people and their societal roles.

That said, if this study were to expand to include currently airing Disney Channel programs, we hypothesize that we would see a marked shift in both the number and line frequency of characters of color, and a reduction in the number and line frequency of white male characters. *Bizaardvark*'s main cast features two girls of color, one white girl, and two white boys as main characters. *Andi Mack* features two girls of color, two women of color, two white boys, and two white men as main character cast. *Stuck in the Middle* features a cast that is all Latinx (four girls of color, three boys of color, one woman of color, and one man of color). *Raven's Home* features two female characters of color, one male character of color, two white female characters, and one white male character as main cast. Necessarily, those casts would push the numbers in most, if not all, categories into greater frequency, and reduce the numbers of white characters in general.

Perceived Worth

A superficial coding analysis of race and gender takes into account the important variable of appearance, whereas a deeper narrative analysis of main versus secondary storyline roles and number of lines expands upon the first analysis by indicating the value one places on a character based on his or her appearance. Disney makes specific choices in representation that directly correlate with identification, and the company expands upon these representations to include a value judgment that viewers actively absorb. While the number of black or female characters inexorably contributes to a construction of reality that communicates problematic assertions regarding the presence of minorities in Western culture, ascribing secondary roles and significantly less spoken words to characters that are not white or male disseminates binary evaluations and normalizes Othering.

As a collective whole, Disney live-action tween programming ascribes the most main storyline roles to white male characters, and the least main storyline roles to person of color male characters (Table 3). This essentially means that those characters essential to the progression of the plotline are most often white and least often people of color. Such character roles communicate very specific messages regarding who matters most in these stories—without white characters, there is no plotline; without person of color characters, the plotline is relatively unchanged. In fact, if taken *together*, the number of both person of color male and person of color female main storyline roles are less than the number of both white male and white female main storyline roles *separately* (Table 3). People of color are consistently at the bottom in regard to necessity to the storyline, and their presence does little to drive plotlines forward. For tweens that not only exist in a culture where appearance largely determines social status but also develop through and identify with those that look and behave as they do, witnessing shows where white males and females tell a story that can be told without people of color communicates their own worth in society. Hundreds of episodes that consistently place white characters into the heart of the narrative suggest over and over that people can and do function effectively without people of color, creating a displacement of ethnic characters internal to plotlines as well as ethnic viewers external to plotlines. Still, the inclusion of diverse characters in other roles would provide some level of representation for people of color—nonetheless problematic in the insignificance to narratives; Yet, white male characters continue to fill *all* storyline roles to a higher degree (Table 4). Through the placement of characters in main and secondary storyline roles, Disney live-action teen programming presents hundreds of accounts where people of color not only offer little in the way of narrative advancement, but are further relegated to secondary roles.

Within these positions, an examination of who speaks more often correlates speech and opportunities to speak with one's value. White characters speak over twice as often as people of color, with person of color males occupying the lowest number of speaking roles and lines (Tables 1 and 2). Through the significant divide in distribution of main and secondary storyline roles emerges a correlation between role and chances to speak—with less representation and integration into narratives comes less opportunities for expression and fewer words to communicate. Spoken words become just as essential to character development as visuals, given that images and the interpretation of images are polysemic, with multiple meanings and perspectives. The use of language, then, aids in the anchoring of characters as to solidify their identities and evaluation (Kozloff, 2000). In order to stress the inherent importance of specific characters, dialogue is used more or less often in purposeful ways; an examination of dialogue in Disney shows reaffirms the assertions the company makes visually regarding an individual's presence and worth in Western culture.

Narrative Analysis

This leads us into a space where, perhaps, numbers are not enough to give us a clear picture of the Disney Channel over time. As has been shown in a myriad of ways and in countless instances, one of the most important engagements scholars can undertake in popular culture scholarship is that of textual critique—making an argument for what a particular artifact is attempting to *do* is a vital exercise in understanding the nature of popular culture within any society. This work is necessarily interpretive by nature, which means, as previously stated, there is no singular "correct" way to analyze a text. Textual artifacts are polysemic; they encompass many simultaneous meanings that are in no way mutually exclusive or "correct." However, bringing to bear the lens of the analytic scholar on a popular culture artifact can often be illuminating as to the nature of that text.

Coupled with the quantitative data of this introductory study, a more holistic view of the Disney Channel's programming can be constructed, and this could be quite useful in making determinations about the Disney Channel Universe. To that end, assembled in these pages are a formidable collection of some of the most interesting popular culture scholars from around the world, both new and established. Their insight into the Disney Channel's programming over time will prove to be most illuminating. The essays are organized (mostly) chronologically, beginning with a discussion of *Lizzie McGuire* and ending with a conversation about *Andi Mack*. In between, every major Disney Channel program receives consideration. In the end, a complete picture of the Disney Channel Universe should become clear. What that picture ultimately means is the purview of the reader.

REFERENCES

Anderson, L., Tufte, B., Rasmussen, J., & Chan, K. (2007). Tweens and new media in Denmark and Hong Kong. *Journal of Consumer Marketing, 24*(6), 340–350.

Azmi, N.J., Ab Rashid, R., Rahman, M.A., & Safawati Basirah, Z. (2016). Gender and speech in a Disney princess movie. *International Journal of Applied Linguistics and English Literature, 5*(6), 235–239.

Baker-Sperry, L. (2007). The production of meaning through peer interaction: Children and Walt Disney's Cinderella. *Sex Roles, 56*(11–12), 717–727.

Bakir, A., Palan, K.M., & Kolbe, R.H. (2013). A comparative content analysis of advertising practices to children. *Journal of Current Issues & Research in Advertising, 34*(2), 247–262.

Blue, M.G. (2017). *Girlhood on Disney channel: Branding, celebrity, and femininity*. New York: Routledge.

BoxOfficeMojo (n.d.). Box office by studio—Disney. Retrieved from: https://www.boxoffice mojo.com/studio/chart/?studio=buenavista.htm&debug=0&view=parent&p=.htm.

Centers for Disease Control (2000). *Audience insights: Communicating to tweens*. Retrieved from: https://www.cdc.gov/healthcommunication/pdf/audience/audienceinsight_tweens. pdf.

Cole, T., & Leets, L. (1999). Attachment styles and intimate television viewing: Insecurely forming relationships in a parasocial way. *Journal of Social and Personal Relationships, 16*(4), 495–511.

"Common sense media." (2015). *The Common sense census: Media use by tweens and teens*. Retrieved from: https://www.commonsensemedia.org/sites/default/files/uploads/ research/census_researchreport.pdf.

Cook, D.T., & Kaiser, S. (2004). Betwixt and be tween: Age ambiguity and the sexualization of the female consuming subject. *Journal of Consumer Culture, 4*(2), 203–227.

Coyne, S.M., Linder, J.R., Rasmussen, E.E., Nelson, D.A., & Birkbeck, V. (2016). Pretty as a princess: Longitudinal effects of engagement with Disney princesses on gender stereotypes, body esteem, and prosocial behavior in children. *Child development, 87*(6), 1909–1925.

Craven, A. (2002). Beauty and the belles: Discourses of feminism and femininity in Disneyland. *European Journal of Women's Studies, 9*(2), 123–142.

Dale, L.P., Higgins, B.E., Pinkerton, N., Couto, M., Mansolillo, V., Weisinger, N., & Flores, M. (2016). Princess picture books: content and messages. *Journal of Research in Childhood Education, 30*(2), 185–199.

Do Rozario, R.A.C. (2004). The princess and the magic kingdom: Beyond nostalgia, the function of the Disney princess. *Women's Studies in Communication, 27*(1), 34–59.

Fought, C., & Eisenhauer, K. (2016, January). *A quantitative analysis of gendered compliments in Disney princess films*. Paper presented at the annual meeting for the Linguistic Society of America, Washington, D.C.

Garlen, J.C., & Sandlin, J.A. (2017). Happily (n) ever after: The cruel optimism of Disney's romantic ideal. *Feminist Media Studies, 17*(6), 957–971.

Giges, N. (1991). Global spending patterns emerge. *Advertising Age, 62*(48), 64.

Graser, M. (2013). How TV has replaced animated films as Disney's biggest brand ambassador. Retrieved 21 November 2016 from http://variety.com/2013/biz/features/how-tv-has-replaced-animated-films-as-disneys-biggest-brand-ambassador-1200324380/.

Greenwood, P.M. (2007). Functional plasticity in cognitive aging: Review and hypothesis. *Neuropsychology, 21*(6), 657–673.

Guo, J. (2016). Researchers have found a major problem with "The Little Mermaid" and other Disney movies. *The Washington Post*. [online] 25 January. Retrieve from: https://www. washingtonpost.com/news/wonk/wp/2016/01/25/researchers-have-discovered-a-major-problem-with-the-littlemermaid-and-other-disney-movies.

Holcomb, J., Latham, K., & Fernandez-Baca, D. (2015). Who cares for the hids? Caregiving and parenting in Disney films." *Journal of Family Issues, 36*(14), 1957–1981.

Hulan, D. (2007). Mistaking brands for tween identity. *The McCaster Journal of Communication, 4*(1), 31–36.

Hymowitz, K. (2000). *Ready or not: What happens when we treat children as small adults*. San Francisco: Encounter Books.

Jenkins, E. (2013). Seeing life in Disney's mutual affection-images. *Quarterly Review of Film and Video, 30*(5), 421–434.

Kissell, R. (2015, December 30). Ratings: Disney channel edges Nickelodeon in 2015 for first-ever No. 1 total-day finish. Retrieved from http://variety.com/2015/tv/news/ratings-disney-channel-beats-nickelodeon-2015-1201669852/.

Kozloff, S. (2000). *Overhearing film dialogue*. Berkley: University of California Press.

Lindstrom, M., & Seybold, P. (2003). *BRANDchild*, London: Kogan Page.

Llyod, B. (2002). A conceptual framework for examining adolescent identity, media influence, and social development. *Review of General Psychology, 6*(1), 73–91.

Martin, A. (2014). Television media as a potential negative factor in the racial identity development of African American youth. *Academic Psychiatry, 32*(4), 338–342.

McGladrey, M.L. (2014). Becoming tween bodies: what preadolescent girls in the US say about beauty, the "just-right ideal," and the "Disney girls." *Journal of Children and Media, 8*(4), 353–370.

Nielsen, L.B., Patel, N.A., and Rosner, J. (2013). "Ahead of the lawmen": Law and morality in Disney animated films, 1960–1998. *Law, Culture and the Humanities*.

Northup, T., & Liebler, C.M. (2010). The good, the bad, and the beautiful: Beauty ideals on the Disney and Nickelodeon channels. *Journal of Children and Media, 4*(3), 265–282.

Padilla-Walker, L.M., Coyne, S.M., Fraser, A.M., & Stockdale, L.A. (2013). Is Disney the nicest place on earth? A content analysis of prosocial behavior in animated Disney films. *Journal of Communication, 63*(2), 393–412.

Pallant, C. (2010). Neo-Disney: Recent developments in Disney feature animation. *New Cinemas: Journal of Contemporary Film, 8*(2), 103–117.

Patrikakou, E. (2016). Parent involvement, technology, and media: Now what? *School Community Journal, 26*(2), 9–24.

Prince, D., & Martin, N. (2011). The tween consumer marketing model: significant variables and recommended research hypotheses. *Academy of Marketing Studies Journal, 16*(2), 31–46.

Telotte, J.P. (2007). Crossing borders and opening boxes: Disney and hybrid animation. *Quarterly Review of Film and Video, 24*(2), 107–116.

Tomaz, Renata. (2014). The invention of the tweens: youth, culture and media. *Intercom: Revista Brasileira de Ciências da Comunicação, 37*(2), 177–202.

Van Wormer, K., & Juby, C. (2016). Cultural representations in Walt Disney films: Implications for social work education. *Journal of Social Work, 16*(5), 578–594.

"The Walt Disney company." (n.d.) American advertising federation. Retrieved from: https://www.aaf.org/AAFMemberR/Membership_Information/Corporate_Membership/Corporate_Member_List/Advertiser_CorpMem_WaltDisney.aspx.

Wasko, J. (2013). *Understanding Disney: The manufacture of fantasy*. John Wiley & Sons.

What Dreams Are Made Of

Hilary Duff and the Illusion of Girl Power

CARY ELZA

Lizzie McGuire begins with a strong sense of a split identity, a distinction between what Lizzie (Hilary Duff) knows, rationally, to be true, and what she wants all the same. The series opens with a pan across cheerleading posters on the walls of Lizzie's junior high hallway that stops on Lizzie herself, then cuts, as the show often does, to the image of cartoon Lizzie, who tells us what Lizzie is thinking. Hauling a big duffel bag and pulling outfits out to illustrate her points, she says, "Okay. I know what you're thinking. Me, Lizzie McGuire, cheerleader? What up with that? I mean, nothing could be more superficial, demeaning, and shallow. Cheerleading is like this plot to make girls feel bad about themselves" (Gould & Israel, 2001). Cut to what Lizzie is looking at: the hallway doors swing open, accompanied by an edgy guitar riff, and there, backlit with blinding brightness, are two older, cool-looking cheerleaders, who perform a slow pom-pom routine while floating down the hallway on a moving sidewalk. Lizzie looks, she stares, she covets. The series emphasizes repeatedly that Lizzie is smart, she's kind, she values her independent mind, and yet, all the same, she wants that dazzle, that chance to be *seen*.

I begin with this moment in the show not just because it's the first sense we get of Lizzie as a character and the challenges of her world, but because it encapsulates the struggle played out over the course of the entire series: the split between Lizzie's internal voice and her external image, between Lizzie's third-wave understanding (*vis à vis* her mom) of the tools of patriarchal repression and her very natural tween desire to be seen as a valued member of her community, and even a star. This dilemma is at the core of this series—indeed, at the core of a number of Disney Channel series during the heyday of the Girl Power movement, but here I will examine *Lizzie*

McGuire, the series and the movie, as well as Hilary Duff's star persona, as a way of teasing out some of the issues at stake during the formation of the "tween" as an ideal of girlhood, a consumer demographic, and an affective category in the early 2000s.

Amid the deluge of female teen stars in American popular culture at the turn of the century, Duff made a name for herself as the relentlessly perky, upbeat, and squeaky-clean alternative to the sexually charged antics of figures like Lindsay Lohan and Britney Spears. Blonde, pretty, and likeable, she parlayed her phenomenal success as the star of Disney's top-rated series *Lizzie McGuire* (2001–2003) into a career in film, fashion, and pop music. As Dave Kehr (2003) noted at the time in the *New York Times*, "If you have never heard of Lizzie McGuire, you are almost certainly not a female resident of the United States between the ages of 8 and 14, and you are unlikely to be related to one" (p. E16). *The Lizzie McGuire Movie* extended the series in 2003, and although Hilary Duff declined to continue her stint as Lizzie after salary negotiations failed following the movie (Blue, 2017, p. 23), she used the character as a jumping-off point for film roles which, while ostensibly departures from Lizzie's clumsy, charming, girl-on-the-verge-of-womanhood uncertainty, nonetheless capture that same spirit of a moment of transition from awkward girlhood to self-made womanhood.

The uniformity of Duff's image, from the character of Lizzie to the everyteen persona she constructed in interviews, suggests that she represents a distinct version of feminism at a particular moment. On the surface, her can-do attitude and refusal to become just a face in the crowd appear to privilege the idea of independence and personal choice. But dig a little deeper, and Hilary Duff's star qualities and characters encourage pre-teen and teen girl audiences to work within the system, rather than challenging the system itself. I contend that Duff can be seen as emblematic of a cycle of popular culture texts which internalized the third wave maxim that the personal is political; Duff shows her viewers that if they make changes in their own lives, they do not need to worry about making larger changes in society. The encouragement (and perceived necessity) for real change is thus diminished, allowing a patriarchal society to continue exerting its dominance with the illusion of individual autonomy.

At the same time, the widespread discussion of post-feminism and third wave feminism in the early 2000s invited the consideration of texts like *Lizzie McGuire* in the context of personal choice, articulations of self, and what it meant to grow up, as Jennifer Baumgardner and Amy Richards (2000) wrote, with feminism just "in the water," in the sense of a completed project (p. 17). In retrospect, *Lizzie McGuire* is worth our critical attention as a key text in the spread of the ideals of choice and self-fashioning that helped inform the development of neoliberalism and the affect economy. Recent scholarship

(Blue, 2017; McRobbie, 2009; Kearney, 2015; Coulter, 2013, among others) has contributed to our understanding of how a particular construction of femininity, and a particular construction of liminal girlhood, came to prominence over the course of the late 1990s and early 2000s. Morgan Genevieve Blue (2017) discusses the production of girlhood on Disney channel shows, particularly *That's So Raven, Hannah Montana*, and *Wizards of Waverly Place*, while Natalie Coulter (2014) analyzes the cultural and especially marketing forces surrounding the "crystallization" of the "tween" girl beginning in the 1980s.

This essay seeks to add to those important works by interrogating another key figure and text in the formation of the tween girl as an ideal of girlhood in the early 2000s, Hilary Duff. By examining the foregrounding of the acts of performance, transformation, and self-display in both Duff's film and TV appearances and her real-life star persona, I hope to show that in the early to mid–2000s, Duff functioned as a spokeswoman for a white, heteronormative girl culture which privileged the appearance of independence over working towards societal change.

The Crystallization of the Tween Postfeminist

Duff's version of Girl Power for tweens doesn't come out of a vacuum; in Natalie Coulter's (2013) terms, the tween girl as a persona "crystallized within an environment of radical social, political and cultural changes of the 1980s and early 1990s—in the marketplace, in media and in the everyday family life and ideology within which girls came to know themselves as consumers" and as images to be consumed by others (p. 5). Key to this crystallization was the understanding of what feminine power looked like in popular discourse, and in the early to mid–2000s, that conversation was dominated by the concept of post-feminism.

Astrid Henry (2004) writes that the term "post-feminism … signals both failure and success, both an anti-feminist critique of the misguidedness of feminism and a pro-feminist nod to feminism's victories," and goes on to note that one of the most visible characteristics of third wave feminism is its "stress on individuality and individual definitions of feminism" (pp. 19, 43). Likewise, Leslie Heywood and Jennifer Drake (1997) point to "languages and images that account for multiplicity and difference, that negotiate contradiction in affirmative ways, and that give voice to a politics of hybridity and coalition" as valuable works of third wave feminism, works which privilege individual voices and allow for a variety of definitions of feminism (p. 9). Yet this emphasis on personal choice and the ability to couch almost any lifestyle in the language of feminism also has a darker side: is any choice a "feminist" choice? Hilary Duff's target audience in the early 2000s grew up with the idea of feminism as a given; Henry (2004, p. 39) cites Jennifer Baumgardner and Amy Richards' contention (2000) that "'the presence of feminism in our lives is taken for granted. For our generation, feminism is like fluoride. We scarcely notice that we have it—it's simply in the water'" (p. 17). Angela McRobbie (2009) addresses and expands upon this concept, terming it "feminism taken into account," which has resulted in distance and "utterances of forceful non-identity with feminism" which have "consolidated into something closer to repudiation rather than ambivalence" (pp. 14, 15). In other words, while the benefits of having feminism "in the water" are no doubt manifest, the absence of feminist discourse from popular culture means that during this period, American tween girls got a sense of what it meant to be female from texts which sent mixed messages to girls about "Girl Power" and the limiting factors of female independence in society.

Furthermore, this repudiation of second-wave feminism came along with an emphasis on the choices a girl makes as a neoliberal subject. McRobbie (2004) notes that although "the apparent capacity to choose in a more individualized society" receives much critical attention these days, it is important to take into account "how subject formation occurs by means of notions of choice *and* assumed gender equality coming together to actually ensure adherence to new unfolding norms of femininity" (pp. 10–11). McRobbie (2009) further clarified her position in her book *The Aftermath of Feminism*, in which she analyzes the process by which elements like "'empowerment' and 'choice'" are "converted into a much more individualistic discourse, and … are deployed in this new guise, particularly in media and popular culture, but also by agencies of the state, as a kind of substitute for feminism" (p. 1). In other words, just because one decides to call their lifestyle feminist does not necessarily make it so, and by extension, just because dominant American culture fills the airwaves with images of "Girl Power" does not necessarily mean that the images empower girls. Jessica K. Taft (2004) describes Girl Power as a post-feminist, or even anti-feminist movement which presents "a world with no need for social change," which "fails to provide girls with tools to understand and challenge situations where they experience sexism and other forms of oppression. Thus, girls are discouraged from seeing inequality and from engaging in challenges to such inequalities" (p. 73). The pop quintet the Spice Girls received much critical attention in regard to this questionable meaning of Girl Power in the mid– to late 1990s; Taft (2004) writes of the Spice Girls that "while their version of Girl Power may indeed be empowering, celebratory, and affirmative of girls' strength, it also contains anti-feminist messages" (p. 71). At the turn of the century, a similar critique could be leveled at Hilary Duff, with regard to both her onscreen roles and her public image.

Hilary Duff Is Just Like You

While the character of Lizzie McGuire functioned as a springboard for Hilary Duff's popularity, her real-life star persona helped. Duff's public image, with its heavy-handed emphasis on presenting teenage life as fun and wholesome, but with enough edge to appeal to a broad audience. As I will discuss later, the success of her image and her onscreen roles relied upon the ability to manufacture the illusion of edge, or gutsy independence, while maintaining a backbone of conservatism. After all, Duff did perform at the Youth Concert celebrating George W. Bush's inauguration ceremony. It must be noted here, however, that Duff's target demographic during the run of *Lizzie McGuire* and immediately thereafter was 8 to 14 (the tween demographic), not older; as Natalie Coulter (2013) notes, "The tween is a complicated lifestyle and developmental construct," both "predominantly defined as female" and linked to the image of "a consumer, in the largest possible sense of the word" (pp. 8, 9). Furthermore, the tween as a construct "does not have many of the responsibilities or pressures of adulthood; she has some of the sophistication and freedoms of adolescence, while being able to access the frivolity and playfulness of childhood" (Coulter, 2013, p. 12). Coulter argues that the very category of the tween "crystallizes" during the time period under consideration here; in other words, as Duff's star persona indicates, the definition of this stage of life and consumer demographic happens contemporaneously with the rise of figures like Duff, who are intentionally positioned as liminal in popular discourse. Instead of foregrounding teen rebellion and budding sexuality, as so many other stars her age did (see Lindsay Lohan, Miley Cyrus, Britney Spears), Duff's publicity team toed the line between childhood and girlhood, moral and edgy, normality and fame—addressing the fears and desires of the tween girl demographic. An examination of articles and interviews with Duff reveals that she and her team worked hard to establish three main points of appeal for potential audiences, which can be boiled down to (1) Hilary Duff is just like you; (2) Hilary Duff loves her family; and (3) Hilary Duff *could* be you, if you were discovered.

First, they sought to show viewers that Duff is a normal girl, just like her fans. Often she comes right out and declares her normality in the popular press. In a 2003 *USA Today* interview, Duff marvels at the strangeness of having her own fashion line: "It's weird that my name would be on something and make someone want to buy it…. It's crazy, because I'm such a normal teenager" (p. B3). In other cases, interviews focus on mundane elements of her daily life. *Rolling Stone* (Binelli, 2003) mentions that "[a]fter our interview, Duff has a photo shoot. 'Then I have to go home and clean my room,' she says, sighing" (p. 41). In addition to maintaining a normal life, the press points out, Duff also has to deal with relationships, like the much-publicized one with pop star Aaron Carter, which was on-again off-again for over two years, and incited a minor gossip rag skirmish with fellow pop star and Carter ex-girlfriend Lindsay Lohan. In 2003, she told *People* that "'[h]e messed up big last time … [but] he's being good this time'" (p. 83). Most articles in the early to mid–2000s tended to foreground her age and her desire to stay out of gossip columns, making sure that her fans know that she is one of them, young, prone to making romantic mistakes, impressionable, and dependent on her parents.

And indeed, Duff's relationship to her family forms the backbone of the second major tenet of her projected star persona: Hilary Duff is nice, wholesome, and kind—someone who would be your friend. In order to project this image, Duff's team emphasized her strong family values and the intense morality which distanced her from the Lindsay Lohan/Britney Spears paradigm of pop stardom. The publicized story of Duff's rise to fame emphasizes her parents' sacrifices; *Newsweek* (Stroup, 2003) notes that "the Duffs are from Texas. A makeup artist turned rancher, Susan [Duff] insists she 'never wanted to be a stage mom'…. But, five years ago, when the kids begged to be performers, she loaded them all into the family Acura—along with a hermit crab, a gerbil, two goldfish and a rabbit—and drove the 20 hours from Austin to L.A." (p. 56). And as *Teen People* (Amodio, 2004) insists, what keeps Duff grounded is "her close-knit family…. Hilary credits them with helping her steer clear of the wild Hollywood scene that brings down a lot of stars" (p. 93). By foregrounding Hilary Duff's roots in the heartland and her strong family ties, her publicists make sure her image appeals to more conservative audiences. Duff herself writes in *Texas Monthly* (2004) that "[b]ack when we lived out in the Hill Country, in Boerne, we had so much land that I ran wild" (p. 80). The image of a tomboy running wild in hill country runs counter to the typical persona of a teen pop star, but it is precisely this background which lends Duff her every-girl appeal.

Furthermore, Hilary Duff, during the run of *Lizzie McGuire,* projected an aura of morality. Quoted in the *New York Times* (Ogunnaike, 2004), Duff insists that "I think growing up means different things for different people,' she said, her slight five-foot frame wrapped snug in a fluffy pink cardigan. 'I don't think it means taking your clothes off and going out and partying'" (p. E1). *Seventeen* magazine (Grigoriadis, 2005) adds that Duff "definitely tries not to be judgmental of others, but you can tell she's bothered by what some other artists do for attention. 'When people try to rip off their clothes because they want to grow up so fast, it isn't a sign of maturity. That's a sign of immaturity. It's not a very good example either,' she says, and then quickly adds, 'But if they feel comfortable doing that, then more power to them'" (p. 120). Duff and her publicity team intentionally dissociated her from her pop star peers, but always with the caveat that Duff refused to pass judgment on the choices that others make. Articles on Duff refer to her unwillingness to be sexualized as a positive message for teens, some even going so far as to point out that this morality sets her apart from other teen stars. Hillary Frey (2003) in the *New York Times* writes that "Ms. Duff ... appears to be in no hurry to grow up—and that's refreshing" (p. B13), just as Mark Binelli in *Rolling Stone* (2003) notes that "she comes off as refreshingly innocent as her TV counterpart" (p. 40).

Finally, Hilary Duff's public image was designed to suggest to her fans that they, too, could be just like her—all it takes is being discovered. Anita Harris (2004) writes that "[i]t is in a world of celebrities, pop stars, supermodels, actresses, and entertainers that young women are encouraged to become somebody. Indeed, it is often these kinds of figures who are supposed to illustrate how young women have made it; they are emblematic of the arrival of the can-do girl in the public world" (p. 127). Duff's success positioned her as a role model for girls who dream of stardom; as Harris points out, young girls especially are socialized into the belief that becoming a star is the best way to demonstrate their self-worth. It involves hard work, but if you pay your dues, Duff suggests, you are rewarded. She writes in *Texas Monthly* (2004), "I struggled a lot with auditioning until I finally got the TV show Lizzie McGuire" (p. 80). And, as *Teen People* (Amodio, 2004) states, she "is no spoiled brat. 'I feel like the luckiest person on the [planet],' she says. 'My entire world is upside down in a good way, but I work my butt off for this'" (p. 94). But fame does not exempt one from the fears of performance, and her admitted stage fright humanizes her in a way that allows young fans to imagine themselves in the same situation. She writes in (2004), "When I performed at the American Music Awards last November, it was the first time I felt like I had hit the big time, because I had to sing in front of my peers. I was, like, 'I can't believe I'm doing this.' I had never performed in concert before. I didn't sleep the night before the show, I was so nervous" (Duff, p. 80). Her interest in pointing out her own flaws—nervousness, self-doubt— and her apparent success in overcoming these flaws positions her as a role model for young girls interested in entering show business. And indeed, as McRobbie (2009) points out, the visibility of girls requires active engagement in "the production of self. They must become harsh judges of themselves" (p. 60). Self-deprecation, here, becomes a means to connect with fans, but also exemplifies an ideal of girlhood that foregrounds performance as a key component of individual worth.

The fact that she shares her fears with fans also exemplifies the "confessional style" of entertainment, which Harris (2004) describes as having "become a particularly common mode of engaging young women in popular culture" in the 2000s (p. 128). The emergence of the confessional narrative was evident at the time in shows like *The Ashlee Simpson Show* (2004), which turned its title star's frailties into assets by foregrounding the ways in which her flaws made her more of a real person. This confessional mode of speaking characterizes virtually all of Duff's onscreen characters, particularly on *Lizzie McGuire*, where the cartoon version of Lizzie informs viewers what live-action Lizzie is truly thinking. Particularly during the early days of her singing career, Duff was an early adopter of using social media to connect to her audience, letting fans know how new the act of performance was to her. The use of blogging before the advent of social media was evidence of her sophistication when it came to the manipulation of this culture of confiding, of making the private public. It should be noted that Duff remains very active on Twitter and Instagram. This blending of the public and private with regard to not only Duff's life, but the lives of her characters, held appeal for tween fans encouraged to covet lives lived in the spotlight.

The above tenets lent her credibility to teenage and tween girls, even as the wholesome image she and her handlers cultivated allowed parents to feel comfortable in letting their children idolize Duff and use her as a role model. Even with a multi-platform entertainment career, Duff's interests in fashion, shopping, hanging out with friends, and maintaining a good relationship with her family painted her as a normal teenager—so normal, in fact, that the universalized adolescent experience she projected allowed a wide variety of potential fans to find points of identification with her. *People* (Schneider, et al., 2003) cites Duff's fans as attracted to her projection of normality: "fourth-grader Alexandria Elbaz likes her because 'she's nice and pretty.' And funny, adds her friend Gailann Singh, 9, who loves Duff because 'she's a real kid'" (p. 83). In the same article, the creator of *Lizzie McGuire*, Terri Minsky, states that Duff was given the role of Lizzie "because she could 'make all those early teen traumas seem not so scary, very relatable'" (p. 83). It is this element of "relatability" which made Hilary Duff so influential in the tween girl market in the early 2000s, and worth studying for the complexities of stardom, transformation, and performance in her film and TV appearances.

The Promise of Performance

One of the most pervasive film genres of the 2000s was the teen movie, though as Catherine Driscoll (2002) points out, "what has been called the teen flick or the teen film has been a staple of cinematic production since the 1940s, becoming widely recognized in the 1960s and then reemerging as a hypersuccessful genre in the 1980s" (p. 216). She further notes that "[r]egardless of their audience and even in spite of some of their content, teen films are received as girl films because of the transience of their form and content—their romantic narratives of transformation mediated by overt commodification" (p. 217). One of the most common narratives of the genre consists of a female adolescent, through her own machinations and/or the help of others, transforming herself from a pre-sexual ugly duckling into a desirable teen girl. While male-oriented coming-of-age narratives often center on the protagonist's drive to overcome adversity and learn the ways of the world, the female-targeted coming-of-age film is almost always concerned with finding one's place as a girl in mainstream society through the mastery of physical appearance, the demonstration of talent (usually artistic), and the pursuit of heterosexual pairing. This description is as accurate today as it was in the 1980s (and indeed, the 1950s; films like *Gidget* [1959] and *Tammy and the Bachelor* [1957] foreground all three of these elements), suggesting that dominant American culture still produces narratives of visual and behavioral transformation for a willing audience.

As I mentioned at the outset of this essay, Duff's roles in the early to mid–2000s all fit into the female coming-of-age narrative, which typically chronicles a moment of transition from girlhood to womanhood that involves the negotiation of identity and the successful completion of three aspects of femininity: the mastery of physical appearance, the demonstration of talent (usually artistic), and the pursuit of heterosexual pairing. For the sake of brevity, I will focus on Lizzie McGuire in *Lizzie McGuire* (2001–2003) and *The Lizzie McGuire Movie* (2003), but it's worth noting that *Cadet Kelly* (2002), *A Cinderella Story* (2004), and *Raise Your Voice* (2004) all adhere to a template of personal growth.

Narratives of transition to participation in dominant society involve several levels of change which rest upon the initial establishment of the character as a tomboy in need of growing up. As Lynn Peril (2002) writes in regard to "pink think," the process of hyper-feminine indoctrination at work in 1950s and 1960s popular culture, "By the middle of the twentieth century, most experts agreed that it was all right for girls to follow in Jo [March]'s footsteps [be a tomboy], but only to a certain point—usually adolescence" (p. 44). After that, a girl would need to adopt feminine traits or risk becoming a social outcast. And although in these post–Title IX days, the sanctioned participation of girls in organized sports does not preclude societal acceptance, such athleticism does not always connote tomboyness. As a result, in order to establish Duff's cinematic characters as tomboys in need of change, each film must find creative yet clear ways to demonstrate the immaturity of its protagonist.

To begin with, Lizzie McGuire is frequently defined by moments of transition. On the series, episodes focus on events like babysitting for the first time, shopping for a first bra, sneaking into an R-rated movie, and going steady for the first time, to name only a few. *The Lizzie McGuire Movie*, though, which is set at the end of the show's run, foregrounds change in an even more dramatic way. The film begins with Lizzie's graduation from middle school, where she is forced to give a spur-of-the-moment graduation speech, chokes, and trips off the stage, thereby destroying the curtains and decorations and essentially ruining graduation. Since news of her mishap aired on *Good Morning America*, she is understandably eager to set out on her school graduation trip to Rome and drown her embarrassment in the anonymity of a foreign country for two weeks. Here, a modern rite of passage marks a moment of change in Lizzie's life, and a desired escape from mundane life motivates her growth.

Yet a perceived failure of femininity on the part of the character up until this point also motivates the action. Lizzie herself voices concerns to this effect; as stated earlier, a "confessional" style characterizes much of entertainment for girls today, and in addition to Duff's extratextual confessions, her filmic characters tend to employ methods of personal confession. *Lizzie McGuire* is the most obvious example of this, since the show delivered Lizzie's internal monologue by way of an animated version of herself who pops into the frame and makes editorial comments which punctuate her successes and failures, but overall indicate the character's extremely low self-esteem.

But how Lizzie reveals herself directly only comprises a small fraction of her motivation for change—the reactions of other characters to Lizzie's assumed naiveté and failure to assimilate are based on indicators of appearance and/or class, and the desire to move past these social stigmas helps convince her to undergo a transition. At the outset of *The Lizzie McGuire Movie*, popular girl Kate immediately notices the sleeves of Lizzie's dress peeking out from under her graduation gown and disgustedly accosts her: "You're an outfit repeater! You wore that dress to the spring dance!" (Rogow & Fall, 2003). Such an accusation of fashion transgression points to both fashion and class inferiority; ostensibly a more "together" girl would know not to wear the same dress to two major school events. Kate is the primary antagonist in the *Lizzie McGuire* universe; her snide comments regarding fashion, makeup, and the elements of popularity are designed to remind the viewer of Lizzie's low place in the social hierarchy and her oft-stated need to win the approval of her peers. Although Lizzie has demonstrated competence in some traditionally tomboy areas, like physical strength ("Just One of the Guys")[1] and sports ("I've Got Rhythmic"),[2] these athletic endeavors are typically abandoned by episode's end. Clearly, the way to avoid the scorn of others and the implication that Lizzie is not a fully realized (read: feminized) young woman, she must make changes that address deficiencies in both social class and physical appearance.

In true American fashion, social success is largely determined by one's earning potential, and this generally means stardom for little girls. Harris (2004) quotes Susan Hopkins' contention that "'[t]he new hero is a girl in pursuit of media visibility, public recognition and notoriety. She wants to be somebody and 'live large.' In the postmodern world, fame has replaced marriage as the imagined means to realizing feminine dreams … fame is the ultimate girl fantasy'" (pp. 126–127). Other scholars have commented upon the drive for performativity in popular culture for and about girls, including Sarah Projanksy (2014), who notes that "media incessantly look at and invite us to look at girls. Girls are objects at which we gaze, whether we want to or not. They are everywhere in our mediascapes. As such, media turn girls into spectacles—*visual objects on display*" (p. 5). The process of becoming a spectacle, she writes, is "a discursive and economic strategy of turn-of-the-twenty-first-century celebrity culture easily applied to girls" (p. 5). Morgan Genevieve Blue addresses the way in which this spectacularization and emphasis on performance appears specifically in programming for tweens on the Disney channel: "Individualizing discourses in contemporary postfeminist girls' culture are driven by incitements to perform, which are rampant in Disney's efforts to sustain and grow its tween-aged consumer base" (p. 31). Blue further explains, "The construction of a tween girl idol relies on discourses of aspirational fantasy directed at and produced by girls. And girls' dreams, wishes, or fantasies of becoming famous entertainers are in part fueled by constructions of girls as possessed of natural talents just waiting to be discovered and made visible" (p. 32).

The *Lizzie McGuire* series, as stated earlier, opens with Lizzie's desire for fame, for the dazzling luminosity that characterizes those girls who attract others' attention. Elsewhere in the show, similar imagery appears again. In episode 23 of season one, for instance, Lizzie is chosen as a *Teen Attitude* model to walk the catwalk for a fashion show at the local mall. During the fashion show sequence, the upbeat music declares "everybody wants ya, when everybody sees ya" while Lizzie struts her stuff and spins with confidence. Canted angles in medium close up and close up, top lighting, and strategic photography flashes on Lizzie's face emphasize that she's reveling in her to-be-looked-at-ness. The rest of the episode, of course, deals with Lizzie's difficulty in managing her sudden celebrity. The positive feeling of fame gives way to cartoon Lizzie screeching "stop staring at me!" when she feels overwhelmed by the looks people give her in the hallway and the obsequious way her friends are acting. Eventually she intentionally bombs her next fashion show by dressing up as a slovenly bumpkin with a turkey leg and staging a mock fight with her friend Miranda. A similar sequence of shots, but without the flashbulb effect this time, suggests that Lizzie is also enjoying her dubious fame.

Furthermore, as episode 22 of season one exemplifies, Lizzie frequently wears shimmery or sparkly clothes to "stick out." In this episode in particular, she wants to catch the attention of a documentary filmmaker visiting the school. But in nearly every episode, Duff wears costumes that exemplify what

Mary Celeste Kearney (2015) has articulated as "sparkle." Kearney articulates the ubiquitousness and the implications of visual tropes of sparkle and luminosity, noting that "*[e]ither embodying or surrounded by light, young female characters are stylistically highlighted today in ways that make them visually superior to virtually all else in the frame*" (pp. 264–265). Blue notes, as does Kearney, that these aesthetic norms are especially visible in Disney Channel's depiction of girlhood (p. 40). Duff is frequently the shiniest figure in any given frame of the series, and by the end of *The Lizzie McGuire Movie*, her association with a luminous mise-en-scene is even more obvious.

Within narratives that focus on Duff's characters' singing talents, the act of being photographed or videotaped stands in as an indicator that success will come to the protagonist in the form of stardom. *The Lizzie McGuire Movie* opens with Lizzie's brother Matt affixing a video camera to a radio-controlled car, which he maneuvers into her room while she dresses for graduation. Scenes of animated Lizzie trying on clothes are interspersed with scenes of real-life Lizzie trying on outfits, dancing, lip-synching "The Tide Is High (Get the Feeling)" into a hairbrush, and falling into the bathtub—all of which Matt captures on videotape. In keeping with his diabolical characterization from the show, Matt plans to use the tape for blackmail, but this simply gives the sequence its narrative causality. Its real purpose is threefold: to establish Lizzie's aptitude for performance (she sings into the hairbrush, and we hear that she actually can sing), to mark her as a character worthy of being a cinematic spectacle, or worthy of an audience, and to suggest that this behavior—singing into a hairbrush, dancing as one gets dressed—is normal for a teenager and also indicative of the first two functions. Therefore, in one short credits sequence, the film sends the audience the message that (1) Lizzie McGuire, like Hilary Duff, is just like you, (2) Lizzie McGuire, like Hilary Duff, has performative potential, and (3) if Lizzie and Hilary can perform, you probably can, too.

Finding Your Voice

Of course, one of the most frequently discussed side effects of the digital age is the ability of a user to assume an alternate identity with little or no difficulty. While playing with notions of identity has remained at the center of teen movie narratives since the genre's inception (even Gidget has a secret identity), Duff's films often feature a literal trying-on of a completely different persona. This rite-of-passage exploration of selfhood also involves an element of rebellion, since any secret identity requires deception. The Roman adventure in *The Lizzie McGuire Movie* begins when Lizzie is mistaken for Italian pop star Isabella, half of the popular singing duo Paolo and Isabella. Due to

Lizzie's resemblance to Isabella (also played by Hilary Duff), Paolo recruits her to fill in for the mysteriously absentee Isabella at the International Music Video Awards, performing Isabella's part by lip-synching. In order to spend each day of her class trip learning dance moves, getting fitted for a dress, and going on Vespa trips around Rome, Lizzie pretends to be sick every morning until her chaperone leaves the hotel. Her best friend Gordo and former popular girl enemy Kate keep her secret and distract the chaperone. Interestingly, technology both helps and exposes Lizzie as an impostor before the climax of the film; her ability to lip-synch will help her deceive the IVMA audience, as Paolo points out, but once the Italian paparazzi start taking pictures of Lizzie-as-Isabella, Matt discovers them on the Internet and manufactures a reason to get the McGuire parents to take him to Rome so that he can expose her as a fraud.

The discovery of one's true voice, of course, is what the film suggests we should want for Lizzie. Although "true voice" is as vague a term as "Girl Power," the two phrases appear to be synonymous here, suggesting that the expression of voice, or standing up for yourself, is more or less an updating of Girl Power for audiences, as will become evident in the climax of the film. Before the final transformation, however, Lizzie must make changes in her physical appearance, addressing the criticisms of her peers and adopting a more feminine style which reflects her transformation into a sexual object. One of these changes, naturally, involves a fashion makeover. Driscoll (2002) notes that "[f]ashion provides a range of already sanctioned codes for coherence and recognition to be cited by the girl in pursuit of identity. In synthesizing this unified character, the beauty routine and the fashionable look are synecdochic of the process of adolescence" (p. 245). In other words, by changing clothes, an adolescent girl experiments with the ways in which she wants the world to perceive her according to pre-established meanings of dress. As stated earlier, Duff's public insistence that she had no intention of sexing up her image distanced her from contemporary pop stars like the similarly aged Lindsay Lohan (and even Britney Spears, though by the time of Duff's ascent, she was in her early twenties), who used eroticized self-display at the time as a means of self-expression. In her film roles, Duff largely rejects fashion trends that overtly expose the body; the act of exposure happens through the public exhibition of inner feelings, often mediated through technology, as discussed earlier.

Duff's unwillingness to sexualize her image in a predictable way forced her stylists to use fashion creatively to express her characters' moods and imply processes of identity transformation. Reflecting Hilary Duff's own self-proclaimed penchant for fashion experimentation, many of her films include at least one montage in which other characters dress her up in crazy outfits, the end result of which is Duff's character's own declaration of self through fashion. When Lizzie agrees to impersonate Isabella in *The Lizzie McGuire Movie*, Pablo takes her to Franca, a colorful Italian designer, who takes one look at Lizzie and shrieks, "I cannot put clothes on this! You, fix the hair, fix the eyebrows, fix the lips, fix the ears … jewelry!" (Rogow & Fall, 2003). What follows is a dress-up montage to "Supermodel," as Franca sends Lizzie down the runway in ridiculous concept dresses: a tabloid hat, a dress made out of Christmas lights, a plastic igloo dress, and a lime-green Louis XVI wig (cartoon Lizzie says, "Diva, good. Tacky, bad") (Rogow & Fall, 2003). But when Pablo tells her that she can dictate her own fashion choices, she stands up for herself, announcing, "I am not your Barbie doll! Choices, I need choices!" (Rogow & Fall, 2003). The sequence ends out on the street, where she says, "Goodbye Lizzie McGuire, hello fabulous," and signs autographs as Isabella (Rogow & Fall, 2003). Viewers do not see the final dress until the climax, making the image of transformed Lizzie all the more powerful.

If one of the underlying currents of the teen movie genre is that deep down, everyone wants to be popular, then the final outcomes of *The Lizzie McGuire Movie* certainly does nothing to challenge the importance of popularity. Celebrity, of course, means extreme popularity. As Harris (2004) writes, "the regular young person is able to work on him- or herself as a celebrity project and gain some kind of public profile in the process. With determination and effort, visibility and therefore success can be accomplished. Living outside the public gaze is for those who do not try hard enough" (p. 127). Indeed, in keeping with the idea that society teaches girls the value of a "life lived large," one of the most important components of a successful transformation in these films is the presence of witnesses—not just the audience, witnessing the film, but peers within the film who both legitimate and applaud the protagonist's triumph.

In Lizzie McGuire's case, a taste of false celebrity gives way to real celebrity, once she performs on the IVMAs as Lizzie, not Isabella. Lizzie's best friend Gordo (who has been in love with her throughout the entire series) keeps her secret by telling the chaperone that he is the one who has been sneaking out, not Lizzie, and gets kicked off the trip. At the airport, he runs into the real Isabella, who tells him that Paolo has designed the IVMAs performance as a way to sink Isabella and embark upon his own solo career; in fact, Paolo plans to lip-synch to a vocal track and leave Lizzie with an active microphone in order to publicly embarrass both her and Isabella. At the last minute, Gordo and Isabella intercept Lizzie and orchestrate a way to reveal Paolo as the bad guy—Isabella will sing on Lizzie's mike while they turn off the voice track for Paolo. Lizzie walks onstage in front of a massive audience at the Colosseum in a lavender, lacy, full-skirted dress, which looks like a small girl's fantasy of glamour. Her parents and brother have arrived in Rome, and they and everyone on the school trip have managed to sneak their way into the IVMAs, and are sitting in the front rows. Once Paolo, publicly humiliated as a horrendous singer, runs off the stage, Isabella walks onstage and explains the plot, introducing Lizzie and asking the crowd, "Would you like to hear her sing?" (Rogow & Fall, 2003). Isabella and Lizzie begin to sing together, then Isabella walks off the stage and leaves Lizzie by herself. She considers making a run for it, but offstage, Gordo gestures for her to stay and sing a song. Alone in the center of the stage, she is initially terrified, but quickly finds her feet and does the entire song, complete with choreography and backup dancers. At the end, a medium shot from behind of the huge cheering crowd, with blinding lights shining on her rapturous singing, signifies her total triumph. I would argue that, in keeping with the transition Kearney describes, as well as the narrative trope of transformation in popular culture aimed at teens and tweens, Lizzie's transition from awkward adolescent admiring other girls' shine to dazzling pop star in her own right signals the character's completion of a journey sanctioned by mainstream values.

The fact that this scene represents the culmination of two years' worth of TV episodes and a film adds to its satisfying quality; Duff's fans have seen her transition from an awkward pre-teen who trips over her feet and lands in garbage cans into a full-fledged celebrity. In addition, although most of the film centers on her attraction to Paolo, and most of the TV show focuses on her pursuit of hunky Ethan Craft, she finally realizes that the boy she has been looking for is right in front of her. Like Jay and Austin, Gordo has encouraged her to follow her dreams throughout the entire narrative, and indeed, Gordo has been one of her primary supporters for two years of a TV series.[3] The film ends as she finally kisses Gordo on a balcony overlooking Rome. Although they are both embarrassed and quickly go back inside, this scene, a confirmation of heteronormativity, acts as a capper for the *Lizzie McGuire* franchise.

Taft (2004) writes that Girl Power tells young female consumers that success comes to a girl "Through hard work, standing up for what she believe[s] in, and following her dreams," yet such pervasive messages in media "place the responsibility for achievement on the shoulders of each individual girl. Not only can this lead to feelings of inadequacy and low self-esteem, but this meaning of Girl Power as individual power could serve to inhibit girls' connections with one another, reduce the possibilities for social analysis and critical thinking, and thus hinder girls' social and political engagement" (pp. 73–74). Although it seems extreme to suggest that telling girls to follow their dreams could have a negative impact, it indeed discourages the idea that society itself could be a factor in their inability to achieve those dreams.

The climactic song in *The Lizzie McGuire Movie* tells girls that having "somewhere [to] belong" and "somebody to love" is "what dreams are made of" (Rogow & Fall, 2003). For those of us who grew up with feminism "in the water," as Jennifer Baumgardner and Amy Richards (2000) put it, the idea that we can achieve anything if we follow our dreams was instilled in us from a very early age (p. 39). But where are those dreams coming from? In each of these films, and in Duff's own life, she has not needed to change the system, because she has managed to change herself to work within the system. As a girl who presents herself as the epitome of normality, Duff suggests that if a postfeminist society, a heteronormative lifestyle, and even conservative politics worked for her, it ought to work for her fans, as well. The success of the new Girl Power—finding one's own true voice and shouting it to the world— relies upon the media's images of which "voices" will help girls to achieve appropriate dreams. The onscreen and offscreen personas of Hilary Duff tell girls that having and pursuing dreams make life worth living, if those dreams involve finding heterosexual romance and expressing "voice" through socially acceptable channels.

NOTES

1. Bargiel, N. & Bargiel, J. (Writers), & De Jarnatt, S. (Director). (November 21, 2003). One of the Guys [Television series episode]. In S. Rogow (Producer), *Lizzie McGuire*. Los Angeles, CA: Disney Channel Original Productions. This episode shows Lizzie's upper body strength during the Presidential Physical Fitness Test, when she beats everyone on the chin-up bar. Her athleticism leads resident heartthrob Ethan Craft to challenge Lizzie to arm-wrestling (she wins) and then invite her to play touch football. After she proves that she is skilled at football, she undergoes a crisis of gender identity in which she expresses horror that people might think of her as a "guy-girl," and spends extra time doing her hair and makeup and choosing her outfit in the morning. No one notices a difference. After a talk with the gym teacher Coach Kelly, Lizzie decides to help her team win the game.

2. Neufeld Callaway, N. (Writer), & Myerson, A. (Director). (February 9, 2001). I've Got Rhythmic [Television series episode]. In S. Rogow (Producer), *Lizzie McGuire*. Los Angeles, CA: Disney Channel Original Productions.

3. Although this is not addressed in the film, on the show *Lizzie McGuire*, Gordo is figured as a budding Steven Spielberg, and videotapes Lizzie quite a few times over the course of the series, even having her star in an amateur music video.

REFERENCES

Amodio, R. (2004, Nov.). Hangin' out with Hilary. *Teen People*, Vol. 7, Iss. 9, pp. 92–96.

Baumgardner, J., & Richards, A. (2000). *Manifesta: Young women, feminism, and the future.* New York: Farrar, Straus and Giroux.

Binelli, M. (2003, Sep. 18). Teenager of the year. *Rolling Stone*, Iss. 931, pp. 40–41.

Blue, M.G. (2017). *Girlhood on Disney Channel: Branding, celebrity, and femininity.* New York: Routledge.

Coulter, N. (2013). *Tweening the girl: The crystallization of the tween market.* New York: Peter Lang.

Driscoll, C. (2002). *Girls: Feminine adolescence in popular culture & cultural theory.* New York: Columbia University Press.

Duff, H., & Vine, K. (2004, Apr.). Teeny popper. *Texas Monthly*, Vol. 32, Iss. 4, p. 80.

Frey, H. (2003, Apr. 27). How Hilary Duff made off with your daughter. *New York Times*, p. B13.

Gould, M. (Writer), & Israel, N. (Director). (January 12, 2001). Rumors [Television series episode]. In S. Rogow (Producer), *Lizzie McGuire*. Los Angeles: Disney Channel Original Productions.

Grigoriadis, V. (2005 Jun.). Hilary Duff. *Seventeen*, p. 120.

Harris, A. (2004). *Future girl: Young women in the twenty-first century*, New York: Routledge.

Henry, A. (2004). *Not my mother's sister: Generational conflict and third-wave feminism.* Bloomington: Indiana University Press.

Heywood, L., & Drake, J. (1997). *Third wave feminism: Being feminist, doing feminism.* Minneapolis: University of Minnesota Press.

Hopkins, S. (2002). *Girl heroes: The new force in popular culture.* Sydney: Pluto Press, qtd. in Harris, A. (2004). *Future girl: Young women in the twenty-first century.* New York: Routledge.

Just can't get enough of Duff. (2003, Jul. 16). *USA Today*, p. B3.

Kearney, M.C. (2015) Sparkle: Luminosity and post-girl power media. *Continuum*, vol. 29, no. 2, 263–273.

Kehr, D. (2003, May 2). First rule for a class trip: Shuck the chaperone. *New York Times*.

McRobbie, A. (2004). Notes on postfeminism and popular culture: Bridget Jones and the new gender regime. In Anita Harris (Ed.), *All about the girl: Culture, power, and identity* (pp. 3–14). New York: Routledge.

McRobbie, A (2009). *The aftermath of feminism: Gender, culture and social change.* Los Angeles: Sage.

Ogunnaike, L. (2004, Oct. 13). Hilary Duff has no plans to go the steamy, risque route. *New York Times*, E1.

Peril, L. (2002). *Pink think: Becoming a woman in many uneasy lessons.* New York: W.W. Norton.

Rogow, S. (Producer) & Fall, J. (Director). (2003). *The Lizzie McGuire Movie* [Motion Picture]. USA: Walt Disney Pictures.

Schneider, K., Dagostino, M., Labossiere, R., & Wang, C. (2003, May 19). 'Tween queen. *People*, Vol. 59, Iss. 19., p. 83.

Stroup, K. (2003, Mar 17). Girl power. *Newsweek* Vol. 141, Iss. 11, 56–57.

Taft, J. (2004). Girl power politics: Pop-culture barriers and organizational resistance. In Anita Harris (Ed.), *All about the girl: Culture, power, and identity* (pp. 69–78). New York: Routledge.

Weeks, L. (2005, Jan. 20). Enthusiastic parties to a second term; Celebrity-studded galas peak tonight with inaugural balls. *The Washington Post*, p. A42.

That's So Afrofuturist

That's So Raven,
Black Radical Imagination
and Afrofuturist Tweens

Terah J. Stewart

The cultural impact of *That's So Raven* within the Disney tween television universe is undeniable. Raven Baxter has been studied, written about, and analyzed in terms of her cultural significance both within and outside of the academy (Bell, 2015; Curtis, 2018). Raven-Symoné Pearman was one of the first African American women to star in a Disney Channel series, and *That's So Raven,* which first aired January 17, 2003, would go on to be the first Disney Channel original television series to reach 100 episodes (Alston, 2016). Scholars and researchers have studied the importance of minoritized children seeing people that "look like them," citing that it helps develop more confidence, self-esteem, and pride in their racial and ethnic identities (Stroman,1991; Ward, 2004), and *That's So Raven* was a show that offered important representation.

Raven Baxter was the original "awkward Black girl," and as such, she provided an example of one way Black girls could *be* in the world. *That's So Raven* also served as a representation of what a Black family could be in the new millennium, especially on the Disney Channel, where, up until that point, there were limited examples. Throughout the course of the show, there were vivid moments when it seemed that writers and showrunners were interested in centering a deliberate representation of Blackness. An example of this is when actress T'Keyah Crystal Keymah (Tanya Baxter) intentionally wore her natural hair in nearly every episode. These efforts were further achieved through the way Raven and her family spoke, engaged each other, through their mannerisms, and through music and pop-culture references.

Finally, Raven's gift as a psychic was not only foundational to the story, but I argue, foundational to Black tweens and their early conceptualizations of Afrofuturism, what it meant to dream, imagine, and self-define/create as an act of resistance.

In this essay, I will argue that *That's So Raven* was key in developing radical imaginations for Black tweens who watched the series. I position Afrofuturism and radical black imagination as important concepts to examine the representations offered on and through the show. I will also discuss critiques of the show, including considerations about the problematic nature of some of the representations, including the way Raven was racialized, which troubles her archetype as a Black girl on television (Bell, 2015). I will also discuss the legacy of the show, as well as the implications and dissonance of Raven-Symone's contemporary (and often contrary) identity-politics to the legacy.

Afrofuturism

Afrofuturism is a conceptual undertaking that involves how Black people imagine possible futures for themselves against dominant narratives about who they are and who they are supposed to be (Womack, 2013). Usually, these imaginings include science, technology, historical fiction and science fiction that position African ascendants in ways that break away from a violent and oppressive past. This (re)visioning of past and future often includes cultural critique while centering re-definition and self-definition as an act of resilience and a buffer to the harsh realities of life (Womack, 2013).

The term Afrofuturism was first coined in 1994 in an essay titled "Black to the Future" written by Mark Dery. In his essay, Dery explored why there were so few Black science fiction writers, and if the dearth of representation in art related to science, technology, and mysticism had implications for Black people:

> Can a community whose past has been deliberately rubbed out, and whose energies have subsequently been consumed by the search for legible traces in history, imagine possible futures? Furthermore, isn't the unreal estate of the future already owned by the technocrats, futurologists, streamliners and set designers—white to the man— who have engineered our collective fantasies? [Dery, 1994; p. 180].

Dery alludes to a critical imperative in that, the violence of colonialism and the transatlantic slave trade nearly *requires* that Black people—as an historically subjugated people—determine ways to visualize themselves beyond the scope of such terror and dominance. One might critique the perception that we must break away from the dark and violent parts of our history; however,

Afrofuturism suggests that an Afrofuturist does not need to ignore or be ignorant of their histories and legacies *and* that history should not confine their creativity or imagination (Womack, 2013).

While Afrofuturism did not receive explicit terminology until the '90s, Black women have been writing about Afrofuturism and centering Black women and girls in those futures for many years (Butler, 1989; Butler, 1993). In fact, Dery names Octavia Butler as one of the pioneers and prominent writers of Black science fiction which renders visible imaginations and possibilities of Blackness in dynamic and material ways. As a Black woman, Womack (2013) speaks to the importance of Afrofuturist work, and, I argue, specifically for Black women and girls. She articulates the symbolic and material value of representations:

> Afrofuturism is a great tool for wielding the imagination for personal change and societal growth. Empowering people to see themselves and their ideas in the future gives rise to innovators and free thinkers, all of whom can pull from the best of the past while navigating the sea of possibilities to create communities, culture, and a new, balanced world. The imagination is the key to progress, and it's the imagination that is all too often smothered in the name of conformity and community standards [Womack, 2013; p. 191].

In the case of Raven Baxter, I posit that tween psychic powers and abilities also fit within this realm of Afrofuturism through mysticism, wonder, and magic, which provided a powerful foundation for Black tweens to nurture their imaginations.

At the Intersection of Black, Teen and Psychic

The major premise of *That's So Raven* is that she is a young Black girl with psychic powers simply trying to figure out the world and her place in it. Given that the psychic aspect of her character arc was the main premise of the show, in this section, I intend to highlight examples of deliberate representations of Blackness that were represented throughout the series. Her psychic abilities, taken together with my illustration of Blackness, will demonstrate just how Black tweens benefited from such representation and positions them to do so across time.

That's So Raven Theme

At the onset of the show is the original theme song. Raven Symone—a known singer/songwriter—performed her own theme song, which was a type of rap/pop fusion. In addition to the verse sung by Raven and the chorus sung by Raven and Annaliese van der Pol (Chelsea), the theme also included a bridge rapped by Orlando Brown (Eddie), a distinct and unique decision for a Disney Channel original theme.

In the formal promotional video for the show—which included the full-length version of the theme song from the series soundtrack—the cast and extras performed in a music video shot in a studio designed to be reminiscent of New York City. That particular marketing and creative decision communicated that while this show was for everyone, there is a particular demographic the showrunners wanted to be seen: Black people and people of color.

Language

Throughout the show, there are countless examples of representation through the use of, naming, and centering of language. For example, in S1E21, "To See or Not to See," Chelsea and Raven engage in conversation after gym class and Chelsea confesses that she thinks Raven smells bad. Raven, a little shocked at Chelsea's honesty, offers a distinct and disapproving look:

> CHELSEA: I know. I mean, my hair is all a mess and I'm like really sweaty … and FYI, you kinda smell a little. [laugh track]
> RAVEN: [inaudible].
> CHELSEA: Actually, you smell a lot. [laugh track]
> RAVEN: …
> CHELSEA: …Just keepin' it real Rae, just keepin' it real.
> RAVEN: Hey Chelsea, I taught you that phrase … don't use it against me [laugh track] [Banks-Waddles & Savel, 2004].

While Chelsea was the one to deliver the specific line, the scene demonstrates that Raven, as a Black girl, has very distinct vernacular and language which, had she not been Black, the dynamic of the scene would have been lost in translation. Further, there is a deliberate demonstration of Raven engaging in cultural exchange with Chelsea, indicated by her reminding that *she* taught Chelsea the phrase and likely what it meant.

Another scene that helps to situate and illustrate the importance and relevance of the Baxters as a Black family was conveyed in S1E12, "Teach Your Children Well." During this episode, Tanya Baxter is selected as a substitute teacher for Raven's English class. During the episode, Tanya delivers a reading of *Romeo & Juliet*; however, her lesson is not particularly interesting to the students, to which she states:

> TANYA: Ok, let me try and make this a little easier. If Shakespeare were writing today, it might sound more like this, "Yo! Romeo! Where you at? Ok. Tell your daddy if he don't like us together then that's just too bad. Cuz this Juliet ain't waiting around for some fool in tights named Romeo. You hear what I'm saying?"
> And uh, Romeo might sound like this, [reminiscent of Chris Tucker] "Do you

believe the words that are comin outta her mouth? Should I speak up and make a fool of myself? Or just let her go on and on about how fine she think I am?" [Seriff, Tarson & Singletary, 2003].

Through this scene, actress T'Keyah Crystal Keymah truly shines, and her performance is reminiscent of her previous work on the sketch comedy show *In Living Color*. While Tanya Baxter is simply trying to relate course material to students in more accessible terms, she does so through a re-interpretation in modern times that directly reflect aspects of AAVE (African American Vernacular English). This is much to the dismay of Raven's character; however, her dismay is based in the fact that it was her mother—as teens are supposed to be embarrassed by their parents—and not necessarily her choice to represent *Romeo and Juliet* that way. These are two of countless examples of how language is utilized as a cultural device to situate and not shy away from the Blackness of characters.

To be clear, I do not suggest that Blackness is a monolith or a singular experience. I do argue that there are certain aspects of Black experiences that networks, throughout history and across time, have been shy in embracing. In these examples, language—although probably situated as being more "cool" or relatable to tweens and teens—is in fact an indicator of Black expression. In some ways, it could be argued that the show engages in *stereotypes* of Blackness at times, and I explore that criticism later.

Tackling Race

That's So Raven was courageous in the various issues that it tackled on the show, particularly for a teen/tween audience. Through the episode "Royal Treatment" (S3E12), the show addresses bullying, but specifically within a cultural context, as an exchange student from the continent of Africa is teased for wearing his traditional garb. In the episode "That's So Not Raven" (S2E8), the show addresses body image and the importance of being comfortable in one's own skin and at any size. Through the episode titled "Five Finger Discount" (S3E5), the show explores peer pressure and decision-making when Raven attempts to prevent her little brother Cory from stealing after hanging with a new group of friends. Indeed, *That's So Raven* addresses many important topics, and the issue of race and Blackness was also a critical subject.

The episode that illustrates a deliberate centering of Blackness and the Black experience aired as S3E10, "True Colors." This episode follows two different arcs: the first is Cory's, who struggles to see the significance in Black History Month, celebrating Black culture, and acknowledging his heritage. Later in the episode, Cory is visited by Frederick Douglass, Bessie Coleman, Scott Joplin, Harriet Tubman, Jackie Robinson, Thurgood Marshall, Sojourner Truth, Madame C.J. Walker, Althea Gibson, Marcus Garvey, Mary McLeod

Bethune, and Jessie Owens. During the course of these visits, Cory finally understands the importance of Black history, culture, and the contributions of several pioneers.

The other primary story arc follows Raven and Chelsea as they attempt to apply for jobs at a clothing store that they often frequent. During the course of their interview, the subsequent tests, and evaluation, it is clear that Raven exceeds all expectations—while Chelsea does not—and Raven is set to receive the offer. However, the next day at school, Chelsea is offered the job and Raven is not. Bewildered by the news in that moment, Raven receives a vision where she sees the hiring manager state: "The truth is, I don't hire Black people." Eddie responds to Raven that the manager's decision is discriminatory.

Raven's parents encourage her to advocate for herself, and as a result, she partners with Chelsea and Eddie to catch the store manager stating on camera that she does not hire Black people, the same statement that Raven saw in her vision. The manager is ousted on the local news and ultimately fired. This particular episode is successful in both uplifting Blackness, its histories, and legacies, while also naming in a visible and deliberate way the realities of discrimination and prejudice Black people experience. While these topics are commonplace for many of us today, for the tweens and teens in the early to mid–2000s, "True Colors" highlighted, in accessible terms, an example of those harsh realities.

The synthesis of both Raven's Blackness as a site of racial prejudice and her reality as being psychic become so blended in the "True Colors" episode that the viewer *almost* forgets. The violence of discrimination *almost* renders her powers invisible and we, for a small still moment, let the magic of Raven slip away. The salvation, however, comes in the form of her vision, a "gift" most of us do not have, and yet, we are filled up by Raven's possession of it. This particular moment/episode is an apex example of Afrofuturism; a moment that both uniquely indicts the realities of oppression/dominance but helps uncover it and subsequently find a way *through* it; leaning on her magic and mysticism.

That's So Radical Black Imagination

Connected to this idea is the concept of Black Radical Imagination (Kelley, 2003). In his text *Freedom Dreams*, author Robin Kelly (2003) highlights and centers the ways Black people have created art and tapped into imagination as a matter of sustenance and resistance. I contend that the ability of tweens to bear witness to a show such as *That's So Raven* allowed them to resist oppressive structures through their imaginings, similarly to how Raven was able to resist oppressive structures with her psychic powers. Further, Kelly contends that a requirement for liberation goes beyond "merely a refusal of victim status" (p. 191); on the contrary, Kelley (2003) argues, "I am talking about an unleashing of the mind's most creative capacities, catalyzed by participation in struggles for change" (p. 191), which is illustrated in the episode "True Colors." Raven embraces the struggle in which she finds herself, precipitated *by* her psychic vision. In this way, imaginings and of and with Blackness serve as precursors to revolution; and, as such, creativity, not rationality, is the imperative. Kelley (2003) states:

> any revolution must begin with thought, with how we imagine a New World, with how we reconstruct our social and individual relationships, with unleashing our desire and unfolding a new future on the basis of love and creativity rather than rationality [p. 193].

There are countless examples of a representative Blackness that operates in tandem with Raven's psychic powers. From music, to fashion, to familial gifts passed down—Raven's grandmother, played by Jennifer Lewis, also possesses psychic powers—in 100 episodes, the Baxters are a fascinating representation for Black tweens, one that will not soon be forgotten. A representation that allowed tweens to imagine themselves out of difficult—and at times discouraging—realities, yet still embrace the beauty and wonder of their Blackness.

The Conundrum of Representation

Throughout this essay, I have suggested *That's So Raven* served as an important and necessary representation for Black tweens, particularly as it relates to those tweens needing representations of themselves in a universe where people that look like them are literal magic. This representation, however, is not without problematization or critique.

To begin, there are some that might argue that a Black woman character who has psychic powers is both a fictional stereotype and legitimate archetype often assumed by Black women. Typically, this archetype is situated as part of a history and legacy of African Indigenous practices and religions related to voodoo, hoodoo, and witchcraft and *perceptions* of traditional African religions interpreted as witchcraft or "black magic" by colonizers. An early example of the consequences of this archetype can be traced back to the 1600s as the famous Tituba, an enslaved woman from the Caribbean, was accused of practicing and teaching witchcraft during the infamous Salem witch trials (Magoon, 2008). I believe the combination of her Blackness and corresponding white supremacy found her swiftly guilty as the genesis of the witchcraft that erupted in Salem, specifically within the household of her slaver, Minister Samuel Parris. She was an easy target *precisely* because of the perception of Black women and magic, witchcraft, and supernatural powers and gifts.

In more contemporary times, Black women have been the "face" of this type of mysticism, such as Youree Dell Harris (better known as "Miss Cleo" [Andrews, 2016]), Dionne Warwick and her Psychic Friends Network (Errico, 1998), and Latoya Jackson and her Psychic Friends Network (Ryan, 1998). This archetype is so prevalent that showrunners parodied Raven serving as a TV/hotline psychic by the name of Ms. Talula. In S1E17, "Psychics Wanted," Raven takes a job as a hotline psychic to make money so she can take a guy at her school out on a date. After the previous star of the Psychic Sidekicks show—Ms. Cassandra, played by Niecy Nash—quits, Raven is promoted to the star of the show. She is ultimately fired for telling the truth about the fake psychic network. While there are limited writings on the relevance and significance of these representations, what I would suggest is a show like *That's So Raven* would not have been as successful had Raven not been Black. Whether this reality is a result of the aforementioned stereotypes or archetypes deserves an analysis all its own.

That's So Stereotypical

Scholars and writers have critiqued *That's So Raven* for how Raven and her best friend Chelsea were juxtaposed within the show, citing that some of Raven's representation was achieved through stereotypical Blackness. Bell (2015) critiqued five episodes that explored the racialization of Raven, and found a pattern in that representation:

> First, the friendship between Raven and Chelsea set the context for these episodes. In fact, their relationship is a major component of the show. Secondly, conflict arises in which each character not only expresses opposing sides, but their divergent positionalities represent a certain value and belief system. Finally, Chelsea disagrees with Raven's views on social and political issues, and in the end, it is Chelsea, according to the show's narrative, who is right and thus Raven places her friend's position and desires before her own. The viewer is lead [*sic*] to believe that Chelsea is not only right, but her whiteness, much like a colonial model, serves as a calculated greater good for all the students, particularly the Black students [Bell, 2015; p. 58].

The types of issues that Raven and Chelsea disagreed on included health and wellness, as evidenced by the "Food for Thought" episode (S3E29), where Chelsea advocates for healthy options, and Raven and Eddie initially celebrate the stereotypical "unhealthy" options. Another example cited by Bell (2015) is illustrated in the episode "On Top of Old Oaky" (S3E16) or "Skunk'd" (S2E16), where Raven and Eddie either show a lack of interest in environmental justice, or they project a simple blithe unawareness. This representation, of course, is set in contrast to Chelsea who, despite *her* dunce-like character trope, always seems to be the person that holds the moral compass or invites the other cast members to take the moral high ground on some political or social issue (Bell, 2015).

There is a natural tension between authentic and stereotypical representations of Blackness within *That's So Raven* which I referenced through the previous illustrative examples of how language—particularly AAVE—is often used as a device to situate cultural identity. Bell's critique is a compelling one, and admittedly a critical perspective from the gaze of a critical scholar and parent who fairly asks the question, "How is this representation harmful?" On the other hand, for the vast majority of tweens—and perhaps some of their parents—this level of critical analysis is likely lacking. So, it begs the question about whether a problematic representation is more helpful than no representation (in this case, on the Disney Channel specifically)? In regard to this tension, I think about the work of bell hooks and her philosophies and teachings on media, representation, and what it means to be an "enlightened witness" to those representations. hooks borrowed the term enlightened witness from Psychoanalyst Alice Miller (hooks, 2003), and applies/d it in many different ways. Within the context of media and representation, she offers:

> the issue is not freeing ourselves from representation. It's really about being enlightened witnesses when we watch representations, which means we are able to be critically vigilant about both what is being told to us and how we respond to what is being told. Because I think that the answer is not the kind of censoring absolutism of a right-wing political correctness but in fact of a proactive sense of agency that requires of all of us one, a greater level of literacy [hooks & Jhally, 1997; DVD].

From this perspective, I argue that despite the problematic aspects of Raven's racialization—and the representation of Blackness more generally on the show—as Black teens and tweens learned and grew in their understandings of social identity, they were likely able to reconcile the complicated and competing truths. To this end, a less than perfect representation such as *That's So Raven* still serves as a critical component in the development of Black tweens/teens media literacy generally, and more specifically cultivates a desire for Afrofuturistic representations that nourish their radical Black imaginations.

A Tale of Two Ravens

Raven Baxter served to ground important conceptualizations of Black tweens in ways they could imagine themselves, and those imaginings served as important reframes of possible futures. In the early 2010s Raven-Symoné, however, came under fire for some of her questionable politics around race and social identity that stand in contrast with some of the Black representations the show represented.

In a 2014 interview with Oprah Winfrey, Raven shared that she is someone who doesn't believe in "labels." She went on to say, "I'm tired of being labeled, I'm an American. I'm not African American; I'm an American" (OWN, 2014). Raven went on to indicate that her inability to trace her roots to the continent of Africa is/was a point of contention for her, and that she identified with her Louisianan roots; she sees herself as connecting with "each culture." Raven was heavily criticized for her rhetoric, namely that it served to diminish and distance herself from her Blackness. Further, identifying as a Black person does not necessarily preclude anyone from connecting with other people and cultures. In this way, Raven's articulations were clearly about not wanting to be labeled Black, because, as it turns out, to be labeled an "American" is still a label.

In 2015, while serving as a co-host on the ABC daytime talk show *The View*, Raven engaged with her co-hosts around an offensive comment made by a Univision TV host Rodner Figueroa. During the segment, the hosts revealed that Figueroa compared the appearance of Michelle Obama to that of an ape from the film *Planet of the Apes*. Raven seemingly defended Figueroa stating:

> Was he saying it racist-like? Because he said that he voted for her later, and I don't think he was saying it racist…. Michelle, don't fire me from this right now but some people look like animals. I look like a bird. So can I be mad if somebody calls me Toucan Sam? [Gennis, 2015; para 3 & para 6].

A number of people criticized Raven and her line of thinking, citing that regardless of if Figueroa meant it as a joke or not, there is a history of racial violence connected to comparing Black people to monkeys and apes which is problematic. Further, it should not be understated that Figueroa is of Latin American heritage; he is fair-skinned, and his comment invoked issues around colorism more broadly both within and across racial groups including, and especially, communities of color. The fact that the multiple dynamics related to this moment were lost on Raven made many people begin to question and wonder about her racial and identity politics. She later went on to say she was not defending Figueroa, but stated, "Some comments are rude, some are disrespectful, and some are racist. Try not to exchange one for the other" (Fallon, 2015).

Finally, in 2015—again while co-hosting *The View*—Raven came under fire for her suggestions that *everyone* should be able to use the N-word. The topic came about because actor Terrence Howard expressed to showrunners that he wanted to use the term—because it made contextual sense to him—in the environment of the show, *Empire*. Raven suggested that it should not be a big deal and that:

We [young/er people] don't look at is as racism as the way your [older] generation does. You guys worked hard and fought hard and went through a whole bunch of [redacted] to make sure we live a better life. And when we do, "You need to remember what happened." We're trying to move forward [*The View*, 2015].

Once again, Raven illustrated that her beginnings squarely and firmly within a Black experience, on television, through her roles on *The Cosby Show* and later on *That's So Raven,* were out of step with her more contemporary understandings and articulations of Blackness, experiences related to racism and dominance, and what those things meant in a contemporary context.

To be clear, actors are not the characters they play, and certainly Raven-Symoné is not the first actor/artist to disappoint fans or supporters related to socio-political opinions she harbors. However, it is worth mentioning that throughout her career, she has participated in critical representations of Blackness and Black families on TV and in film, including the reboot of *Dr. Doolittle, The Cosby Show, Hanging with Mr. Cooper, My Wife and Kids, College Road Trip, That's So Raven,* and the admittedly watered-down TV adaptation of *The Cheetah Girls.* As such, it is troublesome that such a legacy is marred by her contemporary politics, and while it is disappointing, her impact on a generation of tweens is undeniable. In representation, politics, and popular culture, these are complicated and competing truths we must wrestle with.

Conclusion

Raven Baxter, the relatable teen from California, was a character many of us came to know and love. So much so that, 10 years later, *Raven's Home* premiered—a series sequel that explores Raven's experience navigating her psychic powers, her career, divorce, and motherhood. *That's So Raven* became a possibility model for Black family/tween programs that went beyond situational comedy, and incorporated elements—mysticism, powers, psychic abilities and Blackness—in meaningful and material ways. I believe Queenie, the human voodoo doll/witch—Gabourey Sidibe's character—on *American Horror Story: Coven* was made possible, in part, because of Raven Baxter. Bonnie Bennett from the *Vampire Diaries,* Abbie and Jenny Mills from *Sleepy Hollow,* were/are all powerful on TV because a generation of Afrofuturist tweens once knew a Black girl psychic; one that was real, imperfect, and just trying to figure it all out. They once knew a Black girl psychic, and through knowing her, those later representations were not only desired by audiences writ large, but they were also normalized. While Raven Baxter was certainly not the first representation of this type, within the context of the Disney Channel tween-verse, she made a mark and forged a path that is undeniable.

Given the current socio-political climate, imagining futures for Black people and Blackness are at a premium. The major box office smash success of the 2018 film *Black Panther* (as an example) shows evidence that the African American community continues to yearn for representations of ourselves that break away from the violence of our histories and legacies. While it would be difficult to pinpoint, I argue that the community and market around Blackness, Afrofuturism, and representation in TV and film is connected to early representations such as *That's So Raven*. We continue to seek representations that serve to sustain and refill; they remind us that there are possible futures filled with joy and freedom. There was a time when *That's So Raven* took up needed space in the imagination of Black tweens all over the United States and the world, and it allowed them to "gaze into the future" and see one filled with imagination, possibility, and wonder.

REFERENCES

Alston, J. (2016, May 16). That's So Raven changed Disney Channel in ways no one could have predicted. Retrieved April 30, 2018, from https://tv.avclub.com/that-s-so-raven-changed-disney-channel-in-ways-no-one-c-1798247263.

Andrews, T.M. (2016, July 27). The many lives of Youree Dell Harris a.k.a. the "psychic" Miss Cleo, dead at 53. Retrieved from https://www.washingtonpost.com/news/morning-mix/wp/2016/07/27/the-bizarre-legacy-left-behind-by-the-actress-who-played-miss-cleo/?noredirect=on&utm_term=.9f946f23ea23.

Banks-Waddles, C., & Savel, D. (Writers), Correll, R. (Director). (2004, March 5). Too See or Not to See [Television series episode]. In *That's So Raven*. Burbank, CA: Walt Disney Television.

Bell, R.J.J. (2015). Racializing Raven: Race and gender in That's So Raven. *Humboldt Journal of Social Relations*, 55.

Butler, O.E. (1993). *Parable of the sower*. New York: Four Walls Eight Windows.

Butler, O.E. (2000). *Lilith's brood*. New York: Aspect/Warner Books, ©1989.

Curtis, T. (2018, January 17). Raven Baxter of "That's So Raven" was the OG awkward Black girl. Retrieved April 28, 2018, from https://hellogiggles.com/reviews-coverage/tv-shows/hats-so-raven-og-awkward-black-girl/.

Dery, M. (1994). Black to the future: Interviews with Samuel R. Delaney, Greg Tate, & Tricia Rose. In M. Dery (Ed.), *Flame wars: The discourse by cyberculture*. Durham, NC: Duke University Press. 1994.

Disney Channel (2015, December 10). That's So Raven theme song | Disney Channel [Video file]. Retrieved from https://www.youtube.com/watch?v=gpH_PIqT-q8.

Errico, M. (1998, February 5) Dionne's psychic friends go under. Retrieved from https://www.eonline.com/news/35903/dionne-s-psychic-friends-go-under.

Fallon, K. (2015, March 18) Raven-Symone: I'm not going to back down from comments on The View. Retrieved from: https://www.thedailybeast.com/raven-symone-im-not-going-to-back-down-from-comments-on-the-view.

Gennis, S. (2015, March 18) Raven-Symone defends Univision host's Michelle Obama comments: "Some people just look like animals." Retrieved from https://www.tvguide.com/news/raven-symone-michelle-obama-ape-racist-comments/.

hooks, b. (2003). *Teaching community: A pedagogy of hope*. New York: Routledge.

hooks, b. (Director), & Jhally, S. (Director). (1997). *Bell hooks: Cultural criticism & transformation* [DVD] Media Education Foundation. London: University of Westminster.

Kelley, R.G. (2002). *Freedom dreams: The Black radical imagination*. Boston: Beacon Press.

Magoon, K. (2008). *The Salem witch trials*. Edina, MN: Abdo Publishing.

Morris, S. (2012). Black girls are from the future: Afrofuturist feminism in Octavia E. Butler's "Fledgling." *Women's Studies Quarterly, 40*(3/4), 146–166.

[OWN]. (2014, October 5) Raven-Symoné: "I'm tired of being labeled" | Where Are They Now | Oprah Winfrey Network [Video File| Retrieved from https://www.youtube.com/watch?v=QXAho8vlmAI.

Ryan, J. (1998, January 16) LaToya bummed out by psychic friends. Retrieved from https://www.eonline.com/news/35799/latoya-bummed-out-by-psychic-friends.

Seriff, B., & Tarson, G. (Writers), & Singletary, T. (Director). (2003, May 2). Teach Your Children Well [Television series episode]. In *That's So Raven*. Burbank, CA: Walt Disney Television.

Stroman, Carolyn. 1991. Television's role in the socialization of African American children and adolescents, *Journal of Negro Education, 60* (3): 314–327.

[The View] (2015, March 17) Raven-Symoné on "n-word" & different generations [Video File] Retrieved from https://www.youtube.com/watch?v=uJhHsX0xZQw.

Ward, Monique L. 2004. Wading through the stereotypes: Positive and negative associations between media use and Black adolescents' conceptions of self. *Developmental Psychology, 40* (2): 284–294.

Womack, Y. (2013). *Afrofuturism: the world of black sci-fi and fantasy culture*. Chicago: Chicago Review Press.

Hannah Montana

The Best of Both Worlds
During the Rise of Facebook

Claudia Lisa Moeller

The Disney Channel's original series have inspired millions in younger generations. The Disney Channel produced and is still today producing shows that set moral examples for future generations. The Disney Channel wants, with its original series, to broadcast positive messages to their younger viewers who will one day be adults.

Over the past few decades, female protagonists have been portrayed more and more. They are strong, confident, and independent (Krishna & Taylor 2015). We might even consider some as role models for younger female generations, a soft version of female empowerment to teach girls to be always true to themselves.

New statistics show us that Disney has chosen, in the last few decades, more female characters over male characters, but despite this choice, women speak less than the male colleagues (Guo 2016; see also the first essay of this volume). Many articles point out this duality: women are protagonists, yet they do not talk very much, and most of the time, they can only follow their parents' will—e.g., the female protagonist Merida does not want to get married, and after an entire film, she persuades her mother to postpone her wedding day (Veritas & Cowan 2017). Disney Princesses have evolved in recent years, yet they are still a controversial topic in terms of feminism and female empowerment. Actress Keira Knightley has worked for Disney; nonetheless, she has publicly stated that she does not allow her daughter to watch certain Disney classics due to the moral lessons they teach ("TheEllenShow" 2018). According to the actress, Ariel from *The Little Mermaid* renounces her voice for a man, and this is not a lesson she likes her daughter to learn ("TheEllenShow" 2018).

Recently, the Disney Channel also tried to update its television programming, having more strong-willed and controversial female protagonists (Lauf 2017). This choice and new direction led older classics, such as *Boy Meets World*, to create a revival set almost fifteen years later, focusing on the former protagonist's daughter; consequently, the series' name was *Girl Meets World*. The original series was a success; the revival disappointed many and the series was canceled (Murtha 2017; for more in-depth analysis of *Girl Meets World*, see the "Girl Meets 'Woke'" essay in this volume).

In a period where Disney is losing its grip on and hype with younger generations (Flint & Fritz 2017), it is helpful to focus our attention on one of the classic, major successes of the channel. From 2006 to 2011, *Hannah Montana* was a hit show and one of the most watched programs on the Disney Channel ("The Hollywood Reporter" 2011d).

Hannah Montana caught our attention because of the double identity of the protagonist. She does not seek to find a balance between these two aspects of her life. She does not want to choose to cease lying; indeed, she drags her best friends into her world full of lies and duplicity. My theory is that *Hannah Montana*'s big success is not connected to the plot; instead, the show became one of the biggest successes for the Disney Channel because the show presents the question of having a double identity and life.

While social networks were being born and growing (McKenna 2017), *Hannah Montana* was teaching kids that it is not a big problem to be yourself (under a fake name, pretending to be someone else). This essay will analyze the structure of *Hannah Montana*, its music texts, and episode construction to demonstrate that this type of series has always pushed and praised being someone else (Miley Stewart vs. Hannah Montana). Furthermore, during the same years, the Disney Channel promoted and encouraged a certain stereotyped female figure who is not able to choose; whenever it comes time for the female character to make a decision, a male character interferes and overrides the female character.

Hannah Montana and the Best of Both Worlds

Hannah Montana was a huge hit show on the Disney Channel between 2006 and 2011 (McDowell 2016). The main character, Miley Stewart (Miley Cyrus[1]), is a normal California teenager: she attends school, she has normal friends, and she lives with her father (Billy Ray Cyrus) and awkward brother (Jason Daniel Earles). However, at night, Miley Stewart becomes the teen idol Hannah Montana, a pop singer. A blond wig protects Miley's secret identity (!), and in this way, Miley can lead a normal life. On the surface, the plot might appear a bit worn out: how many heroes and heroines have a double life? The shy journalist Clark Kent is the mighty and dashing Superman (Rodriguez 2017), the decadent playboy Bruce Wayne is behind Batman's mask (Sims, n.d.), and we could name many different heroes whose dual identity has already been the object of movies, films, comics, and other shows.

Yet, *Hannah Montana* differs from all these other movies or fictional products. *Hannah Montana*'s plot might appear dull and repetitive (Sparatori 2015[2]), but this Disney program has a different, new element that makes *Hannah Montana* different from all the other copycat and similar shows of that period (Lufkin 2012). Miley (or Hannah) does not seek to combine the two identities together. She keeps faking a double existence, possibly one completely estranged from the other. In this way, as the opening song explains, she will get "the best of both worlds."

Miley Stewart does not seek to have a normal life. She does not want to choose an identity; she wants only to continue swinging between the two options of her double life. She is both a normal student and a superstar. She wants to sell millions of records, but at the same time, she wishes to be anonymous. She does not want to have any "downside" from her choice. Fame comes at price, but not for Hannah/Miley.

In addition, Hannah Montana was a real popstar in our world, too. Hannah Montana toured all over America, and her concerts were always sold out (Goldsmith 2007). The fictional character was a real money machine (Casserly 2010), and real superstar who sold records and went on tour. Real fans were listening to her music, and buying whatever merchandise bore Hannah Montana's face (Tirella 2008). But it was the actress under the blonde wig, Miley Cyrus, who decided that it was time to "kill" Hannah Montana.

After ending her rich collaboration with Disney (Reagan 2010), Miley Cyrus continued her music career. She changed her look ("ET" 2012); she scandalized the world (Mallenbaum 2013) with a provocative MTV performance (Montgomery 2013). In the music video for "Wrecking Ball," she swings naked on a demolition ball and licks a hammer ("Wrecking Ball"). Cyrus declared openly that Hannah Montana was dead (Hare 2013; "Saturday Night Live" n.d.). This sudden change of brand and new scandalous lifestyle led to some particular fan conspiracy theories that posited that the real Miley Cyrus was murdered (in different scenarios, and for different reasons), and a new clone had overtaken her identity (White 2016).

Miley Cyrus has, multiple times, attacked the Disney Channel after having abandoned the show. Her father, who also plays her father and manager on the show, has said that *Hannah Montana* ruined his family (Heath 2011). Miley Cyrus claimed that it was a nightmare to work on set of the show. The time schedule was so chaotic, the responsibilities too many for a child, that Disney did not allow her to have a normal childhood (Pasquini 2017). In addition, she confessed that living for years as another person, by wearing

Hannah Montana's clothes and look, caused her major problems with her body image (Friedman 2015). Miley Cyrus has, more than once, expressed her point of view on being a celebrity kid and what it meant to work for the Disney Channel (Bacharach 2016).

In 2019, Miley Cyrus portrayed, once again, the teenage pop idol in an episode of the British television series *Black Mirror*. In "Rachel, Jack, and Ashley, Too" (S5E3), Ashley (Miley Cyrus) is a pop sensation whose life might appear golden and perfect from the outside, but is not really like this. Her manager/aunt manipulates Ashley by making her take drugs, and eventually puts her into coma in order to maintain total control of her creative work. Many have seen in this episode several references to Disney, even in the structure of the episode itself ("u/hmcconie" 2019): for example, Rachel and Jack's father is building a new system to chase mice by controlling their minds with neurotechnologies; the plot and the development of the episode itself reminded many of the Disney Channel's movies ("lillycrack" 2019); references to other existing teen idols (N. Clark 2019; Chambers 2019). Cyrus herself commented on the episode, saying that "[i]t's just that no one else can play this because this is my life" (Lambert 2019). In the same interview, she added that her previous scandals disappointed many of her fans (Cutter 2011), because they thought she was a "Disney mascot," but she is a person and not a merchandising object.

Indeed, *Hannah Montana* is different from any other show that one might watch on television. The show does not try to describe the importance of making up one's own mind when one grows up as a dilemma. The show portrays a teenager who is a pop singer, but this is her father's idea and plan, not Miley's. She seems unable to make any decision from the beginning of the series to the end.

The opening song of *Hannah Montana* (a hymn of the show) is a clear proof of this mentality. In the text (DisneyChannelIT 2018), Hannah/Miley sings about having the best of both worlds without any downside or negative consequences. The intro song is about being popular, famous, and leading a luscious lifestyle, all while pretending to be a normal, anonymous kid. Be the star of a television show, and, at the same time, go to school and chill with friends on the beach. That is the best of both worlds, and Hannah/Miley invites her fans to be like her. Do not be afraid of consequences; embrace duplicity to be the "real you." The song praises double identity. In the lyrics, we read that having a double secret identity allows one to be whomever one wants to be. One can be popular, sign autographs, be in magazines, and invited to the most important parties. One can be famous, but it is essential that this identity remains a secret in order to realize one's true nature. In the text, we read at least three times that it is better to have two identities, and to live undercover, rather than being openly one's self.

This double life is not just a strategy to protect family members or friends; on the contrary, it is again a solution to allow the protagonist to get everything without any major, bad consequences. In the first verse, Hannah/Miley sings that the one under the spotlight is the "real you." To be truly "you," different from one's friends, one must have two identities. Only as the second identity, the superstar and the celebrity, one can finally show one's true colors. The "true" Miley Cyrus is Hannah Montana, not simply an alter ego, but the confident, famous pop singer who everybody loves. In this way, it is clear that the show's opening song encourages audiences that there is no possibility to put together the two souls, and only leading a double life can one be truly "yourself": better than one's friends (as the song states), because one is more popular and beloved than ever. Hannah Montana can do everything, better and more successfully, than others can thanks to her brilliant strategy of leading two independent lives. This double life, where no decisions are ever made, is not only displayed in the song, but also in the plot of numerous episodes of the series. The plot of an average episode of the series is the following: Miley and her friends get into some minor problems. Hannah Montana (Miley's alter ego), or Miley's friend, or a parental figure helps her to get out of trouble.

In S2E18, "That's What Friends Are For," Miley and her ex-boyfriend, Jake (Cody Linley), agree to be only friends after their breakup. A couple of days later, Hannah Montana's enemy, Mikayla (Selena Gomez), lands a role beside Jake. They will play a romantic couple in a movie. Miley is jealous of this situation, yet she does not want to admit that she is, and she keeps telling herself and her friends that it is over with Jake. During the episode, Miley and her friend Lilly sabotage the film. They succeed, and Miley does her worst to ruin Mikayla's reputation in the movie industry. Before being fired, the real Mikayla escapes and warns the set of the fraud. Later, Miley asks Jake to forgive her, and they remain good friends. Mikayla forgives Miley, too, and becomes best friend with her (and not with Lilly, she specifies) because they both hate (?) Hannah Montana. In this episode, Miley tries to ruin two of her colleagues' professional lives. Only after being caught does she apologize for her misconduct. Both Jake and Mikayla (for mysterious reasons) forgive her, and they are happy to again be friends with her. Miley drags Lilly into her plan, and makes her kidnap Mikayla, who will later accept only Miley's apologies. Miley pushes her best friend into doing something illegal, and after being manipulative and mean towards others, she is forgiven and everybody is keen to be her friend. Again, others must repair her damage.

In another episode, "Miley Hurts the Feeling of the Radio DJ" (S3E17), Miley's best friend, Oliver (Mitchell Musso), is working at a radio station. When the DJ quits his job, Oliver has his chance to become a DJ. His first attempts as a DJ are terribly awkward, so Miley decides to help him. Together they have chemistry as DJs, and the producers of the radio station ask Oliver to repeat the show. Oliver asks Miley to help him again, but her father and manager reminds her of her multiple events and appointments as Hannah Montana. However, Miley does not want to let one of her best friends down, so she accepts this other job. After different inconveniences due to the lack of sleep, Miley must make a decision. Her father repeats her that she cannot help her friend anymore, and Miley tells Oliver that she cannot work with him at the radio station. At the end of the episode (as a last gag), we find out that Oliver has the job, but the radio producers do not want Miley in the show. Miley is furious about being canceled from a show she did not want to take part in. Again, in this episode, we see how Miley is able to make neither plans nor decisions. Her father and manager, then her friend Oliver (or his bosses), makes her quit the job at the radio station. Miley does not opt for anything; she is passive in the entire episode. When she decides something (after having followed her father's advice), it is too late because someone else has already made the choice for her.

Even in the last episode of *Hannah Montana*, Miley's last line is interesting. Miley and Lilly have several arguments during the last episode (Sorich 2011). At the beginning, Miley and Lilly plan to go together to college.[3] Even as Miley is about to go to college, she accepts a new film project that will bring her to Europe. She does not offer for her best friend to come with her, nor mention it to her. This leads to a big fight. Lilly decides to "break up" with Miley, but then Miley asks Lilly to join her on her trip to Paris. Lilly is happy, and she forgives her best friend. They are about to leave, but Lilly realizes that Miley will get to keep working as a popstar/actress, while Lilly must put her dream (going to college) on hold. After having realized that Miley's aims are not hers, Lilly opts to stay in the U.S. and go to college. The last sequence takes place in Lilly's dormitory; she is chilling in her room when someone knocks on her door. Miley is back and explains to Lilly: "You are right: there are going to be a million concerts, and tours, and movies; but I only get one chance to go to college with my best friend!"[4]

As we can read (and watch), Miley does not believe that college is the best option for her. She considers college with her longtime friend an opportunity that she cannot pass up, because it happens only once in life. She is sure that she will get plenty of other chances in show business, so she is not giving up anything to be with her friend. Her choice is again a product of a compromise, in which she can get both stardom and friendship. She does not value her friendship more than her career; she only recognizes that her friend has to attend college now and cannot wait a year.

So as we have seen, the series wants Miley, most of the time, to be either completely passive or simply mean towards others who are having success.

Hannah Montana could be considered her best part: she is popular, beloved, rich, and wise. Hannah Montana has not only been a role model for many young girls (*Daily Beast*, "Time for Warning Labels"), but first of all, she is a role model to Miley Stewart.

However, *Hannah Montana* did not want its protagonist to grow old. The show represents an eternal teenager, not only because of her young age, but also because of her lack of ability to take responsibility. She does not opt for something else; she does not even consider the possibility that she might not be able to take back her choice. She opts for a comfortable option that will not affect—according to Miley—her life. Nor does she consider the possibility mundane, namely abandoning the spotlight, the glitter, and the fame.

This type of character and popularity makes us think and reflect. Is it possible that *Hannah Montana* forecasted something else? Her popularity—her empire—was not due to the plot, nor the protagonist, but a symptom of a cultural change.

Internet and the Double Life

The Internet has become, in recent years, an intrinsic part of our everyday life (Il Sole 24 Ore, "Il boom di Amazon"). We cannot live without it; from purchase to common interaction, our lives have completely changed in the last dozen years.

In this perspective, we should remember that in the same years *Hannah Montana* was on air, social networks were developing. The father of them all, Facebook, became the most important and widespread social network of recent history (Sedghi 2014). Facebook was born in 2004, but within a few years, Facebook became the most famous and popular social network in the world. Only after several scandals (Perrin 2018), and increasingly competitive offers of new platforms, did Facebook start looking old (Greenwood, Perrin & Duggan 2016). Yet what interests us for purposes of this essay is the fact that Facebook was born and had its biggest moments in the same years as *Hannah Montana* was on air.

Facebook was one of the first social networks to create new links and possible contacts with individuals that have common interests and passions. For this purpose, Facebook needs as much (and the most accurate) possible amount of information of its users (Kevin Ludlow, "Bayesian Flooding"). Facebook provides contacts and possible friendships. This works while all of the members of this community are honest and trustworthy (Zimmer 2010), but in the last few years, it appears clear that not all users are telling the truth (Hough 2013). At least, they tend to exaggerate some aspects of their lives to impress others (Greenfield 2014; Renzulli 2017).

Social networks and other social platforms allow us to interact and get to know other people. We could be ourselves or we could be someone else. In a recent study in which 272 adults were surveyed, scientists found out that overall 32 percent were "completely honest" online, especially on social networks (Seidman 2016). Other studies describe many of the white lies that we are likely to tell on the telephone most of the time, or online to embellish ourselves, especially on dating applications and websites (Dourish & Bell 2011, pp. 147–149). Facebook has discovered over the last few years that Internet users are not always completely honest (Eler 2012): 7.5 million children under the age of 13 are online and have a Facebook profile without any parent's consent ("Consumer Report" 2011). First, this means that there are underage users of a platform that is not designed for them (Sweney 2013); secondly, there are very young users who do not see having to lie to get an account as a problem.

Younger generations are eager to create and use multiple identities online, for different purposes and goals—and not always morally good ones. Finstas (Molina 2017) and trolls are different typologies of fake identities that are built online to achieve different targets. In a recent study concerning the role of trolls in online games (Cook, Shaafsma & Antheneunis 2017), researchers found that being a troll may not always be negative and harming behavior. In a particular setting (for example a war game) players might enjoy these particularly aggressive behaviors and jabs. Double identities are not synonymous with being mean and false, but they show us a particular sensibility younger generations have for their privacy and problems in expressing themselves. In a world where social media are part of our identity and might jeopardize our chances to land the job of our dreams ("Facebook," n.d.) it is essential to protect ourselves, particularly our dumbest and naivest part.

Even if cases of people getting fired because of something they posted online might be false or controversial (Price 2016), this fear of negative consequences lead younger generations to be more cautious about their "real" account (Madden, Lenhart, Cortesi, Gasser, Duggan, Smith & Beaton 2013), and prefer having two or more accounts online (Orlando, n.d.).

Indeed, younger generations seem to be under pressure when it comes to their online reputation; the English charity Ditch the Label studies bullying ("Ditch the Label," n.d.). Online, the charity found out that women are not less aggressive than male users; girls and women are keener to use pejorative words referring to other women. Women judge other women's bodies and looks. Furthermore, Ditch the Label asked younger users in 2014 to answer different questions about applications and their use ("Ditch the Label," n.d.). Twenty one percent of 2,732 British people, aged between 13 and 25, answered that they were bullied by anonymous accounts. Online, one might meet and talk to a "catfish": a person who sets up a false personal profile on a social networking site for fraudulent or deceptive purposes ("Merriam-Webster" n.d.). Catfishes chat with people online and avoid any direct contact with their targets. Most catfish are female, and they tend to create false accounts for different reasons, from insecurity to revenge (Lacapria 2103).

We have seen that younger generations might be using fake accounts for multiple reasons, both good and bad. We should also consider the development and expansions of the sex industry online, where "normal" women and men can perform sexual activities online. The BBC wrote that the webcam market grew from around £730 million in 2006 to £1.1 billion in 2008 (Crawford 2009). Webcam models or "girls" are a relatively new industry that allows selling erotic or pornographic pictures or movies independently (Stuart 2016). In the last decade, young adult "sexting" is getting to be more and more of a wider phenomenon. Ditch the Labels states that almost 30 percent of 17-year-old youngsters have sent a naked selfie of their bodies ("Ditch the Label," pp. 21–26).

We should also consider the enormous porn industry that Internet has created. Pornhub, one of the largest pornographic websites, states that they have enough material to last 173 years. After ten years online, they have more than 10,059,213 videos uploaded ("Pornhub Insights" 2017). Sex workers online, also known as indirect sex workers, have found in the Internet a possibility to earn money with their bodies with fewer risks compared to their colleagues that work on the streets or in clubs (e.g., prostitutes and strippers). Some university students have especially found, in the sex industry, a new alley to quickly and easily pay off student loans. In 2015, Swansea University conducted a study among 6,773 university UK students, and 5 percent of the students answered that they worked in the sex industry. The main reason was connected to the fact that they wanted to repay their university debt, or at least a great part of it (Sagar, Jones, Symons, & Bowring p. 21). In the same study, the sex workers stated that the biggest downside of their work was the secrecy; even if their peers say that there would not be a social stigma to have taken part in the sex industry, most of those who worked in the industry hid this decision from their relatives or friends (p. 24). This study reflects the popularity in recent years of dating websites and applications where sugar daddies and mamas can meet sugar babies (Rodriguez 2017).

Here we come to my point: *Hannah Montana*'s success is correlated to the rise of social networks. In a period where social networks and Internet were getting more and more predominant in our lives, *Hannah Montana* showed a normal teen being someone else. Her alter ego is better, "cooler," beloved, and always trendy. Hannah Montana embodied, in a very innocent way, a particular form of secret identity. A woman can only be her true self, her winning and rich self, undercover—her double identity.

Conclusion

As we have seen in this essay, *Hannah Montana* was an enormous success despite the questionable plot. We tried to figure out why *Hannah Montana* (and similarly, other Disney Channel shows featuring double identities, like *Wizards of Waverly Place* [see Ackerman, in this volume]) had such a success. We analyzed the plot of *Hannah Montana* and highlighted the structure of the episodes: in every episode, we can find a pattern where the main female protagonist does not make any decisions. The final happy conclusion of each episode is the result of someone else's decisions. Hannah/Miley is, most of the time, passive and the final episode of the entire series proves it. She does not choose to go to college because she wants to get higher education. Hannah/Miley opts to attend university because she says that this experience can happen only once in life, and she does not want to miss it. Hence, Hannah/Miley does not choose anything; she will be both a superstar and a normal student. *Hannah Montana* praises the double identity: during the day, she is a normal teenager; after the sunset, she becomes a popular popstar. Throughout the series, Miley justifies her double identity because she wants to have a private life. It seems that Hannah is somehow a public alter ego of Miley, and Miley is the private and more intimate part of this identity.

We noticed that in the same years that *Hannah Montana* was on air, our society was changing. Social networks were born, in particular, Facebook. All over the world, Facebook has more than 2,200 billion users. Facebook is one of the biggest and more popular social networks available, and users check their status and updates more than once a day (Perrin 2018). Everybody seems to be online and has social networks. Those new platforms were born to be "private," or, at least, a safe place in which one can carelessly post opinions, messages, and pictures. But online, where there is no option to be forgotten, the question of being one's self without any possible negative consequences in the future is becoming more and more challenging.

We have seen that especially younger generations are using fake accounts to interact and "peacefully" use the Internet and the upsides of social media. We have seen that the phenomenon of having dual or multiple identities online is not always a choice made for negative and malicious purposes. For example, in online war games, we have read a study in which being a troll is part of the roleplaying game itself, and in this way, friendships can blossom under the bombs or flying bullets.

Double identities are not always a synonym of vicious, mean, and doubtful conduct. Double identities might be an essential trick to preserve identities and their multiple facets. Especially, younger generations will face (and are already dealing with) the problem of growing up online. If our lives will be online, and we will share with or without our consent ("Stern" 2013) images or text concerning our private life (and body) that will be online potentially forever, it seems logical and even wise to have multiple accounts.

We started asking ourselves what kind of moral lessons *Hannah Montana* taught. We could summarize two aspects: On one hand, *Hannah Montana* praised multiple identities and each of them allows the protagonist (Miley) to express herself and explore her different potentialities and abilities. We could here quote Nietzsche: "Without forgetting, it is impossible to live." To live, we have also the right to forget and "get over it." The online world does not forget, and still remembers our traces and data, potentially for eternity.

On the other hand, Miley is completely passive and does not make any decisions. She follows other dreams and aspirations; even her choice to be a singer is something she pursues because her father told her to. The impossibility to choose something, to exclude one possibility, makes Hannah passive. Somehow, she can never be an adult. Not even her last episode portrays a responsible and mature Miley who can finally do what she wants. Hannah/Miley dreams, but she is not able to live her own life. To quote another philosopher, Kierkegaard described possibility and all of the consequences that are in front of us before we make up our mind: "Anxiety is the dizziness of freedom." This famous quote explains that the particular is put in the eternal perspective. In this way, this range of possibilities may prevent someone from choosing and following one path.

Hannah Montana wanted to portray why a teenager may wish to have two (or more) identities. In the same years, social networks were getting popular and made every user a potential Hannah Montana with two or more identities. Identities are essential to investigating curiosities, tendencies, and interests without being judged by peers, relatives, and potential bosses. Still, being unable to make any decision and, consequently, being unable to proudly be one identity is ta lack of freedom that can only be expressed by our actions and words.

NOTES

1. The main actress and singer's name at the time was Destiny Hope Cyrus. Her father was the famous country singer Billy Ray Cyrus, who plays her father also in the show. Miley Ray Cyrus changed her name as her fictional character in 2008 (https://people.com/celebrity/miley-cyrus-makes-name-change-official/).

2. In the Italian article, the author compares the series *Hannah Montana* and *L'incantevole Creamy* (in English, "Creamy Mami, the magic angel") and *Magica, Magica Emi* (in English, "Magical Emi, the magic star"). The first Japanese cartoon has been popular in Italy since its debut in 1985. The author praises *L'incantevole Creamy*'s structure and character development. Yu suffers from the fact that she cannot confess to being Creamy, the charming popstar. Yu and Creamy can only be together for a limited period, and Yu is happy to get back to her normal life at the end of the comic/anime. In the other, Mai becomes the Magical Emi, an older and more skilled magician thanks to a magical wand. After becoming famous thanks to her alter ego, Mai chooses to abandon her fake identity, because Emi wants to be only herself and does not want to live in a lie anymore.

3. In the episode "I'll Always Remember You" (S04E09), Miley has to face reality: sometimes things do not go as one wishes. Indeed, Hannah's current boyfriend ends up being caught kissing Miley; therefore, fans assume that he is cheating on Hannah. He cannot handle this sudden hate, and asks her to confess to the entire world who she really is. She does not want to help, and he dumps her. At the same time, Miley and Lilly are waiting for Stanford University acceptance letters. Lilly is accepted, while Miley is rejected. However, Miley does not give up the idea of getting into Stanford, and she drives to Stanford three times to prove that she is better than her best friend. She even suggests to the board commission that it is unfair that her friend got into the prestigious college and not her. After multiple conversations and trips to Stanford, the commission tells Miley/Hannah that only the popular pop singer could get straight into the university. Since Miley is depressed, Lilly is about to say no to Stanford because she is thankful that Miley made her part of her glittery Hollywood world. In addition, Miley's boyfriend comes back and serenades her. They are all there for Miley. Miley is happy, but her conscience is not. The following day, she confesses to the world that Miley Stewart is Hannah Montana.

4. https://www.youtube.com/watch?v=q6IHAq_O5z0.

REFERENCES

Addams Rosa, J., Bennett, W., & Orentein, H. (2018, June 18). Here's a timeline Selena Gomez & Justin Bieber's rocky relationship, from start … to finish? *Seventeen*. Retrieved from: https://www.seventeen.com/celebrity/g1108/justin-bieber-selena-gomez-relationship-timeline/?slide=57.

Agency (2015, June 19). Daft Punk: Being robots helped us to be normal humans. *The Telegraph*. Retrieved from: https://www.telegraph.co.uk/culture/music/music-news/11685709/Daft-Punk-being-robots-helped-us-to-be-normal-humans.html.

Amed, I. (2017, September 11) Inside the millennial mind of Selena Gomez. *Business of Fashion*. Retrieved from: https://www.businessoffashion.com/articles/people/inside-the-millennial-mind-of-selena-gomez.

The annual bullying survey 2018. (N.D.). Ditch the label. Retrieved from: https://www.ditchthelabel.org/research-papers/the-annual-bullying-survey-2018/.

Bacharach, E. (2016, September 16). 9 Times Miley Cyrus went savage on Disney. *Cosmopolitan*. Retrieved from: https://www.cosmopolitan.com/entertainment/celebs/a3324821/miley-cyrus-disney-quotes/.

Barlaam, R. (2018, Marzo 3). Il boom di Amazon spiegato con cinque grafici. *Il Sole 24 Ore*. Retrieved from: https://www.ilsole24ore.com/art/finanza-e-mercati/2018-03-03/amazon-spiegata-cinque-grafici-forte-aumento-vendite-142847.shtml?uuid=AEZJidAE.

Blue, M.G. (2017). *Girlhood on Disney Channel: Branding, celebrity, and femininity*. New York: Routledge.

Casserly, M. (2010, September 8). The Disney star machine. *Forbes*. Retrieved from: https://www.forbes.com/sites/meghancasserly/2010/09/08/the-disney-star-machine/#58943926e61dd.

Catfish. (N.D.) In *Merriam-Webster*. Retrieved from: https://www.merriam-webster.com/dictionary/catfish.

Celebrating 10 years of porn … and data! (2017, May 25). In *PornHub Insights*. Retrieved from: https://www.pornhub.com/insights/10-years.

Chambers, H. (2019, June 5). Miley Cyrus's "Black Mirror" episode is actually about Jojo Siwa, and you can't convince me otherwise. *Cosmopolitan*. Retrieved from: https://www.cosmopolitan.com/entertainment/tv/a27757252/miley-cyrus-black-mirror-episode/.

Clark, M. (2016, July 22). Tiffany Trump might actually be Hannah Montana, *Huffington Post*. Retrieved from: https://www.huffingtonpost.com/entry/shes-just-being-miley_us_579260f5e4b00c9876cf53ce.

Clark, N. (2019, June 6). Miley Cyrus's "Black Mirror" episode is a creepy dive into how we ruin pop stars. *VICE*. Retrieved from: https://www.vice.com/en_us/article/7xg7q4/miley-cyruss-black-mirror-episode-is-a-creepy-dive-into-how-we-ruin-pop-stars.

Cook, C., Schaafsma, J., & Antheneunis, M. (2018). Under the bridge: An in-depth examination of online trolling in the gaming context. *SAGE*, 2018, Vol. 20 (9), 3323–3340.

CR survey: 7.5 million Facebook users are under the age of 13, violating the site's terms. (2011, May 10). *Consumer Report*. Retrieved from: https://www.consumerreports.org/mediaroom/press-releases/2011/05/cr-survey-75-million-facebook-users-are-under-the-age-of-13-violating-the-sites-terms-/.

Crawford, D. (2009, September 14).Number of webcam models "on the rise." *BBC*. Retrieved from: http://www.bbc.co.uk/newsbeat/article/10001612/number-of-webcam-models-on-the-rise.

Cutter, K. (2011, July 21). The life of Miley Cyrus. *Marie Claire*. Retrieved from: https://www.marieclaire.com/celebrity/a11786/miley-cyrus-interview/.

Cyberbullying and Hate Speech. (N.D.). Ditch the label. Retrieved from: https://www.ditchthelabel.org/research-papers/cyberbullying-and-hate-speech/.

Cyrus, M. (2013, September 9). *Wrecking ball*. Retrieved from: https://www.youtube.com/watch?v=My2FRPA3Gf8.

DisneyChannelIT. (2018, October 3). *Hannah Montana* | The best of both worlds—Music Video—Disney Channel Italia. Retrieved from: https://www.youtube.com/watch?v=N2ubfMZNrwQ.

Dourish, P., & Bell, G. (2011) *Divining a digital future: Mess and mythology in ubiquitous computing*. Cambridge, MA: MIT Press, 147–149.

Drouin, M., Miller, D., Wehle, S.M.J., & Hernandez, E. (2016) Why do people lie online? Because everyone lies on the internet. *Computers in Human Behavior, 64*, 134–142.

Eler, A. (2012, January 23). Why people have Facebook profiles. *Readwrite*. Retrieved from: https://readwrite.com/2012/01/23/why_people_have_fake_facebook_profiles/.

TheEllenShow. (2018, October 16). *Keira Knightley's daughter has a wild ambition for when she grows up*. Retrieved from: https://www.youtube.com/watch?v=jkS0Lz3JAjU.

ET. (2012, August 13). Miley Cyrus haircut: Twitter reactions to the star's platinum pixie cut. *The Huffington Post*. Retrieved from: https://www.huffingtonpost.com/2012/08/13/miley-cyrus-cuts-hair-rec_n_1773153.html.

Flint, J., & Fritz, B. (2017, July 4). Disney's Channels: Children are tuning out. *The Wall Street Journal*. Retrieved from: https://www.wsj.com/articles/disneys-channels-kids-are-tuning-out-1499166003.

Friedman, M. (2015, August 13). 9 things you never know about Miley Cyrus, courtsey of her Maire Claire cover interview. *Marie Claire*. Retrieved from: https://www.marieclaire.com/celebrity/news/a15514/miley-cyrus-marie-claire-september-cover/.

Goldsmith, B. (2007, October 18). Parents go to extremes for Hannah Montana tickets. *Reuters*. Retrieved from: https://www.reuters.com/article/us-hannah/parents-go-to-extremes-for-hannah-montana-tickets-idUSN1731159520071017.

Greenfeld, K.T. (2014, May 24). Faking culutral literacy. *New York Times*. Retrieved from: https://www.nytimes.com/2014/05/25/opinion/sunday/faking-cultural-literacy.html.

Greenwood, S., Perrin, A., & Duggan, M. (2016, November 11). Social media update 2016. *Pew Research Center*. Retrieved from: http://www.pewinternet.org/2016/11/11/social-media-update-2016/.

Guo, J. (2016, January 25). Researchers have found a major problem with "The Little Mermaid" and other Disney Movies. *The Washington Post*. Retrieved from: https://www.washingtonpost.com/news/wonk/wp/2016/01/25/researchers-have-discovered-a-major-problem-with-the-little-mermaid-and-other-disney-movies/?noredirect=on&utm_term=.fadc77ed65d7.

Hare, B. (2013, October 7). Miley Cyrus on "SNL": "Hannah Montana" is dead. *CNN*. Retrieved from: https://edition.cnn.com/2013/10/06/showbiz/celebrity-news-gossip/miley-cyrus-snl/index.html.

Headscratchers—Hannah Montana. (n.d.) Messages posted to: https://tvtropes.org/pmwiki/pmwiki.php/Headscratchers/HannahMontana.

Heath, C. (2011, February 15). Mr. Hannah Montana's achy breaky heart. *GQ*. Retrieved from: https://www.gq.com/story/billy-ray-cyrus-mr-hannah-montana-miley.

The Hollywood Reporter. (2011, January 19). 'Hannah Montana' finale sets Disney ratings record. *Billboard*. Retrieved from: https://www.billboard.com/articles/news/473581/hannah-montana-finale-sets-disney-ratings-record.

Hough, A. (2013, March 12). Why women constantly lie about life on Facebook. *The Telegraph*. Retrieved from: https://www.telegraph.co.uk/technology/facebook/9925072/Why-women-constantly-lie-about-life-on-Facebook.html.

How young people between the ages of 13–25 engage with smartphone technology and naked photos. (N.D.) Ditch the label. Retrieved from: https://www.ditchthelabel.org/research-papers/the-wireless-report/.

Jones, A., & Brooker, C. (Producers). (2011–present). *Black Mirror*. [Television series]. United Kingdom: Channel Four (2011–2014) and Netflix (2016–present).

Kierkegaard, S. (1981) *The concept of anxiety*. (Thomte, R., & Anderson, A.B.) Princeton: Princeton University Press. (Original work published 1844.)

Kinderbilder bei Facebook: "Sie kannten keine Scham." *Stern*. (2013, September 13). Retrieved from: https://www.stern.de/familie/kinder/kinderbilder-bei-facebook-18-jaehrige-klagt-sie-kannten-keine-scham-7056006.html.

Krishna, P., & Taylor, K. (2015, June 4). 50 Disney Channel original movies, ranked by feminism. *BuzzFeed News*. Retrieved from: https://www.buzzfeednews.com/article/priya krishna/50-disney-channel-original-movies-ranked-by-feminism.

Lacapria, K. (2013, March 23). Catfishing is bigger than you might think, study reveals trucks used by fraudsters *Social News Daily*. Retrieved from: https://socialnewsdaily.com/11296/catfishing-infographic/.

Lambert, M. (2019, July 11). Miley Cyrus has finally found herself. *Elle*. Retrieved from: https://www.elle.com/culture/music/a28280119/miley-cyrus-elle-interview/.

Lauf, J. (2017, July 22). Disney Channel's "Discendants 2" allows girls to be heroes, villains, & often, both. *Bustle*. Retrieved from: https://www.bustle.com/p/disney-channels-descendants-2-allows-girls-to-be-heroes-villains-often-both-67279.

Lawrence, J. (2014, February 25). Time for warning labels on Miley Cyrus's licking and twerking contest? *The Daily Beast*. Retrieved from: https://www.thedailybeast.com/time-for-warning-labels-on-miley-cyruss-licking-and-twerking-concerts.

lillycrack. (2019, June 7). I feel like people are missing that the episode is supposed to feel like a cheesy Disney movie. You can still dislike it but don't act like it was accidental. [Post in a web discussion] *Reddit*. Retrieved from: https://www.reddit.com/r/black mirror/comments/bxqpcy/rachel_jack_and_ashley_too_was_overlooked_by_90/.

Ludlow, K. (2012, May 23). Bayesian flooding and Facebook manipulation. Retrieved from: http://www.kevinludlow.com/blog/1610/bayesian_flooding_and_facebook_manipula tion_fb/.

Lufkin, B. (2012, June 28) The "Hannah Montana" effect: Why are so many kids' tv shows about fame? *The Atlantic*. Retrieved from: https://www.theatlantic.com/entertainment/archive/2012/06/the-hannah-montana-effect-why-are-so-many-kids-tv-shows-about-fame/259067/.

Madden, M., Lenhart, A., Cortesi, S., Gasser, U., Duggan, M., Smith, A., & Beaton, M. (2013, May 21). Teens, social media, and privacy. *Pew Research Center*. Retrieved from: http://www.pewinternet.org/2013/05/21/teens-social-media-and-privacy/.

Mallenbaum, C. (2013, August 27). Miley's VMAs performance shocks celebs. *USA Today*. Retrieved from: https://eu.usatoday.com/story/life/people/2013/08/26/miley-cyrus-vmas-twitter/2699021/.

McDowell, J. (2006, November 30). A Disney star is born. *Time*. Retrieved from: http://content.time.com/time/arts/article/0,8599,1564394,00.html.

McKenna, J. (2017, May 10). Facebook is about to hit 2 billion users. Here's a closer look at the rise of the social giant. *World Economic Forum*. Retrieved from: https://www.we forum.org/agenda/2017/05/facebook-is-about-to-hit-2-billion-users-here-s-a-closer-look-at-the-rise-of-the-social-giant/.

Molina, B. (2017, October 20). Does your kid have a "finsta" account? Why it's a big deal. *USA Today*. Retrieved from: https://eu.usatoday.com/story/tech/talkingtech/2017/10/20/does-your-kid-have-finsta-account-why-its-big-deal/783424001/.

Montgomery, J. (2013, September 3). Exclusive: Miley Cyrus Breaks silence over VMA performance, *Mtv.com*. Retrieved from: http://www.mtv.com/news/1713414/miley-cyrus-vma-performance-interview/.

Murtha, P. (2017, June 1). Why "Boys Meets World" succeeded and "Girl Meets World" failed. *Study Breaks*. Retrieved from: https://studybreaks.com/culture/girl-meets-world/.

Nietzsche, F. (1978). *Werke. Nachgelassene Fragmente Sommer 1872 bis Ende 1874* (Vol III/4), Berlin: Gruyter, p. 314.

Orlando, J. (N.A.). How teens use fake Instagram accounts to relieve the pressure of perfection. *The Conversation*. Retrieved from: https://theconversation.com/how-teens-use-fake-instagram-accounts-to-relieve-the-pressure-of-perfection-92105.

Over 50% of couples will meet online by 2031. (n.d.) Retrieved from: https://www.eharmony.co.uk/dating-advice/online-dating-unplugged/over-50-of-couples-will-meet-online-by-2031#.W9h1ntVKjIU.

Pasquini, M. (2017, October 29). Miley Cyrus reflects on "Hannah Montana": "That's a lot to put on a kid." *PEOPLE*. Retrieved from: https://people.com/celebrity/miley-cyrus-reflects-hannah-montana-thats-lot-put-on-kid/.

People Staff (2008, January 29). Miley Cyrus makes name change official. *People*. Retrieved from: https://people.com/celebrity/miley-cyrus-makes-name-change-official/.

Perrin, A. (2018, September 5). Americans are changing their relationship with Facebook. *Pew Research Center*. Retrieved from: http://www.pewresearch.org/fact-tank/2018/09/05/americans-are-changing-their-relationship-with-facebook/.

Peterman, S., & Poryes, M. (Producers). (2006–2011). *Hannah Montana*. [Television series]. Hollywood, CA: Disney Channel.

Price, L. (July 8, 2016). 20 Tales of employees who were fired because of social media posts. *PEOPLE*. Retrieved from: https://people.com/celebrity/employees-who-were-fired-because-of-social-media-posts/.

Primogeniture and ultimogeniture. (N.D.). In *Encyclopedia Britannica Online*. Retrieved from: https://www.britannica.com/topic/primogeniture.

Reagan, G. (2010, March 22). Miley Cyrus "rejoices" in killing Disney's $1 billion star: Hannah Montana. *Business Inside*. Retrieved from: https://businessinsider.com/miley-cyrus-rejoices-in-killing-disneys-1-billion-star-hannah-montana-2010–3?IR=T.

Recruiting survey: Social media helps connect job seekers with employers. (N.D.) In *Facebook*, Retrieved from: https://www.facebook.com/notes/social-jobs-partnership/recruiting-survey-social-media-helps-connect-job-seekers-with-employers/404484379619706.

Renzulli, K.A. (2017, June 20). More than 33% of men say they've faked a vacation photo. *Time*. Retrieved from: http://time.com/money/4823463/men-women-vacation-spending-social-media/.

Rodriguez, C. (2017, October 29). "Sugar baby" or student loan? Ad campaign strike rage in Paris. *Forbes*, https://www.forbes.com/sites/ceciliarodriguez/2017/10/29/sugar-daddy-or-student-loan-ad-campaign-sparks-outrage-in-paris/#7a74a73f56a7.

Rodriguez, G. (2017, July 5). 5 reasons why no one knows that Clark Kent is Superman," *The Odyssey*. Retrieved from: https://www.theodysseyonline.com/why-no-one-recognizes-clark-kent-as-superman.

Sagar, T., Jones, D., Symons, K., & Bowring, J. (2015 March). The student sex work project. *The Student Sex Work Project*. Retrieved from: http://www.thestudentsexworkproject.co.uk/wp-content/uploads/2015/03/TSSWP-Research-Summary-English.pdf.

Saturday Night Live. (2013, October 7). *Monologue: Miley Cyrus on the 2013 VMAs—SNL*. Retrieved from: https://www.youtube.com/watch?v=Cr_9-Rikttg.

Sedghi, A. (2014, February 4). Facebook: 10 years of social networking, in numbers. *The Guardian*. Retrieved from: https://www.theguardian.com/news/datablog/2014/feb/04/facebook-in-numbers-statistics.

Seidman, G. (2016, September 6). Is everyone really lying online? *Psychology Today*. Retrieved from: https://www.psychologytoday.com/us/blog/close-encounters/201609/is-everyone-really-lying-online.

Sims, C. (N.D.). Most bizarre things Batman did to keep his identity secret. *Looper*. Retrieved from: https://www.looper.com/79379/bizarre-things-batman-keep-identity-secret/.

Smith, A., & Anderson, M. (2016, February 29). 5 facts about online dating. *Pew Research*

Center. Retrieved from: http://www.pewresearch.org/fact-tank/2016/02/29/5-facts-about-online-dating/.

Smith, A., & Anderson, M. (2018, March 1). Social media use in 2018. *Pew Research Center.* Retrieved from: http://www.pewinternet.org/2018/03/01/social-media-use-in-2018/.

Soldani, B. (2015, February 10). Who is the real Sia? The story behind the wig—wearing singer who refuses tho show her face and once contemplated suicide while battling alcohol and drug addiction. *The Daily Mail.* Retrieved from: https://www.dailymail.co.uk/tvshowbiz/article-2946583/Who-real-Sia-story-wig-wearing-singer-REFUSES-face-contemplated-suicide-battling-alcohol-drug-addiction.html.

Sorich S. (2011, January 16). Hannah Montana series finale 2011: How did the last Hannah Montana Forever episode end? *Ledger Enquirer.* Retrieved from: https://www.ledger-enquirer.com/entertainment/article29171236.html.

Sparatore, A. (2015, June 8). Gira e sfera. *Nerdface.* Retrieved from: http://www.nerdface.it/it/magica-emi-con-creamy-ed-evelyn-quando-la-magia-era-una-cosa-seria.

Stuart, R. (2016, 21 December). Webcomming: The sex work revolution that no one is willing to talk about. *The Independent.* Retrieved from: https://www.independent.co.uk/lifestyle/gadgets-and-tech/features/webcamming-the-sex-work-revolution-that-no-one-is-willing-to-talk-about-a7485176.html.

Sweney, M. (2013, July 26). More than 80% children lie about their age to use sites like Facebook. *The Guardian.* Retrieved from: https://www.theguardian.com/media/2013/jul/26/children-lie-age-facebook-asa.

Temple JR, P.J.A., van den Berg P., Le VD, McElhany A, & Temple, BW. (2012). Teen sexting and its association with sexual behaviors. *Arch Pediatr Adolesc Med.,166(9)*, 828–833.

Tirella, J.V. (2008, February 8). Hannah Montana crowned new queen of 'tween. *NBC News.* Retrieved from: http://www.nbcnews.com/id/23051344/ns/business-us_business/t/hannah-montana-crowned-new-queen-tween/#.W83zq3szbIU.

u/hmcconie. (2019, June 7). Rachel, Jack, and Ashley Too was overlooked by 90% of you. [web discussion] *Reddit.* Retrieved from: https://www.reddit.com/r/blackmirror/comments/bxqpcy/rachel_jack_and_ashley_too_was_overlooked_by_90/.

Veritas, V., & Cowan, M. (2017, January 4). 5 ways modern Disney is even more sexist than the classics. *Cracked.* Retrieved from: http://www.cracked.com/article_24452_5-ways-disney-has-actually-gotten-more-sexist-over-time.html.

White, C. (2016, November 22). Celebrity clone theories mad enough to break the internet. *BBC.* Retrieved from: https://www.bbc.co.uk/bbcthree/article/9c869b31-e229–4742-bcf9-c99a780f7867.

Zimmer, M. (2010, March 14). Facebook's Zuckerberg: "Having two identities for yourself is an example of a lack of integrity." *Michael Zimmer.* Retrieved from: https://www.michaelzimmer.org/2010/05/14/facebooks-zuckerberg-having-two-identities-for-yourself-is-an-example-of-a-lack-of-integrity/.

Family, Hard Work and Magic

The Skewed Working-Class Sensibilities *of* Wizards of Waverly Place

COLIN ACKERMAN

With the worldwide popularity of magic, witches, and wizards created out of the *Harry Potter* series in the early 2000s, other popular culture outlets unsurprisingly sought to capitalize by putting time and effort into developing TV shows, movies, and books around the booming economic potential bestowed upon magical stories and characters. Popular culture proliferation around a particular topic or theme is unique to neither the early 2000s nor the subject of magic; however, this particular instance occurring in the throes of the digital revolution afforded by the internet gave magic-related content previously unmatched potentials for profitability.

Disney Channel's *Wizards of Waverly Place* was one such example of exploiting the marketability of magic and, as I will argue in this inquiry, is an excellent site within popular culture to discuss the implications of hegemonic discourses around class and neoliberal values presented as part of a show marketed for tweens. A textual analysis grounded in the public pedagogy theory of H.A. Giroux will illuminate hegemonic discourses present within the show. The potential implications of those discourses' presence will be defended as notable because of the stage of psychological development of the tween viewing audience. Before getting into the analysis, this essay provides an overview of the show itself, and pre-existing literature studying *Wizards of Waverly Place* (and similar shows). Additionally, there is an explication of the public pedagogy and Piagetian developmental lenses that frame my arguments; namely that a show such as *Wizards of Waverly Place* has the potential for being a rationalizing agent for hegemonic discourses about class and neoliberal values in the developing minds of tween viewers, and how to leverage more democratic outcomes from that potential.

Working Class Wizards on TV

Wizards of Waverly Place premiered on the Disney Channel on October 12, 2007, and ran for 106 episodes (including a made-for-TV movie), ending on January 6, 2012. It stars a post–*Barney the Dinosaur* but pre-music fame Selena Gomez (who also sings the theme song) as Alex Russo, a teenager living in the Greenwich Village neighborhood of Manhattan with her family above their family-owned sub shop, called Waverly Sub Station. Her family includes father Jerry and mother Theresa (played by David DeLuise and Maria Canals Barrera, respectively) and brothers Justin and Max (played by David Henrie and Jake T. Austin, respectively). The main cast is rounded out by Jennifer Stone playing Alex's best friend, Harper.

Alex's father, Jerry, descends from a long line of wizards and acts as his children's wizard instructor, holding daily lessons on how to responsibly use magic. Jerry no longer has any magical power because he gave it up years prior, so he could marry his wife Theresa, a mortal. Jerry trains Alex, Justin, and Max because according to the wizarding laws of the show's universe, only one of the siblings will be able to keep their magical powers. An eventual competition between the siblings determines who gets to keep their powers. The show portrays The Russo Family as a solidly blue-collar, working-class family who runs a family business in the service industry. The Russo parents consistently emphasize the importance of family, responsibility, and hard work with their children.

Each episode generally follows the same basic structure: Jerry teaches his children a new magical spell and consistently warns them always to use magic responsibly. Inevitably, one of his children (usually Alex, but not always) uses the new spell as a shortcut to make something about average teenage life more comfortable (e.g., using a spell to boost her intelligence to impress a boy she likes at her school's quiz bowl). The siblings usually band together to solve the problem before their parents find out (which they always do) and the siblings learn a valuable lesson about not taking shortcuts. Though the show is typical tween-oriented fare on the Disney Channel and seemingly innocuous in its social implications, these kinds of shows do receive a modest level of attention in scholarly research.

Existing Literature and Inquiry
About *Wizards of Waverly Place*

There has been a relatively small amount of academic inquiry examining this show, and none which focus on this text solely. Existing research uses *Wizards of Waverly Place* as one of the multiple tween-oriented programs analyzed for a particular study. This includes content analyses examining instances of heteronormative plots and dialogue (Kirsch and Murnen, 2015), underrepresentation of female characters (Gerding & Signorelli, 2013), non-hegemonic representations of masculinity (Myers, 2012), handling and representation of sex and sexuality (Signorelli & Bievenour, 2015), promotion of disrespectful behavior (Brown, 2011), depictions of violence (Bramwell et al., 2010), and the portrayal of physical activity (O'Reilly-Duff, Best, & Tully, 2018).

Outside of the usual limitations of content analysis regarding measurement, interpretation, representation, and indication (Weber, 1990), these studies also lack diversity in how they theoretically operationalize the findings. Some of the studies lack a theoretical grounding of why the collect data matters entirely, while the ones that do solely reference either cultivation theory (Gerbner et al., 1994) or social learning theory (Bandura, 1977) (or both). While using these theories is not without merit (as will be discussed in a later section of this essay), this inquiry aims to incorporate theories of childhood to development to broaden the argument of why analysis of teen-oriented shows such as *Wizards of Waverly Place* is useful and warranted.

Additionally, qualitative analyses analyzing tween-oriented shows (including *Wizards of Waverly Place)* examine the prevalence of anti-feminist messages (Myers, 2013) and a discrepancy between demographic and represented realities of ethnic minorities in TV (de Tirado, 2016). These provide more nuanced accounts of tween-oriented programming compared to the content analyses mentioned above; however, they similarly only examine *Wizards of Waverly* as part of broader trends in teen-programming. This inquiry intends to provide an in-depth critical analysis of *Wizards of Waverly Place* on its own while exploring previously unstudied dynamics of class, privilege, and neoliberal values. The present research grounds itself in theories of public pedagogy and Piagetian development as a means of making a unique analytical contribution to this category of media text.

Public Pedagogy: A Complex Term in Need of Narrowing

Public pedagogy is a slippery term with various and differing uses of the concept. Due to this lack of an agreed-upon definition, before delving into an analysis of *Wizards of Waverly Place* using a public pedagogy lens, it is necessary to explicate the meaning of the term public pedagogy as well as precisely how the present inquiry is utilizing it.

What Does Public Pedagogy Mean?
It's Complicated

Generally, research and scholarship broadly categorize inquiry and research into how children learn under the umbrella of "educational research." While this is not an inaccurate classification, it tends to limit the research to examine how students and teachers interact in a school/classroom environment. A subgenre of educational research emerging from critical traditions focuses on learning occurring outside the traditional school setting, referring to these alternate sites of learning as public pedagogy. According to Sandlin, O'Malley, and Burdick (2011), "The term public pedagogy first appeared in 1894 and has been widely deployed as a theoretical construct in education research to focus on processes and sites of education beyond formal schooling, with a proliferation of its use by feminist and critical theorists occurring since the mid–1990s" (p. 388).

The reason for this developing perspective on learning is the underlying notion that mainstream educational research was not doing enough to identify and analyze alternate sites of learning and this omission could have consequences on research's ability to understand all ways in which children learn. Mainstream education research tends to operate under the assumption that schools are the most salient and therefore most substantive site of learning. Theorists have argued that operating under this false assumption of schools being a closed system results in incomplete accounts of how and where learning takes place (Pinar, 2006; Giroux, 2000; Ellsworth, 2005).

Public pedagogy research involves learning in institutions alternative to schools, such as museums, zoos, or libraries, as well as learning in informal education sites, such as popular culture, the internet, or commercial spaces (Sandlin, Schultz, & Burdick, 2010). Since the term's proliferation in the mid–1990s, the use of public pedagogy has engendered widespread use. Unfortunately, frequently the term is used without explicating on its exact definition or how its use compares to other uses of the term (Sandlin, O'Malley, & Burdick, 2011). This characteristic has led to a cheapening of the term public pedagogy which in turn has stunted the development of research.

Sandlin, O'Malley, and Burdick (2011) sought to remedy this by conducting a meta-analysis of 420 articles which use the term public pedagogy and derived five broad categories of public pedagogy research to "provide a preliminary but needed methodologically rigorous organizing schema for reviewing and theorizing public pedagogy and welcome alternate perspectives" (p. 341). The five categories are (a) citizenship within and beyond schools, (b) popular culture and everyday life, (c) informal institutions and public spaces, (d) dominant cultural discourses, and (e) public intellectualism and social activism. Of these categories, "popular culture and every life" and "dominant cultural discourses" broadly inform how and why this inquiry uses the term public pedagogy. *Wizards of Waverly Place,* being a popular culture text, constitutes a non-traditional site of learning which warrants it as a rich site for observing and analyzing messages which may contribute to dominant cultural discourses. This study examines discourses regarding class and neoliberal culture explicitly.

Public Pedagogy, Popular Culture and Dominant Cultural Discourses

Gramsci's (1971) often-quoted idea that "every relationship of hegemony is an educational one" (p. 350) can serve as a broad framing of where much of the popular culture related inquiry into public pedagogy resides. Public pedagogy theorists see popular culture as a site where children can be exposed to dominant social/cultural norms. While public pedagogy research involving popular culture has encompassed texts marketed for all ages, work looking at popular culture aimed specifically for youth has found it can impart oppressive constructs of race, class, gender, heterosexism, and consumerism (Giroux, 1998, 1999; Trifonas, 2006).

H.A. Giroux (2000, 2001) is a leading scholar looking at popular culture as public pedagogy. Giroux draws from the theoretical frameworks of Hall (1997), Gramsci (1971), and Freire (1973) to demonstrate that popular culture does not automatically reproduce dominant cultural norms, but rather provides an arena for people (including children) to struggle against hegemonic forces—sometimes succumbing and sometimes transcending. Giroux's work in this area shows popular culture texts are critical aspects of culture which require examination due to their implications with cultural norms (social and economic). This brief explication of Giroux's theory serves to specify further how I will be grounding my analysis of *Wizards of Waverly Place* as public pedagogy.

In observing the text itself, this inquiry seeks to elucidate content which indicates questionable dealings with issues of class, privilege, and neoliberal values. Due to the popularity of the show itself, it is reasonable to assume observed problematic discourse partly contributes to dominant cultural discourses viewed and internalized by young consumers of popular culture. These observed discourses within *Wizards of Waverly Place* will not be viewed solely from a deficit perspective, or how the show potentially *negatively* impacts children and their sensibilities, but also how this text specifically could be utilized to resist against the dominant cultural discourses presented within it.

Child Development Theory: Why Is Looking at This Show Worthwhile?

As mentioned previously, existing inquiry and analysis involving *Wizards of Waverly Place* (and similar shows) overwhelmingly are grounded in the perspectives of cultivation theory and social learning theory. Cultivation theory (Gerbner et al., 1994) posits the more time people spend consuming television, the more likely they are to believe social reality aligns with the reality portrayed on television. Social learning theory (Bandura, 1977) claims TV can potentially offer models of behavior which can be imitated (social learning theory has historically been used to speak of the potential promotion of sexual and violent discourse in children's programming). These grounding theories would be appropriate for the present inquiry; however, for the sake of diversifying perspectives as to why teen shows such as *Wizards of Waverly Place* are useful to observe, analyze, and discuss, in addition to public pedagogy this analysis grounds itself in child development theories of Jean Piaget. Additionally, the Piagetian perspective aligns well with the tenets of this inquiry's use of public pedagogy.

Piagetian Developmental Stage of the *Wizards* Audience

The traditional developmental theory of Piaget (1969) classifies children aged 7–12 as being in the *concrete operational* stage of development, where "schemas develop that enable the child to engage in mental transformations in interactions with the concrete world" (Lemish, 2014: p. 43). This conception of child development fits well with this inquiry's use of public pedagogy which pushes to understand what schemas and understanding develop through the child's interaction with the cultural discourses within a particular popular culture text. Based on television ratings put out by Nielson, it can be assumed *Wizards of Waverly Place*'s largest audience was children within or close to the concrete operational stage.

In 2009, *Wizards of Waverly Place* was the most-watched scripted show across all of television amongst children aged 6–11 (average 1.81 million viewers per episode) and tweens aged 9–14 (1.63 million viewers per episode) (Seidman, 2010). Naturally, one cannot assume *all* viewers were within the Piagetian concrete operational stage, but one can assume *the largest group of viewers* likely fell within this stage. Meaning they were at a point in their development where mediated messages could potentially have an influencing presence in the formation of a child's schemas and their understanding of the social world.

Additionally, public pedagogy is an excellent lens to use in conjunction with this framing of childhood development because it addresses a perceived shortcoming in Piagetian theory. Some criticize Piaget's developmental stages for not putting enough emphasis on social contexts and different modes of interaction with one's environment (Casper & Theilheimer, 2009). Public pedagogy views popular culture texts as potentially tantamount in their socializing functions to traditional socializing agents such as school and family. This approach contributes to a more catholic understanding of the influencers in students' lives and advocates for engaging with more contemporary influencers of youth in addition to traditional ones. According to Lemish (2014), "[Media are] major socializing agents in children's lives, ones that complement and often compete with other more traditional socializing agents" (p. 135). If this is accepted to be true, public pedagogy is a useful lens for complicating traditional conceptions of childhood development to address media and popular culture's role in a child's lived experience in the social world.

Methods for Data Collection and Analysis

For this inquiry, I viewed all episodes of *Wizards of Waverly Place* (106 episodes total, including one made-for-tv movie). Initially, the first season (21 episodes) was viewed to delineate what social discourses were most prevalent in the show. A viewing of the first season uncovered messages about class as a potential point of analysis and three areas of discourse emerged: the socioeconomic reality of Greenwich Village as opposed what the show presents, the conflation of neoliberal values with family values, and the use of magic as a stand-in for privilege. These three broad categories guided the observation and analysis of the rest of the episodes.

The media ecology research traditions pioneered by theorists such as Marshall McLuhan (1971), Neil Postman (1985), Elizabeth Eisenstein (1980), and Camille Paglia (1990) influence analysis of the episodes. According to Jupp (2006), media analysis through a media ecology perspective "divert[s] analysts' attention away from the sheer content of media and towards the particular relationships human subjects had with the various media" (n.p.). The actual content of *Wizards of Waverly Place* will be merely a starting point for putting the show in a broader context. Through the public pedagogy lens, content (such as specific scenes, episodes, or storylines from the show) will be discussed as potential sites of struggle against or passive receiving of contemporary dominant cultural discourses. Additionally, there will be ideas presented on how to leverage a child's relationship with a text such as *Wizards of Waverly Place* towards social progress.

Issues of Class and Privilege on Waverly Place

Wizards Thriving in One of the United States' Most Expensive Zip Codes

The most salient asynchrony between the actual lived-social world and the version presented in *Wizards of Waverly Place* is the depiction of life and community in the Greenwich Village neighborhood on the lower west side of Manhattan. An inaccurate depiction of a neighborhood or region is not inherently problematic nor is it anywhere near unique to this show; however, based on the assumptions of the public pedagogy lens and child development theory described above there could be unseen implications. Youth could potentially view, internalize, and rationalize a skewed representation of how to be successful in what is one of the most expensive zip codes in the world. The misrepresentation of Greenwich Village includes an apparent disregard for the socioeconomic makeup of the neighborhood and the experiential reality of small businesses.

Greenwich Village has a rich history of being a cultural hub for art, music, performance, and progressive values and is considered a cradle for the development of LGBT-rights movements, 1960s counterculture, and the Beat Generation of authors. The historical significance of the area in addition to its walkability, proximity to institutions such as New York University, and preservation of historic buildings have made the four zip codes which make up Greenwich Village (10011, 10012, 10003, and 10014) regularly ranked among the top–20 most expensive zip codes in the United States for the past 20 years (DePietro, 2018). By comparing the depiction of the neighborhood in the show to real-life statistics about the area, an apparent discrepancy between representation and reality presents itself; it is particularly evident when considering the depicted efficacy of the working class Russos and their peers in what is considered a lavish place to live for highly financially successful people.

Within the 10014 zip code (where the real street "Waverly Place" is and where the show is purported to take place), the average household income for families, according to the U.S. Census Bureau, in 2011 was $264,028 per year and estimates indicated an increase to $298,732 by 2016 (2011). The Russo Family owns and runs the Waverly Sub Station restaurant, which is located on Waverly Place, a prime real estate location only a few blocks away from

Washington Square Park. While the show never explicitly states how much money the Russo Family takes in from the restaurant, it is safe to assume they are not making anywhere near the mean income for the area. This fact is especially misleading as the Russos not only work in the neighborhood but live in a four bedroom/four bathroom two-story apartment directly above the restaurant. Public records show a comparable apartment near Waverly Place currently has a monthly rent of $28,000 (Zillow, n.d.); a rate few outside the top-echelon of earners in NYC could afford, let alone a family who runs a sub shop.

The Russos are not the only occupants of the show's fictional version of Greenwich Village who do not make sense given the real-life milieu of the neighborhood. The show repeatedly depicts the Russos' community as a thriving hub for small, family-owned businesses. For example, in the episode "Racing" (S2E4), Alex Russo gets a new boyfriend, Dean, whose family runs an auto repair shop just up the street. In "Wizards vs. Vampires" (S2E26), a family moves to the neighborhood and opens an immediately successful late-night snack shop, and a local business competition sees the community banding together to resist corporate development in the neighborhood in "Wizard School, Pt. 2" (S1E14). These ideal representations of community ties are indeed a positive representation of working outside of the mainstream neoliberal capitalist system, but ignorance to the lived-reality of Greenwich Village misleads young viewers of the efficacy of small business ownership, especially service-based ones, in an upscale urban neighborhood.

The depiction of the Russos' restaurant and the other service-based small businesses in the neighborhood particularly skirt reality in light of the well-documented rise in rent prices and the proliferation of boutique fashion stores in Greenwich Village specifically. In 2000, the HBO series *Sex and the City* featured a scene at Greenwich Village's own Magnolia Bakery (located at 401 Bleecker Street), which brought unprecedented commercial attention to the neighborhood (Morris, 2001). The growing attention to the neighborhood prompted an effort by renowned designer Marc Jacobs to create a retail corridor throughout Greenwich, opening his boutiques and attracting many others. This shift in the culture of the neighborhood contributed to rent for commercial spaces to rise from around $75 per square foot in the late 1990s to an average of $300 a square foot, driving out the majority of businesses which did not have significant financial backing from outside investors (Kurutz, 2007). The plethora of family-owned businesses thriving within the fiction of *Wizards of Waverly Place* would not exist in the real world. These differences between reality and what the show presents may seem inconsequential, but as will be explored in the analysis, the reality of the show should be viewed as a site presenting hegemonic cultural discourses which young minds may rationalize as truths.

The Russos Always Put Family
(and Goods and Services) First

Wizards of Waverly Place's version of Greenwich Village as a safe-haven for small businesses partially contributes to another problematic aspect uncovered during a critical watching of the show: a consistent conflation of working-class family values with neoliberal success. Greenwich Village historically (before the gentrification described in the previous section) prided itself on its work-class culture, particularly in the role local merchants played in supporting fellow community members. According to Duneier (2001), small business owners and vendors in Greenwich Village historically not only supply goods for purchase but "serve an important function in the lives of their customers," offering them an attentive ear and conversation and exuding ideals of self-worth and mutual reliance (p. 19). The fictional version of Greenwich Village in the show seemingly attempts to exude these values in portraying a robust local-business community, but simultaneously betrays it in the clear neoliberal capitalist logics driving the relationships between those businesses. Additionally, the Russo children's frequent coveting and pursuing of consumer goods (at the encouragement of their parents) belie the end of episode "lessons" which attempt to expound the importance of family and community further.

The Russos show neoliberal capitalist-driven aggression towards their neighboring local vendors frequently and consistently throughout the show, undercutting attempts to portray the family and the neighborhood as community-focused and supportive. In S4E7, "Everything's Rosie for Justin," the Russo parents and Alex's friend Harper (who is living with the Russos at this point in the series) think up a punch-card system to bring in more customers to Waverly Sub Station. This plan is not mentioned to be driven by a need to support the Russo family or community, but rather to "squash" the competition from nearby restaurants. In S3E2, "Halloween," the Waverly Place Merchants Association (portrayed as a local organization of businesses whose goal is to further the interests of businesses, similar to a Chamber of Commerce) stops by Waverly Sub Station to discuss the Russos' contribution of hosting a haunted house for the neighborhoods Halloween festival. Because the festival is "important to the brand, image, and commercial growth" of the neighborhood, the head of the association threatens to ban the Russos from operating their business during the festival unless their haunted house is made scarier.

These examples (amongst others throughout the show) demonstrate the Greenwich Village portrayed in the show is driven more by neoliberal values of expansion, growth, and profit rather than family/community support and sustenance. In addition to neoliberal values being apparent in the way the neighborhood businesses operate, the repeating story structure of most episodes and lack permanent character development contradicts the family-oriented, value-driven lessons learned at the end of most episodes.

The majority of *Wizards of Waverly Place* episodes follow a similar structure: one of the Russo children uses magic to get something they want, their plan somehow goes awry, and other family members help bail them out, and everyone learns a valuable lesson. For example, in S2E1, "Smarty Pants," Alex Russo impresses a boy she likes by stealing magical "smarty pants" to boost her intelligence. After she is found out, her parents tell her that being herself, not changing her image, is the best way to get a boy's attention. This lesson is pretty standard fare for a tween-oriented show like *Wizards of Waverly Place*. Unfortunately, Alex and her siblings making the same kinds of mistakes and then hearing the same kinds of lessons in almost every episode undercuts any potential positive impact on viewers. Throughout the series, the episode structure described above recurs with one or more of the Russo children using magic to do things like get tickets to a concert, get a shopping advantage at a 10-minute clothing sale, make the baseball team, win a marathon, silence a rival, or start a rock band (to name only a few). They then seemingly forget the lessons they learn and make the same mistakes and learn the same lessons episode after episode.

The repeating episodic structure of *Wizards of Waverly Place* is similar to most sitcoms. Writers sacrifice long-term character development in service of creating new plots based off of a few core characteristics of the characters/traits (e.g., Joey from *Friends* never seeming to get any smarter or Mr. Roper on *Three's Company* never catching on Jack was not gay). Alex Russo, in particular, never matures past her core characteristics of being unknowingly selfish, materialistic, and manipulative to get her way yet not worried about losing the trust of family and friends in the process. We must consider the neoliberal desires of the Russo children around things like consumer goods, image, changing one's identity, and the importance of measurable achievement in the context of Giroux's (1998) public pedagogy. He argues

> media culture becom[ing] a substantive, if not the primary, educational force in regulating the meanings, values, and tastes that set the norms and conventions that offer up and legitimate particular subject positions—what it means to claim an identity as a male, female, white, black, citizen, non-citizen, successful, or unsuccessful as well as to define the meaning of childhood, the national past, beauty, truth, and social agency [p. 254].

A Magical Take on Privilege

Consumer-driven values are not the only component of the neoliberal age to be rampant within the storylines of *Wizards of Waverly Place*, with power and privilege manifesting in the show's use and framing of the magical powers the Russo children possess. Giroux argues "media culture is central to understanding how power, privilege, and social desire intersect to structure daily life" (Doyle & Singh, 2006: p. 41). In the show, the social desires of the Russo children (as argued in the previous section) are rooted in neoliberal/consumer-driven values, and their magical abilities and heritage embody their power and privilege.

As described in the previous section, most episodes contain one or more of the Russo children desiring to attain something that without magic would otherwise be unattainable. Whether it is Alex casting a spell to get a boy to pay attention to her friend, Justin bewitching a zit so it will disappear before a date, or Max secretly using magic to boost sales of the restaurant, the Russo children are quick to utilize their privilege to pursue their desires. The show's theme song (sung by lead actress Selena Gomez) sets up the Russo children's relationship to their magical privilege nicely; the theme contains a warning to take care with one's powers and to be responsible in their use. They are allowed to use their magic to make their lives more comfortable, but when they use their powers irresponsibly, things get out of hand. Unfortunately, the lessons learned are not usually, "check your privilege and don't abuse it" but rather "when you do use your privilege, be smart about it, so you don't bring attention to your unearned privilege." Mainly, as the theme song suggests, Alex and her brothers are taught to make their privilege invisible, so others do not know they are exerting it.

The link between magic and family heritage further complicates the relationship between the Russo siblings and their magical privilege. The sole storyline that recurs throughout the entirety of the series is father Jerry teaching his three children magic to prepare them for a competition against each other. According to the magical laws of the show, the winner of the competition will keep their powers forever while the others will permanently lose their powers. Jerry frequently bemoans when his children abuse their magic because he is worried they will not be able to function without their powers; however, there are never consequences.

Learning to exist without magic is a frequent end-of-episode lesson which, like the other "lessons" discussed previously, is never taken to heart by the Russo children. In the show's final episodes, Alex (the most common offender of abusing magic throughout the show) becomes the family wizard and keeps her powers through the competition. Older brother Justin is still able to keep his powers through his connections in the wizard world, and younger brother Max loses his powers but takes over the family sub shop and brings it to new heights of success through investments from the wizarding world. The entire, series-spanning lesson from their father about not abusing their magical privilege so they can learn to live without it is rendered moot.

All three benefit from their privilege and are set-up to have prosperous adulthoods.

The consequence-free notion of living fully through one's inherited privilege is a problematic one. The argument here is not that children watching this show will be interpellated into full-on neoliberal values or irreversibly primed to exploit one's privilege. The argument is children in the concrete-operational stage of development regularly consuming shows like *Wizards of Waverly Place* has the opportunity to rationalize those messages as truth. The exact consequence of this is unclear (and possibly unknowable), but by identifying texts containing problematic dominant cultural discourses, such as *Wizards of Waverly*, there also presents an opportunity for intervention to "interrupt" that rationalization.

Discussion

Utilizing a Pedagogy of Interruption in Popular Culture

The preceding section lays out some of the dominant cultural discourses found within the text of *Wizards of Waverly Place*. The question then becomes, "So what?" So what if the show does not accurately depict life and class in Greenwich Village? So what working-class values conflate with neoliberal one? So what if magic presents conflicting messages about privilege? It is only a show made for tweens about magical wizards after all. Giroux (1999), through his public pedagogy lens, would find this show particularly problematic as it is a product of the Walt Disney Company. He claims Disney not only "mystif[ies] its corporate agenda with appeals to fun, innocence, and purity" but also represents a threat "to a vibrant democracy in their control over information" (pp. 259–260). Giroux's approach to public pedagogy tends to favor more macro-level analyses of the modes of production for popular culture and how they manifest in texts in a general way. The present analysis fits in as a small piece to the broader arguments Giroux makes.

Earlier in this essay, I argued *Wizards of Waverly Place* (as well as the other shows discussed in this volume) as an appropriate point of focus in understanding how and why dominant societal values and discourse (in this specific case, values, and discourse around class and capitalism) reproduce in our society. This argument grounded itself in Giroux's conception of the public pedagogy, namely that popular culture presents an arena to rationalize or react against dominant cultural discourses. Additionally, the target audience being youth in the concrete-operational Piagetian stage of development provides justification and support for this text and similar ones being of particular importance when considering the development of citizens through mediated discourse in our 21st-century society. Now that I have laid out what cultural discourses are present in *Wizards of Waverly Place* and the developmental potential for rationalizing them, it is worth exploring the other side of Giroux's public pedagogy of popular culture: how can the text be a site for resistance and dissent against those discourse?

Biesta (2006), writing about K–12 teacher pedagogy, claims a pedagogy of interruption is necessary to counteract the subjectifying capabilities of media culture and technologies. A pedagogy of interruption must prime students to approach mediated interactions in a democratically responsible way. While Biesta is explicitly referring to the K–12 classroom space, I believe the contemporary interwoven nature of media and society necessitates bringing these sensibilities outside of the classroom as well. So who should "interrupt" the rationalization of cultural discourses by viewers of *Wizards of Waverly Place?* Parents seem like a logical place to start.

Co-viewing, or the practice of parents and children consuming content together, has been found to increase engagement with the text on the part of the child (Haridakis & Hanson, 2009). This increased engagement, in my opinion, presents a prime opportunity for the parent to "interrupt" the discourses of the show and prompt youth to approach media consumption in a democratically minded way. This interruption does not have to be complicated or planned. Simply asking children a question like "Do you think it's right that Alex manipulates people with their magic?" as a conversation starter and having a brief discussion off of that could develop a child's understanding about the differences between the social world presented through fictional media and the actual lived-social world and why understanding those differences is essential. Simple questions like this could potentially interrupt Giroux's worry of the potential rationalization of hegemonic discourse and create space for dissent and the beginnings of critical cultural awareness in young viewers.

Are Class, Neoliberalism and Privilege All We Can Talk About?

To close this essay, placing this discussion in a broader context is necessary. While I focused on problematic discourses of class, neoliberalism, and privilege in *Wizards of Waverly Place* for this study, I am not claiming this is the only salient area needing exploration. There are indeed questions about identity formation, hegemonic masculinity/femininity, race, and heteronormativity (to name a few) to be asked and explored through academic research, but more importantly in the context of the home. The present analysis is one example of a much-needed intellectual shift in how we frame popular culture's role in our lives. Academics, parents, and teachers alike must think of the implications of unchecked cultural discourses presented to youth not just through *Wizards of Waverly Place,* but all youth-oriented programming. The content itself does not necessarily need to be adjusted (nor is it pragmatically conceivable that Disney would suddenly entirely change how they make their shows), but rather how we talk about the content is where the shift needs to happen.

REFERENCES

Adair, J. (2009). Everything is not what it seems [Recorded by Gomez, S.]. On *Wizards of Waverly Place Soundtrack* [CD]. Burbank, CA: Walt Disney Records.
Bandura, A. (1977). *Social learning theory.* Englewood Cliffs, NJ: Prentice Hall.
Biesta, G.J.J. (2006). *Beyond learning: Democratic education for a human future.* Boulder, CO: Paradigm Publishers.
Bramwell, V., Herr, A., Sickles, C., & Kugath, J. (2010). Violence in children's popular television programs. *FHSS Mentored Research Conference.* Retrieved from https://scholarsarchive.byu.edu/fhssconference_studentpub/257.
Denzel de Tirado, H. (2013). Media monitoring and ethnicity: Representing Latino families on american television (2000–2013). *Nuevo mundo mundos nuevos. Nouveaux mondes mondes nouveaux—Novo mundo mundos novos—New world new worlds.* https://doi.org/10.4000/nuevomundo.66165.
DePietro, A. (2018, July 31). Housing 1998–2018: America's most expensive zip codes, then and now. Retrieved October 22, 2018, from https://www.forbes.com/sites/andrewdepietro/2018/07/31/housing-1998–2018-most-expensive-zip-codes/#187f96801aea.
Doyle, C., & Singh, A. (2006). *Reading & teaching Henry Giroux.* Peter Lang.
Duneier, M. (2001). *Sidewalk.* New York: Macmillan.
Eisenstein, E.L. (1980). *The printing press as an agent of change.* Cambridge University Press.
Ellsworth, E. (2005). *Places of learning: Media, architecture, pedagogy.* New York: Routledge.
Freire, P. (1973). *Pedagogy of the oppressed.* New York: Seabury Press.
Gerbner, G., Gross, L., Morgan, M., & Signorielli, N. (1994). Growing up with television: The cultivation perspective. In J. Bryant & D. Zillman (Eds.), *Media effects: Advances in theory and research* (pp. 17–41). Hillsdale, NJ: Erlbaum.
Gerding, A., & Signorielli, N. (2014). Gender roles in tween television programming: A Content analysis of two genres. *Sex Roles, 70*(1), 43–56. https://doi.org/10.1007/s11199-013-0330-z.
Giroux, H.A. (1998). Public pedagogy and rodent politics: Cultural studies and the challenge of Disney. *Arizona Journal of Hispanic Cultural Studies, 2,* 253–266.
Giroux, H.A. (1999). *The mouse that roared: Disney and the end of innocence.* Lanham, MD: Roman & Littlefield.
Giroux, H.A. (2000). Public pedagogy as cultural politics: Stuart Hall and the "crisis" of culture. *Cultural Studies, 14,* 341–360.
Giroux, H.A. (2001). *Stealing innocence: Corporate culture's war on children.* New York: Palgrave Macmillan.
Gramsci, A. (1971). *Selections from the prison notebooks.* New York: International.
Hall, S. (1997). The centrality of culture: Notes on the cultural revolutions of our times. In K. Thompson (Ed.), *Media and cultural regulation* (pp. 208–238). Thousand Oaks, CA: Sage.
Haridakis, P., & Hanson, G. (2009). Social interaction and co-viewing with YouTube: Blending mass communication reception and social connection. *Journal of Broadcasting & Electronic Media, 53*(2), 317–335. https://doi.org/10.1080/08838150902908270.
Jupp, V. (2006). *The SAGE dictionary of social research methods.* London: SAGE Publications Ltd doi: 10.4135/9780857020116
Kirsch, A.C., & Murnen, S.K. (2015). "Hot" girls and "cool dudes": Examining the prevalence

of the heterosexual script in American children's television media. *Psychology of Popular Media Culture, 4*(1), 18–30. http://dx.doi.org/10.1037/ppm0000017.

Kurutz, S. (2018, January 20). Bleecker street's swerve from luxe shops to vacant stores. *New York Times*. Retrieved from https://www.nytimes.com/2017/05/31/fashion/bleecker-street-shopping-empty-storefronts.html.

Lemish, D. (2014). *Children and media: A global perspective*. Somerset: Wiley. Retrieved from http://ebookcentral.proquest.com/lib/ucb/detail.action?docID=1887115.

McLuhan, M. (1971). *The Medium is the message*. Penguin Books.

Morris, B. (2001, June 3). The age of dissonance: Babes in adultland. *New York Times*. Retrieved from https://www.nytimes.com/2001/06/03/style/the-age-of-dissonance-babes-in-adultland.html.

Myers, K. (2012). "Cowboy up!": Non-hegemonic representations of masculinity in children's television programming. *The Journal of Men's Studies, 20*(2), 125–143. https://doi.org/10.3149/jms.2002.125.

Myers, K. (2013). Anti-feminist messages in American television programming for young girls. *Journal of Gender Studies, 22*(2), 192–205. https://doi.org/10.1080/09589236.2012.714074.

Paglia, C. (1990). *Sexual Personae*. Yale University Press.

Pinar, W.F. (2006). Relocating cultural studies into curriculum studies. *Journal of Curriculum Theorizing, 22*(2), 55–72.

Piaget, J. (1969). *The origins of intelligence in the child*. New York: International University Press.

Postman, N. (1986). *Amusing ourselves to death: Public discourse in the age of show business*. New York: Penguin.

Sandlin, J.A., O'Malley, M.P., & Burdick, J. (2011). Mapping the complexity of public pedagogy scholarship 1894–2010. *Review of Educational Research, 81*(3), 338–375. https://doi.org/10.3102/0034654311413395.

Sandlin, J.A., Schultz, B.D., & Burdick, J. (2010). *Handbook of public pedagogy*. New York: Routledge.

Seidman, E. (2009, December 22). Disney Channel sets new viewing records in 2009. Retrieved September 20, 2018, from https://tvbythenumbers.zap2it.com/network-press-releases/disney-channel-sets-new-viewing-records-in-2009/.

Signorielli, N., & Bievenour, A. (2015). Sex in adolescent programming: A content analysis. *Communication Research Reports, 32*(4), 304–313. https://doi.org/10.1080/08824096.2015.1089856.

Trifonas, P.P. (2006). Engaging the Disney effect: The cultural production of escapism and utopia in media. In J. Weiss, J. Nolan, J. Hunsinger, & P.P. Trifonas (Eds.), *The international handbook of virtual learning environments* (pp. 1107–1119). New York: Springer.

U.S. Census Bureau. (2011). *2012–2016 American community survey 5-year estimates*. Retrieved from https://factfinder.census.gov/faces/tableservices/jsf/pages/productview.xhtml?src=CF.

Weber, R. (1990). Quantitative applications in the social sciences: Basic content analysis Thousand Oaks, CA: SAGE Publications Ltd doi: 10.4135/9781412983488.

Zillow. (n.d.). 12 E 9th St, New York, NY 10011 | Zillow. Retrieved October 23, 2018, from https://www.zillow.com:443/homes/for_sale/Greenwich-Village-Manhattan-New-York-NY/condo,apartment_duplex_type/2094191153_zpid/195133_rid/4-_beds/2-_baths/40.74064,-73.98496,40.721778,-74.015859_rect/14_zm/0_mmm/1_fr/.

"Disney is ruining my kid!"

A Case for Cultivation and Social Learning in Tween TV

RACHEL GULDIN, JANELLE APPLEQUIST
and TRAVIS R. BELL

Since the metaphorical dawn of mass-mediated time, critics have condemned media as causes of social ills and destroyers of the fabric of society. From Addams' *The House of Dreams*, to the Payne Fund Studies, to Wertham's *Seduction of the Innocent*, media are criticized for corrupting youth. The essence of this conversation has not changed dramatically over decades, though the medium under fire varies. This study addresses television content and its perceived threat to children.

The concern surrounding media effects on children is unsurprising. According to Nielsen, more than 95 percent of children watch more than 20 hours of television each week (Grow & Tell, 2015), clocking in an average of 1,200 hours per year (Television Watching, 2016). With all this time in front of the TV, what do many children find themselves watching? Evidence indicates the Disney Channel. In 2015, the Disney Channel had an average of 1.234 million viewers every minute, pulled in the largest share of audiences aged 6–14, and was the most-watched cable network (Kissel, 2015). The Disney Channel also accounts for a large amount of international viewership, with its reach encompassing 166 countries and a significant increase recently in popularity in Europe, the Middle East, Latin America, and Asia (Graser, 2013). Among both cable and broadcast networks, the Disney Channel ranks 24th among all viewers (Schneider, 2017). Even with the advent of popular streaming services, Disney refuses to be left behind—it developed its own streaming service, Disney+, which launched in late 2019. Its prominence makes it no wonder the network has come under scrutiny for what the programs show children.

Parents and popular press alike criticize the effects of the Disney Channel's shows on children, and their complaints reverberate: Disney shows make children rude and disrespectful. Parent bloggers have written that the Disney Channel shows were "garbage" (megpoulinindeed, 2014, para. 15), encouraged "indulging in an awful lot of sassy back-talk" (From There, 2011, para. 8), and glorified when children "deceive, avoid, or outsmart their parents" (DiGiovanni, 2014, para. 8). Simply, "Disney has been ruining my kid" (megpoulinindeed, 2014, para. 1). Popular press shares these sentiments. *The New York Post* criticized the disrespectful nature of the Disney Channel characters as barriers for parental approval of the shows (Riley, 2016), and *LA Weekly*'s Schager (2013) opined, "When adults are around, they're depicted as buffoons, and their threats of punishment are toothless, mere narrative devices designed to provide drama while also underscoring the kids' awesome and lionized do-what-I-wanna-do behavior" (para. 6). With both parents and press calling Disney disrespectful, we must ask if this is adult alarmism and moral panic, or if there is real cultural concern.

The purpose of this study is to examine the presence of displays of negative and disrespectful interactions (social aggressions) performed by characters on the Disney Channel's live-action television shows and to determine the differences in frequency of verbal versus nonverbal social aggressions. The study uses content analysis to analyze the types of socially aggressive interactions between characters of different ages and sexes, as well as the frequency of socially aggressive interactions over the course of an individual series. We add to the current body of literature on children's television via contributions explaining trends in children's programming, specifically how child characters are aggressing in live-action the Disney Channel television shows.

Literature Review

While studies of children's media are many, research focused on social aggression as shown via the Disney Channel shows is limited. To best understand the research supporting this study, it is essential to first consider works and theories that address children and television, then studies focused on children's television programming, and finally, research that examines Disney's films and television content.

Whether it is acting as a form of cultural capital among peers (Kampf & Hamo, 2015) or as a teacher of socialization (Callister, Robinson, & Clark, 2007), television impacts social and cultural aspects of childhood. Concern over what children take from TV consumption is well established because television is often considered capable of teaching. Thirty years ago, Comstock and Strzyzewski (1990) posited that behaviors on television shows acted as suggestions for viewers and would "increase the viewers' repertoire of behaviors" (p. 264). Research continued to support this notion through studies that television could stimulate children to perform specific imitations of aggressive behaviors they viewed (Martins & Wilson, 2012b) and that frequent displays of aggression on television may be influencing how children come to understand acceptable interactions and behaviors in everyday life (Coyne, 2004). A comprehensive review of the media effects literature from the 1990s indicates that viewing violence in television shows and movies demonstrates impacts on children's aggressive behaviors (Villani, 2001).

Researchers have examined how children and family characters interact on primetime television. Kaye and Sapolsky's (2004) study on profane language used during primetime shows with child-friendly ratings reflects the arguments that inspired this study: "a new nemesis has appeared: young characters acting like adults. Children on television are [...] seen engaging in aggressive behaviors and other activities that are unacceptable for that age group" (p. 431). Other studies indicate that primetime television families display prosocial (or at least not antisocial) behaviors (Comstock & Strzyzewski, 1990; Skill & Wallace, 1990) with two important considerations. First, television provides portrayals of family living that are "seductively realistic" and may be foundational to a cultural understanding of the ways in which this social organism operates (Skill & Wallace, 1990, p. 244). Second, situational comedy shows have the highest occurrences of conflict during primetime programming slots (Comstock & Strzyzewski, 1990).

Studies of aggression in children's media have diverged from media effects concerning physical aggression by including nonphysical aggression in studies on television, specifically indirect aggression. Indirect aggression (used here in concert with "social aggression") does not inflict physical violence against another but is instead based in manipulation (Coyne & Whitehead, 2008). Studies suggest that indirect aggression is the most frequently depicted form of aggression (Coyne & Archer, 2004; Coyne & Whitehead, 2008), occurring in 92 percent of the 50 most popular children's television shows (Martins & Wilson, 2012a), and that viewing indirect aggression has limited predictive power for actual performance of indirect aggression (Coyne & Archer, 2005).

Martins and Wilson (2012b) note that performing socially aggressive behaviors is "positively correlated with overall television exposure and exposure to both physical and socially aggressive programming" (p. 59). Performances of socially aggressive behaviors on children's television shows are overwhelmingly direct and verbal (Martins & Wilson, 2012a). A study of indirect aggression in Disney films showed that animated Disney films exhibited approximately nine acts of social aggression every hour, a statistic comparable to social aggression as seen on television shows in prior research (Coyne & Archer, 2004; Coyne & Whitehead, 2008). In addition, the literature suggests that indirect aggression may be gendered. Females tend to be most closely tied to indirect aggression: more female characters are shown committing acts of indirect aggression (Coyne & Archer, 2004; Luther & Legg, 2010; Martins & Wilson, 2012a), female viewers prefer shows that tend to display more indirect aggression (Coyne & Archer, 2005), and females demonstrate a relationship between viewing indirect aggression and engaging in said aggression at school (Martins & Wilson, 2012b). Compounding these findings, additional research suggests that children's television shows portray social aggression committed mostly by attractive characters, arguably making these attractive behaviors (Martins & Wilson, 2012a).

Little work has been done specifically on aggression in the Disney Channel television shows, though one study shows that displays of nonphysical aggression on the Disney Channel do not differ significantly from peer channels Cartoon Network and Nickelodeon (Hentges & Case, 2013). Yet two studies provide insight with exclusive focus on the Disney Channel series and suggest they warrant further research in this area. Brown (2003) focused on disrespectful acts in six live-action Disney Channel shows that were popular in the early 2000s. Results of the study indicated that disrespectful acts—verbal, nonverbal, and physical—occurred about once per minute, and out of all disrespectful acts, 73 percent were verbal. In addition, child characters performed the majority of acts coded as disrespectful; often these actions were directed at other child characters. Weaver (2012) examined the portrayal of school in popular Disney Channel television shows. The findings indicate that students often take on the role of being an adult and supplant teachers' authority. Teachers (i.e., adults), then, are often shown as immature or incompetent when compared to child characters.

There is a dearth of research about Disney live-action shows in the context of indirect aggression. Additionally, there is a lack of longitudinal work examining patterns of indirect aggression in children's television shows (Martins & Wilson, 2012b). This research will help to fill these gaps by focusing exclusively on how the Disney Channel's live-action shows depict social aggression and providing a launchpad for further analysis.

The extent to which television can act as a teacher for children has remained a topic for the popular press and an inquiry focused on by researchers. While it is widely held that direct effects are unlikely, television's indirect effects and role in socialization and teaching are generally accepted: "television is an effective tutor" (Bandura, 1978, p. 15). Bandura's (1978) social learning theory, originally applied to aggression, purports that learning occurs from both personal experience and observation. Observation of behaviors—as well as subsequent consequences—can incite action of repeated behaviors (Bandura, 1978). In the context of television, because children may not have extensive experiences or interactions with the world at large but likely do consume television, impressions of social reality can be drawn from mediated experiences and build foundations for how children understand and interact with the world (Callister et al., 2007).

Unlike social learning theory's attention to specific instances, cultivation theory concerns overarching, long-term, and repeated mediated messaging. In an early piece developing this theory, Gerbner (1970) asserts that through symbols and recurring messages, mass media create narratives that resonate with publics. In addition, cultivation is a long and invasive process: "Viewers are born into that symbolic world and cannot avoid regular exposure to its recurrent patterns" (Morgan, Shanahan, & Signorielli, 2008, p. 36). Cultivation proposes that a lifetime surrounded by repeated mediated messages that transcend specific shows and incorporate television in totality creates predominant notions or assumptions about social reality. Cultivation also recognizes that traditionally localized sources of socialization, such as family and school, are preempted by television's storytelling function and with great intensity: "children are born into homes where mass-produced stories can reach them on average more than seven hours a day" (Gerbner, 2012, p. 238). Applying cultivation theory helps researchers better understand the "shared representations of life" (Gerbner, 1970, p. 81) that publics hold across physical spaces. The primary contribution provided by cultivation theory is its support for further understanding of the ways in which our surroundings influence our perspectives of the world, society, and reality (Morgan et al., 2008).

Some recent work has taken a more psychological approach to this topic, employing Huesmann's (1988) information processing model (Coyne & Archer, 2005) or Anderson and Bushman's (2002) General Aggression Model (GAM) (Coyne & Whitehead, 2008; Luther & Legg, 2010), yet both theories extend beyond the scope of this study. Previous research has incorporated only social learning theory (Buerkel-Rothfuss et al., 1982; Kaye & Sapolsky, 2004) while other work has paired cultivation theory with GAM (Luther & Legg, 2010). The use of social learning theory in tandem with cultivation theory fits the scope of the current investigation and has previously been used and established for studying children's television phenomena (Brown, 2003; Callister et al., 2007; Comstock & Strzyzewski, 1990; Hentges & Case, 2013; Robinson & Anderson, 2006; Robinson, Callister, Magoffin, & Moore, 2007; Skill & Wallace, 1990).

Based on the reviewed literature, this study proposes three hypotheses. Because the literature suggests that social aggression is present in most popular children's shows and that it is most often portrayed by child characters, this study predicts:

H_1: In the Disney Channel's live-action television series, social aggression is committed more frequently by child characters than by adult characters.

Because the literature shows that children's television shows contain acts of social aggression and that social aggression is often gendered female, this study predicts:

H_2: In the Disney Channel's live-action television series, social aggression is committed more frequently by female characters than by male characters.

The literature shows that adults are portrayed as immature and infantile in children's television and films at large, but that child characters are recipients of most aggressive behavior performances in live action Disney shows. Thus, based on Brown's (2003) findings that indicate social aggression is most often directed by children toward other child characters, this study predicts:

H_3: In the Disney Channel's live-action television series, acts of social aggression committed by child characters are most frequently directed at other child characters.

In addition, this study seeks to further understand how often verbal and nonverbal social aggression is occurring in the Disney Channel live-action shows. While the literature does support the notion that social aggression is likely to occur, the likelihood of which kind, that is verbal or nonverbal, is less clear, as is how this may change over the course of a series. As such, the following research questions are posed:

RQ_1: Across both series, how have frequencies of socially aggressive behaviors changed over the course of the series?
RQ_2: How do verbal social aggressions and nonverbal social aggressions differ in frequency of occurrence, and by age and sex of aggression initiators?

Method

This study used content analysis to analyze displays of aggression on live-action Disney Channel television shows. To operationalize social aggression, it is important to consider other nonphysical forms of aggression. Three similar yet highly nuanced terms are used to refer nonphysical forms of aggression: indirect aggression, aggression for which the aggressor may not aggress directly at the intended victim; relational aggression, direct or indirect aggression among friendships and relationships; and social aggression, direct or indirect nonphysical aggression among social groups (Coyne & Archer, 2004). Social aggression is used less commonly (Coyne & Archer, 2004), but because it casts the widest net and creates the least limitations by not limiting aggression to "behind-the-back" (Coyne & Archer, 2004, p. 255) acts or occurring between friends and family members, this is the approach to nonphysical aggression the study will use. In this study, based on Martins and Wilson's (2012b) definition, social aggression is operationalized as both verbal and nonverbal acts of aggression performed to harm "a target's self-esteem or social standing" (p. 49). Some examples include name-calling, standing behind someone's back and mimicking behaviors, sticking out one's tongue, or using sarcasm. Coders were given clear and specific examples of what constitutes both verbal and nonverbal acts of social aggression based on Brown's (2003) coding scheme.

Sample

A purposive sample was selected to determine the series for the study. In order to be timely while recognizing the importance of studying content collected over the course of an entire series (Riffe, Lacy, & Fico, 1998), only the Disney Channel live-action original shows with at least three seasons that began and ended production between 2007 to 2017 were considered. This allowed for analysis of complete series. Based on this, we analyzed *Austin & Ally* and *Jessie*. Though others fit the criteria, these shows demonstrate international reach and recognition as culturally significant, self-contained series (Ng, 2011; Schneider, 2010; Wagmeister, 2015) that are currently being re-aired in syndication nationally and internationally via the Disney Channel, thus continuing to reach tween audiences and maintaining social and cultural significance for this demographic.

The study used a stratified random sample to collect 21 episodes from each series for analysis, seven from the first season (beginning), seven from the second and third season (middle), and seven from the fourth season (final). In total, 42 episodes were analyzed. Based on prior findings (Brown, 2003; Weaver, 2003) and our own trial test of the coding scheme, we anticipated a high volume of socially aggressive incidents per minute. Drawing on Baruh's (2009) sampling method, we divided each episode into three blocks (beginning, middle, and end) and sampled two minutes from each block, yielding a six-minute sample per episode that accounted for more than 25 percent of the average 22–23 minute episode runtime and provided 252 total minutes of analyzed programming.

For consistency, we coded minutes 4:00–6:00, 10:00–12:00, and 17:00–

19:00 of each episode to avoid coding the theme song and the end credits, as well to avoid any bias favoring the beginning or end of commercial breaks that might not be immersed in the narrative of the storyline. Based on Baruh (2003), we allowed minimal deviation from the coding start time to ensure that a full line of dialogue or a full action was observed.

Unit of Analysis

The unit of analysis for this study is an individual act of social aggression. For the purposes of this study, social aggression is divided into verbal social aggression and nonverbal social aggression. Though this study's hypotheses and research questions do not differentiate between verbal and nonverbal social aggression in its analysis and both were used to address social aggression, coders were asked to code these separately. Acts of aggression were also analyzed for the age of the act's initiator (child, adult) and sex of the act's initiator (male, female). Finally, the acts of aggression were analyzed for the age of the act's recipient (child, adult, mixed ages) and the sex of the act's recipient (male, female, mixed sexes).

Because the series under study have four seasons each, the series' seasons were coded as first season, middle season, or final season to consider individual series' changes over time in RQ_1. For RQ_2, dates of episodes by year were divided into three categories, 2011–2012, 2013–2014, and 2015–2016, to more effectively reflect the beginning, middle, and end of the demi-decade under study. The years at the extremes of the range (i.e., 2016) might have only a few episodes from a single series left to define the entire year, while the other years could have samples from both series to define them. Grouping the years helped to create more evenly sized categories and reduce any skewing that might have resulted from limited data in analyzing the years individually.

Training and Reliability

Two coders performed the coding for this project. Coders familiarized themselves with the coding scheme and its specific instructions, then trained together. First, they coded episodes from similar non-sample series (*Good Luck Charlie* and *The Suite Life on Deck*), then coded non-sample series' episodes individually, and finally coded non-sample episodes from *Austin & Ally*'s and *Jessie*'s seasons one and two. Training included more than 30 hours of practice. Final intercoder reliability, measured using Cohen's kappa (κ), ranged from .81–1.00 for each of five total coded categories (aggression type, initiator age, initiator sex, recipient age, and recipient sex). Overall reliability was .92 (very good).

It was determined during training that because of the likelihood of multiple instances of aggression occurring simultaneously, the necessity of coders to individually find and identify each unit for analysis within the sample, and the chance that timestamps may vary by a second between coders, it was essential to include a short written description of the behavior that occurred to establish intercoder reliability. Because the hypotheses and research questions in this study did not require that level of detail, the general category of the aggression was coded and the act itself was noted in a written description that could be referenced if discrepancies arose. Though time is one measure to determine if coders found the same incident, a short description helped to ensure reliability was accurately measured.

Results and Discussion

In total, 1,522 acts of social aggression were recorded in the 252-minute sample. This averaged to approximately six acts of social aggression per one minute of programming. Results indicate that acts of aggression occurred consistently across both programs, with *Austin & Ally* accounting for 766 acts and *Jessie* accounting for 756 acts. RQ_1 asks how frequencies of socially aggressive acts have changed over time. Results show a similar, but not identical, downward trend in frequencies of socially aggressive acts. Both series combined featured a decrease in the number of aggressive acts present over time during the progression of each season, with the percentage of these acts in total going from 36.9 percent (first season) to 32.7 percent (middle seasons), to 30.4 percent (last season). However, individual series results for total acts of combined verbal and nonverbal social aggression over time indicate that *Austin & Ally* and *Jessie* differed in the amount of aggression presented at different points within the series. The first season of *Austin & Ally* accounted for 36.9 percent of the program's coded aggressive acts, with the middle and last seasons featuring 40.5 percent and 22.6 percent respectively. Thus, this program featured an overall decrease in its inclusion of such acts from first season to last. Although content analysis can only account for the occurrence of events, and not necessarily *why* such events take place, it stands to reason that fewer acts of aggression are present as main characters in each series mature and develop over time. Alternatively, the first season of *Jessie* featured 36.9 percent of the program's total coded aggressive acts (identical to the amount featured in the first season of *Austin & Ally*), with the middle and last seasons featuring 24.5 percent and 38.2 percent respectively. In this case, the amount of nonverbal and verbal social aggressions in *Jessie* increased over time.

Combined content blocks for both programs (minutes 4–6, 10–12, and

17–19) featured nearly consistent amounts of socially aggressive acts, with less social aggression taking place in earlier portions of episodes. Minutes 4–6 featured 474 socially aggressive acts total, with minutes 10–12 and 17–19 featuring 525 and 523 respectively. This finding aligns with the progression of a narrative story arc, where exposition presents foundational content and introduces a storyline, perhaps explaining why fewer aggressive acts occurred at this point in programming.

RQ$_2$ asks how verbal and nonverbal social aggressions differed when considering frequency of occurrence. When looking at the total number of socially aggressive acts present in the context of each series, results indicate that of all 1,522 acts of aggression recorded, both *Austin & Ally* and *Jessie* included slightly more acts of verbal aggression (404 and 448 acts respectively) when compared with coded instances of nonverbal aggression for each program (362 and 308 acts respectively). Results show that verbally aggressive acts occurred at a higher rate than nonverbal (56 percent versus 44 percent) when looking at both series combined (see Figure 1).

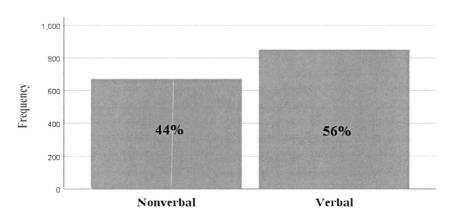

Figure 1. Frequency of aggression by type.

RQ$_2$ also asks how verbal and nonverbal social aggressions differed when considering the age and sex of the aggression initiator. When looking at age, between both shows, children committed a total of 1,051 acts of social aggression with 478 nonverbal acts (45.5 percent) and 573 verbal acts (54.5 percent). Adults committed a total of 471 acts of social aggression, of which 192 (40.8 percent) were nonverbal and 279 (59.2 percent) were verbal. Within age group, types of aggressive acts were similarly distributed. But it is essential to note that children performed 71.3 percent of all nonverbal social aggressions compared to 28.7 percent by adults, and children performed 67.3 percent of all verbal social aggression compared to 32.7 percent by adults. This follows as there are more child characters in the show than adults.

Next, we consider sex of the aggression initiator. Between both shows, male characters committed 227 acts of nonverbal social aggression (42 percent) and 314 acts of verbal social aggression (58 percent). Female characters committed 443 acts of nonverbal social aggression (45.2 percent) and 538 acts of verbal social aggression (54.8 percent). While these frequencies may seem nearly equivalent, it is important to note that of 670 total nonverbal aggressions, male characters accounted for 33.9 percent of acts while female characters accounted for 66.1 percent. Additionally, of 852 verbal acts of social aggression, male characters performed 36.9 percent and female characters performed 63.1 percent.

Thus, to answer RQ_2, we found that acts of nonverbal and verbal social aggression may look similarly distributed *within* age (child, adult) and sex (male, female) categories, yet clear differences appeared when comparing *between* age and sex categories. That is, children performed nearly three times as many nonverbal acts as adults and almost twice as many verbal acts as adults. Female characters performed nearly twice as much nonverbal social aggression and twice as much verbal social aggression when compared to male characters.

Children initiated aggressive acts more than twice as much (69.1 percent) as adults (30.9 percent), meaning that H_1 was supported (see Figure 2). This finding is not entirely surprising given that there are more child characters in each show when compared to adults, but the finding is important because it indicates that child characters are not the only characters engaging in social aggressions. That being said, it is important to note that the character makeup in *Austin & Ally* has nearly no adult main characters, whereas

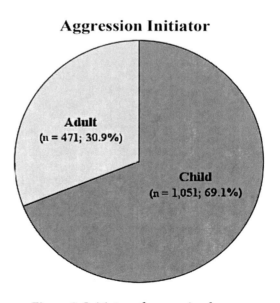

Aggression Initiator

Adult
(n = 471; 30.9%)

Child
(n = 1,051; 69.1%)

Figure 2. Initiator of aggression by age.

Jessie includes the presence of at least three regularly featured adult main characters. This information is important in considering the context of the following findings. In *Austin & Ally*, children initiated aggressive acts 88.5 percent of the time, whereas children in *Jessie* initiated such aggression 49.3 percent of the time. Viewed alternatively, this means that adults were the initiators of aggression in *Austin & Ally* 11.5 percent of the time, with adults in *Jessie* initiating such acts 50.7 percent of the time.

H_2 was also supported, indicated by the finding that female characters initiated aggressive acts nearly twice as often (64.5 percent) as male characters (35.5 percent) (see Figure 3). This finding raises important points regarding the cultivation of narratives related to female characters. In looking at individual programs, findings indicate that the rate at which female characters initiated aggressive acts was consistent across both *Austin & Ally* (65.8 percent) and *Jessie* (63.1 percent). Thus, male characters in *Austin & Ally* initiated such acts 34.2 percent of the time, with those in *Jessie* doing so 36.9 percent of the time.

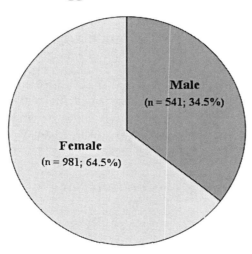

Aggression Initiator

Male
(n = 541; 34.5%)

Female
(n = 981; 64.5%)

Figure 3. Initiator of aggression by sex.

Overall, recipients of socially aggressive acts when combined across both programs were primarily male (50.9 percent), although female recipients had a similar number of occurrences at 41.9 percent (with 7.2 percent of recipients in mixed sex groups) (see Figure 4). In accounting for individual shows, *Austin & Ally* featured a higher percentage of male characters receiving aggression (59.0 percent) when compared with *Jessie* (42.6 percent). Alternatively, female characters in *Austin & Ally* were the recipients of aggression 35.3 percent of the time, whereas female characters in *Jessie* were 48.6 percent of the time. *Austin & Ally* featured a lower amount of aggression directed toward mixed sex groups (5.7 percent), with *Jessie* accounting for 8.9 percent of this occurrence.

Recipients of socially aggressive acts were most often children (67.1 percent), with adults receiving the aggression 31.2 percent of the time and mixed age groups being on the receiving end 1.7 percent of the time. Thus, H_3 was

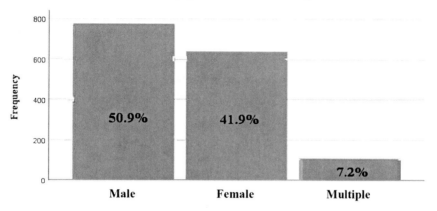

Figure 4. Frequency of receiving aggression by sex.

also supported. A breakdown based on individual series revealed that *Austin & Ally* featured a much higher frequency of children being on the receiving end of aggression (82.8 percent) when compared with adults (16.4 percent) and mixed age groups (0.8 percent). Alternatively, *Jessie* featured a nearly equal occurrence of children (51.2 percent) and adults (46.2 percent) being receptors of nonverbal and verbal social aggressions. Mixed age groups received social aggression 2.6 percent of the time. As discussed above, the variation in this category of findings based on main character demographic makeup is an important consideration.

To summarize, in attempting to holistically analyze what these results mean in the context of aggression types, overall, verbal acts of social aggression occurred at a slightly higher rate (56.0 percent) than nonverbal (44.0 percent), with female characters initiating a greater number of aggressive acts most often directed at male characters. Previous research has shown that forms of socially aggressive behavior are more common among female characters than male characters, helping to validate our results (Archer & Coyne, 2005).

Conclusion

The results of this study shed light on the occurrence of social aggression in the Disney Channel live-action television shows. A sample from *Austin & Ally* and *Jessie* indicated that an average of approximately six acts of social aggression occur per minute of programming. Each series had effectively an equivalent number of aggressive acts in the sample, but the series differed in how those acts were distributed over the course of each series. Data indicate that both series had more acts of verbal social aggression than nonverbal social aggression; child characters performed two times more acts of social aggression than adult characters; female characters performed two times more acts of social aggression than male characters; and male characters were primarily the recipients of social aggressions.

Previous research has concluded that when assessing media influence on children, an investigation of the type of content being shown is often more important than an analysis of the amount of content being consumed (Wilson, 2008). As such, studies have documented the degree to which children's media content acts as a source of learning for children regarding their emotions and interpersonal skills they wish to acquire, meaning that children have the unique ability to transfer to real life the lessons they are learning from television programs (Calvert & Kotler, 2003; Weiss & Wilson, 1996). Previous research related to this topic has found that 92 percent of television programs popular with teens contained acts of relational and social aggression (Coyne & Archer, 2004), and another found that teens who viewed such content were more likely to exhibit that same behavior (Coyne, Archer, & Eslea, 2004). The present study is the first of our knowledge to examine specific live-action shows of the Disney Channel, helping to expand the available literature. An investigation of the Disney Channel programming merited an important opportunity for analysis, as it is the only cable network with programming aimed at young people, rather than featuring content aimed at children during the day and families/adults at night like many other networks (Beail, Lupo, & Beail, 2018).

Tied closely with both cultivation theory and social learning theory, this study aimed to provide a foundation of the content that tween audience members are exposed to when watching *Austin & Ally* and *Jessie*. In alignment with these theories, our findings provide important points for consideration among parents and policymakers alike, as tween audiences viewing this content may come to perceive verbal and nonverbal socially aggressive acts as consistent with the ways in which they should act in the real world (Gerbner, Gross, Morgan, & Signorielli, 1994). Anecdotal evidence provided while watching the analyzed the Disney Channel programs showed that in nearly all instances, recorded acts of both verbal and nonverbal social aggressions occurred without consequences (e.g. a child rolled their eyes at an adult but was not reprimanded for doing such). Interestingly, previous research has shown that, in accordance with social learning theory, children are more likely to imitate behaviors that lack consequences as a lack of punishment simultaneously serves as a reward, showing how the present study has important applications for social functioning and behavior (Bandura, 1965; Bandura, Ross, & Ross, 1963).

Limitations

While each act of aggression had to be directed at a human to be counted, we did not consider whether the act was committed as an aggressor or defender. That is, two characters may have called each other names, but the first character attacked, and the second character responded. Our coding did not account for that, just that they occurred. For the purpose of this study, we wanted to code only what audiences see, but this additional context may be more helpful in understanding what the shows mean to young viewers.

Additionally, it is important to note that content analysis requires specific and structured code books for intercoder agreement. Unfortunately, this does not allow for deviation and can result in some acts left unaccounted. Some aggressive acts were performed through behaviors that are usually not aggressive. That is, actions such as smiling or embracing cannot be included in a code book as acts of aggression because they generally are not considered such, but in sample episodes, these actions represented social aggressions and inspired aggressive responses. This inability to deviate for unanticipated or outlier acts may have left a small number of aggressions without account in the study.

Finally, because the study was a pilot examining a small sample of the Disney Channel's live-action original series, we cannot presume that these results are reflective of all shows in the Disney Channel universe. But the results do provide enough evidence to indicate that wider investigation into social aggression on Disney Channel live-action shows is warranted.

Directions for Future Research

Coders anecdotally reported that many of the coded instances of social aggression, both verbal and nonverbal, were punctuated with a laugh track. Because laugh tracks act to signal to an audience what is humorous or replicate an audience's response to humor, we see space for further studies to explore the relationship between laugh tracks and aggression on the Disney Channel's live-action shows, laughter's role in framing aggression on children's sitcoms, and the effects of laughter and laugh tracks on child audiences in understanding social aggression.

This study was meant to provide foundational findings to spur future research questions. As such, our method of content analysis did not account for the purpose of an aggression. That is, this study did not determine if acts were committed as offense to another or as defense of oneself. Because this content analysis was restricted to recording all behaviors that occurred on screen and could not account for the context of the interactions, future research should incorporate qualitative analyses to account for how and why aggressions occur in the narrative. When coupled with this study, such research will provide a more comprehensive analysis of the aggressive acts occurring on the Disney Channel's series.

Finally, future studies can also explore how child viewers assess and interpret aggression in the Disney Channel's shows. Our code book was based on adults' understanding of aggression. Asking children to identify behaviors they see as rude, disrespectful, or unkind could shed light on how children make meaning of social interactions using the Disney Channel's shows.

Authors' note: We thank Joel Guldin for his assistance with this study.

Appendix A: Instructions and Coding Sheet for Coders

Content Analysis Coding Sheet Instructions: Live-Action Disney Channel Television Shows (based on and modified from Brown, 2003)

Unit of Analysis: Act of aggression
Series Name:
   Austin & Ally = 1
   Jessie = 2
Show Date: Year episode was first broadcast
   2011–2012 = 1
   2013–2014 = 2
   2015–2016 = 3
Season: The season the episode being analyzed is from
   First season = 1
   Season 1
   Middle season = 2
   Season 2 or 3
   Final season = 3
   Season 4
Episode Block: The portion of the episode in which the aggression occurs
   If you must start a few seconds before the time range in order to avoid interrupting dialogue or action in progress, use the closest code. (Ex: 09:58 should be coded as 2)
   Minutes 04:00–06:00 = 1
   Minutes 10:00–12:00 = 2
   Minutes 17:00–19:00 = 3

Time Stamp:
Indicate the exact time the incidents begin their occurrence based on the timestamp in the video. Use the format ##:## for minutes:seconds. (ex: 04:14)

General Aggression Type:
Social, Nonverbal Aggression = 1
Social, Verbal Aggression = 2

Specific Aggression Type:
Code for aggressive behaviors displayed by any character. Each aggressive behavior should be coded separately, even if the same character repeats the same behavior more than once in the same episode. It may be possible that more than one code applies for one aggressive event; in this case, please use all applicable codes for the aggressive event. (Ex: Jane rolls eyes and says, "Fred, you stupid cow." This should be coded as aggression-nonverbal and aggression-verbal since both forms of aggression occurred simultaneously. Use a separate line for each aggression with appropriate time stamp.)

If a character states that they did something aggressive (ex: "I pushed her down the stairs,") but it is not shown, do not code.

Only code acts of aggression that occur between humans. Do not code aggression directed at animals, robots, inanimate objects, etc. You should be able to clearly see that both characters involved in the act of aggression are humans. If you are not sure if both characters are human, do not code the aggression.

Do not include any displays of aggression that appear to occur during theme songs.

Tip: Do *not* try to determine if a certain action is or is not aggressive based on the situation surrounding the occurrence. If any of the below actions occur within the episode, code them.

Social, Nonverbal Aggression = 1

- Crossing arms in annoyance
- Sighing/scoffing in annoyance
- Glaring at someone
- Rolling eyes at someone/about someone/behind someone's back
- Mouthing words behind someone's back in attempt to mock, make fun, or show annoyance
- Ignoring
- Sticking tongue out at or behind someone's back
- Making faces at someone or behind someone's back
- Moving toward someone/motioning at them as if one will hit/kick/slap without actually hitting/kicking/slapping

Social, Verbal Aggression = 2

- Character attack: saying unfavorable things about another's character, morality, ethics
- Competence attack: criticizing another's capabilities/way of thinking
- Background attack: saying unfavorable things about another's family, race, age, geographical place of residence/origin
- Physical appearance attack: expressing dissatisfaction with or making fun of the way one physically looks, dresses, appears
- Rejection: disagreeing with another in a rude or disrespectful way
- Dislike: verbal expression of dislike or hate for or toward another
- Sarcasm: saying something ironically with the intent of mocking
- Threat: intimidation of another, threat to harm
- Demand: commanding another to do or not do something
- Mocking: imitating another by speaking in mean-spirited way
- Lying: not being truthful
- Name calling
- Using a "snotty" tone
- Yelling at someone
- Laughing at someone in ridicule
- Interruption

Initiator Age: The age of the character committing the act of aggression
    Child = 1
    Adult = 2
Initiator Sex: The sex of the character committing the act of aggression
    Male = 1
    Female = 2
Recipient Age: The age of the character the aggression was directed at
    Child(ren) = 1
    Adult(s) = 2
    More than one recipient representing more than one age = 3
Recipient Sex: The sex of the character the aggression was directed at
    Male(s) = 1
    Female(s) = 2
    More than one recipient representing more than one sex = 3

REFERENCES

Archer, J., & Coyne, S. (2005). An integrated review of indirect, relational, and social aggression. *Personality and Social Psychology Review, 9*(3), 212–230.
Bandura, A. (1965). Influence of model's reinforcement contingencies on the acquisition of imitative responses. *Journal of Personality and Social Psychology, 36*, 589–595.
Bandura, A., Ross, S., & Ross, D. (1963). Vicarious reinforcement and imitative learning. *Journal of Abnormal and Social Psychology, 67*(6), 601–607.

Baruh, L. (2009). Publicized intimacies on reality television: An analysis of voyeuristic content and its contribution to the appeal of reality programming. *Journal of Broadcasting & Electronic Media, 53*(2), 190–210.

Beail, L., Lupo, L, & Beail, C. (2018). "Better in stereo": Doubled and divided representations of postfeminist girlhood on the Disney Channel. *Visual Inquiry: Learning & Teaching Art, 7*(2), 125–140. doi: 10.1386/vi.7.2.125_1.

Brown, A.B. (2003). Promoting disrespect through children's television (Master's thesis). Retrieved from EngagedScholarship @ Cleveland State University ETD Archive. (Paper 688).

Callister, M.A., Robinson, T., & Clark, B.R. (2007). Media portrayals of the family in children's television programming during the 2005–2006 season in the US. *Journal of Children and Media, 1*(2), 142–161. doi:10.1080/17482790701339142.

Calvert, S., & Kotler, J. (2003). Lessons from children's television: The impact of the children's television act on children's learning. *Journal of Applied Developmental Psychology, 24,* 275–335.

Comstock, J., & Strzyzewski, K. (1990). Interpersonal interaction on television: Family conflict and jealousy on primetime. *Journal of Broadcasting & Electronic Media, 34*(3), 263–282.

Coyne, S.M., & Archer, J. (2004). Indirect aggression in the media: A content analysis of British television programs. *Aggressive Behavior, 30,* 254–271.

Coyne, S.M., & Archer, J. (2005). The relationship between indirect and physical aggression on television and in real life. *Social Development, 14*(2), 323–338.

Coyne, S.M., Archer, J., & Eslea. (2004). Cruel intentions on television and in real life: Can viewing indirect aggression increase viewers' subsequent indirect aggression? *Journal of Experimental Child Psychology, 88*(3), 234–253.

Coyne, S.M., & Whitehead, E. (2008). Indirect aggression in animated Disney films. *Journal of Communication, 58,* 382–395. doi:10.1111/j.1460–2466.2008.00390.x.

DiGiovanni, D. (2014, June 22). Five ways the Disney Channel is undoing your good parenting. *The Good Men Project.* [Web log post]. Retrieved from https://goodmenproject.com.

From there to here: The disrespect of Disney. (2011, January 11). Chambanamoms [Web log post]. Retrieved from http://www.chambanamoms.com/.

Galen, B.R., & Underwood, M.K. (1997). A developmental investigation of social aggression among children. *Developmental Psychology, 33*(4), 589–600.

Gerbner, G. (1970). Cultural indicators: The case of violence in television drama. *The Annals of the American Academy of Political and Social Science, 338,* 69–81.

Gerbner, G. (2012). The stories we tell and the stories we sell. *The Journal of International Communication, 18*(2), 237–244. doi: 10.1080/13216597.2012.709928.

Gerbner, G., Gross, L., Morgan, M., & Signorielli, N. (1994). Growing up with television: The cultivation perspective. In J. Bryant & D. Zillmann (Eds.), *LEA's communication series. Media effects: Advances in theory and research* (pp. 17–41). Hillsdale, NJ: Lawrence Erlbaum.

Graser, M. (2013, March 15). How TV has replaced animated films as Disney's biggest brand ambassador. *Variety.* Retrieved from http://www.variety.com/2013/biz/features/how-tv-has-replaced-animated-films-as-disneys-biggest-brand-ambassador-1200324380/.

Grow and tell: As children age from toddlers to teens, their media palate changes. (2015, March 3). *Nielsen.* Retrieved from http://www.nielsen.com/.

Hentges, B., & Case, K. (2013). Gender representations on Disney Channel, Cartoon Network, and Nickelodeon broadcasts in the United states. *Journal of Children and Media, 7*(3), 319–333. doi: 10.1080/17482798.2012.729150.

Huesmann, L.R. (1988). An information procession model of the development of aggression. *Aggressive Behavior, 14,* 13–24.

Kampf, Z., & Hamo, M. (2015). Children talking television: The salience and functions of media content in child peer interactions. *Discourse & Communication, 9*(4), 465–485. doi: 10.1177/1750481315576840.

Kaye, B., & Sapolsky, B.S. (2004). Watch your mouth! An analysis of profanity uttered by children on prime-time television. *Mass Communication & Society, 7*(4), 429–452.

Kissell, R. (2015, December 15). Ratings: Disney Channel edges Nickelodeon in 2015 for first-ever no. 1 total-day finish. *Variety*. Retrieved from http://variety.com/.

Luther, C.A., & Legg, J.R., Jr., (2010) Gender differences in depictions of social and physical aggression in children's television cartoons in the US. *Journal of Children and Media, 4*(2), 191–205. doi: 10.1080/17482791003629651.

megpoulinindeed. (2014, March 28). Disney is ruining my kid. *IndeedIAm* [Web log post]. Retrieved from https://megpoulinindeed.com/.

Martins, N., & Wilson, B.J. (2012a). Mean on the screen: Social aggression in programs popular with children. *Journal of Communication, 62*(6), 991–1009. doi:10.1111/j.1460-2466.2011.01599.x.

Martins, N., & Wilson, B.J. (2012b). Social aggression on television and its and relationship to children's aggression in the classroom. *Human Communication Research, 38*, 48–71. doi:10.1111/j.1468-2958.2011.01417.x.

Morgan, M., Shanahan, J., & Signorielli, N. (2008). Growing up with television: Cultivation processes. In J. Bryant & M.B. Oliver (Eds.), *Media effects: Advances in theory and research* (3rd ed.). (pp. 34–49). New York: Routledge.

Ng, P. (2011, October 11). Disney Channel's "Jessie" premiere posts record ratings. *The Hollywood Reporter*. Retrieved from https://www.hollywoodreporter.com/live-feed/disney-channels-jessie-premiere-posts-242864.

Riffe, D., Lacy, S., & Fico, F.G. (1998). Analyzing media messages: Using quantitative content analysis in research. Mahwah, NJ: Lawrence Erlbaum Associates.

Riley, N.S. (2016, June 14). How Disney teaches contempt for dads. *New York Post*. Retrieved from http://nypost.com/2016/06/14/how-disney-teaches-contempt-for-dads/.

Robinson, T., & Anderson, C. (2006). Older characters in children's animated television programs: A content analysis of their portrayal. *Journal of Broadcasting & Electronic Media, 50*(2), 287–304.

Robinson, T., Callister, M., Magoffin, D., & Moore, J. (2007). The portrayal of older characters in Disney animated films. *Journal of Aging Studies, 21*, 201–213.

Schneider, M. (2010, December 8). Teens go showbiz for Disney Channel. *Variety*. Retrieved from https://variety.com/2010/tv/news/teens-go-showbiz-for-disney-channel-111802 8677/.

Schneider, M. (2017, December 28). Most-watched television networks: Ranking 2017's winners and losers. *IndieWire*. Retrieved from http://www.indiewire.com/2017/12/highest-network-ratings-2017-most-watched-hbo-cbs-espn-fx-msnbc-fox-news-1201911363/.

Schrager, N. (2013, June 20). Disney TV is poisoning your daughters. *LA Weekly*. Retrieved from http://www.laweekly.com/.

Skill, T., & Wallace, S. (1990) Family interactions on primetime television: A descriptive analysis of assertive power interactions. *Journal of Broadcasting & Electronic Media, 34*(2), 243–262.

Villani, S. (2001). Impact of media on children and adolescents: A 10-year review of the research. *Journal of the American Academy of Child and Adolescent Psychiatry, 40*(4), 392–401.

Wagmeister, E. (2015, February 25). Disney Channel's "Jessie" wrapping after season 4—Spin-off ordered to series. *Variety*. Retrieved from http://variety.com/2015/tv/news/jessie-spinoff-disney-channel-peyton-list-skai-jackson-karan-brar-1201441742/.

Weaver, C.E. (2012). *Studying school: Depictions of education on the Disney Channel.* (Master's thesis). Retrieved from University of North Carolina Wilmington ETD Archive.

Weiss, A., & Wilson, B. (1996). Emotional portrayals in family television series that are popular among children. *Journal of Broadcasting & Electronic Media, 40*, 1–29.

Wilson, B.J. (2008). Media and children's aggression, fear and altruism. *The Future of Children, 18*(1), 87–118.

"There's no way I can make it without you?"

Austin & Ally's *Vision of Gender/Race Equality*

ALLISON SCHOTTENSTEIN

Busty bodacious bikini-wearing girls on the beach describes, in a nutshell, the plot line of almost every single beach party film. By the early 1960s, the film industry brought attention to young Americans that female sexuality was real and penetrable. Beach party movies of the 1960s dripped with sexual overtones and promoted teenage sexual rebellion. The depiction of white teens surfing the waves in California emphasized the freedom of the sandy oasis. The downside of the beach party genre was that it did not promote female empowerment, diversity, or tolerance. Often in the beach genre, liberation of sexuality came with a price, as it encouraged objectification, whiteness, and static characters. The beach party genre began with the first *Gidget* film, in 1959, and took off when American International Films began to realize that the beach party films were great money-makers. The beach party genre would reach its height between 1963 and 1968 (McParland, 1992). These films left an impression on popular culture. Although one will see the image of the beach in film and television after the 1960s, interest in the beach party genre dwindled.

In the 2000s, the Disney Channel began to show an interest in the beach genre; however, it was through a clean-cut pluralistic lens. In the hit television series, *Austin & Ally,* Disney recreated the beach party genre by deemphasizing the beach and sexuality at its center and instead focusing on the lives and the aspirations of the teens who lived adjacent to the beach. Through this approach, Disney teaches their tween to teen audience the value of friendship, diversity, and respect between boys and girls. Although Disney created two *Teen Beach* films—which featured *Austin & Ally* star, Ross Lynch—it is *Austin & Ally* that propels us to rethink the entire beach genre and encourages a new generation to not think of the beach as the epicenter of sexuality, but instead as a location where teens can make lasting relationships and express their musical abilities. Disney does not entirely ignore stereotypes of gender or race; however, the show tries to create a vision where a team of multiple identities can exist on equal terms, and the beach helps to promote this idealistic image. One can see this transformation if one examines the Beach Party films of the 1960s in relation to *Austin & Ally*, with an in-depth examination of *Austin & Ally*, Trish, and Dez. *Austin & Ally* reinvent the romantic duo of the beach party narrative in that *Austin & Ally* do not conform to a typical heteronormative narrative in that their relationship is not based on fulfilling traditional gender roles—boyfriend and girlfriend. A new character in the beach genre is Trish, who is Latina and proud—and not exoticized for her ethnicity—but instead acts as a feminist support for Ally as well as presents herself as a role model for other Latinas. Dez is an example of a boy who does not exemplify uber masculinity, like the beach heroes, but rather who is gender bending, yet also heterosexual. Through this analysis, one will see that teens who live in this beach city are not vapid, sex-consumed individuals, but instead real teenagers seeking to carve out an existence that has more durability than sand castles.

Post–World War II marked the emergence of teenage culture (Tropiano, 2006, p. 18). Teens became the prime consumer. In the 1950s, there was an explosion of teen-related media (Tropiano, 2006, p. 20). The teen identity emerged. Television shows, music, dance, and even the automobile industry became teen-centric (Tropiano, 2006). In addition to the growing teen culture, Dr. Alfred Kinsey's reports *Sexual Behavior in the Human Male* (1948), and *Sexual Behavior in the Human Female* (1953) revolutionized the West's understanding of male and female sexuality (Tropiano, 2006). Kinsey brought sexuality to the forefront. More studies on sexuality further uncovered that both men and women were not "saving themselves" for marriage. In fact, in the 1960s, sociologist Ira L. Reis discovered that "over 50 percent of women were not virgins on their wedding night and the majority who were had engaged in 'deep kissing' or were the recipient of heavy petting" (Tropiano, 2006, p. 67). On top of consumerism and this sexual awakening, teens also became interested in flexing their bodies and surfing the waves, especially in sunny California (Tropiano, 2006).

Teen films were more interested in the lives and the adventures of teens than in family dynamics (Doherty, 2002, p. 159). Parents were irrelevant. Alan Betrock calls it the "Peter Pan Syndrome"; in other words, these teen films'—like beach films—sole purpose was for teens not to grow up and become boring adults, but to continue to dream and stay perpetual teens (Qtd. in Shary, 2005). When Columbia Pictures Cinescope introduced the world to a blond, petite, surfer wannabe named Gidget, American teens flocked to the theater to escape and enjoy love between two beachgoers, the waves, and the endless fun on the beach. In 1959, *Gidget* drew teens to the beach through the silver screen. The popularity of *Gidget* not only caused the creation of more *Gidget* films, but it also sparked a beach craze (Lisanti, 2005). American International Pictures, not long after *Gidget,* created a series of B-films starring actors Frankie Avalon and Annette Funicello. These plots seemed to follow a romance between a teenage boy and a girl, a mishap, and adults who are bumbling idiots that get in the way (Lisanti, 2005). All these films emphasized the importance of music. On the beach, there was usually a rad band or random singing among lovebirds. Some of the popular beach films included *Beach Party, Muscle Beach Party, Bikini Beach, Beach Blanket Bingo,* and *How to Stuff a Wild Bikini* (Lisanti, 2005). AIP would also include films that followed this same beach party plot, but the actual beach space played a lesser role. The Beach Party films would also look outside the beach area, such as in *Pajama Party, Ski Party,* and *The Ghost in the Invisible Bikini* (Lisanti, 2005).

In the iconic film *Gidget,* Frances Lawrence, a pre-pubescent young blond girl, falls in love with the beach and surfing. Gidget gets her first taste of the beach when her female friends take her on her first official "manhunt" (Wendkos, *Gidget*). Frances (Gidget) is not interested in searching for men or becoming a feminist. Gidget is perplexed as to why her friends want to spend their beach time finding a "hunk of male" (Wendkos, *Gidget*). She cringes when her friends inform her there are many available men on the beach worth picking from—"almost enough for second helpings" (Wendkos, *Gidget*). The girls parade around in their bikinis to flaunt their breasts. They strategize as to how to attract a boy. The girls' actions become known as "manhunting." The men catcall the women. The beach men taunt Gidget because she does not look like a real woman—budding breasts. The guys call her the "Jailbait caper" (Wendkos, *Gidget*) because they cannot mess around with the young Gidget.

Gidget ventures off from her friends. She discovers surfing after she encounters a gaggle of surfers. Although Gidget rides the waves and learns the sport, like the guys, she also becomes a damsel in distress instead of a strong, empowered woman. When Moondoggie saves Gidget from drowning, she develops feelings for him. He becomes the object of her affection. At this point, she morphs into one of the beach babes in search of a man. She becomes consumed with Moondoggie. The only difference between Gidget and her female peers is that she can surf. Moondoggie also falls for Gidget. The audience knows Moondoggie's intentions because he sings to Gidget— as she lays unconscious—about marrying her. This song does not talk about

Gidget as a person; they frame her in terms of her size and her looks, but nothing of any substance (Wendkos, *Gidget*). Although the viewer knows that Gidget and Moondoggie like each other, Gidget's insecurity causes her to create a half-witted plot to make Moondoggie jealous.

She flirts with the head of the surfers, Kahuna, who is much older and a war veteran, to make Moondoggie jealous. He willingly goes along with Gidget's ruse. He takes her back to his apartment where he offers her beer. He says to her, "How about one of our little private parties" (Wendkos, *Gidget*). Gidget follows him willingly for the sake of proving she is a desirable woman—even though this scenario is creepy. He asks her, "Are you sure that is what you want?" (Wendkos, *Gidget*). When she agrees, he places himself on her and begins touching her. His lust for Gidget almost overtakes him, and he expresses a certain attachment for her—"Before I forget it is just a game" (Wendkos, *Gidget*). He almost falls for her and comes close to taking advantage of her sexually. He entertains the idea of rape. However, he stops himself. Not long after he makes this decision, Kahuna engages in a fighting match with Moondoggie. The police find Gidget, and she goes home. Her mother does not advise her on sexual predators, but instead comforts the torn Gidget who is worried at age fifteen that she will "die an old maiden" (Wendkos, *Gidget*). Gidget is concerned she will never take the "next step" and will remain "pure as the driven snow" (Wendkos, *Gidget*). Her mother advises her "to be a real woman is to bring out the best in a man." In other words, a woman's identity is dependent upon a man. In the end, she and Moondoggie realize they should be with each other despite Gidget's ruse. The movie ends with them embraced in each other's arms, in love, standing on the beach.

The controversial film *Where the Boys Are* shows a less glamorous image of the beach; however, the theme of oversexed teens and objectification of women on the beach is still apparent. Four college-aged Midwestern women (Merritt Andrews, Melanie Tolman, Tuggle Carpenter, and Angie) head to Fort Lauderdale in hopes of meeting a man and having fun. The girls feel pressured to make out. In *Where the Boys Are,* spring break is like a mating call for all eligible boys and girls, who overtake the beach in the hunt for the perfect date. Indeed, the girls want to know *where the boys are.* One of the characters, Tuggles, believes her destiny is to be a mother: "Girls like me were not meant to be educated," but to have children (Levin, *Where the Boys Are*). In this film, men treat women as pleasure objects. The most profound example is the scene when Yale student, Dill, rapes Melanie. She tells him "no," but he does not stop (Levin, *Where the Boys Are*). Melanie is shell-shocked. Her friends report the rape to the police. Melanie goes to the hospital, where she is under the care of a male doctor. The doctor says to her friends, "she'll get by," and smokes a cigarette (Levin, *Where the Boys Are*). The viewer does not know what will happen to Melanie except that she will go home. The film does not end on a grim note or to warn girls of the dangers of this beach culture, but instead, viewers must forget what happened to Melanie and refocus their attention on Meritt and Ryder. In the last scene, like Gidget and Moondoggie, they promise to stay committed to each other despite that each has to go back to school in their own state. The romance of spring break is over.

The more popular beach party films were more light and fluffy than both *Gidget* and *Where the Boys Are*. These films lack a dynamic female lead. *Beach Party* (1963) emphasized the need to surf and to ogle. Everyone is on their surfboards. All the college students live in a house divided between boys and girls. Guys are so obsessed with the female body that when they see a woman in a bikini, they lose their balance. Dolores's main preoccupation is on her boyfriend Frankie. Her ultimate goal is to convince Frankie to propose to her. Her dream is for Frankie to see her as a wife (Asher, *Beach Party*). Her matrimony aspiration causes Frankie to flee. He decides to find someone else who rather have fun than to settle down. There are a lot of dance scenes, singing, and making out to fill space in the film. The one adult who could have been the voice of reason, Professor Sutwell, is as nonsensical as the teens he desires to study. His study of the subculture of teens is meant to mimic outdated anthropological studies of "primitive" tribes (Stenger, 2008, p. 37). At the same time, there is a Biker group called the Rats who wants to spoil the fun. The chauvinistic Eric von Zipper, head of the Rats, tries to force Dolores into a lip lock. The professor defends her and accuses him of "molesting" Annette (Asher, *Beach Party*). He calls von Zipper a "stormtrooper"—a Nazi—but the reference becomes lost (Asher, *Beach Party*). There are nonsensical mishaps and no dynamic character development. In the end, Frankie and Dolores get back together. The films that followed did not differentiate much in the plot, with only a few subtleties. *Muscle Beach Party* promotes the glorification of both male and female bodies. The premise of the film centers on male bodybuilders. In several scenes, we see the male bodybuilders flex their muscles as they are auctioned off. A young Italian countess falls for one of the bodybuilders and later Frankie. When the plots became too familiar, the AIP beach movies took liberties and featured mythical creatures such as mermaids, ghosts, and ghouls.

One of the problematic features in all these films is the sea of whiteness and the lack of diversity. During the 1960s, these hierarchies and privileges were clearly defined since in America, equality was only granted to the white and privileged. Although California's beaches desegregated after the 1960s (Burdsey, 2016), the beach films perpetuated a segregated beach culture that did not welcome African Americans. As Josh Stenger concluded, these films enabled whites to escape to idyllic white-only beaches where middle-class whites could ignore the chaos of the Civil Rights Movement or the pleas of minorities (Stenger, 2008). According to Grace Palladino, the lack of representation of African Americans was ironic considering that teens rocked to Black music, which inspired rock and roll. Yet, African American teens were absent from the screen (Palladino, 1996). Ultimately, these films did not cater to all teens.

In the beach party films, African American women were not seen in bikinis or seen as the object of anyone's affection. There were no male African American beach leads. There are African Americans in the background, but barely noticeable, except for Stevie Wonder in *Muscle Beach,* who sings "Happy Street" (Stenger, 2008, p. 42)—a song that only emphasizes dancing ("stomp your feet" "clap your hands") (Asher, Muscle Beach Party). Stenger defines the beach as the place of "white flight" (Stenger, 2008, p. 28) that "resonated with white suburban audiences as an historically specific, utopian geography of whiteness" (Stenger, 2008, p. 28). In the film *Pajama Party,* one of the characters is a white man (Buster Keaton) who plays a Native American man, Chief Rotten Eagle. Keaton's stereotypical portrayal as a "comic witch doctor" (Bukowczyk, 2018, p. 98) epitomized the practice of "Red Face" (Antelyes, 2009). After all, he wears stereotypical costume-like Native American apparel. Even the way he sits appears like a stereotypical Native American figurine in a cigar shop. To compound this, he carries around a bow and arrow. He has an affair with a Swedish woman named Helga. He smothers his face in her bosom. Their relationship emphasizes exoticism. Not only is he consumed with sex, but he is also seen scheming to gain money. The beach becomes a place of exclusivity and perpetuates the belief that on the beach, whiteness and sex are more important than personhood.

Austin & Ally does not follow the same plot line as the beach party films of the 1960s, but instead provides the viewer with insight into the teens who live near the beach all year round. The popular tween series came at the time of President Barack Obama's "Yes, We Can" era, which according to Jennifer Gilman's *Television Brandcasting: The Return of the Content—Promotion Hybrid*, inspired new Disney programming (Gilman, 2015, p. 160). Disney tried to emphasize the concept that teens can make a change and focus on their careers. In the case of *Austin & Ally,* Disney promoted the idea that Austin's "success depends on the continuing support of Ally, Trish, and Dez on their respective skills as songwriter, publicist, and filmmaker" (Gilman, 2015, p. 162). In *Austin & Ally,* the concept of sexuality is traded in for tolerance and acceptance.

Set in Miami Beach, *Austin & Ally* explores the personal awakening of a middle-class teen named Ally, who with her best friend Trish and her two male counterparts, Austin and Dez, revolutionize the entertainment industry. In the opening scene, we see a beach. The viewer who is aware of beach party films may presume that *Austin & Ally* would become a reboot of the 1960s beach party films; however, the beach is secondary to the music store located adjacent to the main beach area. In the pilot episode, *Rockers and Writers*, the camera does not focus on women in tight bikinis with their breast hanging out, but instead, the first scene of dialogue centers on a conversation between a petite teenage girl, modestly dressed, working at her father's music store, talking wither her friend Trish, an outspoken Latina teen. Trish reveals to Ally her newest job, working at the cupcake shop, "Cupcake City." Trish does not want to settle for just any job. In fact, in the first episode, she has three different jobs. Ally does not appear to be a woman in the same way as the women of the beach or even Gidget—though she fits the size. When she first encounters Austin, he wants to bum musical instruments off her father's store; however, Ally stands her ground and tries to kick him out of the store, along with his friend Dez. Before the viewer sees what happens with the foursome, the episode cuts to the opening theme song, "Can't Do It Without You," which sets the stage for the entire series, leading the viewers to believe that a story of friendship will soon transpire.

The theme song depicts the individuality of each character as well as how they work as a team, or, as Gilman says, an "entourage" (Gilman, 2015, p. 162). It does not mention the beach, bikinis, or romance, but instead the need to rely on one's friends. Austin Moon reveals honestly in the theme song "Can't Do It Without You" that he did not achieve stardom alone. Austin becomes a superstar because he had the support of his male and female friends. Most of all, Austin expresses his commitment to his friend Ally, who he fully acknowledges is the person responsible for transforming him into Austin Moon. He wants to share his fame with her without sexual expectation (McGarity, Belle, & Michaels, 2011–2012, track 12). In fact, in the last episode, Austin and Ally sing the song "Two in a Million" to imply that, together, Austin and Ally are both one in a million (Tishler & Reid, 2016). Ally is not the woman in the backdrop, but an equally talented partner by Austin's side. In the first three seasons, Austin sings, "Can't Make it Without You," and later, both Austin and Ally sing this song together. This song is also the last song played at the end of the series, when Austin and Ally sit in the music room, married (McGarity, Belle, & Michaels, track 12). This song, "Can't Make It Without You," sets the foundation, so when the viewer watches the pilot, *Rockers and Writers,* they are prepared to see how these bonds of friendship will form. The first relationship that develops is one between Trish and Ally, not Austin and Ally. The viewer observes the power of sisterhood when Trish pushes Ally not to allow a boy to dictate her life. In *Austin & Ally*'s pilot, Trish encourages Ally to rebel against the traditional beach narrative and embrace her womanhood and personhood. Trish encourages Ally not to position herself as a passive being until she experiences the major stages to empowerment. In accordance to Feminist Standpoint Theory, women can relate to other women, and share a united perspective of oppression because of their common struggle under a patriarchal society. Keeping in mind Standpoint Feminism, in the first episode, Trish forces Ally to come to terms with how she is being subordinated to Austin, the main male protagonist—who steals her song, even if by accident—which enables Ally to gain confidence to seek experiences in the music industry and rebel against patriarchy as a way of gaining dominance. Austin comes across Ally's song "Double Take" when he invades her personal space. In the music room, she sings about her, desire to become a singer/songwriter but expresses her struggle with stage fright, how nobody knows her work and her hope that one day everybody will recognize her (Lurie, Archontis, & Neeman, 2011–2012, track 6). Austin interrupts her and gives her a suggestion on how to fix her song. She does not want to take Austin's advice. It is *her* song and *her* songbook. Austin wants the song to have more pep. Austin, who appears more as a bumbling, pretty boy accidentally steals the song and turns Ally's song into an overnight success.

Ally is furious that he stole her song. She needs assistance from Trish to fight back, but Ally is still unsure as to how to defend herself. Trish encourages her, builds up her confidence, and pushes Ally to tell Austin he was wrong for taking her song on public television. Although Ally's plan to embarrass Austin on television goes awry, Austin realizes that he does not have the talent to write a song and crawls back to Ally for help. Ally does not embrace him and calls him a "weasel" (Kopelow & Seifert, "Rockers and Writers," 2011). However, Austin reveals to her that he needs her songs to be successful because his father does not believe in his talent. Ally relates to this discouragement from her father. According to Psychoanalytical Feminist theory, adolescent boys and girls both want approval from their parents respectively. Boys want to emulate their fathers, while girls need their father's approbation, but also strive for independence. In relation to Psychoanalytical Feminism theory, Ally needs first to recognize the unbeneficial nature of her relationship with her father before rebelling against him as a way of embracing her musical ability and become an independent rocker/music writer. When Austin apologizes, and recognizes that she is the one with the talent, he asks her to become his partner—not his ghostwriter. Austin and Ally stay confined in the music store instead of going to the beach to write Austin's new song. He is not afraid of commitment, like Frankie. Austin tries to encourage Ally to perform with him on *The Helen Show*; however, Ally cannot get over her fear. Austin surprises Ally with the cameras, which causes Ally to panic and accidently destroy the set.

Ally's battle with stage fright is the emphasis of Season One. Her friends work with her on her disabling stage fright. At one point in "Bloggers and Butterflies," Austin is willing to give up his blossoming career so Ally does not have to perform in public. Austin is concerned that the world will not recognize Ally's talents because of her fear and therefore she will not receive the attention she rightfully deserves ("Deejays & Demos"). He becomes especially concerned after hearing her sing "You Don't See Me" alone. Ally's stage fright causes her to feel like a girl lost in the crowd and desperate for people to recognize her talent (Marano, "Austin and Ally," 2011–2012).

The fact that Ally emphasizes that she is a "girl" shows that Ally recognizes that as a shy woman, she runs the chance of being a man's sidekick, which she does not want to be—unlike the beach babes. Austin convinces Ally she is not submissive, that she is his "partner" (Christiansen, "Deejays and Demos," 2012). He tells her, "I could never do this without you, you're awesome" (Christiansen, "Deejays and Demos," 2012). He wants to share the spotlight with Ally when he goes to perform for a special Beach edition of *Miami Mac*. On *Miami Mac*, he brings Ally's song so the radio station can play it for everyone to hear. He tells her, "I want the world to know who Ally Dawson is" (Christiansen, "Deejays and Demos," 2012). Ally cannot appear in public, so Trish lip sings as Ally. Trish leads the world to believe that she is the talented songwriter and partner of Austin. Trish even gets a picture of herself in the magazine, "Miami Music," next to Austin. In the Disney universe, Trish and a white blond male could be successful partners. Ally does come close to fighting her insecurity in the Season Two episode "Costume and Courage" when she pretends to be Taylor Swift dressed as Galexis Nova, a female superhero, after Swift becomes injured.

Ally finally overcomes her stage fright when her mother, anthropologist Penny Dawson, comes back from Africa to Miami Beach in the Season Two episode "Chapter and Choices." She inspires Ally as well as her friends to seize the day. At the same time, Ally is dealing with her own romantic feelings for Austin ("Girlfriends & Girl Friends," "Campers and Complications," "Chapters and Choices"). Austin, oblivious to Ally's feelings, becomes involved with Kira, the daughter of the head of Star Records, Jimmy Star. The head of Austin's label is African American, which is different dynamic as opposed to the beach movies which lacked African American characters, let alone a powerful one. Ally does not jeopardize their partnership or friendship, even when she is frustrated that Austin chooses Kira. There is no mention of this as an interracial relationship. Ally does not tell Austin she has secret feelings for him because she does not want to ruin their partnership or get in between Kira and Austin. Austin and Kira's relationship is short-lived when Austin realizes he has feelings for Ally after he sees her with Elliot, an old camp friend of hers. Austin tries to deny his feelings for Ally and even promises to take her to the beach to see Katy Perry, but Austin fails to keep his promise of having a romantic beach date with Kira because he cannot stop thinking about Ally. He is drawn more to Ally than to the beach with Kira. These feelings come to a head when Penny Dawson comes and reminds her daughter to come to terms with what she wants from life. This prompts her to sing a duet about her friendship with Austin at the Jungle Club, "You Can Come to Me," and overcome her stage fright. In this song, Austin and Ally do not conform to gender roles, like in *Gidget*. Neither Austin nor Ally take a lead role in the song, instead they promise to help each other in life with no disparity between the sexes. There is no male hero or female in distress (Tishler & Powers, 2013, track 3). Indeed, this song is not gender-specific.

When Austin kisses Ally, it is not romanticized by crashing waves, like in typical beach movies; instead it is backstage at the Jungle Club. At this point, Ally has conquered her biggest fear—stage fright. She has become her own person. There are a few mishaps that prevent them from being together long-term, such as their careers as individual artists. The series demonstrates that Ally does not become who she is because of Austin, but because Ally embraces herself. Her discovery of herself is epitomized in her song "Finally Me," which is about her newfound confidence in herself. She may not be perfect, but she realizes that she is a star in the making even without Austin (Marano, Tishler & Charles, 2013). Ally has found herself without the assistance of a man. Although Ally is willing to make sacrifices for Austin, throughout the series, Ally will never give up on her dreams, such as making her own album or going off to Harvard.

The beach does bring Austin and Ally together, but not in a sexist way. In the third season, Austin, Ally, Trish, and Dez center their lives at the beach club. Here, Austin and Ally's relationship can freely bloom after holding back their feelings for each other because of their respective careers. However, Ronnie Ramone, the head of Ally's label, bans Ally from working with Austin, in "Austin and Alias," because they work with two competing labels. Dez tries to replace Ally with a Mariachi singer; however, Austin feels torn not to work with Ally. To help Austin, Ally decides to perform disguised as a Swedish pop singer, Roxy Rocket. Her song, performed incognito as Roxy, with Austin, becomes an instant hit on the beach. Everyone at the beach club can hear their song. Ally, as Roxy, is interviewed by Jett Deely, from *Miami Countdown Live*, on the beach. Deely believes that Roxy is better qualified to be Austin's songwriter than Ally. Amazed and more confident, the event brings out Ally's "moxie." As Roxy, Ally realizes she needs to stand up for herself more and tells Ramone that she will not abandon Austin, pushing him in the sand.

The beach's romantic landscape pushes Austin and Ally to express their love for each, in the purest sense, not regarding Austin's desire to bed Ally. In "Princess and Prizes" in Season Three, Ally becomes jealous when Austin goes on two beach dates with another girl after he agrees to auction himself off for a date for Ally's manatee fundraiser. Ally destroys, by accident, a little girl's princess beach party because she is jealous. Austin and Ally struggle with their feelings for each other; however, they do not allow it to break their friendship and musical partnership. Ally and Austin do battle with jealously but not in efforts to sabotage one another. Unlike in *Austin & Ally*, in many beach films, jealously amongst the main characters is often the main plot line. In "Critics and Confidence," Austin suffers from stage fright after receiving a bad review. All of Austin's friends encourage him to ignore the critic's comment. However, the only way that Austin can overcome his insecurity is to sing a song on the beach to Ally. The reason is because Austin, unlike Moondoggie or Frankie, can admit his weakness in the presence of Ally and everyone at the beach club. In the song "Stuck on You," Austin does not try to be uber masculine, but rather expresses his vulnerability on the beach. His love and affection for Ally are pure and not sexual. This concept is distinctly different from male beach characters like Moondoggie, who express their machismo rather than their lack of confidence (Anders, Anders, & Astrom, 2012–2013, track 8).

Ally's and Austin's relationship transforms the beach party narrative, i.e., where a woman gives up everything, like Gidget is willing to give up her whole identity for Moondoggie. In *Austin & Ally*, Ally does not epitomize, as Radical feminist Bonnie Kreps would claim, as the "Other," and Austin is not the "Subject" (Kreps, 2003, p. 48). Ally may like *girly* things, but she does not appear as though she is programmed to conform to her gender (Kreps, 2003). Kreps believes that as young "ladies," girls are socialized to be neat and to play with "dolls" instead of to be "dirty" and adventurous (Kreps, 2003, p. 46). According to Kreps, "Women's immediate social environment puts enormous pressure on [them] to submit to male dominance. She is exhorted to play out the role of Cinderella"—that is, her destiny is to marry "Prince Charming" at the expense of fulfilling her true potential (Kreps, 2003, p. 46). In short, society's expectations of women contribute to their oppression. However, Ally defies this by fulfilling her passion for becoming a songwriter, for learning how to dance, and for her commitment to her schoolwork. Although Austin is her "Prince Charming," she does not act as his "Cinderella."

When Austin and Ally fully commit to each other in the fourth season, the beach becomes non-existent in the series. The series concentrates on the group's music factory. Austin sacrifices his career so he can be with Ally, but not because Ally asked him to. He knows that he cannot have both, and Ally trumps everything. The show reverses their gender roles. Eventually, Austin finds his way back to the music industry only to lose Ally to Harvard. Ally and Austin reunite on television during *The Helen Show*, where she and Austin decide to become a duet. This marks the beginning of their new musical careers as partners in music and in life. The absence of the beach in the final scene shows that their relationship did not need the waves and the sand castles to constitute a whirlwind romance. Unlike beach party films, where the beach unites characters or encourages sexual liaisons, the beach is part of Austin and Ally's past, and their future is their friendship and their careers—because, in the end, love transcends the waves.

In the *Austin & Ally* universe, one can get ahead by creating partnerships and alliances regardless of race and gender. Women and minorities do not play a sidekick role in *Austin & Ally*, as is typical in beach party texts. The show may center on the rise and fame of two musicians, Austin and Ally, but this program also emphasizes the power of the dynamic foursome—Austin, Ally, Trish, and Dez—who interact at the beach, but do not need the beach to succeed. However, the four of them do not let the beach party scene convince them to objectify or belittle minorities. In the traditional beach movies, the friends of the leading romantic duo are either irrelevant or underdeveloped; in *Austin & Ally*, Trish and Dez play not only a significant part in the shaping of the series, but also they are dynamic characters themselves, providing additional story plots that could relate to all types of fans in the Disney universe. Trish provides the voice for Latinas and minority tweens, whereas Dez is a non-conformist and does not stay within the confines of his gender. These characters would not have existed in the beach movies, but in *Austin & Ally* world, they play a role in bringing the beach to marginalized tweens.

Trish

The relationship between Ally and Trish stands out as different than Ally and Austin's bond. One should consider their relationship in terms of standpoint theory, which considers a woman's experience regarding patriarchy. Although not all women share the same background—each is different socially, economically, and racially—all women must embrace one another's experiences and find commonalities to perceive how patriarchy has oppressed them. Ally and Trish do not expose their bodies for the sake of a boy. In S1E11, "Songwriting and Starfish," Ally and Trish wear conservative bathing suits to the beach. There is nothing sexual about their interactions on the beach. They are not bimbos. Ally is a klutz and awkward, and Trish is dynamo who believes she is beautiful without showing off her skin. Their relationship is solidified, not through "man-hunting," but through sisterhood.

In her article "The Feminist Standpoint: Toward a Specifically Feminist Historical Materialism," Nancy Hartsock uses the Marxist Standpoint on the proletariat to convey her feminist position. To articulate this, she discusses how "women's work in every society differs systematically from men" (Hartsock, 2003, p. 293). In *Austin & Ally*, Trish and Ally have different experiences than Dez and Austin. They have to prove themselves. Trish must prove herself to be a manager/actress and Ally as a songwriter/musician. Different than the typical beach genre, *Austin & Ally* does not highlight what Hartsock would call "sexual division of labor" between men and women (Hartsock, 2003, p. 293). In the beach films, women are men's toys, and they aspire to become wives and mothers. Even though Ally and Trish have different identities, they both, as Hartsock noted, share some kind of commonality because they are women. In the case of *Austin & Ally*, Ally and Trish share the commonality of wanting to express their talents and further their independence.

Hartsock may claim that women share similar experiences when it comes to traditional "women's work," but in the case of *Austin & Ally*, she and Trish find commonality in their quest for fame (Hartsock, 2003, p. 293). A woman's experience is therefore different from a man's because of her gendered socio-economic duties; outsiders in the patriarchal world, they have opinions and understandings different than men (Hartsock, 2003, p. 295). Thus, in *Austin & Ally*, Trish and Ally's alliance prevents them from falling prey due to their sex. Hartsock suggests that although on a global scale woman are divided by a myriad of social and cultural experiences, the fact that society universally subordinates women enables them to find commonalities with each other and promote a sisterhood, which demolishes existing patriarchal hegemonies. Trish is a confident, petite, Mexican American teen who is the voice of reason for Ally. She inspires Ally to think about her career and how she can fulfill her dream as an artist.

The show briefly explores Trish's pride in her Latina identity. The viewer never sees Trish question her Latina roots. In fact, in the episode on Trish's Quinceanera, Trish does not spend the event reflecting on her difference, but instead how she—as Austin's manager—can find a way to get the most presents and convince one of her cousins, who she believes is "club" owner—not a "golf club" owner—to listen to Austin's song "Billion Hits" (Seaton, "Club Owners & Quinceaneras," 2012). One sees through different episodes through the years, Trish is comfortable speaking Spanish (her Spanish edition of *Romeo and Juliet*, speaking Spanish during the episode "Fanatic and Favors" [S3E14], or Austin coming to her for Spanish tutoring). Throughout the series, Trish has over thirty jobs. Her longest job was working as Austin and Ally's manager, which she self-appoints. She also has a job at Shredder Beach Club and eventually becomes the party planner. Trish's confidence and belief that her future is bright enables her to pursue a successful career in acting.

Though Trish is not tall, blond, and busty, like "perfect" female beach bodies, she is not threatened. Trish has relationships with several boys—all different races—but she does not sacrifice herself for them and urges Ally not to either, even if she may love Austin. At one point, Trish gets terrible advice from Austin and Ally not to be herself; however, Trish realizes that she is only happy in her intimate relationships when she can be the boss. In

Austin & Ally, the show creators play with Trish's extreme confidence as opposed to Ally when she, Ally, and Dez envision an alternate world where Trish is the famed pop singer with her hit song, "I'm Better Than You." Trish is uncomfortable with this reality, not because she sees herself as less than her white friend, Ally, but instead, because she knows her ego would overtake her.

Trish does become jealous of Ally's freedom to spend time on the beach with her new friend Kira, Austin's ex-girlfriend. She worries that she has lost Ally to another girl. To prove that Trish is the most important person to her, Ally dedicates a song to Trish at the beach club. The song "Redial" is about how Trish, not Austin, is her main confidant. Here, Ally does not sing a love song to a boy, but rather her best friend—a girl. In this song, she marks the importance of sisterhood. It is not Austin who is the first person she wants to call, but Trish. As they hold hands and Ally sings to Trish, it illustrates that on the beach, there can be love between two female friends (Lurie, Archontis, Neeman, & Michaels, 2012–2013, track 9). In Austin and Ally's vision of the beach, a girl can enjoy the company of her female friend without worrying about finding a boy. This relationship stands in contrast to Gidget, whose primary goal is to catch Moondoggie, who she thinks completes her as a woman as opposed to her female counterparts.

One of the most significant episodes in *Austin & Ally* is when Trish is bullied and made to feel ugly. The show does not stipulate the cause of Trish's bullying is out of prejudice; however, the viewer could presume there is some relation. After all, Trish becomes the subject of intimidation when she is selected to be Sleeping Beauty. In this episode, Disney wants us to question the concept of beauty. According to Dorothy Hurley, "the images found in fairy tales, therefore have particular importance for children of color in relation to the internalization of White privileging" as seen in Disney fairy tales (Hurley, 2005, p. 221). This is compounded by how whiteness has come to dominate what is beautiful. According to Peggy McIntosh, in her article "White Privilege and Male Privilege: A Personal Account of Coming to See Correspondences Through Work in Women's Studies," America is a white supremacist society that focuses on whiteness. In other words, in America, to be white is to be privileged. McIntosh demonstrates that she has certain privileges just because she is white—the idea of "white privilege" (Mcintosh, 1988, p. 100). In popular culture, whiteness typifies beauty. As McIntosh notes, one "can turn on the television … and see people of [the white] race widely and positively represented" (Mcintosh, 2005, p. 279).

Ally and Austin have a hard time convincing Trish to have confidence in herself. Austin even sings a song that he and Ally wrote for her on the beach. Ally says to Trish, "I keep trying to tell you that we're here for you, but you don't seem to be hearing me. You left us no choice we had to write you a song." (Kopelow & Seifert, "Beauties & Bullies," 2012). In the song "Super-hero," which Austin sings, but Ally wrote, both want to save Trish from her despair and convince her to come back to school and face her bully. They want her to rely on them for help. The duo says she has permission to become passive. The song does not help Trish deal with what happened at school (Tishler, Kay, & Shaw, 2012–2013, track 4). She has to find the strength in herself. Her white friends cannot become her protector. By the end of the episode, Trish stands up for herself and reclaims the title of Sleeping Beauty. Her friends support her. Peggy McIntosh would argue that Trish needed to find her voice and her friends needed to "unpack [their] invisible knapsack of white privilege" (Mcintosh, 2005, p. 280). Trish remains the glue that holds the foursome together. In the S4E19, when the team wants to break up because everyone is going their separate ways, Trish sings, "You've Got a Friend," which convinces the four friends that "friends are supposed to be there for each other no matter what" (Craig Wyrick-Solari, "Musicals & Moving On," 2016). She encourages her friends to find their voices, even if this means leaving the security of their friendship because it supersedes Miami Beach. In other words, life does not begin and end on the beach.

Dez

Austin and Ally's friend, Dez, exhibits characteristics that do not conform to his gender identity, and his affection for Austin does border on homoerotic. He is nonsensical; he texts his dogs, carries around random objects like hams, wears mismatched clothes, and is willing to eat moldy food. His piercing screams are un-masculine, but become a defining part of his personality. He has a strong attachment to romantic films and openly cries at the end of them. When Dez wears Trish's tiara from her Quinceanera in Season One, he is secure in his masculinity. In Season Two, when Austin begins to date Kira, Dez is regretful that Austin cannot spend more time with him. He is even willing to go to the spa with Trish and have all the treatment she would have done with Ally. In S3E6, "Glee Clubs & Glory," Dez reveals his ultimate dream is to be in the glee club. At the end of the episode, he performs in a glee competition with his friends. In his performance, he chooses to sing Ally's song of female empowerment, "Finally Me." Dez even goes to great lengths to become a cheerleader in Season Three as he states, "What little boy doesn't want to grow up to be a cheerleader?" (Wayne Conley, "Sports & Brains" "Sports & Sprains," 2013).

Dez's gendered identity is fluid. He defines himself as heterosexual as he falls in love with a girl named Carrie, but at the same time, Dez is willing to break normative heterosexual behavior. He does not hide his fascination and his homoerotic devotion towards his friend Austin, who he worships. He does everything for Austin. He even dresses up as him for Halloween. In Season Three's "Fanatics and Favors" (S3E14), the gang meets Austin's number one fan: Dez's cousin and NBA player Dwayne Wade. Dwayne has a shrine dedicated to Austin, from storybooks to cuckoo clocks, and all kinds of Austin memorabilia. He is obsessed with Austin. Eventually, when Dwayne no longer idolizes Austin, Dez asks Dwayne if he can have all of Austin's memorabilia.

Dez also has no qualms with playing a female role. When Austin wants to help Ally in season one get a date with Dallas, Dez insists on playing Ally. Austin replies, "Dez, we talked about this" (Seaton, "Club Owners & Quinceaneras," 2012), which implies that Dez likes to play the feminine role. This desire is best seen in Season Four, when Austin wants to show Ally his ballroom dance moves. Dez insists on dancing with Austin and cutting in line. He also passes out when he sees the boy band *Boynado* in Season Four.

Dez enjoys being a spectator on the beach and enjoys watching Austin preform. Dez even directs his film, *The Claw*, with Austin as his first star. The film is a horror film about a claw. It is reminiscent of the 1960s beach horror films like *Blood Beach*. He casts Austin and Trish as the main leads. But Dez also follows the traditional beach narratives of the 1960s—in that Austin must save a white, blond woman—but Trish still has an important role, regardless of the fact that she does not fit the image of the beach beauty. Austin's belief in Dez enables him to further Dez's passion for the film industry when he lands Dez an internship with Spike Stevens in *The Pilot and the Mermaid*, whose movie set is also on the beach. Austin, Ally, and Trish come up with an elaborate plan that enables Dez to replace Stevens so he can direct his own film with Austin as the main star. It is a musical about a pilot, Austin, who falls in love with a mermaid—possible reference to *Beach Blanket Bingo,* a film that explores a mermaid love story.

Conclusion

The story of *Austin & Ally* transforms the beach narrative from a space that exclusively promoted sexuality, and objectification to a place where characters of both genders can enjoy friendships without trying to seduce the other. Indeed, *Austin & Ally*'s beach does not epitomize the oversexed lily-white experience of the past. *Austin & Ally*'s characters are dynamic and portray each's struggles and distinct experiences on their road to fame. *Austin & Ally* rejects the traditional beach genre story plot of the 1960s, which separated individuals based on their gender and race. The show does not have a constant outside villain, a flirtatious girl or boy who tries to distract the primary love interest, and surfing is not a sport that the main male character can use to express his masculinity and manhood. Indeed, on this beach, men do not lurk around and exert their sexuality. Teens listen to music on the beach, for the sake of the beat, and not to rub up close against a person of the opposite sex. *Austin & Ally* may incorporate slapstick dialogue like in many of the beach genre films, but in the end, the songs are used to move along the plot—for the most part—to emphasize the value of friendship, falling in love, and music. The characters do not embody beauty, but instead show off their talent and how working together can ultimately break down boundaries. As Austin said himself, "There is no way I can make it without you" (Lynch, "Austin and Ally," 2011–2012).

REFERENCES

Antelyes, P. (2009). "Haim afen range": The Jewish indian and the redface western. *MELUS*, 34 (3). 15–42.
Asher, W. (Director). (1963). *Beach Party* [Motion Picture]. United States: American International Pictures.
Austin & Ally. (2012). Walt Disney Records.
Austin and Ally: Turn It Up. (2013). Disney.
Bukowczyk, J.J. (2016). California dreamin', whiteness, and the American dream. *Journal of American Ethnic History*, 35 (2), 91–106.
Burdsey, D. (2016). *Race, place and the seaside: Postcards from the edge*. London: Palgrave Macmillian UK.
Disney Channel Play It Loud. (2014). Aec.
Doherty, T (2010). *Teenagers and teenpics: The juvenilization of American movies in the 1950s*. Philadelphia: Temple University Press.
Gillian, J. *Television brandcasting: The return of the content-promotion hybrid*. New York: Routledge, Taylor & Francis Group.
Hartsock, N. (2003).The feminist standpoint: Toward a specifically feminist historical materialism.In C. McCann and S.K. Kim (Eds.), In *Feminist theory reader: Local and global perspectives* (pp. 45–49). New York: Routledge.
Hurley, D.L. (2005). Seeing white: Children of color and the Disney fairy tale princess. *The Journal of Negro Education*, 74 (3), 221–232.
Kopelow, K. and Seifert, H. (Producer). (2011–2016). *Austin and Ally* [Television Series]. Irving, CA: Disney.
Kreps, B. (2003). Radical feminism. In C. McCann and S.K. Kim (Eds.), In *Feminist theory reader: Local and global perspectives* (pp. 45–49). New York: Routledge.
Levan. H. (Director). (1960). *Where the Boys Are* [Motion Picture]. United States: Warner Bros.
Lisanti, T. (2012). *Hollywood surf and beach movies: The first wave, 1959–1969*. Jefferson, NC: McFarland.
Mcintosh, P. (2005). White privilege: Unpacking the invisible knapsack. In M.B. Zinn, et al. (Eds.), *Gender through the prism of difference* (pp. 278–284). New York: Oxford University Press.
McParland, S.J. (2015). *It's party time: A musical appreciation of the beach party film genre*. North Strathfield, NSW: California Music, CA: John Blair.
Palladino, G. (1999). *Teenagers: An American history*. New York: Basic Books.
Shary, T. (2005). *Teen movies: American youth on screen*. London: Wallflower.
Stenger, J. (2008). Mapping the beach: Beach movies, exploitation film and geographies of whiteness. In D. Bernardi (Ed.), *The persistence of whiteness: Race and contemporary Hollywood cinema* (pp. 28–50). New York: Routledge.

Tropiano, S. (2006). *Rebels and chicks: A history of the Hollywood teen movie.* New York: Back Stage Books.

Wendkos, P. (Director). (1959) *Gidget* [Motion picture on DVD]. United States: Columbia Pictures.

Adopting Diversity and Ignoring Race

Representations of Race in Jessie's and K.C. Undercover's Families of Color

Rebecca Rowe

Disney has a race problem. From classic racist caricatures of crows (see Towbin et al., 2004), "red men" (see Willets, 2013), and singing slaves (see Miller & Rode, 1995; Willets, 2013), to the more recent slate of problematic princesses of color (see, for example, scholarship on *Pocahontas* by Ono & Buescher, 2001; Sardar, 1996), Disney continuously fails in its attempts to depict race. Even when Disney actively attempts to avoid racist portrayals, they fail by ultimately erasing and commodifying race, as can be seen in *The Princess and the Frog*, a film that Disney believed would "fix" their racial issues and yet just ignores whatever racial implications they seemingly attempt to engage (see, for example, Gehlawat, 2010; Gregory, 2010; Turner, 2013). More distressingly, race has a Disney problem. Dorothy L. Hurley (2005) argues that small children internalize the problematic representations of race in Disney fairy-tale movies *before* children are taught critical thought processes to withstand racist images. In other words, while Disney may not be the only source of racism children imbibe, it is one of the most ubiquitous and harmful sources in most American children's lives.

Yet almost all of the conversation about Disney and race focuses on animated feature films, with little scholarship focusing on portrayals of race on the Disney Channel. The Disney Channel releases more content than Walt Disney Animation Studios and Pixar Animation Studios combined and is continuously streaming, so it is important that we analyze the racial messages children receive daily from this source, especially since the Disney Channel

129

has included people and characters of color almost since its inception. One of the few scholarly treatises on race and the Disney Channel, Valdivia's "Mixed Race on the Disney Channel: From *Johnnie Tsunami* Through *Lizzie McGuire* and Ending with *The Cheetah Girls*" (2008), argues that Disney, "never one to fall too far behind the curve on these issues … has gingerly begun to address issues of difference as it seeks to maintain ratings prominence and economic returns in the form of increasing revenues and profits for its shareholders" (p. 270), suggesting that the surprising amount of diversity on the Disney Channel is primarily motivated by ratings rather than ideological morals. Valdivia ultimately claims that "Disney has come a long way since its lily-white days" with "representational changes that, at least temporarily, normalize an ethnically diverse universe with a happy ending" (p. 286). While recognizing that Disney is prompted by economics, Valdivia is cautiously optimistic that Disney's racial representation seems to be improving, at least at the time of her writing in 2006.

Thirteen years later, little seems to have changed: the Disney Channel is still populated with shows with diverse casts of tweens and teens, bopping through life towards their happy ending, with little to no hint about very real race issues such as discrimination, police violence, or activism. The Disney Channel's programming, designed for tween audiences, largely revolves around the family, so this essay analyzes how race and family collide, focusing on two shows: *Jessie* (2011–2015) and *K.C. Undercover* (2015–2018). These two shows approach race differently: *Jessie* follows a multiracial family created primarily through adoption, demonstrating people of different races and cultures existing within one family, and *K.C. Undercover* follows an upper-middle-class Black family, demonstrating that Black people can succeed in White-dominant areas, no matter their race. Yet, each of these tactics ultimately fails, often due to the depiction of the family unit: *Jessie* is built on drastic racist stereotypes that many viewers scorn, and *K.C. Undercover* ignores the very real racism people of color face today, suggesting that our society is past racism and thus implying that people of color are exaggerating or creating their own problems. Both of these shows echo televisual race portrayals from decades ago, demonstrating that even in the surprising diversity of the Disney Channel, Disney is still behind the times in racial representation.

Ultimately, I suggest that the Disney Channel regurgitates such portrayals because it is largely viewed by children and their families and so does not receive the same amount of attention, and thus possible activism, as some of Disney's other properties that have a larger adult audience. This suggestion has an uncomfortable implication: media clearly directed to children, without an implied adult audience, does not seem worth attention, from Disney nor activists. In other words, until adults are interested in a property, there seems to be no reason to make racially progressive material, inculcating a new generation with ideas that many adults no longer support.

Adopting Diversity

Jessie follows the misadventures of Jessie Prescott, a White eighteen-year-old who nannies for Morgan and Christina Ross, a White affluent couple who have four children. Emma, their eldest, is their only biological child. Luke,[1] their second oldest, is a White boy they adopted from Detroit. Ravi is the next oldest but the most recently adopted, adopted approximately six months before the show begins; he was born and raised in India, and the Rosses adopted him when he was ten, meaning he is fluent in Hindi and has memories of his Indian homeland. Zuri, the youngest, is a Black girl the Rosses adopted from Uganda as a baby. The show predominantly focuses on the close-knit multiracial family and their upper-class problems.

It is not hard to imagine why Disney would create a show like this. Children's literature scholars, professionals, and activists have been calling for children of color in children's literature and media since even before 1965 when Larrick released her groundbreaking "The All-White World of Children's Books." Black children's literature author and activist Myer (2014) argues that, without representation of *all* children

> when kids today face the realities of our world, our global economies, our integrations and overlappings, they all do so without a proper map. They are navigating the streets and avenues of their lives with an inadequate, outdated chart, and we wonder why they feel lost. They are threatened by difference, and desperately try to wish the world into some more familiar form.

This article, published three years into *Jessie*'s airing, demonstrates the very real need for diverse lives in children's media: children need to see different people in different situations so they learn how to navigate their world. By showing an adoptive multiracial family, *Jessie* can help children from blended families—families blended by adoption or remarriage or multiracial marriage—navigate their own lives and help other children understand and empathize with those children. Setting the economic lure aside, this is a worthy goal.

However, the response to the representation of race in this show is far from positive, predominantly because the characters, especially the Ravi character, are built on stereotypes. Many viewers explain online their displeasure with the racist portrayal of Ravi. Viewers have pointed out that *Jessie* "makes Ravi's Indian culture the entire joke" which is "both racist and unfunny" (Jeff 2012). In particular, one viewer argues that "Ravi is awkward, weak and constantly bullied by other characters on the show," a harmful stereotype that leads Americans to think that Indians are weak and can be pushed around, as the viewer shares from personal experience (Sharma 2017). These concerns echo scholarship on the harm of the "model minority" stereotype of Asian men and women which "does *not* protect them from prejudice and racism" and in which "Asian American men feel the brunt of emasculating white stereotypes that place them at the bottom of a U.S. masculinity hierarchy," making Asian men, like Ravi, appear weak in our masculine-strength based culture (Chou & Feagin, 2015, pp. 2, 10). In fact, as another viewer points out, Ravi seems to be based firmly in colonialist stereotypes of Indian culture famously deconstructed in Edward Said's *Orientalism* since "a majority of the stereotypes Ravi embodies in the show aren't even real stereotypes of India" and instead work to increase the mysticism around anything, and anyone, from the "Orient" (kayfil, 2013). All of these responses, and many more, appear on just the first page of Google when searching the terms "Jessie," "Ravi," and "race" (though the list continues on the second page and further), pointing to the glaring problems with *Jessie*'s depiction of Ravi.

Many of these responses come from viewers who identify themselves as Indian American. Jeff (2012) talks about raising his Indian children in America; Sharma (2017) discusses his experiences as an Indian man living in America; Fatima (2017), who points to the problems of having Ravi being adopted from India, talks about being a person of color longing for Indian characters. One self-identified Indian American explained in a message for "Top 10 Reasons 'Jessie' Is a Terrible Show":

> [The] Disney Channel is teaching kids that Indian people are all nerdy, weak, uncool, and know nothing about America. Ravi is always talking in a clearly fake accent, which no Indian people ever talk in, and is always wearing Indian clothes. Disney is showing that it's cool to make fun of people who prefer to stay true to their culture by wearing traditional clothes and eating traditional food [Msg 1].

The viewer ends his comment by talking about his own experience growing up Indian in America and how he and his friends, not to mention several cultural icons, break these stereotypes. All of these viewers tie their own Indian identity to their disgust with the show's representation of Ravi. In contrast, none of the major creators or producers for *Jessie* are Indian or claim Indian descent. Many theorists and activists argue that diversity behind the camera can help avoid racist representation on screen (see, for example, Foster, 1997; Donalson, 2003), and *Jessie* demonstrates why this is necessary: the racist images that Indian Americans watching *Jessie* cannot help but see are all but invisible to the non–Indian creators.

While this not-so-subtle racism is problematic, I argue that the family structure of the show exaggerates the problem. For example, the problems with Ravi's character may be slightly less obvious if he did not live with White affluent Americans; his actions contrast to those around him, highlighting the stereotypes of Indian culture. Moreover, this family structure is built on a harmful transnational adoption system that preys on existing power inequalities. Briggs and Marre (2009) explain that "this new form of transnational adoption has been marked by the geographies of unequal power, as children move from poorer countries and families to wealthier ones" because "transnational adoption has been shaped by the forces of colonialism, the Cold War, and globalization," meaning that this form of adoption is built on "a transnational system of power relations that enables privileged women to bear and nurture children while disempowering those who are subordinated by reason of class, race, and national origin" (pp. 1–2, 17). In effect, the Rosses, like real-life famous couple Brad Pitt and Angelina Jolie, revitalize old power structures by repeating mercantile flow, where raw material (i.e., children) move from impoverished/colonized areas (i.e., India and Uganda) to wealthier areas where they become commodified goods (i.e., family). I do not mean to suggest that people engaging in transnational adoption are twirling their moustaches and laughing about depleting India of their children; hopefully, they are only seeking to give children a good home. However, transnational adoption relies on the belief that *here* is better than *there*, reaffirming the believed affluence of the adopted country and poverty of the adoptee country. This feeling is reinforced by the show any time the Rosses visit areas like Ravi's or Zuri's home countries. During a vacation ("We Are So Grounded," 2012), their plane crashes on an island that has the same flora and fauna as Ravi's home (as explained by Ravi), and they barely survive the ensuing jungle trek. Later, when Jessie and the children visit Africa ("But Africa Is So … Fari," 2015), they have to load their gas tank by hand with dung and then nearly get stampeded by rhinos. Both places are portrayed as savage countries which we, the American characters, actors, and audience, are glad to have escaped. In effect, *Jessie* implies that America *has* to be better than India or Uganda, so the Rosses are saving Ravi and Zuri from their dangerous homelands.

Perhaps the most startling problem with this family structure, however, is the depiction of Zuri's Blackness once she is surrounded by White affluent Americans. Zuri is adopted by the White, affluent Rosses when she is a baby and is raised in their community. Her school and neighborhood suspiciously lack Black people, and she prefers White media, especially White country music singers like Dolly Parton and Rascal Flatts. She mostly watches films and television with her White siblings, watching what they watch: media filled with predominantly White characters and actors made by White people. For all intents and purposes, she is raised as a White child, with no connection to the African American[2] community, not even by birth since she is from Uganda.

Yet, Zuri is quite clearly built around the Sapphire Black stereotype, which is based firmly in the African American community. According to Campbell, Giannino, China, and Harris (2008), the Sapphire stereotype gets its name from *Amos 'n' Andy*, whose character, Sapphire Stephens, is the prototypical sassy, angry Black woman. The Sapphire stereotype is "an emasculating portrayal of Black women" who is "feisty and wisecracking, being bossy, loud, aggressive, relishing in conflict, and at times embodying wisdom" (Brown, 2017, p. 108). Nearly sixty years after *Amos 'n' Andy* was canceled at the behest of the National Association for the Advancement of Colored People, this description perfectly describes Zuri, who speaks African American Vernacular English, is sassy to everyone, is constantly screaming, bosses everyone around, constantly derides men (especially the men Jessie dates), and who, according to the Disney Channel, has the catchphrase of "mmmmh-mmmm" (with hip cocked and hand on hip). She is street smart in a way that her siblings are not, able to navigate New York and general life situations much better than her three older siblings and often even better than Jessie. She is seemingly no more than Sapphire resurrected from the days of black-and-white television, a stereotype that comes from a community that supposedly Zuri is never a part of.

If Zuri is not part of an African American community and not learning about the African American community from her media consumption, *Jessie* suggests that this Sapphire stereotype is genetic rather than social. As kayfil (2013) so astutely explains, "The worst part about her character to me is … not just the stereotypes, but the fact that she is exhibiting urban black stereotypes despite never having been a part of urban black society," suggesting that "[t]hese characteristics of Zuri exist in her genetics just because of the color of her skin." Zuri could not get these characteristics from her homeland of Uganda (which has Black people but few African Americans), her White affluent family, or her predominantly White media. Effectively, *Jessie* suggests that Zuri came with these characteristics, that this stereotype is biologically inherent to Black girls. By placing a stereotypical Sapphire in a White family and neighborhood, *Jessie* makes it seem like stereotypes are biological, implying that stereotypes are not only real but inherent to the Black community rather than placed on them by White creators of media.

Jessie attempts to portray a multiracial blended family which, in theory, could help similar children learn to navigate their own lives and help other children learn about blended families. Yet the show fails because it bundles many problematic stereotypes into one family, juxtaposing the drastically racist stereotypes of Ravi and Zuri with White American society. The show continues the Disney Channel's long history of diversity, but in such a racist way that it feels like it is from the 1950s. Shows like this allow stereotypes to continue unquestioned by the majority of viewers who do not belong to the ethnicity being maligned. *Jessie*, the creators, and the Rosses accept racist stereotypes, so viewers do, too.

Ignoring Race

Even with this viewer unrest against the racist portrayals in *Jessie*, the show lasted for four seasons, demonstrating how little the online critique affected Disney. However, it did finally come to an end, and, as it did so, Disney released a new show about a family of color: *K.C. Undercover*. This new series follows a Black family, the Coopers, who are all spies for The Organization, including parents Craig and Kira, sixteen-year-old K.C., fifteen-year-old Ernie, and their adopted robot, seemingly ten-year-old Judy (whose name is an acronym for Junior Undercover Digital Youth). The family has to navigate living a double life of being undercover spies and living in an upper-middle-class neighborhood in Washington, D.C.

This show takes the opposite tactic to the previous one: whereas *Jessie* acknowledges race and ultimately falls into racist stereotypes, *K.C. Undercover* never acknowledges race. They mostly avoid racist stereotypes this way (although Judy is yet another Sapphire), which might explain why *K.C. Undercover* has received less racial critique than *Jessie*. The show is also extremely multiracial: the family is Black and their high school, Hamilton High, has students of many different races. The series seemingly shows people of color in almost every role, from hero to villain and everything in between, moving away from both the stereotypical "bad" person of color and its foil, the impossibly "good" person of color, as Inniss and Feagin (2002) argue populate series like *The Cosby Show*, also distorting the way audiences understand people of color (p. 189). The series attempts to show that teens, no matter their race, can achieve great things and are, at heart, all alike.

More subtly, *K.C. Undercover* builds a hidden language of meaning through small yet consistent nods to African American culture. These nods exist throughout the series in a myriad of different ways: K.C.'s full name is Katrina Charlotte Coretta Scott Cooper, which references the famous hurricane that disproportionately affected Black lives in New Orleans as well as the famous activist wife of Martin Luther King, Jr.; the Coopers have two prominent pieces of artwork, which are reminiscent of Black artists such as Ernie Barnes and Shakor, in their home that are shown almost every episode, one of which shows three Black women and a Black girl hugging and the other of which shows a Black man playing a trumpet; in the episode "Teen Drama" (2017), their boss Beverly makes a comment about KC getting a degree from Harvard or "if you want to keep it real, Howard," which is, of course, a Historically Black University; they often talk about things like dances established in the African American community, such as the Stanky Legg or Wobble. There are small nods like these throughout the series that tie the family to the African American community for those who know what the references mean. Li (2012) argues that recent media have started using "Race-specific, race-free language" (a term borrowed from Toni Morrison), which means "making racial meaning the site of intimacy between those literate in racial codes" by using language and terms that are predominantly known only within racial communities (p. 12). This creates a new sense of community and understanding, not accessed by outsiders, even when media are consumed by large portions of the population. The nods in *K.C. Undercover* operate in that fashion, gesturing to African American culture without actually talking about race. It is made for a specific community, and, honestly, there is a very good chance that I, a White woman, did not catch all of such language. This allows all audiences to watch the show while adding a layer of meaning for Black audiences inaccessible for those outside the African American culture.

While the message of sameness sounds heartwarming and the subtle language creates a community of Black viewers, these tactics can erase all implication of race, as happens with the Coopers and perhaps the most famous Black TV family, the Huxtables from *The Cosby Show*. As many scholars have shown, "Cosby's version of the Black family … avoid[s] racial realities" because "the Huxtables were *too* much like all the other middle-class White families on TV" (Squires, 2009, p. 229). Likewise, the similarity between White families and the Coopers, always evident as most of their neighbors are White, is especially stark in the final episodes of *K.C. Undercover* when the Coopers discover an enemy spy family living on their block. As they enter the family's house in "The Domino Effect" (2018), they all remark about how they must have found the wrong place because it is too close and looks too much like their own home. K.C. even finds a vase she made for her father in third grade that he sold at a yard sale years ago, now gracing a White home, demonstrating how similar the Coopers are to all the White families around them. The differences between the Coopers and the enemy spies are subtle, just like *The Cosby Show* relies on small details to prove the Huxtables' Blackness, such as a "fictional [HCBU] alma mater … art by African Americans hung on the walls of the living room," and references to "major cultural figures in jazz, Black theater, and other arts" (Squires, 2009, p. 230), all tactics *K.C. Undercover* uses, as described above. The connections between these two Black families is stark, and scholarship on the Huxtables makes it clear why this similarity is so problematic. Many Black viewers claim that "the problem [with *The Cosby Show*] lies with the stereotypical nature of an upper-middle-class Black family that never experiences problems, especially racial problems" (Innis & Feagin, 2002, p. 192). While recognizing that

The Cosby Show, like *K.C. Undercover*, is a sitcom, Innis and Feagin (2002) argue that "[u]pper middle-class Black Americans experience much discrimination, and it is overt, recognizable, and everyday" so "it does not seem unreasonable to expect that a Black lawyer or doctor, and certainly a Black college student," much like K.C., "would experience it and deal with it in daily life" (p. 199). This ignorance of racism especially "becomes negative when Whites take the absence of racism to mean that things are fine for Black Americans" (Innis & Feagin, 2002, p. 200). By so closely mirroring the Huxtables, *K.C. Undercover* ignores race and thus makes racism seem impossible.

In fact, *K.C. Undercover* suggests that race and racism would not be problems for a Black, upper-middle-class family living in Washington, D.C. The Coopers receive no particular treatment, at school or at The Organization, for their race. This implies that race is not a problem in twenty-first century America, as if K.C., a teen Black woman from a prosperous family, can exist in Washington, D.C., without any racial problems, even though Black people make up 46.4 percent of D.C.'s population while White people make up only 36.3 percent and yet the median White household in D.C. makes three times as much as the median Black household, suggesting great racial and economic disparity in the D.C. area (City-Data 2018). While *K.C. Undercover*'s imaginary world beyond race would be a problem in any media representation set in contemporary D.C., it is especially problematic for a show about a family of spies. Spies have to fit into their surroundings if they are to be effective. Most of the Coopers' missions, especially K.C.'s, involve going undercover, meaning that if they stand out, they could be in very real danger. Yet the Coopers' race is never mentioned in the cases they are assigned. The Coopers travel not only all over the United States but all over the world for their missions; there are some places where they would stand out as Black people and some places where Black spies would be able to blend in best. Yet it is never stated that the Coopers are assigned or denied a mission due to their race, even though there are several missions where they are put into such situations. For example, in "Daddy's Little Princess" (2015), the Coopers are put in charge of protecting an African prince visiting America on a diplomatic mission. K.C. and Prince Promomomo (which in itself sounds like a racist joke about African names) become infatuated with each other, and so K.C. starts trying to mimic his African culture, ultimately stereotyping Africa. The episode denigrates K.C.'s backwards notions of Africa, but it never engages the fact that her family might have been put on security detail because they were Black and thus would fit in with the rest of his African entourage the same way that he would blend in with their Black household. Likewise, in "Operation: Other Side, Part 1" (2015), K.C. has to go undercover into a correctional facility for teen delinquents. The inmates are almost all people of color, and it is never addressed that they chose to send a Black spy undercover in prison. Mission after mission, K.C. and the Coopers are put into situations where their race affects what they do, and yet race is never addressed.

The only episode that addresses race in any meaningful way is "The Legend of Bad, Bad Cleo Brown" (2016), which tells the story of the first woman to go on a mission for The Organization. The episode begins with K.C. talking about a history report she is supposed to write on a famous trailblazer. She tells her grandmother, who was the first Black woman spy for The Organization, that she wants to write about her, but her grandmother tells her that there was another Black woman before her who successfully completed a mission, even if she was never made an official spy: Cleo Brown. Most of the rest of the episode takes place in a blaxploitation flashback as we see K.C. and friends and family enact the story of Cleo Brown, with K.C. as Cleo. The story is set in 1974 and does show some of the racism and sexism of the time (while also engaging in racist stereotypes popularized by 1970s blaxploitation films), where Cleo gets looked over for a mission in a Black night club that she, as the only young, Black woman in the office, would be perfect for because she is not only a woman but Black. She ultimately has to quit after successfully completing the mission because she did not follow orders, but the flashback ends with other women of color in the office demanding a chance in the field. The episode ends with K.C. holding a memorial service for Cleo at The Organization, in which she says:

> Cleo Brown kicked down the doors so my grandma could become a spy. My grandma Gail fought discrimination with her head held high so that my mother could become a spy. Then my mother, well, she kind of dragged me into this without asking…. It is thanks to Cleo that all young, Black, female spies can be brave, know our worth, and fly.

The writers stage history very clearly: Cleo had to do the most work, then Gail had it easier, Kira seemingly had no problems, and race was so little a problem for K.C. that she had to do no work to become a spy. Raiford and Romano (2006) argue that people today often represent the Civil Rights movement as a part of the past with "singular, extraordinary individuals who made history by acting in ways that are consistent with longstanding American values" (p. xix). This tactic isolates certain people and relegates them to the past, suggesting that the fight is over due to monoliths that single-handedly changed history. This episode of K.C. Undercover, the only episode to address race, does the same thing, suggesting that race was a problem in the past for women like Cleo, but now, anyone can do anything because race does not matter for the twenty-first-century Coopers. This is especially troubling in contrast with another episode, "The Storm Maker" (2017), in which K.C. has to battle gender discrimination in her own work place. The episode deals with different waves of feminism and how that affects how women approach sexism in a surprisingly nuanced way, demonstrating that the series is capable of tackling complex identity issues. And yet, race is ignored or relegated to the past.

This blatant disavowal of racial issues engages in the concept of post-race. After Barack Obama's election, people claimed that America is post-race, a concept that builds on older colorblind racism to say that we, as an American society, are beyond race. It is the belief that "race is an inconvenient myth, an obstacle that we have at last surmounted because the highest office in the land is open to a member of a historically maligned community" and "also signifies the fantasy that we live in a truly egalitarian society, a rhetorical ruse that quells the necessity for further social change" (Li 2012, p. 2) so that "postracialism, like colorblindness before it, serves to drive any substantive analysis of race underground so that structural or systemic inequality is preserved in the name of neutrality" (Powell, 2017, p. 20). Effectively, *K.C. Undercover* attempts to get away from racism as seen in *Jessie* by getting rid of race as part of the post-race project, but that just erases the real racial issues we have instead of engaging them and thus working through them.

One of the major ways we can see this post-racial project is in K.C.'s actress, Zendaya, who is biracial. Joseph (2013) argues that an important image in the new millennium is the "Exceptional Multiracial" who rises above their race, especially their Blackness, so that "the mixed-race African American has somehow magically transcended race; the logical extension of this idea is that race no longer matters" (p. 26). This is part of the post-racial project, especially as it centers around the biracial Obama, working to erode race by showing someone who is beyond one category of race. There are two major issues with this view of the Exceptional Multiracial. First, "Instead of showing America embracing blackness in messy, hybridized, multiracial forms, the unspoken dictate in contemporary representations of multiracial Americans is that blackness must be risen above, surpassed, or truly transcended" (Joseph, 2013, p. 4). In other words, multiracial African Americans are seen as better partially because they are more than "just" Black, which suggests that there is something wrong with Blackness. The second problem is that, in this view, multiracial Black people "heroically eschew the crutch of race or never play the so-called race card" suggesting "that other black and brown people who cannot get over their racialization are lazily choosing not to" (Joseph, 2013, p. 26). The Exceptional Multiracial,

> as a new model of an imagined-to-be-deracialized population, ha[s] been envisioned as racial bridges to a new United States. They are the sum of all races and, therefore, no race at all. Neoconservative and neoliberal Americans deploy images of mixed-race saviors to soothe white fears of allocating equal authority to people of color [Joseph, 2013, p. 23].

Ultimately, multiracial people are being held up as exemplars of people of color who are not raced, as heroes of a new, post-racial America that is beyond racial concerns. Because of the increasing portrayal of biracial and multiracial characters as heroic or possessing "cultural mastery," there has been "an overall boom in the casting of mixed race actors in contemporary film and television" (Beltrán & Fojas, 2008, pp. 10–11). Multiracial has become the next big thing in Hollywood because it allows media makers to portray race without actually dealing with it.

Disney is not immune to this issue. Valdivia (2008) identifies the use of multiracial characters and actors as one of America's, and specifically Disney's, strategies for depicting race, which she calls "ambiguity and hybridity" (p. 272). Effectively, in order to reach the widest audience, media makers, including the Disney Channel, replace easily identifiable ethnicities with "one or more ambiguous body that can sign in for more than one ethnicity" (Valdivia, 2008, p. 273). Zendaya is that one body. She is the daughter of a Black father and White mother, and her race appears both ambiguous and hybrid. K.C., through Zendaya, thus embodies the Exceptional Multiracial hero: she is a spy, working for the American government, who has brown skin and unclear ethnicity. Zendaya, as K.C., also acts as a bridge between her Black family and her White community through Marissa (Veronica Dunne), K.C.'s best friend since kindergarten who is White. Marissa is often treated like one of the family, the only non-family member who knows what they do. K.C. (Zendaya) creates a bridge between her Black family and the White community through her friendship, even going undercover as Marissa at one point, suggesting that Zendaya-as-KC can take the place of her White colleague (Dunne) as well as the Black characters she usually plays (such as K.C.) because she can transcend Blackness. She is more than Black, so she is a hero.

But Zendaya-as-K.C. does not exist in a void. The actress who plays her mother Kira, Tammy Townsend, is also biracial and likewise is presented as more heroic.[3] Of the two parents, Kira is consistently presented as more capable than her husband Craig who, like his son Ernie, is monoracially Black. For example, in "Spy of the Year Awards" (2016), both K.C. and Kira are nominated for a prestigious spying award, and neither Craig nor Ernie have ever been nominated. In fact, much of the series' humor comes from mocking how incompetent both Craig and Ernie are; even though K.C. and Kira have bad days, they are most often depicted as capable, especially as capable of fixing Craig and Ernie's mistakes. Joseph (2013) argues that women have historically been the multiracial image in America (pp. 4–5), and *K.C. Undercover* perpetuates that connection by casting multiracial actresses as the two Cooper women and monoracial Black men as the two Cooper men. The one exception is Judy, played by Trinitee Stokes, a monoracial Black girl. However, Judy is both a robot and another Sapphire stereotype who is often told she cannot and does not connect with people. In other words, when casting heroic female characters who are bridges to White communities, the creators cast multiracial women; when casting incompetent Black men or annoying sassy Black girls, they cast monoracial actors because they do not fit this new Exceptional Multiracial pattern.

All of this is to say that *K.C. Undercover* tries to strip race of its meaning in order to get rid of racism but ultimately denies the real-lived experience of Black people in our country. It holds up multiracial exemplars who do not complain about racial issues, suggesting that people of color who do are just not trying hard enough. It suggests that race is a thing of the past, negating all of the racial issues we still have today. Optimistically, I would call *K.C. Undercover* a valid yet futile attempt to avoid racism; realistically, I cannot help but see the series as an example of what Valdivia saw in the Disney Channel circa 2006 and what Turner saw in *The Princess and the Frog*: another bid to sanitize race in order to pull in an audience of color while also placating White audiences.

The Lack of Attention to Children's Media

Whereas *Jessie* wears its racism almost as a badge of honor, depicting diversity by compiling stereotypes, *K.C. Undercover* demonstrates the problem with pretending race does not matter in twenty-first-century America— it ignores the very real effects of racism. These racist tactics are not new, but that is the problem. The Disney Channel echoes conceptions of Blackness from *Amos 'n' Andy* and *The Cosby Show*, which were considered progressive by many White people but were often denigrated by the very community they were intended to represent. In other words, *Jessie* and *K.C. Undercover* recycle racism from the 1950s and 1980s and rebrand it for a new generation. While doing research on this project, I kept wondering why these shows would be so stuck in the past when Disney as a whole seems to be *trying* to be more progressive when it comes to race, as can be seen in films like *Moana* (2016), *Black Panther* (2018), or the newest *Star Wars* films (2015–2019), all from studios and franchises owned by Disney. I would like to believe that Disney is trying to use their cultural power for good, that they experiment with race to see how best to represent this complicated concept. Yet, even after *Jessie* ran for four seasons, accompanied by scattered complaints of racism, the Disney Channel created another show, *Bunk'd* (2015–), that follows Emma, Ravi, and Zuri Ross at summer camp, engaging in the same racial stereotypes as *Jessie*. Even after social and academic critics attacked Disney for their erasure and commodification of race in *The Princess and the Frog*, they did the same thing in *K.C. Undercover*.

Sadly, this recurring racism may simply be due to how much audiences do or do not hold Disney accountable. When audiences organize and push back on Disney's practices, things change: the creators of *The Princess and the Frog* removed its most glaring racist depictions as Disney responded to African American activists, critics, and scholars during the creation process, which then led the same filmmakers to create an Oceanic Story Trust of Pacific-Islanders to ensure cultural sensitivity when making *Moana*. A similar process occurred more recently when a trailer for *Ralph Breaks the Internet* (2018) revealed that a redesigned Tiana would be significantly whitewashed, looking more biracial than her original character, leading fans and activists to protest until Disney made a last-minute alteration to make the character look more like the original, dark-skinned princess. The constant call for Black superheroes led to not only the Black Panther as part of the Marvel Cinematic Universe but a *Black Panther* film created and populated with Black people and based in lore and visuals of real African tribes. Similarly, the complaints of the all-white world of science fiction led to several main characters in the new *Star Wars* films portrayed by people of color. When audiences refuse to be silent about Disney's mistakes, Disney changes because they have to in order to keep their image and their audience. But, despite the viewer voices I shared here, there has been no large outcry against the racial depictions of *Jessie* or *K.C. Undercover*, from fans, activists, parents, or even scholars, thus my reliance on only a select number of viewer voices in this essay instead of larger reception representation or scholarship on these shows. In short, the series continue to distort racial representation because there is not an organized presence marring Disney's image. Whereas films made by Walt Disney Animation, Marvel Studios, and Lucasfilm are watched by millions of audience members of all ages across the world, the Disney Channel, like much of children's television, is generally watched by children and possibly their families, a viewership that has largely migrated to Netflix and other streaming services, such as the Disney app and the forthcoming Disney Plus, leaving the Disney Channel more unobserved, and thus unaccountable.

Certain audience groups, specifically White audiences who may not notice the racism, may be more plugged into the Disney Channel than others, as can be seen in the one case of successful activism with these shows. Viewers did force the Disney Channel to change one problematic depiction in *Jessie*: the Disney Channel stopped airing an episode that features the main characters mocking a child with celiac disease for being gluten-fee (though the episode is still available online). According to Castillo (2013), parents of celiac children spoke to newspapers, created an online petition, and gathered on Reddit and blogs to explain the problem with this depiction. The Reddit page (2013) is full of commentary on how the Disney Parks system is extremely sensitive to allergy issues, which is why the Disney Channel's disregard to this issue surprised parents so much. These viewers are noticing the same trend I am: Disney Parks, which are full of adults, must be sensitive to dietary restrictions; the shows watched by children, on the other hand, do not seem to bother. I think there is much to be said about the fact that the issue on *Jessie* that garnered attention was the treatment of a child with celiac disease, *not* the series' racist caricatures. Studies from during *Jessie*'s airing suggest that White people are four times more likely to have celiac disease than people of color (Lehman 2015). In other words, the one issue that produced organized activism and thus change around either of these shows was one that affected White people, not people of color.

The implications here are concerning: media consumed by children and adults of multiple races garner enough interest to make Disney change racial depictions for the better; media consumed primarily by White children do not. Parents of color, like Jeff, may get angry about the Disney Channel's representation, but this anger does not lead to the online and in-person protests that engender change. White parents, on the other hand, do not seem to take racial depictions as seriously as the depictions of children with allergies, or, at least, may simply not know about the harmful stereotypes that Disney uses. Younger and younger children lend their voices to activism, yet seemingly not against the Disney Channel. This media outlet, one still viewed primarily by (White) children, seems easy to ignore and thus flies under the radar of viewers, activists, creators, and executives. Until people, adults and children, viewers and creators, care about race on the Disney Channel, nothing will change.

NOTES

1. The actor who played Luke, Cameron Boyce, tragically died due to health complications during the process of writing this essay. I respectfully acknowledge the death of this young actor whose character was problematic but who, in real life, reportedly cared deeply for all of his co-stars and often engaged in charity, including charities supporting people of color in the fight against gun violence.

2. While the terms "Black" and "African American" are often used interchangeably, in this essay, Black refers to the general conception of Black as a race while African American refers specifically to the communities of Black people in America. This distinction is helpful in discussing the differences between Zuri's birth nation (which is predominately Black, but is *not* African-American) and the African-American culture she seems to epitomize.

3. It should be noted that almost all of the women in the show, besides Judy and one Black female spy that is presented as haughty and mean, have light skin, engaging in colorism that values the least-Black skin tones possible. This is often, though not always, achieved through hiring biracial actresses, but it consistently couples feminine beauty with light skin.

REFERENCES

Beltrán, M., & Fojas, C. (2008). Introduction: Mixed race in Hollywood film and media culture. In M. Beltrán & C. Fojas (Eds.), *Mixed race Hollywood* (pp. 1–22). New York: New York University Press.

Briggs, L., & Marre, D. (2009). Introduction: The circulation of children. In D. Marre & L. Briggs (Eds.), *International adoption: Global inequalities and the circulation of children* (pp. 1–28). New York: New York University Press.

Brown, R. (2017). Mammy, angry Black lady, down ass bitch, and beyond: Representation of Black women in reality television. In J.L. Conyers, Jr. (Ed.), *Africana race and communication: A social study of film, communication, and social media* (pp. 105–119). Lanham, MD: Lexington Books.

Campbell, S.B., Giannino, S.S., China, C.R., & Harris, C.S. (2008). I love New York: Does New York love me? *Journal of International Women's Studies, 10*(2), 20–28.

Castillo, M. (2013 May 20). Disney pulls "Jessie" episode that makes fun of gluten-free child. *CBS News*. Retrieved from https://www.cbsnews.com/news/disney-pulls-jessie-episode-that-makes-fun-of-gluten-free-child/.

Chou, R.S., & Feagin, J.R. (2016). *The myth of the Model Minority: Asian Americans facing racism* (2nd ed.). London: Routledge.

City-Data (2018). Washington, District of Columbia. Retrieved from http://www.city-data.com/city/Washington-District-of-Columbia.html.

Donalson, M. (2003). *Black directors in Hollywood*. Austin: University of Texas Press.

Eells, P., Baker, P., & Vaupen, D. (Creators). (2011). *Jessie* [Television series]. Studio City, CA: It's a Laugh Productions.

Fatima, S. (2017, December 8). Let's talk about Disney's portrayl of Indians [online magazine article]. *Affinity magazine*, retrieved from http://culture.affinitymagazine.us/lets-talk-about-disneys-portrayal-of-indians/.

Foster, G.A. (1997). *Women filmmakers of the African and Asian diaspora: Decolonizing the gaze, locating subjectivity*. Carbondale: Southern Illinois University Press.

Gehlawat, A. (2010). The strange case of *The Princess and the Frog*: Passing and the elision of race. *Journal of African American Studies, 14*(4), 417–431.

Gregory, S.M. (2010). Disney's second line: New Orleans, racial masquerade, and the reproduction of whiteness in *The Princess and the Frog. Journal of African American Studies, 14*(4), 432–449.

Hurley, D.L. (2005). Seeing white: Children of color and the Disney fairy tale princess. *The Journal of Negro Education, 74*(3), 221–232.

Inniss, L.B., & Feagin, J.R. (2002). *The Cosby Show*: The view from the Black middle class. In R.R. Means Coleman (Ed.), *Say it loud: African-American audiences, media, and identity* (pp. 187–204). New York: Routledge.

Jeff. (2012, February 1). Is the portrayal of Ravi on Disney Channel's "Jessie" racist, unfunny, or both? [web log]. Retrieved from http://www.8asians.com/2012/02/01/is-the-portrayl-of-ravi-on-disney-channels-jessie-racist-unfunny-or-both/comment-page-1/.

Joseph, R.L. (2013). *Transcending Blackness: From the new millennium mulatta to the exceptional multiracial*. Durham, NC: Duke University Press.

kayfil. (2013, April 13). Why "Jessie" is the worst show on Disney Channel [web log]. Retrieved from https://kayfil.wordpress.com/2013/04/13/why-jessie-is-the-worst-show-on-disney-channel/.

Larrick, N. (1965). The all-white world of children's books. *Journal of African Children's and Youth Literature, 3*, 1–10.

Lehman, Shereen. (2015 March 18). More evidence for rise, and race difference, in U.S. celiac disease. *Reuters*. Retrieved from https://www.reuters.com/article/us-health-race-celiac-gluten-idUSKBN0ME2SY20150318.

Li, S. (2011). *Signifying without specifying: Racial discourse in the age of Obama*. New Brunswick, NJ: Rutgers University Press.

lumpyspaceprincess11. (2013, May 17). Disney should be ashamed of themselves. Making fun of gluten free children now? Please read and share (x-post from r/celiac). *Reddit*. Retrieved from https://www.reddit.com/r/glutenfree/comments/1ej2uv/disney_should_be_ashamed_of_themselves_making_fun/.

Marshall, C. (Creator) (2015). *K.C. Undercover* [Television series]. Studio City, CA: It's a Laugh Productions.

Miller, S., & Rode, G. (1995). The movie you see, the movie you don't. In E. Bell, L. Haas, &

L. Sells (Eds.), *From mouse to mermaid: The politics of film, gender, and culture* (pp. 86–103). Bloomington: Indiana University Press.

Myers, C. (2014, March 15). The apartheid of children's literature. *New York Times*. Retrieved from https://www.nytimes.com/2014/03/16/opinion/sunday/the-apartheid-of-childrens-literature.html.

Ono, K.A., & Buescher, D.T. (2001). *D*eciphering Pocahontas: Unpackaging the commodification of a Native American woman. *Critical Studies in Media Communication, 18*(1), 23–43.

Powell, A.H. (2017). Reflection: "Postracial." In P. McLaren (Ed.), *Rhetorics of whiteness: Postracial hauntings in popular culture, social media, and education* (pp. 19–21). Carbondale: Southern Illinois University Press.

Raiford, L., & Romano, R.C. (2006). Introduction: The struggle over memory. In R.C. Romano & L. Raiford (Eds.), *The Civil Rights movement in American memory* (pp. xi–xxiv). Athens, GA: The University of Georgia Press.

Sardar, Z. (1996). Walt Disney and the double victimisation of Pocahontas. *Third Text, 10*(37), 17–26.

Sharma, P.R. (2017, May 7). View: One of the main reasons why Indian-Americans are subjected to racial abuse in US. *The Economic Times*. Retrieved from https://economictimes.indiatimes.com/nri/nris-in-news/indian-americans-in-us-find-themselves-in-an-increasingly-strange-situation/articleshow/58554714.cms.

Squires, C. (2009). *African Americans and the media*. Malden, MA: Polity.

Top 10 reasons "Jessie" is a terrible show: Racism [Msg 1]. Retrieved from https://www.thetoptens.com/reasons-jessie-is-terrible-show/.

Towbin, M.A., Haddock S.A., Zimmerman T.S., Lund L.K., & Tanner L.R. (2004). Images of gender, race, age, and sexual orientation in Disney feature-length animated films. *Journal of Feminist Family Therapy, 15*(4), 19–44. https://doi.org/10.1300/J086v15n04_02.

Turner, S.E. (2013). Blackness, bayous and gumbo: Encoding and decoding race in a colorblind world. In J. Cheu (Ed.), *Diversity in Disney films: Critical essays on race, ethnicity, gender, sexuality and disability* (pp. 83–98). Jefferson, NC: McFarland.

Valdivia, A.N. (2008). Mixed race on the Disney Channel: From *Johnny Tsunami* through *Lizzie McGuire* and ending with *The Cheetah Girls*. In M.C. Beltran & C. Fojas (Eds*.) Mixed race Hollywood* (pp. 269–289). New York: NYU Press.

Willetts, K.R. (2013). Cannibals and coons: Blackness in the early days of Walt Disney. In J. Cheu (Ed.), *Diversity in Disney films: Critical essays on race, ethnicity, gender, sexuality and disability* (pp. 9–22). Jefferson, NC: McFarland.

Girl Meets "Woke"

Rowan Blanchard, Intersectionality and Fan Engagement

Christopher E. Bell, Marissa Lammon *and* Hanne Murray

"I believe in my generation. I believe in girls. I believe in women.

    I believe in people of color. I believe in the LGBTQ+ community.

    I believe. I believe."

                —Rowan Blanchard, November 11, 2016

Rowan Blanchard, born in 2001, is a social media superstar. Her daily collage of intersectional feminist thought both reflects the shifting landscape of what it means to be an American teenager in 2017 and presents a whole new way of being a teen celebrity. Initially drawing media attention for her starring role in popular Disney Channel tween show *Girl Meets World*, 15-year-old Blanchard regularly posts a variety of news articles, personal opinions, and emotional reactions to current events through her social media accounts, including original and re-posted pictures, links and status updates. Her 4.7 million Instagram followers share in her content, which extends beyond typical, teenage, superficial concerns. Blanchard primarily avoids displaying preferences for products, discussing physical body aspirations or focusing on appearance—values that often garner status for girls and women, particularly for celebrities in popular media. Instead, she focuses her time on, and constructs her own identity with, posts that highlight problems of privilege: who has it, who does not, and why. Blanchard's commentary delves into issues of race, gender, class, sexual orientation and other barriers that define American power structures. As a 21st-century teenaged American woman of Middle-Eastern descent, Blanchard is simultaneously aware of her privilege and her oppression and advocates for equality. She invites conversations regarding the sublime structures of American popular culture that interact to create hegemonic systems which delegate and manage the acquisition and loss of power. Her social media content, interview subject choices, and transitional character traits shown through her on-screen character, Riley, force passive audiences to pay attention to varying degrees of societal elements of power that are kept beneath the surface and deliberately masked by intensive marketing for performative gender purposes. Through an intersectional feminist lens, Rowan Blanchard uses her platform as a celebrity to advocate awareness of hegemonic forces, perpetuate active participation in defining dominant ideologies, and encourage the understanding of people by looking at their culture.

To view Rowan Blanchard's Instagram and Twitter accounts is to view an emotional journey into defining personal identity by defining the cultural identity of American politics, social norms and systems of privilege and oppression. Blanchard defines who she is publicly by defining who she is not. She actively resists allowing generalizations where specificity exists by displaying uncomfortable content that is uncommon in tween and early teen discourse. Rowan Blanchard is not the typical 15-year-old. To compare her photo and text content to many other teen and tween queens is to see a completely different emphasis on belonging, standing apart, cultural definition and demonstrations of success. Blanchard condemns essentialism, the tendency to discursively reduce a whole group of people to a number of essential and usually negative characteristics. In response to the 2016 presidential election, announcing then President-elect Donald Trump, Blanchard posted a photograph of herself crying, covered in Photoshop scrawls of "We Exist." (Figure 1) Subsequent content derides President-elect

Figure 1. Rowan Blanchard, November 9, 2016, 1:15 a.m. (Blanchard, 2016b).

Trump, but also questions American culture in general. Blanchard comments on accepted American systems of oppression that subjugate women to the inactive function of objects to be viewed. Blanchard is mindful of other contributing distinguishing distinctions, and includes content regarding class, sexual orientation and race to the argument of gender biases, therefore embracing an intersectional feminist lens.

Blanchard's social media feminism is coupled with a starring role on a major Disney Channel network program. This duality of intertextual presence creates a delicate tension between real-life Rowan and on-screen Riley, as both grow up and evolve in the media spotlight. As Rowan publicly delved deeper into her own identity, her own activism, and her own world view, Riley's growth as a character was necessarily affected. This moved the Disney Channel into a space where programming executives had to make a choice—how real should Riley get in a show aimed at the 9- to 12-year-old market?

A Boy Meets World *Revival*

In November of 2012, it was announced that a sequel to *Boy Meets World* had entered development with original creator Michael Jacobs (Roots, 2012). By the end of the month, both original cast members Ben Savage and Danielle Fishel had announced their reprisals of Cory Matthews and Topanga Lawrence, respectively (@BenSavage, 2012; @daniellefishel, 2012). Rowan Blanchard, 11 years old at the time, was cast as Cory and Topanga's daughter, Riley, by January of 2013 (Stransky, 2013), with 13-year-old Sabrina Carpenter taking on the role of best friend Maya (Hibberd, 2013). Although the initial plan was to have the focus of the show float back and forth between Cory/Topanga and Riley/Maya (Schwartz, 2013), the younger pair very quickly became the more compelling duo. Before the pilot was even aired, the Disney Channel expanded its buy from 13 to 21 episodes for a full first season, a remarkable "major vow of confidence" for an unaired project (Arruda, 2014).

Girl Meets World debuted on June 27, 2014, to mostly favorable reviews. In its debut, it was the top original cable program on the air (tvbythenumbers, 2014), and ended its first season as the number one television program among children 2 to 14 years old (Bacle, 2014). Fans of *Boy Meets World* discovered almost instantly that the show was not "for" them; critics complained that "the millennials who couldn't wait for it to begin are the ones who aren't going to bother to watch" and that "it's funny, but not to us. Because we're not 12 years old anymore" (Fallon, 2014). *Girl Meets World* was renewed for a second season in August of 2014, and for a third season in November of 2015. During the third season, it was announced that the program would be canceled at the end of the season; the 2.74 million viewer average of the first season dipped to 2.28 million average in the second season, but plummeted to just above 1 million viewers average in season three (Kraft, 2016). Rumors began to swirl that the show's increasingly mature content forced the Disney Channel to reconsider the program in its lineup, and that an alternate Disney network, such as Freeform, might be a viable and appropriate venue for a fourth season after all (Vishnoi, 2016); a Twitter campaign has formed, begging an outside partner such as Netflix or Hulu to pick the show up and revive it. It should be noted here that aside from the nine seasons of *Kids Incorporated*, which ran from 1984 to 1993, no live action Disney Channel–exclusive fictional show has ever aired for more than four seasons. *Girl Meets World's* three season run is within the standard series length for the vast majority of Disney Channel tween shows.

The increasing maturity of the storylines may be attributed to the increasing age of the show's two main stars, but it may also be attributed to Rowan Blanchard's increasing engagement in feminist activism on social media (particularly Twitter and Instagram). Blanchard's rising feminist awakening has bled back into *Girl Meets World* storylines in ways one might not traditionally expect from Disney Channel tween programming, especially when contrasted with programs that are its contemporaries, such as *Liv and Maddie*, *Stuck in the Middle*, and *Bizaardvark*.

The Tween Market

The tween market is generally considered to be children between the ages of 9 and 12 years old, and has been described as "too old for Ronald McDonald and too young for car keys" (Simpson, Douglas, & Schimmel, 1998, p. 637). The category of "tween" or "tweenager" emerged as a marketing target primarily because they are a "$335 billion market … that's a powerful consumer, so that includes not only her spending, but the influence on the family spending" (Leung, 2004). The term "tween" "refers to the concept of being 'in-between' a child and a teen, which is not necessarily tied to a particular age, but rather connected to a state of mind or behaviors" (Prince & Martin, 2011, p. 96). As a cohort, with considerable disposable income and no bills or necessities on which to spend, the tween demographic is highly prized by corporations such as Disney:

> tweens are a sizeable direct market and they are a market which companies hope to start early with brand loyalty. They are described as hyper brand conscious (in areas of cosmetics, music, apparel, consumer electronics, and film), spend a lot of time with peers and are peer influenced. They grow up faster, are more connected, more direct, more informed, have more personal power, more money, more influence and attention than previous generations [Prince & Martin, 2011, p. 96].

In order to capture this market, Disney has developed a slate of tween sitcoms and mild dramas, dating back to 1988's *Good Morning, Miss Bliss* (which starred Disney icon Haley Mills and eventually was retooled into '90s afternoon staple *Saved by the Bell*). Disney Channel's live action programming really began to take hold in 1998, with programs like *The Famous Jett Jackson* and *So Weird,* but it was the 2001 hit *Lizzie McGuire* that made the most impact in terms of the market. By 2003, *Lizzie McGuire* merchandise was earning nearly $100 million for Disney, and its star, Hilary Duff, was a megacelebrity (Boorstin, 2003). In 2005, live action programming dominated the Disney Channel's lineup: *The Suite Life of Zack & Cody, Wizards of Waverly Place, Good Luck Charlie*, and *Hannah Montana* propelled the channel forward; *Hannah Montana,* in 2006, set the record for the most total viewers of any basic cable series telecast in history with 10.7 million viewers—tweens made up 4.1 million of those viewers (Andreeva, 2007).

Currently, the Disney Channel airs almost exclusively tween programming; *Girl Meets World* airs alongside *Liv and Maddie, K.C. Undercover, Best Friends Whenever, Bunk'd, Stuck in the Middle, Walk the Prank, Bizaardvark*, and *Mako Mermaids*, with reruns of canceled programs such as *Jessie* and *Austin & Ally* still running. Series stars, such as Dove Cameron (*Liv and Maddie*), Zendaya Coleman (*K.C. Undercover*) and Jenna Ortega (*Stuck in the Middle*) are following in the footsteps of Hilary Duff and Miley Cyrus as tween celebrity icons, and it is within this environment that Rowan Blanchard operates. Both *Girl Meets World* as a program and Rowan Blanchard as a celebrity symbiotically work to address identity issues with a tween audience in a way other Disney Channel programming (and, historically, other Disney Channel tween stars) do not.

Girl Meets World

Initially, *Girl Meets World* is a stereotypical Disney Channel tween sitcom. In the pilot, Riley joins a middle school rebellion, meets her long-time love interest Lucas, and establishes the nature of her friendship with Maya. The next few episodes are standard situation comedy tropes: Riley gets jealous that Lucas is paying attention to another girl (Fang & Zwick, 2014); Cory gets upset that Riley would rather go to a school dance than honor their yearly tradition of riding a roller coaster (Barnes & Zwick, 2014). In S1E5, Riley and Maya try to decide if and when it is a good idea to lie (Nelson & Zwick, 2014). These types of issues have been raised in sitcoms aimed at teens for generations, and are nothing out of the ordinary.

In S1E6, titled "Girl Meets Popular," the first glimpses of *Girl Meets World* taking some of these familiar storylines down new paths can be seen. The base plot of the episode is Riley being invited to her first boy/girl party; again, a typical tween storyline. However, the story takes a unique turn when Riley discovers the party is full of boys—unpopular "nerd" boys. The next day, Riley arrives at school in a full Harajuku outfit (or, at least, an American understanding of Harajuku clothing)—because she is the only girl who will talk to these boys, Riley is made their queen (Menell & Rosenbaum, 2014). Harajuku culture "offers a mesmerizing panoply of silhouettes, colors, textures, and labels; the aggressively stylized, the excessively accessorized, the unapologetically restless" (Godoy & Varianian, 2007, p. 10). Harajuku street fashion is one of the most internationally recognizable elements of Japanese culture, uniquely Japanese both in origin and execution (Nakao, 2016). American singer Gwen Stefani's blatant and disturbing misappropriation of Harajuku culture in 2004 was widely reviled (Alexandra, 2016; Dockterman, 2014; Lang, 2014; Russell, 2016), but was largely responsible for introducing Harajuku culture to American audiences. Avril Lavigne similarly grossly misappropriated Harajuku culture with 2014's music video for "Hello Kitty"; Lavigne, like Stefani, brushed off criticism that her use of Japanese women as set dressing was intensely racist (Wells, 2014).

Riley's misappropriation of Harajuku culture is a pointed criticism of white audiences adopting Japanese styles as bourgeois suburban fashion statements; a middle school audience may immediately connect to instances in their own lives of white friends embracing anime, kawaii culture, or Harajuku styles. It is Maya who first and most directly confronts Riley about her cultural misappropriation:

> MAYA: Come on. This is not who you are. What do you know about being a Harajuku girl?
> RILEY: I don't have to know anything except they (*indicates boys*) love it. Sorry, Maya [Menell & Rosenbaum, 2014].

Riley's response that the "nerd boys" love her new style is a double-sided issue for *Girl Meets World* viewers—first, that Riley is willing to change her personal style to attract boys, and second, that the clothes she adopts in order to do so are not okay for her to wear. Later in the episode, Topanga addresses the issue purposefully with her daughter:

> TOPANGA: Is this the best part of you?
> RILEY: I'm extremely popular with five people.
> TOPANGA: Is one of them you? [Menell & Rosenbaum, 2014].

The trope—changing one's self to fit in—is not original. However, the added layer of cultural misappropriation, especially for the tween audience in such a straightforward, unapologetic way, is groundbreaking. Maya never lets up on Riley throughout the episode, culminating in a scene at the city regional spelling bee, in which Maya sneaks a new word into the competition: *Hara-*

juku. When Riley asks for the meaning of the word, Cory responds that it is a real neighborhood in Japan where actual Japanese girls designed a style that is authentic to their own lives. The implication here is clear: this style does not and should not belong to Riley. If the implication is not enough, Maja makes it plain: "Stop pretending to be a Harajuku girl, because you're not" [Menell & Rosenbaum, 2014].

This open rebuke of Riley's cultural misappropriation by her best friend, the character who is most positioned as the "cool girl," makes it crystal clear to a tween audience that adopting the styles of other cultures for one's own personal gain is unacceptable. Riley goes back to her own unique style, Maya reinforces how much she cares about the "real" Riley, and the episode ends on a high note. The message is unambiguous—one's friends like authenticity more than trends that may exploit other cultures.

The remainder of the first season vacillates between tween sitcom tropes (Riley asks Maya to teach her how to flirt with Lucas) (Fang & Zwick, 2014) and more serious issues surrounding identity (Riley and Maya mistake a black woman on the subway for a homeless person; it turns out she is the CEO of a Fortune 500 company) (Otero & Zwick, 2014). In S1E12, "Girl Meets the Forgotten," the kids learn to appreciate their custodians and lunch room workers, to whom they have never taken the time to speak, directly addressing social class (Menell & Zwick, 2014). In "Girl Meets Friendship" (S1E14), there is a frank, open debate about the merits and drawbacks of communism vs. the merits and drawbacks of capitalism (Blutman & Whitesell, 2014).

By the second season, *Girl Meets World* has learned to navigate identity issues without turning the plot into a "very special episode." "Very special episodes" are abnormally serious episodes of a television series in which "the lead confronts some highly emotional or forbidden issue from everyday life[: d]rug abuse, teenage sex, bulimia…. At the end of the episode, the protagonist is <u>enlightened</u>, and the guest character with the Very Special Problem is never seen or heard from again. Often there is an 800 number to call, should you (or someone you love) actually have the Very Special Problem" (tvtropes, 2015). "Very special episodes" are typically maudlin at best, and often downright depressing; "viewers used to cackling audiences wooing over the appearances of the wacky neighbor suddenly [find] themselves faced with sexual abuse, teenage pregnancy, and death by drunk-driving" (Millard, 2015).

Girl Meets World avoids this because, by the second season, it has been established that nearly every episode is essentially a dramedy. Viewers are used to having serious issues inserted into the comedy; even an episode like S2E1, in which the kids move to the eighth grade and have to deal with a new teacher who is not as enamored with them as they are used to, ends with the death of a recurring side character (Barnes & Strong, 2015). This priming of the audience allows *Girl Meets World* to more effectively deal with otherwise

"Very Special Episode" topics, such as Asperger's Syndrome. In *Girl Meets Farkle* (S2E15), it is discovered that Farkle Minkus, one of the main characters of the program, may have Asperger's Syndrome (Blutman & Garson, 2015). Asperger's Syndrome is an autism-spectrum disorder that affects approximately 1 in 250 children (Genetic Home Reference, 2011)—common enough that by middle school, most tweens probably have encountered at least one classmate with Asperger's. The kids initially reject the idea that one of their best friends may have an autism-spectrum disorder; Maya tries especially hard to make excuses for Farkle's behaviors. She rejects the idea that Farkle is "awkward;" she ignores his various obsessions. By the time Farkle implores, "Please don't ever let me not understand love (Blutman & Garson, 2015), Maja is forced to concede defeat.Later, it is revealed that Farkle does not, in fact, have Asperger's Syndrome—but his girlfriend, Isadora Smackle, does. By moving Asperger's from Farkle, a main character, to Smackle, a secondary character, *Girl Meets World* is allowed to continue to bring up disability as an identity narrative without making it necessary to constantly address it with a major character. Smackle's Asperger's Syndrome is a topic of conversation in multiple subsequent episodes, and, most importantly, is prescriptively normalized. It is not a "Very Special Episode"; it is an integral part of the character that adds to the diversity of the show and forces the tween audience to continually confront the reality that people with disabilities are a normal part of society.

Similarly, "Girl Meets STEM" (S2E26) unambiguously challenges the idea that boys are better at science than girls. While this is not the first openly feminist narrative of the series, it is the first time that feminist terminology works its way into the dialogue. The plot opens in eighth grade science class, where the teacher, Mr. Norton, has assigned an experiment: drop a marble into a beaker of solution and record what happens. Immediately, all of the boys open their notebooks to make observations, and all of the girls pick up the marbles to drop them. Riley balks, then complains to Maya as class ends that girls have to drop the marble while the boys get to "do the science," ignoring what Riley calls "social injustice" (Kale, Strong & Strong 2016).

Maya's character has a history of not being invested in school, and therefore is perfectly happy to take the path of least resistance, in order to do the least amount of work. Riley, persists, but is ultimately shut down by Maja:

RILEY: You are not going to drop your marble.
MAYA: Oh, I'm gonna drop my marble, but to make you feel better, I'm gonna drop it like a dude. [Kale, Strong & Strong, 2016].

Maya dismisses Riley's concerns as inconsequential; she is willing to drop the marble "like a dude," which, in her mind, equates boys' behavior with athletics. This is an equally problematic narrative, which positions Maya as

Riley's foil, in addition to being her best friend. The contentious nature of their friendship, as they are two very different kinds of girls, is part of the ongoing *Odd Couple* chemistry of the pair. Later in the episode, the feminist outpouring begins:

> RILEY: It all started with Eve. Women have been treated as second-class citizens ever since. Thank goodness for strong women like Queen Elizabeth, then Susan B. Anthony helped get women the vote, and then Betty Friedan wrote *The Feminine Mystique*, and then Riley Matthews refused to drop the marble, and then here we are [Kale, Strong & Strong, 2016].

Riley not only presents a feminist timeline that links herself to strong women throughout history, but specifically invokes the foundational feminist text *The Feminine Mystique*. The average tween has no idea who Betty Friedan is, but there is a chance that thousands, maybe even millions, of tweens Googled her following this program. *Girl Meets World*'s feminist undercurrent should come as little surprise, especially to now-adult fans of *Boy Meets World*. One of the key draws of the original series was Danielle Fishel's Topanga Lawrence, the daughter of two hippies marching to the beat of her own drummer. Fishel herself has described Topanga as "a feminist [who] was a little different and … incredibly smart" (Murray & Okazaki, 2014).

Eventually, Riley's feminist stand convinces Maya, and the rest of the girls in the class, that their complicity in their own marginalization is unacceptable. This is another theme of the Riley/Maya relationship; they make each other better people, and open up alternative possibilities to each other in nearly every episode:

> MAYA: You think I could be a scientist?
> RILEY: I think if you were a scientist, the world would be a very dangerous place.
> MAYA: Awesome!
> RILEY: But if you don't believe you could become a scientist, then it's even more dangerous [Kale, Strong & Strong, 2016].

The real experiment had nothing to do with marbles or beakers or solutions. The real experiment was designed to test the willingness of middle school girls to actively participate in science. In middle school, as science gets more difficult, there is external pressure on girls to focus elsewhere; Riley's protest is framed as a "good test result" (Kale, Strong & Strong, 2016).

Girl Meets World defines itself as a show explicitly about identity issues by the third season. Nearly every episode has abandoned the typical tween sitcom plotlines for more substantive topics; the show, by the third season, really cannot even be classified as a sitcom—it has fully embraced an existence as a dramedy. In S3E3, Riley invents an online persona named Jexica, who then becomes the most popular girl in school; it is a commentary on social media merged with a commentary on identity (Yeager, Strong & Strong, 2016).

Much of the season is devoted to exploring Maya's socioeconomic status; she is poor, her mother is a struggling actress that works as a waitress, and Maya often alludes to lacking what other characters have. Because she is poor, in "Girl Meets True Maya" (S3E7), it is revealed that she has spent time on the streets. Her former street friends attempt to goad Maya into vandalizing the local park; Maya decides that is no longer who she is (Nelson & Fishel, 2016). "Girl Meets Sassy Haltertop" (S3E11) explores homelessness and the nature of good and evil (Jacobs & Savage, 2016). In S3E13, "Girl Meets the Great Lady of New York," Farkle learns his great-grandparents died in a Nazi concentration camp, and that his family is actually Jewish (Menell, Strong & Strong, 2016). This religious diversity returns in S3E18, "Girl Meets a Christmas Maya," as Riley gives Farkle a menorah for "Secret Santa," which initially offends him, but he later finds the gift comes from a place of love. This particular episode is also noteworthy because it is the first time the program openly acknowledges that in S2E3, the writers added the secondary character of Zay Babineaux. Zay is black, and Lucas's best friend from Texas. From the introduction of Zay until S3E18, almost nothing is done to flesh out Zay's back story or character. The main characters hang out with Zay every day; Zay comes over to their houses and participates in all of their activities for almost two full seasons. He is not a casual friend; he is an essential part of the group. It is unlikely that, after being friends for so long, no one would know anything about Zay Babineaux. During "Secret Santa," this is something that Farkle and Smackle candidly admit; neither of them are even able to figure out something as simple as what he might like as a Secret Santa gift. The recognition that the black character is someone no one else bothered to get to know better is courageous for any program, let alone a tween Disney Channel program. It is doubtful that many other Disney Channel programs could successfully deliver the type of identity narratives that *Girl Meets World* manages, which is partly due to the construction of the show, and partly due to the intertextuality of Rowan Blanchard's celebrity status.

Celebrity and Social Media

Celebrities in popular culture tend to function as opinion leaders and endorsers in the United States and other Western countries (Bell, 2010), particularly for teen and tween audiences (Brown, Lusch, & Nicholson, 1996; Marwick, 2013; Shoham & Ruvio, 2008). This ability to motivate young adult audiences in advocacy is exacerbated in a contemporary new media environment in which social media is king; social mass media create a unique environment in which the individual can, with enough followers, create social movements and cultural power previously reserved for local, grassroots efforts. This mediated environment—the *mediasphere*—has the potential to facilitate "reciprocity, mutual support, participation, intergenerational dialogue, self sufficiency and receptiveness" (Lopez, 2012, p. viii) with much greater success than face-to-face interaction. This more democratic usage of social media, such as Facebook, Twitter, and Instagram, opens a space for social justice advocacy, as the creation of content is placed directly into the hands of the user, without intervention from a corporate entity with a necessity to sell commodities. In short, the individual user can create nearly whatever content s/he pleases, specifically for a self-selected and receptive audience, with little or no real, negative consequence. In the hands of a celebrity, with intertextual appeal (Bell, 2010), a Twitter account can become a vehicle for social justice like few others. Much of the literature surrounding the relationship between tween audiences and celebrities focuses on the marketing of products (Vares & Jackson, 2015; Prince & Martin, 2012; Potter & Hill, 2016; McGladrey, 2014). But if that marketing power was turned to social issues instead of marketing products, the celebrity in question would be well positioned to do a remarkable amount of good through clever use of the combination of the mediasphere and traditional intertexts, such as television and film.

The concept of

"anticipatory enculturation" to teenagerdom … describe[s] the age ambiguity, forward-looking nature, and "in-betweenness" of the Tween market, which results from the tension between trying to meet girls' ever-pressing demands for a sense of autonomy and personhood (i.e., encoded in looking 'older') and yet 'keeping' them in the Tween category and store. Anticipatory enculturation encourages Tweens to experiment with the … consumption practices that advertisers prescribe for teen[s] … allowing retailers to groom a group of new consumers who are responsible for billions of dollars in purchases per year [McGladrey, 2014, p. 355].

A large part of tweens' "consumption and media participation increasingly involve performances in the relatively public spaces of social media, mobile media, and the Internet … so the public sphere of consumption is full of exuberant participation in mass-mediated publics" (Bickford, 2015, p. 66). If tweens do, in fact, "interpret the lifestyles of celebrities … as normative for their everyday behavior and prerequisite for social acceptance" (McGladrey, 2014, p. 354), then the celebrity in the mediasphere has the potential to shape the way his or her followers construct their view of the world. Tweens are an ideal target audience for social media celebrity advocacy, in part because of the normative capability of celebrity, and in part because "86% of girls think that something is cool if they have seen it on the internet; … 81% of boys" (Costa, 2010).

Using One's Power for Good

Unlike television, radio, and film in its intensity and plasticity, social media epitomizes an elaborate network of interminable material in a rapid, perpetual state of flux. At any given time, online content will reflect current trends, conflicts, products, and standards, irrespective of temporal boundaries and restrictions present in other mass media outlets. Yet, regardless of the instantaneous updates, there exists a near antithetical relationship between mass media and the adult versus adolescent interpretation, assimilation, and incorporation of the material presented. The tween social media realm today reflects the very nature of the adolescent mind—anxiety, attachment, and introspection—manifested and developed in social and cultural contexts "segregated from adult society" (Micheli, 2016, p. 567). The tween audience represents a group of developing individuals existing in an equivocal environment, rife with media messages and adult influences coupled with respective adolescent developmental obstacles, making social media platforms like Instagram and Twitter outlets for tweens to uncover what their peers think of them, as well as who and how many people like them (Simmons). With hidden, yet understood, "rules" regarding online behavior aimed to produce the maximum amount of likes, followers, and tweets/re-tweets, the average tween profile includes themes related to personal demographic information, romantic relationships, friends, parents, popular culture, school, and self-expression (Williams & Merten, 2008). These superficial threads have permeated tween social media primarily as a means for adolescents to maintain conflict-free energy while presenting a publicly acceptable version of the ideal self (Williams & Merten, 2008; Erikson, 1994). For Rowan Blanchard, social media serves a far more progressive purpose; unlike her tween peers or celebrity counterparts, Blanchard relies on social media to disseminate political and feminist activism and elicit mobilization and involvement among those she reaches (Rosman, 2016).

Setting aside Blanchard's celebrity status for a moment reveals a teen girl with feminist consciousness "colliding with a postfeminist culture" (Lowe, 2003, p. 125). She undergoes the confusing, chaotic milestones present during adolescence, but reflects on her experience from a higher state of consciousness:

> My co-dependent relationship with self-blame and self-deprecation as a means of self-defense has held me tightly since I can remember. It felt safer and less terrifying to silence myself to a degree than to actually engage with people, and make them take responsibility for their own actions. I have treated, specifically, male feelings and ego as superior to and more fragile than my own [Blanchard, 2016e].

Self-blame, self-deprecation, and gender disparities are not uncommon in adolescence; what separates Rowan Blanchard from her adolescent peers are her levels of introspection and ubiquitous exemplification of *sonder*, which has been accepted and understood as "the realization that each random passerby is living a life as vivid and complex as your own" (Koeing, 2012). Rather than using interview opportunities to increase popularity and engage in frivolous conversation, she comments on patriarchy, oppression, and intersectionality (Kantor, 2016).

Blanchard's social media accounts are filled with social causes; she challenges the stereotypical tween social media content by boldly testing her emerging feminist language, unconcerned with popularity. Stereotypical themes of romantic relationships and friends are replaced with themes of politics, intersectionality, feminism, and sexuality—all with an underlying motif of inclusion. From presidential and congressional nominations to hot topics like gun control and immigration, Blanchard establishes a political presence through an ample amount of posts dedicated to facilitating change. Her passion shines through in each post; for example, her devastation when commenting on gun control:

> How can you not see the news and see we need #GunControlNow? Fifty people are dead. The worst U.S. shooting in history! What will it take? … I can't be light about this anymore because it's terrifying to see my friends too scared to leave the house because of all the shootings [Blanchard, 2016d; Blanchard 2016c].

In instances of immigration and proposed regulations against sexuality, anger and subtle passive aggression take the stage: "NO BAN NO WALL IMMIGRANTS ARE AMERICA NO HUMAN BEING IS ILLEGAL … yr president bragged about sexual assault & now is in the White House & yet u r scared about trans girls who just want 2 go 2 the bathroom?" (Blanchard, 2017l; Blanchard, 2017c). While her passionate tone presents itself in different forms according to different topics, the fervent nature of her posts escalates in efficacy when providing the means necessary to elicit change:

> Republican senators who are on the fence about DeVos—most important to call them—leave a voicemail! … Download the @ACLU's free Mobile Justice app—important to have as police quickly militarize…. Also—another useful resource to start using daily (BoycottTrump) … LA—our senator Dianne Feinstein has remained silent about the nomination of Scott Pruit—her office number is 310–914-7300 [Blanchard 2017d; Blanchard 2017e; Blanchard 2017f; Blanchard 2017a].

By presenting tangible action through phone numbers, mobile applications, and websites, Blanchard takes activism several steps further and supplies the vehicle for social change. This approach extends beyond a political nature and floods her Twitter across all categories, with the most prevalent being women's rights.

Although heavily incorporated into her Twitter, Blanchard saturates her Instagram with images and captions demonstrative of her feminist views.

Posts feature text similar to her tweets: "Girls own power—the power to be your own savior and worst enemy—there is no in between. Girls are forever tied to the metaphorical.... All concrete terms are reserved exclusively for white men" (Blanchard, 2016a) but also utilize the profound influence of images; one post features a photo of a sketched, nude woman with inscribed text, "TAKE UP SPACE," followed by a lengthy caption ending with, "okay ladies now let's get in formation," encouraging female solidarity and equality through voting, donations, and dispersing of information (Blanchard, 2017m). While most tween social media sites are riddled with heavily edited "selfies," Blanchard has nearly 2,000 posts and less than 0.05 percent would be considered a "selfie"—instead, she fills her account with images of powerful, influential women in history: Jovita Idar, Marsha P. Johnson, Angela Davis, and Frida Kahlo, as well as feminist literature that she reads: *Girls on Fire*, *Hope in the Dark*, and *Pioneer Doctor: The Story of a Woman's Work*.

As a teen celebrity, keenly aware of not only the world around her, but her influential role as a public figure in social change, Rowan Blanchard has interwoven her burgeoning enlightenment into social media activism. Celebrities occupy a unique "stopping power" which is viewed as "the capability of drawing attention and interest ... in a very cluttered media environment" (Belch & Belch, 2013, p. 370). Blanchard uses her "stopping power" for good and insists other celebrities to do the same, disheartened by the lack of education and encouragement of social cause on celebrity social media: "Don't understand the mainly celebrity fear of not speaking so u don't lose ur audience—your silence doesn't keep u safe and it never will" (Blanchard, 2017j). She understands that "the internet is an escape for many" but that it ultimately serves a "larger service ... to help educate people to get on the side of the good" and sees "silence for fear of losing followers" as "the saddest use of the Internet" (Blanchard, 2017h; Blanchard, 2017i). While her tween peers and fellow celebrities may be unable to see the role they play in social change, Blanchard takes it upon herself to serve as the educator, tweeting, "Not saying every celebrity has to be an activist, but am saying accountability culture exists and pretending nothings wrong will only hurt u.... YOUR SILENCE WILL NOT PROTECT YOU" (Blanchard, 2017g; Blanchard, 2017k). Not only does she share feminist, political, and inclusive material on all social media accounts, she provides an outlet for change and encourages all others to do the same.

This ambitious call to action for all audiences reflects the very inclusiveness Blanchard aims to achieve in her activism, having made a priority that her "personal feminism includes everyone," through education and discussion (Blanchard, 2015). A particularly notable feature of the tween celebrity is her ability to facilitate productive discussion, primarily through her nondiscriminatory language. Unlike several activists, she does not devote all of her attention and efforts to any one group; instead, she challenges common misconceptions of modern feminism by opening discussion for discrepancies beyond just men and women, but women of different races as well, incorporating intersectionality into her cause and writings:

> The way a black woman experiences sexism and inequality is different from the way a white woman experiences sexism and inequality. Likewise with trans-women and Hispanic women…. While white women are making 78 cents to the dollar, Native American women are making 65 cents, black women are making 64 cents, and Hispanic women are making 54 cents…. To acknowledge feminism from a one sided view when the literal DEFINITION is the equality of the sexes is not feminism at all. We need to be talking about this more. Discussion leads to change [Blanchard, 2015].

Promoting conversations surrounding mainstream social injustices serves as the essence of Blanchard's movement(s) due to her view of activism as "a need to know, a need to explain, and a need to help" (Blanchard & Shahidi, 2016). Yet, despite her articulate, inclusive composition, Blanchard once again proves herself an outlier through the level of introspection she demonstrates on her role in contributing to social injustices. Previously unaware of the privileges she herself occupies over other members of society, she addresses the importance of education and self-reflection on social change, "the thing about privilege is, often times you don't even have to think about the inequality when you don't have to face it…. I am constantly trying to check my privilege … you have to always question your politics: Am I being as inclusive as I possibly can?" (Blanchard & Shahidi, 2016). The self-analysis that Blanchard participates in and publicizes contributes to the strong identification that other girls develop toward her, with Blanchard consistently commenting on her imperfections and encouraging an accepting society. From hoping that the "Internet feminism climate gives room to mess up, correct yourself, and learn" to demolishing praises of superiority exclaiming, "I am figuring this out just as much as you are," she is encouraging deep and distinct discussion that originates from the desire to learn and grow intrinsically and, subsequently, extrinsically (Blanchard, 2017b; Blanchard & Shahidi, 2016).

Unsurprisingly, then, Blanchard's active and galvanizing lifestyle off-screen makes its way into her fictional character role on-screen. Eager to utilize her influential position beyond the social media domain, she clearly invested a significant amount of time and effort into incorporating her real-world advocacies into *Girl Meets World* (Connolly, 2016). Similar to her social media accounts, the show resonates with teenagers through themes of self-discovery and self-forgiveness as well as imperfect characters "struggling to figure out their place in the world," but also features bits of Blanchard's feminist activism with underlying messages of girl solidarity and women role models diverse in age, race, and appearance (Bowman, 2016). Essentially, *Girl Meets World* developed, alongside its female teenage star, into a well-informed, enlightened piece of social change. Of course, this is part of the reason why the show was ultimately canceled early. The program outgrew its audience.

Girl Meets "Woke"

On January 20, 2017, *Girl Meets World* aired its final episode on the Disney Channel. Two days later, Rowan Blanchard took the stage at the Women's March in Los Angeles, California—part of the largest mass protest in American history. She spoke eloquently of her fears of a Trump presidency, and the need for solidarity, particularly among her contemporaries:

> The idea of fighting any fight alone is one that terrifies me, and I am lucky to fall back on a generation that believes in the same morals I do. My generation, who I am so honored to stand representing right now, knows exactly what is going on, despite what many adults tell us. We know what's happening because it's happening to us too. We are so actively engaged in this conversation surrounding intersectionality and what freedom actually means that we are willing to risk our lives for it. It is a time so vulnerable that we see the world in two very honest ways: human rights, or the lack thereof. My generation is made up of activist friends in England, in Japan, in France and more, and we have never met each other in person. We are a generation that recognizes the collective power and potential that can be generated through social media, and we work to educate one another when we do not understand. This is largely overlooked by the news and in general politics simply because we cannot vote.... Speaking about my generation doesn't feel like politics because for my brothers and my sisters, my best friends and myself, it is incredibly personal. This is our life, and I hope, knowing in four years, we will be able to vote for something that is good [Maturo, 2017].

Blanchard tacitly recognizes the incredible amount of power in her intertextuality, the ways in which her celebrity can, through social and traditional media, elicit change. She is speaking directly to her fans, a much more politically and technically savvy generation than those that have come before. This girl has met the world, and is attempting to make it a better place. She is, in today's common parlance, "woke." Being woke means "being aware of the real issues and willing to speak of them in ways that are uncomfortable for other[s]" (Hess, 2016). Woke is not new; "What the general public now knows as woke was once referred to as *conscious*, and it's existed … for a very long time.... There were *conscious* rappers, *conscious* poets, the *conscious* black person—see Ankh and African necklaces, dashikis and a chosen vegan lifestyle as popular *conscious* archetypes" (Koren, 2016). Rowan Blanchard is conscious; Rowan Blanchard is woke. *Girl Meets World* was not woke yet … but it was trying.

Boy Meets World had the luxury of airing on ABC in primetime; its audience was allowed to skew older because of its environment, and therefore, its subject matter could be more robust. *Boy Meets World* dealt directly with sex, socioeconomic disparity, absentee parents, and identity issues ("tv.com," n.d.). *Girl Meets World* did not have such luxury, as it aired not in primetime on a national network, but on the Disney Channel, often during daytime hours. One of the hallmarks of the Disney Channel's current lineup is a sort of vapid harmlessness: programs are not really "about" anything, and generally do not deal with issues with any degree of seriousness. The problems and difficulties faced on this slate of tweenage sitcoms are the garden variety middle school topics: low-level relationship problems, difficulties with parents, sibling drama and school struggles. From *Liv and Maddie* to *Bunk'd*, the stakes in these programs are very low; even the more "action" oriented sitcoms, such as *Lab Rats* or *Mighty Med*, are silly and slapstick by nature. It certainly makes sense that the ratings might fall as sharply as they did; *Girl Meets World* was a different kind of show for a different kind of audience. It must be difficult to maintain a following, opening discussions issues of race, class, and gender, while the programs adjacent are delivering stories of slushy machines gone haywire and how much losing the big basketball game makes one sad.

To be fair, *Girl Meets World* is not the Royal Shakespearean Theater; this is a tweenage dramedy, not *Hamilton*. However, clearly, *Girl Meets World* did not want to be harmless, and Rowan Blanchard is anything but vapid. As a primetime network television program, *Girl Meets World* may have been the standard sort of sitcom that Michael Jacobs has been producing for decades, falling right in line with *My Two Dads*, *Charles in Charge*, *Dinosaurs* and *Boy Meets World*. But entering into the Disney Channel lineup positions the program differently, and opens up a completely different audience to a fledgling activist like Rowan Blanchard. A celebrity using social capital through social media to advance a cause is nothing new. A 15-year-old Disney Channel celebrity using her social capital through social media to advance progressive feminist activism is absolutely a new frontier—a new model for how tween celebrities may interact with their fans on a deeper, more important level than simple fandom.

REFERENCES

Alexandra, R. (2016). Does Gwen Stefani's "Harajuku" cartoon really have zero Japanese characters in it? Retrieved from https://ww2.kqed.org/pop/2016/09/16/does-gwen-stefanis-harajuku-cartoon-really-have-zero-japanese-characters-in-it/.

Andreeva, N. (2007, August 19). "High School" upstages TV records. *The Hollywood Reporter*. Retrieved from http://www.hollywoodreporter.com/news/high-school-upstages-tv-records-148288.

Arruda, C. (2014). Disney Channel expands episode order for anticipated "Girl Meets World." Retrieved from http://www.filmthrasher.com/2014/01/the-news-bundle-disney-channel-expands.html.

Bacle, A. (2014). Disney channel orders second season of "Girl Meets World." Retrieved from http://ww.ew.com/article/2014/08/06/disney-channel-girl-meets-world-second-season.

Barnes, R., & Strong, R. (May 11, 2015). S2E1: Girl meets gravity. [Television broadcast]. In F. Pace *Girl Meets World*. Los Angeles: Michael Jacobs Productions.

Barnes, R., & Zwick, J. (July 25, 2014). S1E4: Girl meets father. [Television broadcast]. In F. Pace *Girl Meets World*. Los Angeles: Michael Jacobs Productions.

Belch, G., & Belch, M. (2013). A content analysis study of the use of celebrity endorsers in magazine advertising. *International Journal of Advertising, 23*(3), 369–389.

Bell, C.E. (2010). *American idolatry: Celebrity, commodity and reality television*. Jefferson, NC: McFarland.

Bickford, T. (2015). Tween intimacy and the problem of public life in children's media: "Having it all" on the Disney channel's Hannah Montana. *WSQ: Women's Studies Quarterly, 43*(1), 66–82.

Blanchard, R. (2016). Sorry not sorry. How I quit apologizing for existing. *Rookie Magazine*. Retrieved from http://www.rookiemag.com/2016/01/sorry-not-sorry/.

Blanchard, R., & Shahidi, Y. (2016). Rowan Blanchard and Yara Shahidi on representation. *Teen Vogue*. Retrieved from http://www.teenvogue.com/story/rowan-blanchard-yara-shahidi-cover-interview-december-issue-representation-activism.

Blutman, M., & Garson, W. (September 11, 2015). S2E15: Girl meets Farkle. [Television broadcast]. In F. Pace *Girl Meets World*. Los Angeles: Michael Jacobs Productions.

Blutman, M., & Whitesell, J. (November 28, 2014). S1E14: Girl meets friendship. [Television broadcast]. In F. Pace *Girl Meets World*. Los Angeles: Michael Jacobs Productions.

Boorstin, J. (2003). Disney's "tween machine": How the Disney Channel became must-see TV—And the company's unlikely cash cow. *Fortune Magazine*. Retrieved from http://archive.fortune.com/magazines/fortune/fortune_archive/2003/09/29/349896/index.htm.

Bowman, S. (2016, 7/30/20016). How "Girl meets world" quietly became one of TV's most feminist shows. *Bustle*. Retrieved from http://www.bustle.com/articles/175843-how-girl-meets-world-quietly-became-one-of-tvs-most-feminist-shows.

Brown, J.R., Lusch, R.F., & Nicholson, C.Y. (1996). Power and relationship commitment: Their impact on marketing channel member performance. *Journal of Retailing, 71*(4), 363–392.

Connolly, K. (2016, 1/18/2016). Girl Meets World: Rowan Blanchard wants to see more representation on show. *Entertainment Weekly*. Retrieved from http://www.ew.com/article/2016/01/18girl-meets-world-rowan-blanchard-queer-representation/?iid=sr-link5.

Costa, M. (2010). Brand awareness comes as part of growing up. *Marketing Week*. Retrieved from https://www.marketingweek.com/2010/06/08/brand-awareness-comes-as-part-of-growing-up/.

Dockterman, E. (2014, October 20, 2014). Before we embrace Gwen Stefani's comeback, she owes us an apology. *Time*. Retrieved from http://time.com/3524847/gwen-stefani-racist-harajuku-girls/.

Erikson, E.H. (1994). *Identity: Youth and crisis*. New York: W.W. Norton.

Fallon, K. (2014, 7/26/2014). "Boy Meets World" fans will hate "Girl Meets World.." *The Daily Beast*. Retrieved from http:// www.thedailybeast.com/articles/2014/06/26/boy-meets-world-fans-will-hate-girl-meets-world.html.

Fang, C., & Zwick, J. (July 18, 2014). S1E3: Girl meets sneak attack. [Television broadcast]. In F. Pace *Girl Meets World*. Los Angeles: Michael Jacobs Productions.

Genetics Home Reference. (2011). Asperger syndrome. Retrieved from https://ghr.nlm.nih.gov/condition/asperger-syndrome.

Godoy, T., & Vartanian, I. (2007). *Style deficit disorder: Harajuku street fashion-Tokyo*. San Francisco: Chronicle Books.

Hess, A. (2016, April 19, 2016). Earning the "woke" badge. *New York Times Magazine*. Retrieved from https://www.nytimes.com/2016/04/24/magazine/earning-the-woke-badge.html.

Hibberd, J. (2013, 1/31/2013). "Boy meets world" spin-off casts Riley's best friend. *Entertain-*

ment Weekly. Retrieved from http:// www.ew.com/article/2013/01/31/boy-meets-world-spin-off-maya.

Jacobs, J., & Savage, B. (August 19, 2016). S3E11: Girl meets sassy haltertop. [Television broadcast]. In F. Pace *Girl Meets World*. Los Angeles: Michael Jacobs Productions.

Kale, T., & Savage, B. (December 2, 2016). S3E18: Girl meets a Christmas Maya. [Television broadcast]. In F. Pace *Girl Meets World*. Los Angeles: Michael Jacobs Productions.

Kale, T., Strong, S., & Strong, R. (January 8, 2016). S2E26: Girl meets STEM. [Television broadcast]. In F. Pace *Girl Meets World*. Los Angeles: Michael Jacobs Productions.

Kantor, J. (2016, 8/3/2016). Rowan Blanchard: "Beyonce's Lemonade changed my life." *Glamour*. Retrieved from http:// www.glamour.com/story/rowan-blanchard-beyonces-lemonade-changed-my-life.

Koeing, J. (2012). Sonder. *Dictionary of obscure sorrows*. Retrieved from http://www.dictionaryofobscuresorrows.com/post/23536922667/sonder.

Koren, O. (2016, June 28, 2016). What we really mean when we say "woke." *Complex*. Retrieved from http://www.complex.com/life/2016/06/woke-meaning-origin.

Kraft, A. (2016, 10/6/2016). "Girl Meets World" news & update: Disney series on the brink of cancellation as the ratings took a dip. *Parent Herald*. Retrieved from http://www.parentherald.com/articles/71502/20161006/girl-meets-world-news-update-disney-series-on-the-brink-of-cancellation-as-the-ratings-took-a-dip.htm.

Lang, N. (2014, December 10, 2014). Gwen Stefani still doesn't know what racism is. *The Daily Dot*. Retrieved from https://www.dailydot.com/via/gwen-stefani-cultural-appropriation-harajuku-girls/.

Leung, R. (2004, 12/14/2004). Tweens: A billion-dollar market. *60 Minutes*. Retrieved from http:// http://www.cbsnews.com/news/tweens-a-billion-dollar-market/.

Lopez, A. (2012). *The media ecosystem: What ecology can teach us about responsible media practice*. Berkeley, CA: North Atlantic Books.

Lowe, M. (2003). Colliding feminisms: Britney Spears, "tweens" and the politics of reception. *Popular Music and Society*, 26(2), 123–140.

Marwick, A.E. (2013). *Status update: Celebrity, publicity, and branding in the social media age*. New Haven, CT: Yale University Press.

Maturo, A. [AugustMaturo] (2017, January 21). *Rowan Blanchard speaks at women's march LA*. [Video file]. Retrieved from https://www.youtube.com/watch?v=IQuXxMBd4H8.

McGladrey, M.L. (2014). Becoming tween bodies: What preadolescent girls in the US say about beauty, the "Just-right ideal," and the "Disney girls." *Journal of Children and Media*, 8(4), 353–370.

Menell, J., & Rosenbaum, J. (August 8, 2014). S1E6: Girl meets popular. [Television broadcast]. In F. Pace *Girl Meets World*. Los Angeles: Michael Jacobs Productions.

Menell, J., Strong, S., & Strong, R. (September 16, 2016). S3E13: Girl meets the great lady of New York. [Television broadcast]. In F. Pace *Girl Meets World*. Los Angeles: Michael Jacobs Productions.

Menell, J., & Zwick, J. (August 8, 2014). S1E12: Girl meets the fogotten. [Television broadcast]. In F. Pace *Girl Meets World*. Los Angeles: Michael Jacobs Productions.

Micheli, M. (2016). Social networking sites and low-income teenagers: between opportunity and inequality. *Information, Communication, & Society*, 19(5), 565–581.

Millard, S. (2015). *So excited so scared: The saved by the bell retrospective*. Seattle: Amazon Digital Services.

Murray, M., & Okazaki, S. (2014, 9/10/2014). Danielle Fishel: 6 things I learned about life by playing Topanga on "Boy Meets World." *Today*. Retrieved from http://www.today.com/popculture/danielle-fishel-6-things-i-learned-about-life-playing-topanga-1D80134028.

Nakao, A. (2016). The formation and commodification of Harajuku's image in japan. *Ritsumeikan Journal of Asia Pacific Studies* (34), 10–19.

Nelson, M., & Fishel, D. (July 15, 2016). S3E7: Girl meets true Maya. [Television broadcast]. In F. Pace *Girl Meets World*. Los Angeles: Michael Jacobs Productions.

Nelson, M., & Zwick, J. (August 1, 2014). S1E5: Girl meets the truth. [Television broadcast]. In F. Pace *Girl Meets World*. Los Angeles: Michael Jacobs Productions.

Otero, L., & Zwick, J. (September 26, 2014). S1E10: Girl meets crazy hat. [Television broadcast]. In F. Pace *Girl Meets World*. Los Angeles: Michael Jacobs Productions.

Potter, A., & Hill, L. (2016). Cultivating global celebrity: Bindi Irwin, FremantleMedia and the commodification of grief. *Celebrity Studies*, 1–16.

Prince, D., & Martin, N. (2011). The tween market niche: An overview of past research, current practices, and a comprehensive research model. *Allied Academies International Internet Conference, 13* 95.

Prince, D., & Martin, N. (2012). The tween consumer marketing model: Significant variables and recommended research hypotheses. *Academy of Marketing Studies Journal, 16*(2), 31.

Roots, K. (2012, 11/2/2012). Exclusive: Disney Channel eyes Boy Meets World sequel series, Ben Savage in early talks. *TVLine*. Retrieved from http://tvline.com/2012/11/02/girl-meets-world-sequel-pilot-disney/.

Rosman, K. (2016, 10/10/2016). Rowan Blanchard: The unlikely evolution of a Disney star. *New York Times*. Retrieved from http://www.mobile.nytimes.com/2016/10/12/fassion/rowan-blanchard-disney-star-it-girl.html?_r=0&referrer.

Russell, E. (2016, September 30, 2016). Kuu kuu harajuku: On growing up with Gwen Stefani, Japan street fashion + cultural appropriation. *Pop Crush*. Retrieved from http://popcrush.com/gwen-stefani-kuu-kuu-harajuku-japanese-fashion-appropriation/.

Schwartz, T. (2013, 2//2013). Michaels Jacobs on "Girl Meets World": We want any "Boy Meets World" cast member who wants to come back. *Screener TV*. Retrieved from http://screenertv.com/news-features/michael-jacobs-on-girls-meets-world-we-want-any-boy-meets-world-cast-member-who-wants-to-come-back/.

Shoham, A., & Ruvio, A. (2008). Opinion leaders and followers: A replication and extension. *Psychology & Marketing, 25*(3), 280–297.

Simmons, R. (2014, 11/10/2014). Instagram: Tween and teen girls' have a secret language. *Time*. Retrieved from http://www.time.com/3559340/instagram-tween-girls/.

Simpson, L., Douglas, S., & Schimmel, J. (1998). Tween consumers: Catalog clothing purchase behavior. *Adolescence, 33*(131), 637–644.

Stransky, T. (2013, 1/28/2013). "Boy Meets World" spin-off: Meet Cory and Topanga's daughter—Exclusive. *Entertainment Weekly*. Retrieved from http://www.ew.com/article/2013/01/28/boy-meets-world-daughter-rowan-blanchard.

TV by the Numbers (2014, 7/30/2014). Friday cable ratings: "Girl Meets World" tops night + "Zapped," "Friday Night Smackdown," "Jessie" & more. *ScreenerTV*. Retrieved from http://tvbythenumbers.zap2it.com/sdsdskdh279882992z1/friday-cable-ratings-girl-meets-world-tops-night-zapped-friday-night-smackdown-jessie-more/277892/.

TV.com. *Boy Meets World*. Retrieved from http://www.tv.com/shows/boy-meets-world/episodes/.

tvtropes.org. (2015). *Very special episode*. Retrieved from http://tvtropes.org/pmwiki/pmwiki.php/Main/VerySpecialEpisode.

Vares, T., & Jackson, S. (2015). Reading celebrities/narrating selves 'tween girls, Miley Cyrus and the good/bad girl binary. *Celebrity Studies, 6*(4), 553–567.

Vishnoi, A. (2016, 10/29/2016). Girl Meets World renewal updates: Season 4 will not feature Sabrina Carpenter. *Movie News Guide*. Retrieved from http://www.movienewsguide.com/girl-meets-world-renewal-updates-season-4-will-not-feature-sabrina-carpenter/302055.

Wells, V.S. (2014, April 27, 2014). Lavigne's celebration of Japan is lost in translation. *Nouse*. Retrieved from http://www.nouse.co.uk/2014/04/27/lavignes-celebration-of-japan-is-lost-in-translation/.

Williams, A., & Merton, M. (2008). A review of online social networking profiles by adolescents: Implications for future research and intervention. *Adolescence, 43*(170), 253–274.

Yeager, M., Strong, S., & Strong, R. (June 10, 2016). S3E3: Girl meets Jexica. [Television broadcast]. In F. Pace *Girl Meets World*. Los Angeles: Michael Jacobs Productions.

Girlhood Voice
in the Disney Family

Liv and Maddie *and* Agents of S.H.I.E.L.D.

J. RICHARD STEVENS

As Disney programming and performances represent an increasingly large percentage of American media offerings, the company appears poised more than ever "to shape national identity, gender roles, and childhood values" (Giroux 1999, 10). Among those values is the construction of the girlhood voice within the American family, as Disney offers contrasting constructions across its different media products.

This essay examines how one such program, *Liv and Maddie*, a live-action Disney Chanel series that aired from 2013 to 2017, contrasts frames of girlhood voice and the role of family in the construction of identity with ABC's *Agents of S.H.I.E.L.D.* Both series were produced by Disney production units, and both featured Disney Channel star Dove Cameron for at least one story arc. *Liv and Maddie* focuses on a nuclear family that contains two parents, two twin girls (both played by Cameron), and two younger boys. In each of the 80 episodes in the series, Cameron plays both sisters: Liv Rooney as an emerging teen Hollywood star who returns home to Wisconsin after finishing the taping of a television series in California, and her twin, Maddie, as her tomboy athlete sister. The "sisters by chance, friends by choice" duo presented competing frames of girlhood femininity to the Disney Channel's tween audience, exploring intersections of childhood and postfeminist commercial success in a media age, and providing empowering messages to young women in a nuclear family setting.

By contrast, Cameron's next role was as the teenage villain Ruby Hale in six episodes of the fifth season of Marvel's *Agents of S.H.I.E.L.D.,* a live action ABC primetime drama about secret agents operating in a world of superheroes. Ruby is the lone daughter of a single mother career military officer (and secret Hydra agent). In the course of pursuing her ambitions, Ruby spends her life honing her body and her skills as an assassin to gain her mother's approval. Her feelings of inadequacy express themselves as increasingly erratic and violent behavior that ultimately leads to Ruby's injury and death.

Though each program targets a different audience demographic, both shows focus on the importance of family, whether biological (the Rooneys) or functional (the Agents of S.H.I.E.L.D.). Despite the consistent portrayals of teenage girls finding a confident, energetic, and assertive voice among their peers and in society, each of Cameron's characters struggle to use their voices effectively in the context of their respective families. For Liv, her entertainment success and professional ambitions place her in a role that is both outside parental authority and struggling to function within it. Ultimately, it is her family (and particularly her twin, Maddie) that provides measure to her experiences in ways that allow her to assert agency in both worlds. By contrast, Ruby's constant drive to win her mother's approval through career and missional success undermine the familial rapport she holds with her mother, and the undermining of the parental model directly leads to failure in her missional ambitions, and her ultimate demise.

Though Disney's films consistently prioritize the depiction of family relationships (Tanner, Haddock, Zimmerman, & Lund, 2003), those products historically have reinforced white, middle-class, patriarchal society. This essay extends this analysis to recent Disney television offerings, finding similar reinforcement despite the new emphasis on girlhood voice.

Developing the Girlhood Voice

For its part, Disney has a long-standing stake in engaging and representing youth consumers. Disney has a well-established corporate image that reflects and amplifies attributes that are appealing to a dominant sense of individualism within America. The company's branding and products convey the importance of ingenuity, resourcefulness, optimism, continual progress, and the taking of initiative (Best & Lowney, 2009; Harrington, 2015; Wasko, 2001). In fact, the Disney corporation has the unique ability to leverage not only these key touchpoints of American self-image, but also to align itself well with many American consumers because audiences associate their products with their pleasurable memories of childhood, in what is almost a "sacred" association between Disney and the individual (Wasko, 2001, p. 222). Over decades, the Disney brand has been positively associated with childhood and family and "seen as standing for what is good, decent, and appropriate in a way that few other corporations are" (Best & Lowney, 2006, p. 443). Scholars have observed, for example, that Disney films have done significant work to transmit the company's desired pro-social values. A content analysis of 61 Disney animated films from 1937 to 2011 found that such films were overwhelmingly prosocial in nature, containing "an average of one act of prosocial behavior per minute…" or about seven times higher than what typically appears in children's television (Padilla-Walker, Coyne, Fraser & Stockdale, 2013, p. 405). A particular focus of pro-social messages associated with girls in Disney movies were on the rise at the end of the 20th century, with female characters increasingly shown as "active, self-motivated, strong-willed, intelligent and independent" (Davis, 2006, p. 225). A more recent study of 54 Disney animations over 70 years revealed that, while earlier Disney films showed girls as inferior, passive, and not fit for entry in the workplace, later Disney films depict girls as being strong and important contributors regarding paid work (Griffin, Harding & Learmonth, p. 2017).

Disney's messaging seeks to amplify its pro-social messaging beyond what appears in its products, with a tone that emphasizes the company's desire to mentor youth and families. While the company projects multiple layers of corporate social responsibility messages within what it calls a "Disney Citizenship Framework," one area of emphasis worth noting is: "Inspire Others: Promote the happiness and well-being of kids and families" (Disney Citizenship Table, 2014, p. 7). Within this area, Disney takes a mentoring stance by offering messages designed to promote healthier living, creative thinking, and advocating ways to strengthen communities. The company operationalized these values by, for example, creating more than 50 new playgrounds (live healthier), setting up problem-solving groups in more than 40 low-income schools (think creatively), and facilitating about 3.7 million volunteerism and fundraising actions by kids and families (strengthen communities) (Disney Citizenship Table, 2016). In 2016, Disney added a "Be Your Best" mentoring theme, offering guidance about healthy eating and exercise (and incorporating these messages into Disney retail outlets, theme parks and some of their entertainment products), encouraging millions of kids to participate in coding through an #HourofCode, and using participative digital initiatives like *Marvel Studios: Hero Acts* and the *Share Your Ears* program that allowed participants to post photos and unlock rewards for needy children around the world (Disney Citizenship Table, 2016).

Scholarly critics, however, point out that Disney's pro-social, helpful image represents a deliberate construct designed to attract and keep customers (Wasko, 2001), and to support Disney's the goals to "addictify the customer" (Harrington, 2015, p. 26). In fact, distinct audiences surfaced over the last two decades to point out that they do not subscribe to the beneficence of Disney: conservative Christians complaining the company has fallen into promoting homosexuality and violence, social scientists pointing to problems with the artificial and inauthentic portrayals at Disney theme parks, and progressives attempting to raise awareness that Disney amplifies the values of capitalism and imperialism and tends to promote sexism in its depictions of female characters (Best & Lowney, 2009).

Sammond (2005) maintained that Disney's marketplace imperative to treat children as a "commodity in the making" (p. 360) has historically predisposed the corporation to prioritize status quo perspectives that "foreclose solutions to immediate pressing social and economic problems—such as institutionalized racism or gendered economic inequality" and simply allow such social issues to be deferred to the next generation (p. 23). Sammond further argued that the corporation attempts to prepare the child for "membership in a culture the primary social metaphor of which is the marketplace, a culture in which persons must be simultaneously and impossibly unique individuals and known quantities" (p. 360). Harrington (2015) suggested that Disney's ethos, in keeping with the American valorization of individualism, is to guide the consumer toward believing they can "administrate their own gratification" (p. 26). He observed that this approach is consonant with the company's touting the iconic image of Walt Disney making his way through adversity in the 1930s to eventually achieving his role in the American Dream. Indeed, Disney's CFO (Disney Citizenship Table, 2014) affirmed that the corporation's role is to "help nurture critical thinking and problem solving skills in young people" because "while our own actions can better the world, the actions we inspire in others can profoundly change it" (p. 5). Critics argue, however, that such affirmations of pro-social values need to be carefully contextualized within the market imperatives (and related stressors) that Disney must manage (Harrington, 2015; Sammond, 2005; Wasko, 2001). It is crucial to remember that these market pressures serve to propel and amplify the presence of the corporation as a mentor figure to younger generations, because corporations have "a commanding role over commodity markets as well as support from the highest reaches of government" and therefore have become "the primary educational and cultural force in shaping, if not hijacking, how youth define their interests, values and relations to others" (Giroux, 2016, p. 234).

The Disney Channel aligns to these corporate goals in obvious ways. In the late 1990s, the number and variety of children's television networks expanded, allowing the segmentation of demographics of children into smaller clusters. The Disney Channel's programming usually features teenage stars in its productions, but the target demographic audience members for programming is younger than the actors (Banet-Weiser, 2004). The tween demographic are aged between children and teens, most commonly defined as 8–12 years of age (Siegel et al., 2004). Advertisers and programmers pursue the tween demographic because it influences family spending (Lindstrom, 2004). As Natalie Coulter (2015) observed, "for the tween of today, there is an entire media machine created specifically for their consumption" (142). Developmentally, the tween years are associated with the development of information processing skills as well as intellectual and social schemas (Van Evra, 1998, 7) and gender identity (Zucker and Bradly, 1995).

And yet, this highly sought-after demographic is positioned at an awkward stage for making use of the attention and power they are given. "Youth voice is far too often absent from important discussions and decision-making processes about issues that impact them" (CYCC Network, 2013, p. 20). Tween girls, in particular, are thought to struggle with their voices, but also with their representations, from which their social identities are largely formed (Callero, 2003). Rebecca Hains (2012) observed that making sense of the media that construct and transmit meanings is a habitual and often unconscious practice that girls carry out as they respond to images, ideas, and sounds while engaging with diverse media forms. And so, the Disney Channel's programs should be of particular interest for scholars, given the channel "has imprinted the Disney brand onto the consciousness of millions of children and teens" (Stein, 2011, pp. 99–100).

Pro-Social Girlhood Voice in Liv and Maddie

Liv and Maddie premiered July 19, 2013, with a pilot episode titled "Twin-a-Rooney." The timing was strategic, as the premiere followed a showing of Disney's hit film *High School Musical,* and 5.78 million total viewers watched, the second highest ratings in Disney Channel show preview history. The format of the show models a fixed set sitcom; both parents work at their kids' school. The show contains fourth-wall confessional breaks in the narrative, which the audience learns, in the final episode, is because the family has been the subject of a reality television show. In addition, Dove Cameron frequently composes and performs pop music arrangements in the context of the narrative. This element resembles the musical comedy formula of *Hannah Montana*, and replicates instances throughout the show of the gendered discourse that links pop music to young femininity (Coates, 1997).

In the series premiere, Liv returns to her home in Wisconsin from four years living in Hollywood, where she has concluded filming of a hit television series (*Sing It Loud!*). She is welcomed by her family, but the narrative tension revolves around her difficulty reconnecting with her twin sister Maddie. Liv is presented as a stereotypical pop star fashionista: always wearing makeup, fussing over clothing and her appearance, and using her celebrity status to her advantage when needed. By contrast, Maddie is a masculine jock, obsessed with competition in sports and academics, never wears makeup, normally dresses in athletic clothing with her hair in a casual ponytail.

The show presents the two sisters as halves of each other. The theme song codifies that intent, with its lyrics (performed by Cameron) describing the sisters as opposite in personality, but complimentary in their support, concluding they are better off together than alone. (Hampson, 2013).

Gender only exists to the extent it is performed (Butler, 1988, 527), and the twin convention lets Cameron play two distinct versions of girlhood at the same time. The confessional segments allow articulation to how different versions of the same person react to situations in different ways. Liv returning home after four years (it appears the two never visited each other) is thus both a reunion of sisters and an uncomfortable examination of the self. The differences in attitudes and personalities clash, and the parents spend the opening episode trying to help the girls reconcile. The two younger brothers (Joey Bragg as Joey Rooney and Tenzing Norgay Trainor as Parker Rooney) exploit their parents' attention on Liv and Maddie's relations to wreak havoc, which forms the base formula for the show.

The sisters argue over their inability to listen and feel heard, Liv trying to help Maddie get a date to prom that seems to go awry, and Liv deciding she wants to move back to Hollywood. The sisters reconcile when they are presented with a second-grade art project that introduces the "Sisters by chance, friends by choice" slogan. Moved, Maddie asks Liv not to move away, and Liv responds, "You couldn't drive me away" (Beck & Hart, July 19, 2013). The show concludes with prom photos (Maddie wears a dress, but insists on wearing tennis shoes).

The second episode ("Team-a-Rooney") didn't air until the series began its prime Disney Channel slot on September 15, 2013. Though it aired almost two months after the premiere, the show is set during the events of the pilot, the day after Liv returns from Hollywood. Maddie is named captain of the girls' basketball team just as the school principal announces he is not funding new uniforms or allowing them to compete in a tournament for the team because he thinks no one seems to care about girls basketball. Determined to change his mind, Maddie voices her concerns to the principal, only to realize her team has abandoned her. Frustrated at her apparent lack of leadership skills, Maddie turns to Liv to help her earn the team's respect.

Liv shares with Maddie her model for leadership:

1. Grab their attention,
2. Get them on the same page,
3. Identify your goal,
4. Lead them into battle and
5. Look great doing it [Beck & Hart, September 15, 2013].

The sisters concoct a scheme to have Liv join the team so that Maddie can show strength by kicking her off, but the teammates rally to Liv's defense and she temporarily becomes an actual member of the team. Liv's advice doesn't seem effective, so Maddie gathers the team and encourages them to "release their inner warrior" (Beck & Hart, September 15, 2013). With spirits improved, the basketball team itself raises money for new uniforms and then impresses the principal, who agrees to fund the competition in the tournament.

This second episode focuses mostly on Maddie and her struggle to use her voice and Liv's attempts to infuse her with her own forms of leadership and voice, which backfire. In the end, Maddie figures out how to use her own voice to inspire her teammates, adopting the "inner warrior" rhetoric, reinforcing the theme that there isn't one path to success, and that identity is important to determining how to act. This introduction to Maddie's competitiveness would frame her character throughout the show, the tomboy who relates better to her male classmates than her sister, but who still learns from Liv's experience.

Like some other Disney Channel characters, Cameron's portrayal of Liv embodies the outward trappings of the "post-feminist masquerade" (McRobbie, 2009), the commercialized trappings of neoliberal heterosexual receptivity that signifies power beyond the rhetorics of feminist discourse. Post-feminism repositions female empowerment into stylized (and commercialized) aesthetics divorced from metrics of progress, relegating the struggles of equality as exclusively a question for legal domains and ignoring the cultural barriers that continue to be reproduced in society daily. Post-feminism is popularly understood as "popular perceptions of gender relations often suggest that feminism can now safely be relegated to the past" (Budgeon, 2011, p. 281) and the notion that feminism is something women should be liberated from in order to focus on consumption and sexuality (Whelehan, 2000). The increased narrative emphasis on clothing, consumer culture and sexuality are hallmarks of postfeminist discourse (Kinser, 2004, pp. 134–135), normally functioning within that discourse to provide superficial symbols of empowerment disconnected from the feminist critique. In this way, "feminism itself is no longer needed—it has become a spent force" (Sarikakis and Tsaliki, 2001, p. 112). By seeming to empower young women with commercial success and attention, post-feminism is generally considered a move against feminism and contrary to feminist goals (Kinser 2004, pp. 134–35).

Blue (2013) extends McRobbie's "post-feminist masquerade" framing to "girliness," the hyperfeminine, performative and performance-based personas exemplified in media culture. Disney, in part, has helped frame expectations with its string of "franchisable girl" characters/actors. Blue (2016) defined the franchisabe girl as "media savvy and multitalented; she acts and sings and dances and sometimes plays a musical instrument; she enjoys her visibility and uses it to grow her fame as well as to benefit others" (p. 35).

The Liv character is constructed on the basic "franchisable girl" formula, but allows Cameron to use her voice for empowerment, to draw attention and frame issues and sentiments through musical expression. Throughout the series, Liv (with helpful prodding from her family and classmates) uses her celebrity status to raise awareness to causes she cares about, and as the series progresses, those causes include some of the critiques common to feminism itself.

Perhaps the most clear example of the use of postfeminism voice to raise feminism concerns occurred in S2E10 ("Rate-a-Rooney"). The female characters all react to discovering that a group of male students are circulating a rating scale to judge the attractiveness of every girl in the school. Early in the episode, several of the female characters gather in the Rooney kitchen to react to the situation. Each has a different insecurity exploited by the ranking system. Willow explains that when she picks up magazines and sees the models on the cover, "I feel like I'm no good if I don't look like those girls. And I don't look like those girls." Alex explains that she's been made fun of for liking science, which is not considered "girl stuff." And Maddie expresses her frustration at the gendered response to her athletic talent:

> MADDIE: You know what I hate? When some guy comes up to me and is like, hey, you're really good at basketball You know, for a girl. Like, what? That's supposed to be some kind of compliment? [Keene, 2015].

Each one of these statements embodies a classic feminist critique of male privilege in driving cultural narratives. Liv points out the role that media play in pushing gendered narratives onto self-identity, Willow raises the concerns about hegemonic body norms driven to accommodate the male gaze, Alex invokes the criticisms concerning the masculinization of "serious" zones more male exclusivity, and Maddie responds to the gendered hierarchy that stilts comparisons between male and female competition (in this case, athletics).

Though the girls recognize the various double-standards that affect how their identities and achievements are filtered and judged by society, they struggle to voice their concerns. At first, the girls try to organize a protest, each of them wearing a paper bag over their heads and declaring all girls at the school "a 10." But Willow breaks ranks, wearing a dress for the first time, trying to court male favor to raise her score. Her dissension brings the issues into sharp focus: though her female friends tell her how they value her, Willow feels pressured to accept the boys' judgment, and leaves the group (with others) so she can attempt to improve her standing in their eyes.

Liv is surprised by this turn of events. She exclaims, "This is the world that we live in, but why can't we change the world?" Alex responds, "Changing the world seems highly improbable," and Lacey agrees, "It does seem like a lot of work" (Keene, 2015).

But Liv becomes determined to change the culture she's witnessing, and so she takes to her laptop to compose and record a song, which she releases on her social media channels with this introduction:

> LIV: Some of the boys there have been rating us girls based on our looks, and that makes us girls feel like we have to change. But you don't have to change who you are to fit someone else's idea of what a girl is supposed to be [Keene, 2015].

She presses play and then the song ("What a Girl Is") begins, which presents a critique of fashion magazines and gendered criticisms reducing girls to dress size and appearance. The song rejects this discourse, calling girls to recognize their value comes from inside instead of the outside, and to use their power to get loud and use their voices. Liv returns to the screen and says, "Thank you for watching, girls, and please don't let anyone tell you who you are. You just keep being you" (Keene, 2015).

As the music plays, interactions are shown on the screen between the male and female student characters. At first, Willow (for example) is chasing male favor, dressing up and wearing makeup, and behaving as she thinks boys might value. But as the song progresses, she begins to resist, and by the end of the song she is wearing comfortable clothes and strutting past a line of gaping boys. She smiles, no longer caring about their judgment. The song ends with all the girls standing shoulder to shoulder, holding signs that declare each one of them a "10."

The performance enacts a classic example of "girl power," a challenge to the "conventional narratives and images about what girls are and who they should be" (Banet-Wiser, 2004, p. 136). Liv's lyrics and rhythm empower the individuals in her circle of friends, and as they reconnect, the music affects the community as a whole. This style of post-feminist discourse, using fame and performance to inspire change, also meets with frames as social justice: Liv was originally highly rated by the boys; her indignation at the rating system is on behalf of her peers. Her outrage is focused on what the rating systems means for her gendered community. But the song was also intended to change than just to the characters within the narrative. "What a Girl Is" was released on iTunes as a Dove Cameron song, the full-length video was posted to YouTube, and the song was eventually incorporated into the show's soundtrack.

The transmedia expressions of this act of performance (the show, the song, the video, and the social media promotion) served to not only raise awareness to individual concerns facing tweens (watching teenagers articulate their awareness of the misogynistic messages they receive from the media culture), but also watching teens finding ways to use their voice to create communal support and effect change. Though the expressions were funneled through the aesthetics and rhetorics of post-feminism, the goals and functions of the action are actually feminist (gathering a female community, empowering them for changes that affect women, etc.).

It should be noted that these negotiations happen exclusively among the peer groups involved. The Rooney parents appear oblivious to all these statements and negotiations (a subplot of the show is the parents' struggles over differences in opinion concerning clutter in the house, another over the two brothers' conflict over room space). The parents seem distracted by domestic concerns involving themselves; they are oblivious to the concerns expressed in their kitchen or the conversations occurring around their daughters.

Another example of this phenomenon can be witnessed in S3E8 ("Ask Her More-A-Rooney"). In this episode, Liv attends a red carpet event with her co-stars, and is dismayed when she realizes the questions and comments she received from media interviewers revolve around her wardrobe choices, while her male co-star is asked questions about the content of the show and his craft. Liv takes her frustration home with her, where this time, her mother engages with her and the topic at hand. As Liv expresses her frustration at not being asked substantive questions by reporters, her mother advises her:

> KAREN: If you want to change the questions, you have to find a way to change conversation [Green, 2015].

In this scene, Karen Rooney validates Liv's observations and connects it to the shared feminine experience of "the way it is." She empowers Liv with the general approach that will resolve the issue in terms of the episode's narrative, but that doesn't directly involve her. Karen primarily serves as a source of feminist community for Liv on this particular issue, the experienced woman providing advice to the teenager struggling to find new ways to use her voice to raise awareness to double-standards of treatment. But Karen's interaction also frames the show's portrayal of parenthood: parents exists in the show to be generally supportive, but mostly in guiding the exploration and growth of young women. The advice does not specify an actual course of action; it merely redirects Liv's thinking.

Liv returns to the red carpet, and this time she encounters actress Kristen Bell. After sharing her concerns, the two actresses conspire to change the conversation. Liv jumps the first reporter who asks about her playing an attractive superhero, pointing out that no reporter had asked about "how I feel about playing a superhero, or how I do the stunts, or what heroes inspired me. You guys have only asked me about my dress and my hair." Kristen Bell interjects support as Liv challenges the reporter, who responds that he's asking "the questions that our audience expects." To that, Bell adds her voice with this rebuttal: "Or is it what they're told to expect by a group of people who don't think to dig a little deeper?" (Green, 2015). Liv concludes the interview by looking into the camera and telling the girls in her audience they more than just their appearances.

Once again, Liv uses her celebrity status to drive a feminist message to teens (and tweens), using the access she has to adult women (her mother and Kristen Bell) to frame her actions. This portrayal not only centers the authority of the action in adult women's perspectives (validating Liv's observations), but models for tweens that mothers and adult co-workers are sources of support, albeit mostly to empower the individual to act. This act appears to be centered more in post-feminism (engaging performance values of success to raise awareness), but consults a female community to for messaging to empower larger female community members.

Other actions and decisions of social justice appear throughout the show, but the finale of the show ("End-a-Rooney," S4E15) provides a simple example of how the family structure portrayed and the parenting role intersect with the decisions of the minors in the household. In the series finale, the brothers and sisters have planned a "Summer of Rooney" with their mother, but each of the children wind up with opportunities that conflict with the freedom of an unscheduled summer. Liv is offered a role on Broadway and seems destined for her successful life in show business. Maddie receives a grant to build small houses for people who need them in New Orleans, with a schedule that would prevent her from attending a basketball training camp that had guaranteed her starting position on her new collegiate team. She talks over the internal conflict with Willow, who is poised to be her teammate, which gives her the opportunity to articulate,: "I just think that helping people is, like, so much bigger than basketball. You know? And this is something that I could do for the rest of my life" (Hoover & Monahan, 2017). Choosing between her personal dreams of competitive achievement and the opportunity to help others, Maddie chooses to help people, sending a message to the tween audience about values. However, this decision brings with itself another conflict: the trip to New Orleans will disrupt the "Summer of Rooney," the last time they would likely be together under the same roof with their mother. The siblings confer about their various conflicts, but before any of them can talk to Karen, a neighbor fills her in, and she addresses them together to give them all her blessing to spend the summer on their individual opportunities, ending with:

> The greatest gift a mother can get is knowing that she raised her kids to be confident enough to pursue their dreams. Watching you guys become the wonderful people you've become has been so inspiring [Hoover & Monahan, 2017].

It's telling that neither Karen nor Pete Rooney (absent from season 4) gives explicit permission to their children concerning their opportunities.

The narrative logic of the show suggests that Liv and Maddie (and their brothers, in many cases) are free to make their own decisions and commitments, even when those decisions thrust them into the adult world without parental presence. Parents in the *Liv and Maddie* world provide support and nurture primarily when their children seek their counsel (though the parents also often work behind the scenes to support their children in extreme ways). In terms of their role, these Disney Channel parents mostly provide security and support for the autonomy of their children (though the brothers do receive off-screen punishments for their frequent antics and stunts). As a result, Liv and Maddie enjoy a tremendous amount of freedom to determine their own lives and careers, and the show allows their experiences to serve as a greater source of instruction for social and moral reasoning than direct instruction from their parents.

Impaired Girlhood Voice on Agents of S.H.I.E.L.D.

As *Liv and Maddie* ended, Dove Cameron approached the transition point that most Disney teen stars endure: finding the appropriate mode to "grow out of her Disney Channel role" (Blue, 2017, p. 165). The branding that goes into growing the fan base for teenage Disney stars becomes an obstacle when that star tries to move on to more "grown up" roles beyond the Disney Channel franchise. Many stars (perhaps most notably Miley Cyrus, Britney Spears, and Lindsay Lohan) all struggled with the tenuous "growing up" frame that quickly gave way to the "fallen" framing of prurient interest in unDisneylike behavior (Blue, 2017, pp. 171–73).

For Cameron, the political economy built up by the Disney Corporation afforded some new opportunities, the chance to transition from the Disney girl past to a more "adult present" form of role within the same company confines. After the growing success of the Marvel Cinematic Universe films (distributed by Marvel Studios, a subsidiary of Walt Disney Studios), the primetime television show *Agents of S.H.I.E.L.D.* was created to extend the popularity of the franchise onto ABC (formerly the Disney–ABC Television Group, a subsidiary of Disney Media Networks). Airing from 2013 through the present, the show centers on the espionage unit charged with providing world security, and focuses on a functional "family" of operatives who rely on each other to achieve remarkable feats. Cameron received the role of Ruby Hale, a villain for a fifth season arc, a role that let Cameron "grow up" by playing a character who is ruthless and violent.

Though the "musculinity" and "action babe" eras framed modern violent female action characters, the more recent rise of female adolescent and teenage action characters that utilize extreme violence don't fit into these roles. Absent the sexualization of older characters or the "girl delinquent" (Shary, 2002) aspect found in crime and horror films, characters such as Hayley Stark in *Hard Candy* (2005), Hit-Girl in *Kick-Ass!* (2010), Mattie Ross in *True Grit* (2010), Katniss Everdeen in *The Hunger Games* (2012), and the title characters in *Hanna* (2011), and *Violet & Daisy* (2013) presented a new form of extremely violent adolescent warrior (Lupold, 2014, p. 11). Violence in these characters seem to stem from a lack of parental reliance, a symbol of the destabilization of the nuclear family. Connected by technology, Millennials and Gen Zs tend to maintain stronger lateral bonds across their peers, diminishing the traditional roles of parents. Each of the characters mentioned perform tropes that Lupold (2014) categorized as "rebellious youth," "unreliable mothers," and "failed fathers" (p. 13).

As Ruby Hale, Cameron performs a version the violent adolescent tropes, though it is her mother that trains and pushes her to become a killing machine. A single mother with a career focus, absent is a nurturing parenting role in Ruby's life. In this way, Hale performs both the unreliable mother and the failed father tropes (Schubart, 2006, p. 198). The audience is first introduced to Ruby in S5E11 ("All the Comforts of Home") as a sullen teenager in her room, locked in an argument with General Hale, who is revealed to be her mother. Hale complains that Ruby missed class, and threatens to limit her screen time if they don't have an appropriate conversation.

Later in that episode, the agents of S.H.I.E.L.D. run into a masked assassin who attempts to kill them. As she throws her razor sharp chakram, and Yo-Yo (an agent with super speed) tries to intervene, but loses both of her arms to the weapon. The masked assassin is revealed to be Ruby, and she has a tense exchange with Hale after the agents escape. During the exchange, Hale says, "Your work is sloppy and incomplete, and you've been trained to do better, which is why you don't skip class." Ruby pushes back, but Hale continues, "You're my daughter. And a disappointment" (Greenberg, 2018).

The word "disappointment" would linger with Ruby throughout her appearances on the show, as she struggled to prove herself worthy of her mother's trust, while at the same time refusing to follow her mother's orders. Daisy Johnson (code-name: Quake) leads the S.H.I.E.L.D. strike team, had previously been publicly known as a hero, and served as a role model for Ruby (a role model she wanted to defeat in combat).

S5E15 ("Rise and Shine") would provide the origin and backstory for both Hale and Ruby. Hale had been a teenage recruit of Hydra, and upon graduation from Hydra's training academy, had been assigned to the Air Force. However, she was also forced to undergo artificial insemination to birth a being genetically engineered to acquire great power and lead Hydra. When Hydra fell apart, Hale saved Ruby to continue the mission in isolation.

The show reveals that as Hale pushes Ruby to hone her skills, Ruby resents her mother's discipline and becomes bloodthirsty. Hale explains to others that Ruby's temperament is too violent to lead Hydra, and wonders if Daisy Johnson would be a better fit.

Ruby would first face Quake in S5E17 ("The Honeymoon"), but Johnson uses her powers and defeats her. Hale saves Ruby, but the two argue over Ruby's desire to acquire the powers she's long pursued, as Hale worries about the process and desires more testing. Ruby is approached by Werner von Strucker, who tries to convince her to undergo the process to acquire her powers now:

> RUBY: I don't have a choice.
> STRUCKER: Of course you do. You could tear her apart if you wanted to. So why don't you?
> RUBY: I don't know [Oliver & Oliver, 2018].

This connection resembles the peer connections from *Liv and* Maddie: teens taking matters into their own hands to solve their own problems. Strucker and Ruby represent the Gen Z generation of Hydra, rejecting the conventions and wisdom of the past in lieu of generational values that favor identity over institutional politics and goals.

Hale approaches the room when she realizes the locked door is ajar, expecting Ruby to be gone. However, upon entering, she encounters Ruby, and the two argue about Ruby's training, mission and their relationship with Ruby concluding:

> RUBY: I'm a disappointment. You said that, Mom. And after everything that you've done to me, I've kept trying, because all I've ever wanted—to do is please you. [Crying]—You're my one weakness, Mom. And I'm yours [Oliver & Oliver, 2018].

Ruby flips her mother onto the floor, and locks her in the room. Having verbalized the failure of the parental role in her life, she rejects her mother's authority. Determined to prove her worth by achieving her mission goals, she flees with Strucker, and the two travel to the facility that houses the technology needed for the transformation. They encounter two of the S.H.I.E.L.D. scientists, and force them to rebuild the machine. In S5E18 ("All Roads Lead…"), Ruby begins the transformation, but begins to scream as gravitonium, a substance that grants a person control over the force of gravity, enters her body. Emerging from the chamber with immense power, she accidentally kills Strucker. As Daisy Johnson and her mother try to reason with her, Ruby lashes out with her gravity powers, and begins to crush Johnson's body. Her mother intervenes, and begs her to release Johnson. The two argue, with Ruby accusing her mother of not being on her side, Hale responding that she only wanted Ruby to reach her potential (Kitson, 2018).

As she reasons with her daughter to de-escalate the situation, Hale tries to validate her. Her single parenting presented to her daughter a set of mission goals, and Ruby's identity, having been tightly wrapped up in mission success, is challenged when the gravitonium proves too difficult for her to control. However, just then, Yo-Yo enters the room and sizes up the situation. She uses her speed to turn Ruby's chakra on her, slashing her throat open. Ruby dies, and Hale escapes to ask an alien force to attack S.H.I.E.L.D.

General Hale and Ruby represent a tragedy in terms of the narrative of *Agents of S.H.I.E.L.D.*, but they also represent the cultural anxieties of poor parenting models and the resulting failure of personal identity. "Prime-time feminism" has been noted to focus more on identity rather than politics (Dow, 1996), and Ruby's journey ties her objectives to her identity (and thus, self-worth). Ruby's fall represents a failure of the nuclear family, and portraying a powerful villain who nearly destroys the world as a failure of parenting fits squarely in the messaging strategy of Disney.

Taken together, *Liv and Maddie* and Ruby's arc create a diversity of portrayed messages that reinforces the Disney messaging strategy. Supportive family structures unlock teenage pro–social agency that improves the lives of others, while strained single-parent structures suppress girlhood voice, impair identity, and threaten the world.

REFERENCES

Banet-Weiser, S. (2004). Girls rule! Gender, feminism, and nickelodeon. *Critical Studies in Media Communication, 21*, 119–139.

Beck, J.D., & Hart, R. (Writers). (2013, July 19). Twin-a-Rooney [Television series episode]. In *Liv and Maddie*. Hollywood, CA: The Disney Channel.

_____. (2013, September 15). Team-a-Rooney [Television series episode]. In *Liv and Maddie*. Hollywood, CA: The Disney Channel.

Best, J., & Lowney, K.S. (2009). The disadvantage of a good reputation: Disney as a target for social problem claims. *The Sociological Quarterly, 50*, 431–449.

Blue, M.G. (2017). *Girlhood on Disney Channel: Branding, celebrity, and femininity*. New York: Routledge.

_____. (2019). "The best of both words?" Youth, gender, and a postfeminist sensibility on Disney's *Hannah Montana*. *Feminist Media Studies, 13* (4), 660–675.

Budgeon, S. (2011). The contradictions of successful femininity: Third-wave feminism, post-feminism and "new" femininities. In R. Gill and C. Scharff (eds.) *New femininities: Post-feminism, neoliberalism, and subjectivity,* pp. 279–292, New York: Palgrave Macmillan.

Butler, J. (1988). Performative acts and gender constitution: An essay on the phenomenology and feminist theory. *Theater Journal, 40* (4), 519–531.

Callero, P. (2003). The sociology of the self. *Annual Review of Sociology, 29*, 115–133.

Coates, N. (1997). (R)evolution now? Rock and the political potential of gender. In S. Whitely (Ed.), *Sexting the groove: Popular music and gender* (pp. 50–64). New York: Routledge.

Coulter, N. (2015). *Tweening the girl: The crystallization of the tween market*. Oxford: Peter Lang.

CYCC Network. (2013). *Youth engagement: Empowering youth voices to improve services, programs, and policy*. Retrieved from: http://cyccnetwork.org/en/engagement.

Davis, A.M. (2006). *Good girls & wicked witches: Women in Disney's feature animation*. New Barnet, UK: John Libbey Publishing.

Disney Citizenship Table. (2014). Report. Retrieved from ditm-twdc-us.storage.googleapis. com/FY14-Performance-Summary.pdf.

Disney Citizenship Table. (2016). Report. Retrieved from ditm-twdc-us.storage.googleapis. com/TWDC-FY16-Data-Table-Final.pdf.

Dow, B.J. (1996). *Prime-time feminism: Television, media culture, and the Woman's Movement since 1970*. Philadelphia: University of Pennsylvania Press.

Giroux. H.A. (1999). *The mouse that roared: Disney and the end of innocence*. New York: Rowman & Littlefield.

_____. (2016). Consuming innocence: Disney's corporate stranglehold on youth in the digital age. In J.A. Sandlin, & J.C. Garlen (Eds.), *Disney, culture and curriculum* (pp. 233–249). New York: Routledge.

Green, S. (Writer). (2015, November 22). Ask Her More-a-Rooney [Television series episode]. In *Liv and Maddie*. Hollywood, CA: The Disney Channel.

Greenberg, D.Z. (Writer). (2018, March 2). All the Comforts of Home [Television series episode]. In *Agents of S.H.I.E.L.D.* Los Angeles: ABC Studios.

Griffin, M., Harding, N., & Learmonth, M. (2017). Whistle while you work? Disney animation, organizational readiness and gendered subjugation. *Organization Studies, 38* (7), 869–894.

Hains, Rebecca. (2012). *Growing up with girl power: Girlhood on screen and in everyday life*. New York: Peter Lang.

Hampson, G.A. (Producer). (2013, July 19). *Liv and Maddie* [Television series]. Hollywood, CA: The Disney Channel.

Harrington, S.J. (2015). *The Disney fetish*. Bloomington: Indiana University Press.

Hoover, D., & Monahan, D. (Writers). (2017, March 24). End-a-Rooney [Television series episode]. In *Liv and Maddie*. Hollywood, CA: The Disney Channel.

Keene, J. (Writer). (2015, February 8). Rate-a-Rooney [Television series episode]. In *Liv and Maddie*. Hollywood, CA: The Disney Channel.

Kinser, A.E. (2004). Negotiating spaces for/through third-wave feminism. *NWSA Journal 16* (3), 124–153.

Kitson, G. (Writer). (2018, April 20). All Roads Lead… [Television series episode]. In *Agents of S.H.I.E.L.D.* Los Angeles: ABC Studios.

Lindstrom, M. (2004). Branding is no longer child's play! *Journal of Consumer Marketing, 21* (3), 175–182. doi:10.1108/ 07363760410534722.

Lupold, E. (2014). Adolescence in action: Screening narratives of girl killers. *Girlhood Studies, 7* (2), 6–24.

McRobbie, A. (2009). *The aftermath of feminism: Gender, culture, and social change*. London: Sage.

Oliver, J.C., & Oliver, S. (Writers). (2018, April 13). The Honeymoon [Television series episode]. In *Agents of S.H.I.E.L.D.* Los Angeles: ABC Studios.

Padilla-Walker, L.M., Coyne, S.M., Fraser, A.M., & Stockdale, L.A. (2013). Is Disney the nicest place on Earth? A content analysis of prosocial behavior in animated Disney films. *Journal of Communication, 63* (2), 393–412.

Sammond, N. (2005). *Babes in Tomorrowland: Walt Disney and the making of the American child, 1930–1960*. Durham, NC: Duke University.

Sarikakis, K., & Tsaliki, L. (2011). Post/feminism and the politics of mediated sex. *International Journal of Media & Cultural Politics, 7* (2), 109–119.

Schubart, R. (2006). *Super bitches and action babes: The female hero in popular cinema, 1970–2006*. Jefferson, NC: McFarland.

Shary, T. (2002). *Generation multiplex: The image of youth in contemporary American cinema*. Austin: University of Texas Press.

Siegel, D.L., Coffey, T.J., & Livingston, G. (2004). *The great tweens buying machine: Capturing your share of the multi-billion-dollar tween market*. Chicago: Dearborn Trade Publishing.

Stein, A. (2011). *Why we love Disney: The power of the Disney brand*. New York: Peter Lang.

Tanner, L.T., S.A. Haddock, T.S. Zimmerman & L.K. Lund (2003). Images of couples and families in Disney feature-length animated films, *The American Journal of Family Therapy, 31*(5), 355–373, DOI: 10.1080/01926180390223987.

Van Evra, J. (1998). *Television and child development* (2nd ed.). Mahwah, NJ: Lawrence Erlbaum Associates, Inc.

Wasko, J. (2001). *Understanding Disney: The manufacture of fantasy.* Malden, MA: Blackwell.

Whelehan, I. (2000). *Overloaded: Popular culture and the future of feminism.* London: Women's Press.

Zucker, K.J., & Bradley, S.J. (1995). *Gender identity disorder and psychosexual problems in children and adolescents.* New York: The Guilford Press.

Stuck in the Middle
of a Flattened Culture

SLOAN GONZALES

In the spring of 2016, the Disney Channel released their first Latinx sit-com; the show focuses on Harley, the middle child of the seven Diaz children. At the show's release, Disney's PR department described the show as

> the single-camera comedy series follows 14-year-old Harley Diaz as she maneuvers her way through the bustle of being a middle child in a family with six other siblings. The heartfelt and comedic stories of a big family find Harley devising creative ways to cope with—and stand out—in her family's busy suburban Massachusetts house-hold. Her ingenuity often wins the day for the Diaz family, even with many different personalities living under one roof [Imdb.com, 2016].

The Disney Channel's description of the show highlights a few characteristics that become major themes throughout the show's three seasons, such as the focus on a large working-class family and their struggles. The show's main character must come to the rescue in every episode to save her family, but the show is centered on their relationships, and Harley as a strong, smart, and creative female character. This essay will discuss how these characteristics come to life in the show, and the impact the show has on its tween audience. Common Sense Media describes the tween audience as "individuals between the age of childhood and teenage years, around the ages of eight to twelve years old who spend about 62% of their time watching television" (2015).

Disney's description of *Stuck in the Middle* highlights many of the major themes that play out in the show's three seasons; however, the network never mentions any other goals for the show outside of growing the tween consumer base. The adolescent Latinx population makes up around 17.9 million (Patten, 2016) and the Disney Channel plans to capitalize on every viewer. Neverthe-less, in the early promotion of the show, the Disney Channel did not make any attempt to connect to the Latinx characteristics of *Stuck in the Middle*.

Throughout the show's three seasons, the network takes time to insert bumpers, 60–90 second commercials that feature actors talking about various topics or promoting their specific show. The bumpers for *Stuck in the Middle* often talk about the cast's Latinx heritage, and along with the cast being interviewed for the show, many of these interviews focus on the pride they feel by working on a show that highlights their Latin culture. For example, Kayla Maisonet, who plays Georgie Diaz, in an interview with *De su Mama*, said:

> My father is Puerto Rican. Growing up, one of my favorite traditions included going to visit my abuela and watching her cook delicious authentic Puerto Rican dishes. 'Stuck in the Middle' embraced my heritage by my character Georgie having a Quinceanera. It's a traditional thing to do when you turn 15, and I thought it was so amazing that our show included that. Such a fun moment [2017].

The episode she is referring to airs in the first season, and Harley also has a Quinceñaera in season three. Both episodes involve this milestone; however, neither episode discusses the cultural significance of the event. These two episodes are two of four instances wherein Latin culture is specifically referenced throughout the show's three seasons.

This essay explores the limitations and possibilities of the Disney Channel's contradictory strategy to representing ethnicity exemplified through the construction of contemporary tween Latinidad in *Stuck in the Middle*. The essay will analyze the repetitive rehearsal of a flattened Latinidad through their Christmas episode—the one episode that specifically deals with what it means to be a Latinx—and the two Quinceañera episodes, along with the overall characteristics of the show and how these cultural lessons impact the show's tween demographic.

The Dynamics of the Show

Wizards of Waverly Place (2007–2012) was a Disney Channel show featuring a biracial, Latinx and White family—a first for the network. After the show ended, it was not until 2016 when *Stuck in the Middle* aired that the Disney Channel's audiences would be able to see a similar family demographic. Similar to *Wizards of Waverly Place*, *Stuck in the Middle* features a strong female lead whose interactions and relationships with her family are the focal point of the series. *Stuck in the Middle* features a working-class family consisting of seven kids and their two parents. The show has key characteristics that shape a cultural framework of not only Latin culture, but also the working-class. The show's main character, Harley, must come to her family's rescue in every episode to save them from themselves; in so doing, the show centers itself around Harley's ingenuity as it relates to her familial relationships. Their relationships are woven into many of the episodes, as well as the development of the main characters.

The Diazes—A Working Class Family

One of the main characteristics of the family that is exemplified in every episode, although it is not directly referenced, is the Diaz family's socioeconomic status—categorized by the Disney Channel as a "Suburban Family" (2016). Stereotypical elements of the show highlight the socioeconomic status of the Diaz family as it contributes to their chaotic lifestyle both socially and financially. The 2005 documentary *Class Dismissed: How TV Frames the Working Class* showcases the ways in which class is stereotyped though television media: bad taste, lack of intelligence, reactionary politics, poor work ethic, and dysfunctional family values (Alper and Leistyna). These stereotypes are used to casually disempower the working class. Television media utilize these strategies to subtly point out flaws of the working class and propagate a picture as to why this group of people have not achieved the "American Dream." All five of these stereotypes are played out in *Stuck in the Middle*.

The first stereotype, as identified by *Class Dismissed*, is bad taste, defined as lack of style, organization, or overall appearance of both the characters and the setting (2005). In every frame featuring the Diaz family's household, there is a messy, disheveled, disorganized and ill-designed house, clearly communicating bad taste for this large family of nine. In the pilot episode, it is shown that the family does not have a dining room table; they have many makeshift tables pushed together. The documentary further describes bad taste as not deserving of finer things, such as a nice dining room table that would fit an entire family. Another way this stereotype is shown is through the state of the house: it is a mess of clothes, toys, and random items—a fact pointed out by the Diazes' neighbor, Bethany Peters, a stereotypical white suburban housewife. She constantly lectures the Diaz family on the state of their toy covered yard, and their gutters filled with leaves and trash. The Diaz family laughs it off, as they do in many episodes of the show when their taste, or lack thereof, is discussed.

The character of Bethany Peters is an example of reactionary politics that the documentary discusses in which the middle class is viewed as close minded, right wing, and/or racist (2005). Throughout the series, Ms. Peters is seen as judgmental of the Diaz family, and even forbids her daughter Lulu, who is Harley's best friend, from going to the Diazes' house. She constantly makes statements that show her as a stereotypical white suburban busybody, and her character is often used to point out the faults and Otherness of the Diaz family.

Other working-class stereotypes that we see in the show are a lack of intelligence and poor work ethic, which are primarily displayed through the parents; mainly the dad, Tom, but often the mom, Suzy, as well. *Class Dismissed* looks at the fact that working-class men are portrayed in television as loveable, laughable buffoons: they are not smart, basic things go over their heads, and they are in constant need of help or direction. This help or direction often comes from the female characters in the household, either the wife or the children (2005). In *Stuck in the Middle*, Harley plays this role. She is always the one correcting her dad and fixing the mistakes he or the family make. Tom, the dad, is constantly being portrayed as needing help or guidance. We see this in the Christmas episode when he drops all of the family's electronics and money for their trip into a fire, making it so the family is not able to complete their road trip to see their abuela, and Harley must create a plan and save the family trip. This theme comes up throughout the entire series, and although Tom is a great dad and husband, he sends the message that working class men are unintelligent and need constant supervision. Throughout the series, a poor work ethic in both parents is shown in how they operate their home and raise their children. The unruliness of their lives highlights the family's need for structure, regardless of how much they love one another. This fact is often pointed out by white sub-characters throughout various episodes, such as the neighbor Bethany Peters, or in various sub-characters that judge and correct this unruliness. This is seen again in the Christmas episode when the bank teller that Suzy is trying to convince to help her after their money is all destroyed feels pity for the family at first, but once the twins, Lewie and Beast, trigger the silent alarm, she quickly changes her mind and demeanor from one of helpfulness to a judging and closed off one. This theme of lack of structure and needing constant support or direction is a stereotype that feeds into the idea of the working class as being both unintelligent and lacking work ethic.

The final stereotype portrayed by the show is the dysfunctional family values that *Class Dismissed* describes as bad parenting that creates two types of children, "the smart talented child or the deviant child" (2005). These two characters portrayed throughout the Diaz children with Georgie, Ethan, and Harley as the smart and talented children, who are usually staying out of trouble or fixing the problems caused by their other siblings. The entire premise of the show is Harley always having to save the day or resolve the conflict created by her family with the occasional help of her siblings, which are usually Georgie, and her BFTF (best friend in the family) Ethan. This usually makes her other siblings (Rachel, Beast, Lewis, and Daphne) look like the "deviant child(ren)." Throughout the series, Rachel, the oldest sibling, is constantly needing to be told what to wear and what to do or not to as a teenage girl. Beast and Lewie are always causing chaos and mess wherever they go, and Daphne, the youngest, is seen as the most deviant of all. She is portrayed as a wild child from the way she dresses, speaks, and overall interacts in the show; this portrayal shows the lack of parenting or control the Diaz family has over their children, primarily the younger ones. However, this bad behavior occurs in all of the Diaz family, even Harley, who often in trying to help her family must manipulate or trick her parents into doing what she thinks is correct. This lack of parenting and behavior of the Diaz children is one of the major critiques of the show by parents. Many parents believe the show promotes bad behavior and makes light of those bad behaviors, based on the fact that the Diaz parents do little to correct these behaviors. One review from Common Sense Media showed these sentiments:

> Shocked at the disrespect!! After watching two episodes (Stuck with a guy on couch and; Stuck with Harley's comet), my ten-year-old is NOT allowed to watch this show. The main character manipulates her parents in an effort to hide that she hasn't done her homework, the older sister brags about only putting effort into her looks and tells her father that the mother handles the discipline and not to get involved as she's about to leave the house on the pretense of going to the library with a friend while dressed in a tight skirt and heels and you hear a engine revving outside. Who writes this stuff—15-year old? Not sure what Disney was thinking with this, but no thank you. Any positive message (I can't remember any) is overshadowed by the blatant disrespect and manipulative undertone [2016].

The show highlights a lot of sweet coming-together family moments and, through Harley, shows a smart and talented young woman; however, the show's use of stereotypes of the working class and particularly the Latinx culture (which will be discussed in the next section) teaches a flawed message to its tween audience. As the Disney Channel's only all-Latinx show, this creates a problem, as it creates a visual stereotype: not of the middle class but of the Latinx community. The audience of the show is being taught that these stereotypes are the norm and that many Latinx families operate in a state of chaos, messiness, and a lack of common sense and positive behaviors.

Stuck in the Middle and the Portrayal of Latinidad

Disney's attempt at representing the Latinx culture in *Stuck in the Middle* is missed through its limited storyline, character development, and lack of true representation of the Latinx culture. The show is a continuous example of *Latinidad*, a term used to explain how the images of Latinx in the entertainment business are constructed as being homogenized, erasing uniqueness and differences amongst Latinx cultures (Aparicio & Chávez-Silverman 1997). Valdivia (2010) defines it as "the state or experience of being Latina/o or the assignment of Latina/o traits to people, culture, and habits" (p. 11). "Notice that Latinidad does not have to be produced by Latina/os, inhabited by

Latina/os, or even consumed by Latina/os" (p. 11). Latinidad is an active social construction by both creators and consumers; Disney has created its own version of a Latinidad construct through the hiring of light brown skinned actors, giving the family the name Diaz, having a non–Spanish speaking family, having a stressed out stay at home mom and a unintelligent father, misbehaved children, and finally having the show open with highlighting the Diaz family as being a loud, busy, chaotic, and self-focused family. All of these elements create a clear definition of what Disney wants to portray in its first official show that features a Latin family and cast.

Guidotti-Hernández (2007), in her analysis of the popular children's show *Dora the Explorer*, suggests that Latino cast-centered programming generates broad discourses of "Latinidad" for primarily Anglo-American audiences attempting to negotiate shifting cultural, demographic, and political dynamics. Guidotti-Herndez analysis brings up the question, who is the true audience for *Stuck in the Middle*? Is it the growing Latinx under-18 population, 17.1 million (Passel, Cohn, & Lopez, 2011) or is it the Anglo-American (white) audience that Guidotti-Hernadez is referencing in her 2007 analysis. According to the Walt Disney Company in their 2014 Citizenship Summary:

> The U.S. Hispanic Initiative is a companywide priority that recognizes U.S. Hispanics as one the largest domestic growth opportunities for the Walt Disney Company and brings to life the role of diversity in driving relevance in the marketplace. The initiative has served as the catalyst for projects across all of our businesses focusing on talent, cultural competency, consumer insights, and product development, and content [p. 62].

Since this 2014 statement, Disney has introduced more Latinx characters and content, including the children's TV show *Elena of Avalor*, the motion picture *Coco*, and *Stuck in the Middle*. Each of these texts strive to connect with the growing young Latinx generation and their families.

Many television and films marketed to Latinos have a common theme of "whitewashed" casting. Arlene Davila, in her book *Latino Spin: Public Image and the Whitewashing of Race*, analyzes the ways in which whitewashing is pervasive in mainstream visual media; the Latino Spin maintains that Latinos are simultaneously subjected to processes of whitening and racialization and the dichotomous frameworks reducing the fate of the totality of the Latinx population to one or another process, especially on the bases of a single variable, be it how Latinx identify racially or whether they speak Spanish(2008). Latin actors being cast to play Latinx characters are expected to look as Caucasian as possible, meaning brown hair, lightly tanned skin, straight or well managed curly hair, and they typically speak English proficiently. In their article *Starlets, Subscribers, and Beneficiaries: Disney, Latino Children, and Television Labor*, Chavez and Kiley (2016) looked at how Disney is not only marketing to Latinx youth, but also how they are employing Latinx youth. Chavez and Kiley found that

> Disney's Latinx are either phenotypically white or light brown and with no traceable accents. In other words, they possess no clear outward signifiers of Latino identity. This is not to say that their Latino heritage is completely erased. Instead, these bodies are commodifiable because their ethnicity can be controlled to reach several different markets. As Molina Guzmán has argued, Latinas who are closer to the mainstream are more desirable and consumable than more ethnically coded actresses [2010].

The cast of the show features a white-looking and English speaking version of the Latinx culture; the characters are lighter skinned with straight brown hair, and all speak English, with looks that naturally blend into society's makeup. Nothing about the Diaz family dramatically stands out as Latin, but they have the basic characteristics, while simultaneously being able to fit strategically into the dominant white culture.

Despite Disney's intentions to develop content and cast actors that represent the Latinx culture, Disney has missed the mark with *Stuck in the Middle*. The content of the show very rarely discusses the Latinx culture, and when it does bring it up in the "Stuck at Christmas" episode, and the Quinceanera episodes—*Stuck in the Quinceanera, Stuck in Harley's Quinceanera,* and *Stuck in a Gold Medal Performance,* the Latinx elements are never discussed or explained in terms of a lesson on the Latinx culture. Instead, they are used more as cultural placeholders, where it is mentioned to remind the audience that the Diaz family, is in fact, Latin. In the Christmas episode, a "normal American Christmas" is shown with Christmas decorations, presents, and the greeting of "Merry Christmas." The two references to the Latinx culture are when the Diaz children call their grandmother their *abuela,* and when they are making their abuela's authentic Mexican meal. This is one of the only times that Spanish is used in the series, and it is a brief feature of the episode; however, nothing else about this episode explores the traditions of a Latinx Christmas.

Another way Latinidad is seen is in the content of the show is in the two episodes about Georgie and Harley's Quinceaneras. According to *My Quince Magazine*:

> Although a Quinceañera may appear at first glance to be simply a festive, lavishly adorned birthday party, it also has a deeper significance that extends to the girl's personal self. The Quinceañera, which literally translates to "the girl who is 15," signifies a young girl's transition in becoming a mature woman who is capable of independence in that she can make her own decisions and symbolizes her transition and growth into womanhood. It also plays a symbolic gesture in that it reaffirms her beliefs to her church and her personal faith. This celebration has a religious ceremony followed by a party and combines a blend of traditional customs with contemporary trends [2016].

The main elements of a traditional Quinceanera are not mentioned in either episode. The elements portrayed in the episode are washed down references. It is big party one has when one turns 15; one wears a big pretty dress, and it is a celebration of becoming a woman. These two episodes could have provided a lesson on the cultural role that this milestone is for young Latina women; however, the Disney Channel utilized the episode as a way to briefly and barely touch on the Diaz family's cultural background.

The only other episode that looks at the Latinx culture is "Stuck in a Gold Medal Performance" (S2E13), which features Olympic Gold medalist Laurie Hernandez. The premise of the episode revolves around Georgie meeting the young Olympian and lying about how "Latino" her family is. Laurie decides to come to the Diazes' house for a traditional family dinner based on the lies Georgie tells her. In a state of panic, Georgie does everything she can to make her family appear more "Latino" by learning Spanish, making her family watch a telenovela, taking a Latin dance class, making a traditional dinner, and then redecorating the house to look more like a traditional Latin home. When Laurie arrives, in the tradition of the show, everything goes awry, and the chaos leads Georgie to tell Laurie the truth about her family not being very "Latino." This leads to a great lesson on culture, when Georgie admits to not feeling like she is a Latina, which Laurie responds with, "All the cultural stuff is great, but to me being a good Latina means being a good person, which you are" (S2E13). It is a simple moment showing that Latinx culture looks different to different families, which a great lesson for all tween viewers, regardless of their ethnicity.

The "Stuck in a Gold Medal Performance" episode has a good cultural lesson; however, it is the only episode of the series that directly talks about the Diazes' Latin culture, and what it means to be a young Latinx. *Stuck in the Middle,* in its three-season run, missed out on the opportunity to truly showcase and educate its tween audience on the diversity and complexity of the Latinx culture.

Harley Diaz the "Future" Girl and the Impact *of* Stuck in the Middle

Throughout the last decade, there has been a shift in media around how young girls are portrayed in television, movies, and books. There has been a surge of new stories where young girls are the central character and these characters are no longer just the sidekick or the girl that needs saving. These new "future girls," as Anita Harris calls them in her 2004 book, *Future Girl: Young Women of the 21st Century*, are young girls that are confident, resilient, and have the world at their feet. These new characters are reimagining how young female stories are being told and shown in popular culture. These new future girls are depicted throughout recent pop culture with characters such as Katniss Everdeen from the *Hunger Games*, along with Disney remakes like *Cinderella* and *Beauty and Beast*, where iconic female characters that were once meek and one-dimensional character, now are brave, smart, creative, and strong. This change in young girl storytelling has had its impact on the Disney Channel with most of their shows being centered around or with these strong new "future girls."

Harley Diaz is no exception—she is imaginative, creative, quick witted, smart, and independent. The main theme of the show is about Harley saving the day through her creative solutions and inventions. Harley is a tween girl who looks her age; she is not overly sexualized or made to look older. She looks like an average tween girl one would see at a local school. She is relatable and someone a young girl would want to be like. Her love for science is clear, and she applies it in everyday problem solving, whether it is in making her family a new dining room table, her Harley Cam, or the countless other inventions she creates. She is always thinking of new creative ways to make her and her family's lives easier. This narrative that is depicted throughout the series helps to construct the ideas that young girls have power, confidence, and the opportunity to take charge of their lives and achieve their goals. It shows young girls what it means to be a girl of the future. *Stuck in the Middle* helps to create a new young female identity that promotes self-invention, where young girls can create the kind of future that is unique to their goals and desires. Harley Diaz is a strong female role model for young tween girls and highlights what it means to be a future girl.

Throughout *Stuck in the Middle*'s three season run, the program covered a wide range of age appropriate topics and influenced many young people in both a positive and negative way. Although the show introduced Harley Diaz, a smart, STEM-savvy, innovative Latina, the show missed the opportunity to truly influence its audience. The opportunity to inform and educate the Disney Channel audience in lessons of culture and differences from their enormous platform was missed, and instead, they presented a one-dimensional look at Latinx culture and the ways in which it operates in American society. This essay analyzed the repetitive rehearsal of superficial Latinidad through *Stuck in the Middle*, and how these cultural lessons, or lack thereof, impacted the show's appeal to the tween demographic. The show's key characteristics emphasized a cultural framework of, not only, Latinx culture, but also the working-class and how these groups are portrayed in popular culture.

REFERENCES

Alper, L., and Leistyna, P. (2005). *Class dismissed: How TV frames the working class*. [Video file]. Retrieved from https://www.filmsforaction.org/watch/class-dismissed-how-tv-frames-the-working-class-2005/.

Bonnie W. (2016). What is a quinceanera and why is it so important. Retrieved from https://www.myquincemagazine.com/what-is-a-quinceanera-and-why-is-it-so-important/.

Bell, V. (2017). Disney actors talk Latino identity and Hispanic heritage month. Retrieved from https://www.desumama.com/disney-actors-bicultural-latino-identity-hispanic-heritagae-month/.

Beltrán, M. (2005). The new Hollywood racelessness: Only the fast, furious (and multiracial) will survive. *Cinema Journal, 44*(2), 50–67. doi:10.1353/cj.2005.0003.

Beltrán, M. (2008). Mixed race in Latinowood: Latino stardom and ethnic ambiguity in the era of Dark Angels. In M. Beltrán & C. Fojas (Eds.), *Mixed race Hollywood* (pp. 248–268). New York: New York University Press.

Chavez, C. (2015). *Reinventing the Latino television viewer: Language, ideology, and practice.* Lanham, MD: Lexington.

Chavez, C., & Killey, A. (2016). Starlets, subscribers, and beneficiaries: Disney, Latino children, and television labor. *International Journal of Communication* (10). 2616–2636. doi:1932–8036/20160005.

Cheu, J. (2013). *Diversity in Disney films: Critical essays on race, ethnicity, gender, sexuality, and disability.* Jefferson, NC: McFarland.

Dávila, A. (2001). *Latinos, Inc.: The marketing and making of a people.* Berkeley: University of California Press.

Dávila, A. (2008). *Latino spin: Public image and the whitewashing of race.* New York: New York University Press.

Disney Channel PR. (2016). Stuck in the Middle storyline. Retrieved from https://www.imdb.com/title/tt4488724/.

Harris, A. (2004). *Future girl: Young women in the twenty-first century.* London: Routledge.

Jayed. (2016). Parent reviews for Stuck in the Middle. Retrieved from https://www.commonsensemedia.org/tv-reviews/stuck-in-the-middle/user-reviews/adulthttps://www.commonsensemedia.org/sites/default/files/uploads/research/census_researchreport.pdf.

Mastro, D., Behm-Morawitz, E., & Kopacz, M. (2008). Exposure to television portrayals of Latinos: The implications of aversive racism and social identity theory. *Human Communication Research, 34*(1), 1–27. doi:10.1111/j.1468–2958.2007.00311.x.

Negron-Muntaner, F. (2016). The Latino media gap: A report on the state of latinos in u.s. media. Retrieved from https://media-alliance.org/wp-content/uploads/2016/05/Latino_Media_Gap_Report.pdf.

Rideout, V. (2015). *Common sense census: Media use by tweens and teens.* Common Sense Media. Retrieved from https://www.commonsensemedia.org/research/the-common-sense-census-media-use-by-tweens-and-teens.

Rodriguez, J. (2016, March 18) Disney Channel's new Latino family in Stuck in the Middle. Retrieved from https://latintrends.com/disney-channels-new-latino-family-in-stuck-in-the-middle/.

Rodriguez, J. (2017, June 23). Here's How Laurie Hernandez's Character dealt with the awkward moment when her friend over compensated her "Latina-ness." Retrieved from https://wearemitu.com/entertainment/laurie-hernandez-was-on-disneys-stuck-in-the-middle-and-there-was-a-powerful-moment-latinos-will-relate-to/.

Ruiz, M. (2015). The taxonomy of the latina body: Adrian Lee in The Secret Life of the American Teenager. *Humboldt Journal of Social Relations* (37) (pp. 30–45).

De-*Bunk'd* and De-Natured

Tweenage TV Comedy
in the Artificial Outdoors

Daniel F. Yezbick

"There are few things 'natural' about adolescence."
—Aimee Rickmann, 2018

Bunk'd represents one of the more derivative examples of the Disney Channel's "retail friendly, mom-approved" situation comedies (Stanley 2006). Premiering on July 31, 2015, and concluding on September 21, 2018, *Bunk'd* endured for three seasons, comprising 58 total episodes. Pamela Eells O'Connell developed the summer camp comedy as a spin-off to showcase several characters from her previously successful *Jessie*, the Park Avenue–themed Debby Ryan vehicle that enjoyed 98 episodes across four seasons between 2011 and 2015. *Bunk'd* builds its campfire farce around what Tyler Bickford identifies as a typically "engineered social production," providing an appealing, aloof "oppositional space" to tweens and teens still under the scrutiny and surveillance of parents and guardians (Bickford 2012). Thus, *Bunk'd* and its many Disney Channel clones offer fantasies of empowerment, pleasure, and belonging that not only encourage allegiance to Disney brand entertainment, but also promote a peculiar form of media-soaked detachment or distraction from real world scenarios and their more complex predicaments (Bickford 2012). In the process, such remediated narratives appeal to both parents and children by foregrounding "rhetorics of safety" that "scrub" the text of "potentially offensive elements" as they bridge the gap between juvenile tastes and "big kid" pre-adolescent trends (Bickford 2012). Like much Disney tween TV, *Bunk'd* presents a mildly amusing and generally benign summer camp farce where kids and counselors share a variety of sanitized misadventures.

Yet, *Bunk'd* also reveals crucial truths concerning the ideological and eco-environmental underpinnings of "key markets of identity and affiliation" within tween cultures, as well as the larger pernicious implications of "youth markets" rooted in distraction, disinterest, and denial of actual or immediate threats to self, community, and culture (Bickford 2012).

Bunk'd does not follow the dominant *Lizzie Maguire/Hannah Montana* formula of exploring "the frothy fun and foibles of a just-like-you-but-cuter middle school girl" who also happens to enjoy pop stardom (Orenstein 2011). Nor is *Bunk'd* particularly musical, trendy, or hyper-commercial in its address, at least not as much as established Disney franchises like *High School Musical* or *Camp Rock*. In fact, very little licensed merchandise for *Bunk'd* or its mother series, *Jessie*, exists, placing both shows outside the typical matrices of the Disney Channel's cross-marketing (Mjøs 2010). *Bunk'd* does reflect the standard Disney formula of up-cycling aging child stars from other contexts: "Each girl's rise became fodder for another media fairy tale, another magical rags to riches transformation, to which ordinary girls could aspire" (Orenstein 2011). In this case, however, Disney's synergistic "one stop shop for talent" evolves in somewhat unorthodox directions that both encourage and misuse diversity-driven drama (Stanley 2006).

Like its many sibling series, *Bunk'd* also develops its narratives around close-knit family, friend, and clique-based conflicts adamantly sanitized for "family friendly" viewing. In this case, the action centers around a familiar "summer camp" scenario crucial to several rituals of American adolescent leisure. This essay examines the broader impact of *Bunk'd* as it relates to Disney's previous efforts to blend tween/teen comedy with camp, scout, or outdoor settings; its role in recapitulating and remediating a variety of summer camp themed traits, types, and traditions; and most importantly, its failure to comment on, connect with, or ultimately enable tweens, teens, and young adults through involvement in and advocacy for the escalating eco-environmental crises facing the natural world in the late Anthropocene.

True Life Fallacies: Disney Media, Nature Narratives and Tween Detachment

For better or worse, Disney narratives have always championed the beauty, balance, and beneficence of the natural world. Early animated homages to the majesty and romance of nature include Ub Iwerks and Carl Stalling's trio of bucolic seasonal shorts, *Springtime* (1929), *Summer* (1930), and *Autumn* (1930)[1] as well as Burt Gillett's 1932 Silly Symphony, *Flowers and Trees.* The 1937 Oscar-winning animated short, Wilfred Jackson and Leigh Harline's *The Old Mill,* is still considered one of the studio's most effective blends of technical achievement and environmental commentary. Similarly, landmark features like 1937's *Snow White and the Seven Dwarfs*, 1940's *Fantasia*, and especially 1942's *Bambi*, based on the novel by Austrian-Jewish nature writer, Felix Salten, each emphasized in their own way, the benefits of loving nature, respecting its creatures, and preserving its contexts.[2] In each case, however, Disney media is also complicit in what Jean Baudrillard conceives as the gradual erasure of actual animal and wilderness-based realities from human epistemologies. As animated flowers, birds, trees, and rabbits become technologically enticing spectacles of human ingenuity, they also erase, erode, or remove our interest or respect for the genuine wilderness and its authentic animal encounters (Baudrillard 1994). Thus animated mice, ducks, and dogs are transformed into anthropomorphized fantasies built around branded corporate personalities with strange and addictive significance.[3] The same process holds true for live action Disney Channel comedies that trade in hyper-real extensions of otherwise comfortable, glamorous, or fun people, places, and spaces. The more polished, professional, and perfected each element of Camp Kikiwaka becomes, the less accurately its tween fans are attuned to the complexities of actual wilderness, the animals that inhabit it, and the human benefits of both.

In terms of TV comedy, *Bunk'd*, like most current Disney Channel "after school" sitcoms, also owes its hokey address to a long tradition of ensemble "big kids" gang comedies, beginning with Disney's own *The Mickey Mouse Club* program, which followed the equally iconic "youth party" show *American Bandstand* on ABC from 1955 to 1958.[4] In some ways, the current Disney Channel trend of developing (predominantly Caucasian female, and insistently straight) marquee talent out of their theme park stables via TV vehicles and Radio Disney also hails back to the rise of midcentury celebrity Mouseketeers like Annette Funicello, Darlene Gillespie, Karen Pendleton, and Sharon Baird. As much as Britney Spears, Christina Aguilera, Hillary Duff, Miley Cyrus, Raven-Symoné Pearman, Selena Gomez, and Demi Lovato have redefined iconic Disney tweenery for the 21st century, *The Mickey Mouse Club* introduced several of the comedic, musical, and character-driven features that continue to influence many Disney shows from *Sonny with a Chance* to *Bunk'd* (Orenstein 2011).

This seems especially true in relation to one particular, recurring *Mickey Mouse Club* feature. Immensely popular in it time, but now largely forgotten, *Spin and Marty* was a summer camp serial featuring David Stollery as the pampered orphan snob, Marty Markham, and Tim Considine as the working class over-achiever, Spin Evans. The story ran across several seasons in 25 segments within *The Mickey Mouse Club's* parade of skits, songs, animated shorts, and Head Mouseketeer Jimmie Dodd's avuncular "Doddisms" on ethical behavior. Like *Bunk'd*, *Spin and Marty* sold simulacral bro-mantic fantasies of class-conscious rivals finding common ground via adventures in the great outdoors. Centering mostly around happenings on the Triple R Ranch, the narrative anticipates much of the camp-driven drama of *Bunk'd*'s Emma and Lou or Ravi and Jorge. Camp Kikiwaka also mirrors the rustic shenanigans of the Triple R, right down to the similar theme songs, "Yippee Yay, Yippee Yi, Yipee Yo" and "Kikiwaka Kikiwaka."[5]

Bunk'd further remediates and absorbs a wide variety of other comedic traditions, from slapstick humor to magical realism as it spoofs camp, scout, and outdoor culture. At times, the whiny campers approach the flagrant desperation of satires like Allan Sherman's "Hello Muddah, Hello Faddah" recordings and Ravi's bursts with authoritarian tyranny expose the same hierarchal hypocrisies as the badge-happy Khaki Scouts of Camp Ivanhoe from Wes Anderson's *Moonrise Kingdom*. While those texts each emphasize the social absurdities and individualized agonies of coming of age, *Bunk'd*—breezily tweeny and scrubbed safe in its address—lacks the ideological depth, satiric bite, and, perhaps most obviously, the interest in anything actually keyed to Emersonian Self-Reliance, Twain-esque "roughing it," or Jack London–esque Naturalistic adversity. Instead, the series encourages a shallow simmering disdain for or detachment from the developmental rituals and responsibilities of camp culture involving the exploration of nature or the acceptance of ecological responsibility. The sets themselves—with impossibly bright and airy cabins and synthetically carpeted green spaces—continually emphasize the simulacral erasure of the real, the natural, and the wild. All are replaced with controlled, contrived, and trite approximations of actual camp culture. Even the interstitial establishing shots of bucolic Maine wilderness brimming with lush evergreens, unspoiled lakes, and rugged mountains appear more jarring and incongruous than in most Disney Channel sitcoms.

Bunk'd's continual distance from actual nature seems odd considering Disney media's historical reliance on thrilling spectacles of hyper-realistic wilderness as well as the brand's perpetual emphasis of idealized animal life in its eco-educational films. Later renditions of *the Mickey Mouse Club* included educational vignettes relating to wild animals, conservation, and ecological awareness. At the same time, Roy E. Disney's True-Life Adventures documentary unit at Buena Vista specialized in cutting edge, thoughtfully narrated, educational films instructing audiences of all ages in the risks and wonders of the natural world. Between 1948 and 1960, True-Life Adventures produced seven documentary features, seven "two-reeler" short features, and nine educational shorts for use in classrooms, libraries, and community centers. Among them were several of the most advanced environmental documentaries of their time, equal to both National Geographic and Jacques Costeau's *Undersea World* productions.

True-Life explorations of *White Wilderness* (1958), *The Vanishing Prairie*

(1954), and *The Living Desert* (1953) each earned Academy Awards for Best Documentary, and Kenworthy and Wright's *Perri*, Disney's squirrel driven sequel to Salten's *Bambi* was eventually folded into the series as its one and only experiment in *True-Life Fantasy*. Most True-Life Adventures were also cross-marketed through Disney's expansive merchandising system, perpetuating their eco-conscious dramas through Dell one-shot comics, a daily single panel syndicated newspaper comic developed by George Wheeler between 1955 and 1971, a variety of picture and chapter book adaptations (including the popular *Worlds of Nature* series), a number of Disney Records phonographic recapitulations, and even the occasional D.I.Y. animal model kit.[6]

Several True-Life two-reelers also earned Oscars and helped to further Disney's commitment to excellence in nature documentary. This interest eventually led to consolidation of multiple conservation efforts around their Animal Kingdom theme park, the international impact of the multimillion dollar Disney Wildlife Conservation Fund (beginning in 1995), and the eventual revamping of the True-Life Adventures brand as its current avatar, DisneyNature (beginning in 2008). After the global success of Luc Pacquet's partially Disney-funded *March of the Penguins*, its DisneyNature branch, centered in Paris and overseen by Jean-Francois Camilleri, continued to produce technically impressive nature documentaries relating to popular species like the Mariella Frostrup-narrated 2008 *The Crimson Wing: Mystery of the Flamingo*. They also continue to produce evocative statements advocating for endangered animals as in the John Krasinski-voiced *Born in China*, a 2017 exploration of concerns surrounding pandas, snow leopards, and chiru (a species of Tibetan antelope). With so many diverse, dynamic fusions of ecology, documentary, and celebrity across so many forms and contexts of Disney media from educational shorts and comic-book one-shot specials to theme park awareness campaigns and internationally produced Imax spectacles, the relative dearth of eco-environmental concerns in *Bunk'd* seems aesthetically odd and perhaps ethically troubling.

"*This one time, at* bland *camp!*": Bunk'd in the Bored Outdoors

Despite its ambivalence concerning outdoor leisure or eco-environmental advocacy, *Bunk'd* invokes and appropriates several inter-related camp-themed narrative traditions. Camps, retreats, and other excursion-based rituals of leisure, craftsmanship, and community building provide highly coded spaces of transition and transformation, and the behaviors and anxieties surrounding them inform every feature of American life, especially their intimate conjunction with seminal children's organizations and activities related to scouting, sports and fitness, ethnic and faith identity, music and theater, and the lauded rites of Armed Forces passage associated with basic training and boot camps.

From trust-building ropes courses to psyche-scarring fundamentalist ordeals like those revealed in Grady and Ewing's 2006 *Jesus Camp*, the camp site is itself a heavily coded and conflicted setting for American "coming of age" and self-discovery narratives ranging from ribald urban legends (themselves often circulated through campfire stories!) to celebrity-making reality TV concepts like *Big Brother*, *Survivor*, or *Naked and Afraid*. In short, camp-themed dramas and documentaries often function as assessments or indictments of diversified communities and their complicated influence on specific individuals. Rich in bonding, romance, and risk, most camp-centered dramas explore similar contrasts between individual and communal growth, leader/mentors and their pupils/campers, and established rules of organization, hierarchy, and achievement in conflict with individual freedoms and free will.

Some camp narratives embrace the establishmentarian elements of their institutional settings such as Bill Melendez's 1977 *Race for Your life, Charlie Brown*, Harry Winner's 1986 *Space Camp*, or the more recent *High School Musical* franchise initiated by Kenny Ortega's 2006 film. Such texts, like Steve Brill's 1995 *Heavyweights* or the Riedell Brothers' 2014 *Camp Takota*, follow a familiar situational formula involving a core set of generic conventions that Brian Moylan defines as "a group of underestimated misfits, an unlikely leader, an overly sincere adversary who likes to cheat, and the renewal of traditional values through adversity" (Moylan 2015). Disney's own variations on such themes include the 1961 and 1998 renditions of *The Parent Trap*. Others, such as Ivan Reitman's 1979 genre-defining *Meatballs* (followed by a 1984 sequel), Barry Sonenfeld's 1993 *Addams Family Values* (itself a sequel to the 1991 original), or the devilishly deconstructive *Hot Wet American Summer* concept initiated by David Wain's 2001 feature and expanded Web TV spin-offs—promote a more rebellious, ribald, inherently defiant assault on the rules and rituals that define collaboration, conformity, and competition.

Some camp media elevate rivalry, romance, and "coming of age" to explicit extremes of athletic, sexual, and violent spectacle. Bawdy romps, like Ron Maxwell's surprisingly reflective 1980 *Little Darlings* or lesser entries like the 2005 *American Pie presents Band Camp* developed by Adam Herz and Steve Rash, examine the "sloppy, grasping, wonderful transition to adulthood" that makes summer camp experimentation a common rite of passage (Moylan 2015). Some texts trade powerfully on erotically charged camp encounters such as Emile Ardolino's 1987 blockbuster hit, *Dirty Dancing*. Still others build cleverly on the exploitative "T&A" traditions that drive 1987's *Party Camp* or 2013's *Man Camp* to provoke commentaries on gender diversity, as in Jamie Babbit's 2000 queer classic, *But I'm a Cheerleader* or Medjuck and Smith's understated 2013 meditation on adolescence and belonging in *Summerhood*.

Summer camps and woodland locales have long been associated with the sadistic extremes and rampage/rape fantasies of slasher franchises. The blood-soaked cabins of *Sleepaway Camp* and *Friday the 13th*'s Camp Crystal Lake blend "humor, and traditional horror conventions with bizarre turns while also making you surprisingly sympathetic for both the heroes and the villains" who strive to survive in the darkness (Cadenas and Khal 2015). Some also interpret the frequent gender-switching or transsexual marauders linked specifically to the summer camp slasher sub-genre as reactionary fantasies that develop monstrous "mutations and slidings whereby women begin to look a lot like men and men are pressured to become like women" (Clover 1992). Both the *Friday the 13th* and *Sleepaway Camp* franchises develop their climactic revelations as rustic outdoor transplantings of Norman Bates' cross-dressing blasphemy from Alfred Hitchcock's *Psycho,* though the updates are more exaggerated and explicit in both cases. Feminist media critic Willow Maclay labels such transsexual horrors as uniquely unnerving moments of slasher camp transmisogyny (Maclay 2015). Alongside masked marauders and serial killers, Sasquatch, Big Foot, and other cryptid missing links are also common to summer camp scenarios, especially when they too can speak to gender-driven anxieties concerning social change and the macho repression of eco-feminist empowerment (Bissette 2017). In such texts, atavistic beast-people are generally used as allegorical statements about the risks of over-technologized convenience and the fears of displaced or de-centered patriarchy (Buhs 2009).

Bunk'd remains mildly or sporadically conversant with most of these themes and conventions. Though the family friendly series avoids most overt references to sexual activity, counselors frequently reference The Spot were campers sometimes indulge in romantic interludes. Clover and Maclay's concerns with monstrous transmisogyny also arises early in the first episode, when Emma, Ravi, and Zuri trade derogatory gender-bending quips with Gladys, the crone-ish owner of Camp Kikiwaka. Thrown over years ago by their father, Gladys has grown old and hideous with regret and envy. Emma quickly mistakes her for a man, even before noticing her hairy legs, and Zuri and Ravi keep up the gender-driven barbs for several episodes. Slasher themes also find their way into *Bunk'd* plots, including the second episode, "Gone Girl," when Ravi mistakenly assumes that Xander and Lou are plotting to murder and mutilate Emma, *Texas Chainsaw Massacre*–style.

Ghosts, hauntings, and angry spirits are also common to *Bunk'd* plots, but one particularly gruesome episode in Season Two, "Camp Kiki-slasher" might stand as the most transgressive single installment of Disney TV yet filmed. *Bunk'd*'s producers were clearly concerned, as they include an adamant warning by Zuri that younger audience members should consider viewing this particularly ghoulish Halloween special with a grown-up. As the show moves forward, a masked menace emerges from the woods and methodically kidnaps campers and counselors alike. Midway through, the threat is revealed as Timmy, the show's perpetual outlier who can never afford the entrance fee to Camp Kikiwaka. He now desperately seeks to scare Gladys as vengeance for keeping him out and the whole cast joins in, coating themselves in fake gore, piercing corpses to archery targets and tool sheds, and masquerading as severed heads and rampaging killers. It is, quite possibly, the funniest and most original episode of the series, and one that clearly savors the heady traditions of slashing, screaming, and surviving that define summer camp horror. Perhaps no other Disney Channel sitcom works quite so hard to explore themes of gendered menace or monstrous vengeance.

Like Timmy the slasher, the Camp's own resident sasquatch, the Kikiwaka, also makes several memorable appearances. The first sightings turn out to be the jilted Gladys in disguise, gleefully frightening children and adding to her already witchy reputation. Later episodes like Season One's "Waka! Waka! Waka!" and Season Three's series finale, "Up, Up, and Away!," introduce actual Kikiwakas who befriend campers, disguise themselves as human children, and even rescue the long suffering Timmy from his isolation in the woods. Associated with both slashers and sasquatches, poor maligned Timmy—the impoverished waif thrown from camp like a Dickensian orphan—finally gains his overdue reward in the closing moments of the series.

Bunk'd seems unique to Disney programming in one other respect. Unlike the majority of its cloned siblings, which are historically developed as customized vehicles for individual rising stars, this camp comedy focuses much of its core humor on the antics of its supporting players. Throughout the series, headliner Peyton List—a fairly talented and charismatic Britney/Christina–esque blond—portrays a mostly blasé straight woman surrounded by the complications and conundrums that assail Camp Kikiwaka. Though she occasionally takes on major roles in episodes like "Friending the Enemy" and "Xander Says Goodbye," she often feels like *Bunk'd*'s star in absentia as an ever-changing ensemble of younger, weirder, and more flagrantly grotesque characters fill in the laughs. Several episodes of Seasons Two and Three prefer the broad stereotyping comedy of Miranda May's Lou Hockhauser and Skai Johnson's Zurianna "Zuri" Zenobia Ross, rather than the fetching flatness of Peyton List's Emma Ross.[7] Lou and Zuri generally rise above the clichéd characterizations that plague Camp Kikiwaka, but they also produce some significant concerns relating to ethnic, gender, and class tensions.

Zuri is possibly the most consistently positive (and funny) character in both *Bunk'd* and its progenitor, *Jessie*. Adopted as a baby from Uganda by wealthy New Yorkers, Zuri is a true alpha girl, leading, coaching, consulting, and conspiring to always gain advantage, make profit, or just generally stay on top of whatever game is afoot. Like her high-strung brother, Ravi, she can occasionally substitute for the antagonist, as when she portrays a ruthless judge in the witch trial episode, "Gruel and Unusual Punishment," but she is more frequently cast as an empowered multicultural update of the wisecracking dames and snarking debutantes of Screwball comedy. Despite her unabashed love of country music, Zuri's wit, originality, and cunning are also associated with streetwise African American hustling. In *Bunk'd*'s pilot episode, she encourages stereotyped Asian overachiever, Tiffany, to defy her domineering Tiger Mom by sharing "with your book smarts and my street smarts, we'll run this camp!"(Eells O'Connell & Koherrn 2015).

Similarly, *Bunk'd*'s second episode, "Gone Girl," finds Zuri partnered with a criminalized Hispanic "scarface," Jorge, as they traffic contraband candy and computer games into Kikiwaka. In one of their deliberations on how best to manage their criminal empire, Zuri hilariously quotes *The Wire*'s romantic (queer) Robin Hood hero, Omar Little, "You come at the king, you best not miss!" (Eells O'Connell & Koherr 2015). While many of the Disney Channel's viewers are probably not familiar with one of television history's most unrelenting explorations of urban vice and civic corruption, Zuri's dialogue alludes to one of Omar's most prophetic lines—one which has become gospel to both middle-class HBO fans and actual Baltimore street gangs. Her reference confirms that Zuri, though an Ugandan orphan adopted into privilege, is still conversant in the African American narratives of urban struggle, hustling, and violent crime. As much as Zuri's blackness defines her tough "street cred" in a supposedly diverse camp where she is almost always the only African American present, she is equally adept at invoking the class privileges of the Ross family whenever Kikiwaka activities become too outdoorsy or arduous for her tastes. Some of her first gags involve escaping back to the familiar comforts of Manhattan in the Ross family limo. Zuri's general demeanor is also the complete opposite of the show's most intriguing original character, Miranda May's charming country bumpkin, Lou Hockhauser.

Head Counselor Lou is a buck-toothed, zaftig goofball brimming with folksy charm and, at times, unfiltered "down home" advice relating to simple country customs. Raised on the family farm, she eagerly facilitates city kids and CITs (counselors in training) adjusting to the more laid back, rustic pleasures of Camp Kikiwaka. In her first appearance before the Ross children, who have all been assigned to the camp's Chipmunk cabin, Lou performs a complex ritual greeting exposing her exaggerated dental features, excitedly promotes the thrills of catching mud dabs, and connects the mosquito scars on her thigh to produce a portrait of Abe Lincoln. To their credit, the uptown Rosses all humor sweet, strange Lou, especially after she sympathizes with Emma's missing fashion week in Milan by explaining that she too is the cover girl of 4H magazine's "flea and tick" special. Loopy Lou remains, for the most part, the ethical heart and true comedic focus of *Bunk'd*, and its producers seem to share the Ross family's charitable adoption of its boisterous tomboy. Over the first few episodes, the Rosses, and Emma especially, all befriend Lou as a capable ally in the Chipmunks' ongoing battle against the scheming camp villainess, Hazel Swearengen[8] and the dowdy denizens of her Weasel Cabin.

Like many Disney Channel sitcoms, much of *Bunk'd* is founded in obvious plotting and lackluster parodies, but Miranda May's peculiar portrayal of the pig-petting farmer's daughter is an unexpected, if somewhat classist, thrill, especially early in the series. Lou's hyper-kinetic entrances lend surprising force to lackluster scenes, particularly in her heart to hearts with Emma or her skirmishes with Hazel. Intentional or not, Loveable Lou's sweet and screwy female tomfoolery provides a 21st century recapitulation of 19th century comedic stock characters closely tied to vaudeville, minstrelsy, and travelling chautauquas. Eventually appropriated by early mass media, these humble but strong nurturers developed surprising cultural power. Sentimentalized female domestics like Marie Dressler' Oscar-winning performance of the titular mother in George Hill's 1930 *Min and Bill* and Marjorie Main's portrayal of "Ma" in the Ma and Pa Kettle franchise (beginning with Chester Erskine's 1947 *The Egg and I*) popularized a certain type of working class maternal grotesque whose "plebian social status" as a lovable but forlorn housekeeper, homemaker, or day laborer is eventually transformed or elevated via bourgeois approval "from common to cultivated" (Crafton 1997).

Variations across mass media have included Kate Smith's patriotic Anglo mammie persona on radio and in early sound film, Bernadine Flynn's homespun wit in Paul Rhymer's charming *Vic and Sade* radio serial, Minnie Pearl's jovial auntie on *The Grand Ole Opry* and *Hee Haw*, and the fiery females in midcentury series that juxtapose high culture with homespun humility like *Green Acres*, *Petticoat Junction*, and *The Beverly Hillbillies*. Even Tyler Perry's Madea, a broad lampoon of African American matriarchs, owes much to such traditions, and represents, in many ways, the neglected elder cousin of the peculiar, pig-loving Lou Hockhauser. Miranda May's adorable Lou builds on several—if not all—of these sources and antecedents, injecting gleeful small town warmth and boundless enthusiasm into an otherwise bland camp comedy concept.

Lou is also among the few recurring characters who genuinely appreciate the natural splendors and communal camp rituals that surround and define them. Her boisterous enthusiasm for nature, outsized physique, working class roots, rural heritage, and folk-derived humor all defy the more aloof, contrived affectations of the usual Disney Channel tween-plate. Unlike the typical "fresh-faced girl next door with just enough gumption to make her interesting to kids but not so much as to be threatening to parents," Lou washes over every scene like a force of nature (Orenstein 2011). In the premiere episode,

Zuri likens her pantomime of making out at The Spot to getting electrocuted and in "Bride and Doom" and "Live from Camp Kikiwaka," we find her draped in primitive grass skirts and headdress, performing ludicrous pagan rituals of pseudo-druidical summoning and supplication. Her ear-piercing, contortion-filled efforts to commune with the spirit of her dead pet pig, Snorty, also mark her upbringing as uncouth and common in contrast to the Rosses, Xander, and even Hazel. Though many episodes disparage her frequent "dating fails," personal disappointments, and protruding teeth, she remains one of the Disney Channel's few unique and exciting characterizations, until of course, they "fix" her in the show's final season.

Miranda May's early performances appear far too real, rotund, and plebeian to fit snuggly within the formulaic "emotional environments" that drive Disney Channel simulacras of American perfection (Chytry 2012). As Chytry observes, most Disney entertainment—from animation to theme parks to TV—is built on carefully prescribed interactive theatric components meant "to engender the almost religious aura of feeling alive," happy, and successful. Thus, in its third season, the show initiates a methodical mouseketeer makeover of Miranda May's kooky character. Lou Hockhauser's gradual softening from raw rural rube to charming country queen speaks powerfully to *Bunk'd*'s aesthetic compromises, the Disney Channel's prefab programming, and their places in media history. Lou's extreme peculiarity also brings *Bunk'd*'s troubled class politics to the fore. The camp's resident plutocrats, the Ross children, and its predominantly middle class patrons accept and respect Lou to a point.[9] Early in the pilot, Lou terrifies Emma by threatening to cage her if she does not behave, then reveals that she is just messing around by unleashing some forced texting lingo: "JK again! I'm all about the JKs!" Emma, still the glib cosmopolitan of *Jessie*, caps off the gag with a concerned aside, "JK! OMG."

Season Three's "Bungle in the Jungle" expands Lou's backstory by introducing Beth Curry as Lou's doting, quilt-crazy mother whose name is, of course, Dixie. By this point, Lou's shtick as a wacky Earth Mother is over. Longing to attend college and become a teacher, a degreed middle class professional, she trades in her outsized overalls for more modish tops and tights. Her hair also becomes longer and more lusciously akin to Emma's, and most noticeably of all, she regularly drops her back country accent in favor of more sophisticated cadences. Yet, May's original over-the-top performances made her a fan favorite, as the continuing coverage of her triumphant "low key" weight loss and more svelte physique suggest (Miranda 2017). Her transition also reveals a more disturbing element of what Orenstein calls the "Girl Power Lite" Disney machine (2011).

The series' final episode exhibits its most disturbing class dynamics and its worst treatment of sweet Lou. To break the news that they have all callously decided to sell Camp Kikiwaka, which their parents bought as a favor in

Season Two, the Ross children indulge Lou in one of her greatest dreams, a hot air balloon ride. The conversations that follow make up the bulk of the last episode's B-story and are indeed filled with uncomfortably hot air involving a variety of apologies for arrogance, selfishness, and privilege. The new, thinner, upgraded Lou's distress is captured dead on as she turns away from the Rosses in grief and disbelief, mourning the imminent loss of her friends, job, and favorite place in the world. By show's end, everything ends up copacetic as Lou decides to buy the camp, and plans to overhaul it completely as a recreation space for underprivileged children. The Rosses once again do what plutocrats do best. They shower pretty, proud Lou with praise and facilitate her dreams by selling her the camp for $1, which, she has to borrow. Everyone celebrates with the usual Disney optimism. Then we are treated to a closing gag where the long denied and disenfranchised Timmy—now coated in filth and living on the outskirts of camp wearing animal skin—gets adopted by a family of Kikiwaka. He too receives somewhat questionable closure as *Bunk'd* signs off forever.

Bunk'd's other supporting characters—who are largely younger campers—run the gamut of stereotypes from endearing to reprehensible. In Seasons One and Two, Nina Lu's Tiffany Chen evolves from a sheltered honors student who lives within a literal tent of books and seeks "very early admission to college," into a warmer, heroic multicultural alpha girl. Tiffany is frequently paired with Zuri developing schemes, hacks, and capers that drive the more slapstick B-plots of many episodes, such as her effort to pass off a stolen salmon as a prize catch in the truly hilarious "The Ones That Got Away." She is also often deployed as an earnest, driven, and studious foil for underachieving Jorge, as in Season One's "Smells Like Camp Spirit" episode, where they spar over how best to teach their CIT—the hapless Ravi—how to swim.

Jorge Ramirez himself is probably *Bunk'd*'s most disturbing and irresponsible characterization of difference and diversity. Though he is portrayed with blithe, *Little Rascals*–*style* enthusiasm by Nathan Ramirez, the obese Hispanic slob who defecates in canoes,[10] stirs sweat socks into his chili, and brags about his "23-minute farts" after burrito night reveals the lack of cultural sensitivity lingering just beneath the Disney Channel's otherwise sanitized rainbow of diversity. There are few other Hispanic characters of note across the three seasons of *Bunk'd*, and although Jorge has several heroic moments of triumph and catharsis in his dealings with Zuri, Xander, Tiffany, and especially Ravi in "Camp Rules," the continual contrast of a self-satisfied "lazy, dirty," fat Hispanic child with the more fit, fashionable, and affluent Ross children seems problematic considering the early 21st century climate of anti–Hispanic sentiment in America.

Ravi, another adopted Ross sibling and a Kikiwaka CIT, doesn't fair much better than his fellow Chipmunk, Jorge. Karan Brar's energetic performances of the Hindi speaking STEM wizard are generally enjoyable, but Ravi always finds himself on the wrong side of physically degrading, quasi-queer humiliations. His fears of swimming, fondness for tight biker shorts, and consistent obsession with dress and decorum (which he shares with prissy Anglo sister, Emma), all reference the stereotypically ambiguous masculinity of "little brown Orientals." Even the blundering bumpkin, Lou Hockhauser finds Ravi's slight physique oddly disconcerting. At one point in the pilot, she finds herself cradling a terrified Ravi in her arms and muses, "Wow! You're even lighter than a chicken and their bones are hollow!"(Eells O'Connell & Koherr 2015). Time and again, Ravi's intelligence, strength, and meticulous dressing habits are coded as excessive, odd, or emasculating. Meanwhile the ripped, jovial Anglo-Saxon heartthrob, Xander McCormick (played with roguish chutzpah by Kevin G. Quinn), retains his hunky sexual appeal, despite secret caches of wart remover, jock itch powder, and related manscaping paraphernalia.

In terms of representation then, *Bunk'd*, like many other Disney Channel farces, encourages diversity and inclusion within carefully prescribed limits. The Ross family itself is a globalized "melting pot" of white, black, and "brown" boys and girls all benefiting equally from their parents' ultra-capitalist noblesse oblige. Emma, Zuri, and Ravi are featured with fairly equal consistency throughout the series.[11] Alongside these generally positive and (the coding of Ravi's gender identity not withstanding) progressive representations, *Bunk'd* also indulges in an assortment of more troublesome, reductive, and disturbing racial slanders. The metamorphosis of characters like Lou and Tiffany reveal the nuanced ambivalence of class, race, and gender tensions within carefully policed family entertainments, while more exaggerated ethnic grotesques like the filthy Jorge amount to little more than strangely indulgent neo-minstrelsy. As noted earlier, even primary antagonists like the shrewish Gladys and her scheming niece, Hazel, are treated with uncomfortable classist disdain and contempt. At Camp Kikiwaka, apparently, the most coveted merit badge is that which promises or protects affluent prestige.

Perhaps that's why Season Three swings the *Bunk'd* concept into strange new magical realist territory? After the devastating conflagration of the Season Two finale, "We Didn't Start the Fire," many elements of the show endure a strategic socio-economic purge. Gladys and Hazel are gone, absconding with the insurance money meant to rebuild Camp Kikiwaka. Jorge and Tiffany also opt out of spending another summer with their fellow Chipmunks, and hunky songster Xander also heads into the sunset to fulfill his dreams. The opening episodes of Season Three also reveal Lou's transformation from raw, chubby rube to fetching fashion plate, though she remains prone to self-deprecating gags about her body, teeth, and love life. Season Three also plunges into a series of outlandish, out of this world adventures involving new campers like ex–pageant pro Destiny; animal-loving simpleton Finn; and OCD, Sheldon Cooper–esque genius Matteo. Several episodes, such as "Bungle in the Jungle" and "Gruel and Unusual Punishment," feature this eclectic trio delving into bizarre, Simpsons-esque satires and otherworldly fantasies of high stakes adventure. In "Bungle," they skewer the gist of Jake Kasdan's 2017 *Jumanji* and "Gruel" introduces a kooky lampoon of the Salem witch trials which features some of the most ingenious dialogue of the entire series as confused Millennials stumble through Early Modern cadences and constructions. In such stories, the younger actors take on roles and challenges well beyond the conventional limits of camp comedies, and often reduce their elder counselors/featured stars to sidebar performers. This is especially true of Emma and Ravi, who tend to merely frame or facilitate their new campers' broader, *Duck Tales*–like expeditions into the absurd. For example, in "Up, Up, and Away!," the series ender, which the *Bunk'd* fandom wiki proudly designates as the "156th and final episode in the *Jessie* franchise," the Ross kids wrap up their business stuck in the B-story balloon, while Destiny, Matteo, and Finn save and befriend an actual Kikiwaka cryptid and pass him off as an eager camper.

Bunk'd *Off: Disney Channel Comedy in the Anthropocene*

Considering the Disney Studios' consistent historical commitment to raising awareness about the beauty, value, and fragility of the natural world, as well as the central role that outdoor experience plays in summer camp themed narratives across various genres, the relative lack of eco-conscious, environmentally aware content incorporated into the three seasons of *Bunk'd* seems surprising. If we consider the ever-increasing urgency of infusing globalized youth markets with sustainable habits of eco-environmental engagement, *Bunk'd*'s lack of attention to the practical conservation of the very scenarios that set it off from other urban, suburban, or magical Disney programming seems almost negligent. Why then, is *Bunk'd*, a summer camp themed sitcom not more directly conversant with such concerns? Why isn't environmental advocacy a Kikiwaka tradition?

As scientists, scholars, and critics debate the urgency of potentially catastrophic environmental collapse in the 21st century, a new interdisciplinary emphasis on Anthropocene studies continues to advocate for stronger, clearer, and more immediately transformative examinations of how human cultures can effectively adapt to cleaner, greener, more eco-responsible lifestyles (Laird 2017). At the same time, children's media related to education, entertainment, and social networks are frequently identified as primary opportunities for introducing Anthropocentric awareness, especially in terms of enhancing the individual learner/viewer/consumer's relationships with nature, outdoor experience, and sustainable living. As Susan Laird argues:

> Conscientious human agency in the Anthropocene will demand much deeper and broader rethinking of educational ends and means that take the myriad complex challenges of Earth habitation and habitability seriously, both locally and globally, with diverse children's needs and situations explicitly in mind [2017].

One such "situation" is certainly the internationally networked, colossally diversified transmedial platform of Disney Channel enter-tweenment.

Laird further recommends "fostering children's growth in ways that sustain both environmental and human health" and "educating children to develop nature-loving life practices" as primary goals of adult role models, teachers, and parents in the Anthropocene. Yet *Bunk'd* rarely references even the most basic outdoor activities such as hiking, swimming, or orienteering, not to mention recycling, global warming, or climate change. Camp fire scenes and canoe disasters are common and several episodes include jokes about traumatic bear encounters. Ravi makes one minor comment about climate change when a freak storm arises in "Bride and Doom." Kikiwaka's resident hottie, Xander, often expounds on his passion for fishing, but the first season's "The One That Got Away" does everything it can to undermine the sport as a viable, fun, and practical outdoor skill.

Sometimes, the series' denial or erasure of actual regional eco-environmental traits seems almost schizophrenic. Little content provokes further interest in the rich ecological diversity or unique climatic elements of the camp's supposed location in rural Maine. Season Three's "Whole Lotta Lobsta" seems more concerned with bizarre recipes and goofy mascots like Larry the Lobster instead of the state's laudable lobstering heritage or urgent issues like over-fishing and ethical harvesting.[12] Nary a lobster roll, blueberry, oyster, or chowder appears in all three seasons of the series, and although the counselors are rescued by a fishing boat off screen in the final episode's fateful hot air balloon ride over the ocean, the sun-kissed stock shots involved in the escapade look more like Santa Monica or Fort Myers than Camden or Kennebunkport.

Many Anthropocene scholars also urge drastic reconsiderations of humanity's interaction with the animal world (Chaplin 2016). Here too, *Bunk'd* is strangely ambivalent in its representation of how campers, counselors, and kids generally interpret and interact with pets, pests, and other wildlife. The series is crammed with typical camp comedy gags concerning mosquito bites, spiders, porcupines, and skunks. The show's theme song also includes the line abouta bear eating a camper's phone, illustrating its continuing contrast between interactive human connectivity and threatening or painful animal experience. Two fairly charming episodes—Season's Two's "Dog Days of

Summer" and "Bad Dog"—focus on the passing of Lou's lifelong canine buddy and her newfound puppy, Chuck, but two other characters push *Bunk'd*'s animal politics into more problematic territory.

First, there is Mrs. Kipling, a seven foot water monitor that Ravi supposed raised from an egg he discovered in the swamps of India. A hold-over house pet also featured in *Jessie*, Mrs. Kipling appears or is referenced in 14 of the show's 58 episodes, and is more entertaining than most gags and antics that surround her. She is also perhaps the show's only commentary on Ravi's postcolonial perspectives as an Indian orphan. His lizard's name is clearly derived from the British cultural traditions associated with Rudyard Kipling's exotic allegories and imperialist romances. Mrs. Kipling's presence emphasizes Ravi's privileged eccentricity and Hindi heritage. Though camp owner, Gladys, is disturbed by the monitor's arrival in the premiere, she agrees to let the lizard stay because the Ross family's checks always clear. Mrs. Kipling eventually becomes the camp's official mascot, often counsels human characters about their problems, and plays a seminal role in several mystery-based episodes including the frantic "Smells Like Camp Spirit."

Much of the humor involving Mrs. Kipling arises from the jungle animal's incongruity with its North American surroundings. While the contrasts appeared even more outrageous with *Jessie*'s penthouse sets, Ravi's pet—kept leashed and often lugged about unwillingly—speaks to a long and troubling tradition of status-driven exotic animal trafficking closely interconnected with networks of exploitation, abuse, and enslavement (Alberti 2011). Though Mrs. Kipling's presence at Camp Kikiwaka remains oddly charming, her very uniqueness introduces a variety of Anthropcentric concerns relating to callous human assumptions of superiority and control over the lives and circumstances of companion animals.

If Ravi's choice of pet confirms or comments on humanity's casual dominance of other species, another character's intense empathy for animals code him as oddly simple, weird, or weak. Season Three's "nature boy," Finn Sawyer, fulfills his lifelong dream to attend Camp Kikiwaka where his cousin, Lou works as a counselor. Named for a mash-up of Mark Twain's two most iconic protagonists, Will Buie, Jr.'s Finn exhibits all of Huckleberry's spunk but little of Tom's intelligence. He does embody both boys' great affinity for nature, and animals in particular. Yet, Finn is generally made into Camp Kikiwaka's "village idiot," confounding his peers and frustrating his counselors with his unorthodox relationships with all aspects of nature. In his first appearance, "We Can't Bear It," his obsession with getting a selfie with a bear cub initiates a Grizzly attack on the camp. In "Gruel and Unusual Punishment," he innocently licks rocks and buys a sweater for an otter. "No Bones About It" finds him driving everyone else to ridiculous ends in his search for unknown, marginalized species. Much like Jorge, he is also constantly portrayed as smelly, unwashed, and uninterested in all forms of hygiene. His relation to Lou also emphasizes his earthy, Nebraska perspective, and, as the *Bunk'd* fandom wiki observes, Emma, the fastidious glamour girl, "is rarely seen with Finn so their relationship is unknown" (Fandom 2018). Finn's intimacy with nature and animals is also presented as anti-intellectual and unscientific. At one point, he cannot comprehend why a metal detector—though made of metal—cannot locate lost plastic and wooden objects. Yet, Finn's close attention to animal habitats introduces a more equitable and compassionate perspective on nature and the wild which mirrors Chaplain, Laird, and others' recent efforts to recalibrate children's instructional and entertainment frameworks to better suit the immediate needs of the late Anthropocene.

Finally, Camp Kikiwaka also uses animal metaphor to add unexpected cruelty to both human and animal relations. Like several camp narratives—and many actual camps—Kikiwaka encourages belonging by organizing its humans into cabin-centered groups of peers and leaders. Each *Bunk'd* cabin is animal themed including Lou, Emma, and Ravi's Chipmunks, Hazel's Weasels, and a variety of others like the Grizzlies, Woodchucks, Badgers, Moose, Bobcats, Eagle, and Salmon. Campers are also identified by color-coded t-shirts that designate their particular Kikiwaka species. Though very few actual woodland animals ever appear on the series, these human communities adopt animal characteristics to better emphasize the show's continuity and character development. Most attention is focused on the rivalry between the Ross' Chipmunks and the Swearengens' Weasels, who are, by all that we see, a very gruesome crew.

If the Chipmunks are affluent, diverse, well mannered, and—with the exception of Jorge and Finn—obviously privileged upper middle class campers, the Weasels are predominantly working class kids who nurse their class conscious grudges against the Ross family offspring. Gladys and her niece, Hazel, are generally jealous, covetous, and conniving and their frequent use of subterfuge, deception, and disguise to confuse or embarrass other cabins fuels much of the humor in the first two seasons. Yet, Hazel's Weasels become unexpectedly monstrous as *Bunk'd* progresses. Early in Season One, they appear as a fairly unpleasant but typical posse, backing Hazel's plays for Xander and executing her schemes against Emma. In later episodes like "Zuri Weasels Out," "Tree House of Terror," "Cabin vs Cabin," and especially Season Three's action-packed "Game of Totems" spoof, House Weasel and their new leader, Lydia, are cloaked in the trashy trappings of under-achieving, alterna-grrrls, Goths, and grungers. Mostly female, they gather around Hazel and Lydia covered in edgy cosmetics, draped in flannel, and sporting crispy fried high hair bigger and badder than most 1980s metal bands.

Though the scheming, stalking, sadistic Hazel leads the wicked Weasels through most of their mischief, her generally silent camp "sisters" seem more prone to obesity, laziness, and vandalism, adding even more nuanced classist commentary to *Bunk'd*'s already problematic identity politics. In many ways, Kikiwaka's wily weasels further emphasize how "queer youth, poor youth, and youth of color are even more commonly constructed as deviant and outsider within the hierarchal American society" whose patronage the Disney Channel so effectively solicits (Rickman 2018). At one point, they duct tape Tiffany—the all–A's Asian over-achiever—to her cabin ceiling like spiders preserving their prey. Eventually, even the vengeful Hazel defects to the Chipmunks, fearing their increasing recklessness and hostility of her own clan. Zuri, ever the entrepreneurial opportunist, also takes her turn as a Weasel, but quickly discovers that she does not share their appetites for destruction and disarray.

Kikiwaka's animal-assisted class and gender rivalries become most aggressive in each season's Camp Competition episodes, which also spill over into incidents involving an entirely different enemy, Camp Champion, situated across the lake from *Bunk'd*'s own colony. Yet, the series places more emphasis on animalized divisions and disparities which segregate and antagonize human difference than it does on actual interspecies understanding or reciprocity. In other words, *Bunk'd*'s camp denominations very much reflect its drastically limited awareness of actual outdoor opportunities and animal issues. They are basic, arbitrary, artificial, and mostly uninterested in actual ecosystems teeming with wildlife, natural beauty, and equitable harmony.

Like the majority of Disney tween comedies, *Bunk'd* promotes a comfortably middlebrow, politically neutral, and generally inclusive platform of slick, upbeat family entertainment. Yet, the summer camp spin-off series develops several surprising variations on typical Disney Channel sitcom formulas, appropriates a variety of generic conventions from a broad range of sources, and—unfortunately—indulges in an assortment of flat and questionable ethnic, gender, and class-driven caricatures. *Bunk'd* is also unique in its highly mitigated representation of children and young adults interacting with a problematic approximation of nature. Other high profile entities within the Disney umbrella such as DisneyNature and Orlando's Animal Kingdom theme park promote ecological outreach and environmental education, yet *Bunk'd* prefers a more inauthentic, oppositional address that both privileges and distances its viewers from the urgent concerns of an environment in crisis. Its summer camp milieu, multi-star ensemble cast, and overtly artificial renditions of humans and animals alike remain as problematic as they are pleasurable.

NOTES

1. Bert Gillet and Bert Lewis would complete the seasons series with *Winter* in 1930 after Iwerks and Stalling left the studio.

2. Two more of Salten's anthropomorphic works would receive popular Disney adaptations: The 1938 novel *Perri, the Youth of a Squirrel* became a feature in 1957, and the 1922 novel, *The Hound of Florence,* was adapted to the 1959 live action comedy, *The Shaggy Dog,* setting off an explosion of sequels and imitators.

3. For extended discussions of the epistemological underpinnings and racial politics of animated animal icons see, Lippit (2000), Sammond (2015), and Willmott (2018).

4. Later versions of *The Mickey Mouse Club* followed a different anthology-derived format.

5. The Triple R buddy narrative was especially popular in multiple series of Dell and Gold Key comics from Western Publishing that extended the characters' appeal and influence well into the late 1960s. *The New Adventures of Spin and Marty* also enjoyed a brief unsuccessful reboot in 2000.

6. For the definitive history of early Disney cross-marketing of film, TV, theme park, and phonograph properties, see Hollis and Ehrbar (2006).

7. Some fan-centered ancillary discourse mirrors *Bunk'd*'s special status as a Disney tween show with four primary stars. Fandom's Bunk'd wiki page classifies Emma, Zuri, and Ravi as the show's "three main protagonists," but separately declares the more charming Lou as the show's "main character" (Bunk'd Wiki).

8. Hazel and Gladys Swearengen, the two prevalent baddies of Seasons One and Two, are almost certainly named for the hardscrabble anti-hero of another brutally realistic HBO series, saloon owner, pimp, and crime boss, Al Swearengen of *Deadwood.*

9. One of the show's strangest running gags involves the continuing, merciless denial of Timmy, a camper whose parents' checks have bounced or whose payment is too often delayed. These somewhat cruel expulsions repeatedly remind viewers that, even though Camp Kikiwaka is racially diverse, only certain castes of privileged children are allowed to access its pleasures.

10. More accurately, a later episode, "Smells Like Camp Spirit," reveals that an incontinent moose is actually responsible for "doing No. 2 in a canoe," and although Xander admits that the camp owes Jorge an apology, the character retains the stigma of filth, stink, and gluttony for the duration of his two seasons on *Bunk'd.*

11. Though, as noted earlier, Emma—the classically blonde, blue eyed American beauty—is regularly upstaged by other characters, especially in Season Three.

12. Even the episode's title betrays its lack of authenticity, as the more common Maine colloquialism is generally spelled "Lobstah," invoking the state's nasal native accent which is never present in *Bunk'd.*

References

Alberti, Samuel J.M.M. (2011). *The afterlives of animals.* Charlottesville: University of Virginia Press.

Baudrillard, Jean. (1994) The animals: Territory and metamorphoses. *Simulacra and Simulation.* Trans. Sheila Faria Glaser. Ann Arbor: University of Michigan Press. 129–141.

Bickford, T. (2012). The new "tween" music industry: The Disney Channel, Kidz Bop and an emerging childhood counterpublic. *Popular Music, 31*(3), 417–436. https://doi-org.ez proxy.stlcc.edu/10.1017/S0261143012000335.

Bissette, Steven. (2017). *Cryptid cinema.* Windsor, VT: Spiderbaby Graphix.

Buhs, Joshua Blu. (2009). *Bigfoot: The life and times of a legend.* Chicago: University of Chicago Press.

Bunk'd Wiki. Main characters. Fandom. Retrieved from http://bunkd.wikia.com/wiki/Cate gory:Main_Characters.

Cadenas, Karensa, and Khal. (29 October 2015). The best horror movie of the 1980s: Two superfans talk Sleepaway Camp. The Complex. Retrieved from https://www.complex. com/pop-culture/2015/10/sleepaway-camp-is-the-best-watch-it.

Chaplin, J.E. (2017). 2016 Arthur O. Lovejoy Lecture. Can the nonhuman speak? Breaking the chain of being in the anthropocene. *Journal of the History of Ideas, 78*(4), 509–529.

Retrieved from http://ezproxy.stlcc.edu/login?url=http://search.ebscohost.com/login. aspx?direct=true&db=afh&AN=125778966&site=ehost-live.

Chytry, J. (2012). Walt Disney and the creation of emotional environments: Interpreting Walt Disney's oeuvre from the Disney studios to Disneyland, CalArts, and the Experimental Prototype Community of Tomorrow (EPCOT). *Rethinking History, 16*(2), 259–278. https://doi-org.ezproxy.stlcc.edu/10.1080/13642529.2012.681194.

Clover, Carol J. (1992). *Men, women, and chainsaws: Gender in the modern horror film.* Princeton, NJ: Princeton University Press.

Eells O'Connell, Pamela (wrtier), & Bob Koherr (Director). (August 7, 2015). *Gone Girl.* Pamela Eells O'Connell and Valerie Ahern (Producers). *Bunk'd.* Burbank, CA: Disney Channel.

_____. (July 31, 2015). *Welcome to Camp Kikiwaka.* Pamela Eells O'Connell and Valerie Ahern (Producers). *Bunk'd.* Burbank, CA: Disney Channel.

Crafton, Donald (1997). *The talkies: American cinema's transition to sound 1926–1931.* Berkeley: University of California Press.

Hollis, Tim, & Greg Ehrbar.(2006). *Mouse tracks: The story of Walt Disney records.* Jackson: University of Mississippi Press.

Laird, S. (2017). Learning to live in the anthropocene: Our children and ourselves. *Studies in Philosophy & Education, 36*(3), 265–282. https://doi-org.ezproxy.stlcc.edu/10.1007/s11217-017-9571-6.

Lippit, Akira Mizuta. (2000). *Electric animal: Toward a rhetoric of wildlife.* Minneapolis: University of Minnesota Press.

Maclay, Willow.(Summer 2015). "How can it be? She's a boy." Transmisogyny in Sleepaway Camp. *Cléo: A Journal of Film and Feminism.* 3:2. Retrieved from http://cleojournal. com/2015/08/10/how-can-it-be-shes-a-boy-transmisogyny-in-sleepaway-camp/.

"Miranda May and her low key weight loss is inspiration!" (10 August 2017). Live Rampup. Entertainment" Retrieved from http://liverampup.com/entertainment/miranda-weight-loss-parents-boyfriend-dating-wiki-2017.html.

Mjøs, O.J. (2010). The symbiosis of children's television and merchandising: comparative perspectives on the Norwegian children's television channel NRK Super and the global Disney Channel. *Media, Culture & Society, 32*(6), 1031–1042. https://doi-org.ezproxy. stlcc.edu/10.1177/0163443710380313.

Moylan, Bryan. (30 July 2015). 15 classic summer camp movies. Vulture Lists. Retrieved from http://www.vulture.com/2015/07/summer-camp-movies-ranked-from-worst-to-best. html.

Orenstein, Peggy. (2011). *Cinderella ate my daughter.* New York: HarperCollins.

Rickman, Aimee. (2018). *Adolescence, girlhood, and media migration.* New York: Lexington Books.

Sammond, Nicholas. (2015). *Birth of an Industry.* Durham, NC: Duke University Press.

Stanley, T.L. (2006). Disney Channel: A fresh-face factory. *Advertising Age, 77*(50), 14. Retrieved from http://ezproxy.stlcc.edu/login?url=http://search.ebscohost.com/login. aspx?direct=true&db=afh&AN=23470603&site=ehost-live.

Williams, Florence. (2017). *The nature fix: Why Nature makes us happier, healthier, and more creative.* New York: Norton.

Willmott, Glenn. (2018). The animalized character and style. *Animal Comics.* Ed, David Herman. New York: Bloomsbury, 53–79.

Diversity at Face Value

Bizaardvark's *"Diversity" Problem*

JAYNE M. SIMPSON

Bizaardvark completed three seasons on Disney Channel, and is available online on Disney Now, as well as YouTube, Amazon Prime, and Google Play streaming platforms. The show is a comedy, and is certified as TV-G, suitable for all audiences (*IMDb,* 2018*)*. Disney Channel first began producing and airing television shows in 1983, with *Good Morning, Mickey!* Throughout Disney's television domination of child media, some of their most popular shows from the 2000s until now include *Hannah Montana, Kim Possible, Lizzie McGuire, Good Luck Charlie, The Suite Life of Zack and Cody, Jessie, Liv and Maddie*, and *Girl Meets World.*

Since 1983, Disney has diversified its character lineup, notably featuring non-white and LGBTQ families in *That's So Raven, The Proud Family, Corey in the House*, and more recently, *Andi Mack* and *K.C. Undercover.* This work focuses on *Bizaardvark*, which features two non-white leads, Asian American preteen social media entertainers, Paige Olvera (Olivia Rodrigo) and Frankie Wong (Madison Hu). *Bizaardvark* first aired in 2016 and ended production after three seasons in April 2019. Throughout their musical adventures, Paige and Frankie maneuver relationships with their families, classmates, and fellow video bloggers. The storyline follows the pair of 12-year-olds across their lives, from their school, homes, and creative space at Vuuugle, and online video-sharing platform. Most often, Paige and Frankie can be found with Amelia Duckworth (DeVore Ledridge), host of lifestyle Vuuugle show *Perfect Perfection with Amelia,* Dirk Mann (Jake Paul), the death-defying prank mind *Dare Me Bro*, or Bernie Schotz (Ethan Wacker), a young but hopeful "agent" to his famous friends.

As Paige, Frankie, and their friends create comedic videos as musicians, life and style gurus, and thrill seekers, *Bizaardvark* shares its own messages with viewers. This essay examines the different popular stereotypes that *Bizaardvark* supports throughout its three-season lifetime. At face value, *Bizaardvark* seems to fit into the class of helping diversify Disney. However, even though Paige and Frankie are considered the center of the show, the plotline does not consistently treat their stories and identities as such. This analysis focuses on the ways that Paige and Frankie are cast as the stars of *Bizaardvark,* but not treated as such as viewers follow the plotline.

Even though Paige and Frankie's diversity serves to act as the primary faces of *Bizaardvark*, the show does not address the topics of race and diversity within its storyline. In fact, instead of using the show to address identity and race, *Bizaardvark* reinforces several different pre-existing popular stereotypes pertaining to race and creates problematic representations throughout their three seasons. This analysis will examine this idea of stereotype perpetuation further, as well as address the lack of diversity over the course of the television show outside of Paige and Frankie.

Bizaardvark *Diversity Problem*

The Disney Company has been producing popular media for children since the mid 1920s, and has produced dozens of shows and over 50 full-length films. Although Disney has been a formidable force in media over time, many of their most profitable endeavors (*Hannah Montana*, *The Suite Life of Zack and Cody*, *Snow White and the Seven Dwarfs*) have featured White lead characters and a largely White supporting cast as well. As media have come to warrant more critical examination, the need for more diverse representation also grew. In recent years, Disney's cast lineup has begun to feature a more diverse set of lead characters, casting non-white leads in productions like *That's So Raven*, *The Proud Family*, *Liv and Maddie*, *K.C. Undercover*, *Bizaardvark*, and more.

Disney's *K.C. Undercover* star Zendaya was outspoken following her return to Disney in 2016 about diversity on the show, telling *Cosmopolitan* magazine:

> The only way I was going to come back to the Disney Channel was if I was in a position of more power. One thing that is really important to me is diversity on the channel. It's hard as a young person of a different ethnicity or background to look at the TV and not see anyone who looks like you. Representation is very important [Sandell, 2016].

Similarly, *Andi Mack* features Disney's first openly gay character, played by Joshua Rush (For an in-depth analysis of *Andi Mack*, see A. Baker in this volume). In an interview with ABC, Rush said he was really proud to be able to play Cyrus. I think it's an exciting role to be able to play for Disney...[but] more than anything, it's an exciting role for these kids that are going to end up seeing Cyrus on their screen and going, "Oh, that's me! I recognize that and I understand that and I resonate with that." think it shows those kids that their stories are valid [Williams, 2018].

In casting Rodrigo and Wu as Paige and Frankie, who were both featured in Disney's commercials about Asian American heritage month, Disney appeared to be following their own trend of mixing up their representation portfolio. While Disney has made strides in their previously straight, mostly white lineup, there are still several notable flaws with their presentation of diversity.

This work focuses on *Bizaardvark,* which features two non-white leads, Asian American preteen social media entertainers, Paige Olvera (Olivia Rodrigo) and Frankie Wong (Madison Hu). *Bizaardvark* first aired in 2016 and is still currently in production. Throughout their musical adventures, Paige and Frankie maneuver relationships with their families, classmates, and fellow video bloggers. The storyline follows the pair of 12-year-olds and their friends across adventures and mishaps in their day-to-day lives.

Ono and Pham (2009) define *media racial hegemony* as "the media's role in both continuing and contesting racial and colonial power relations. Media racial hegemony helps us demonstrate how the ways people think about race, the things people do that are racialized, and people's racial identity are represented through media" (p. 10). In viewing *Bizaardvark*, insights are offered into how the show contributes to or contests the pre-existing and dominant understandings of Asian Americans in children's media.

Drawing from another Disney production and its problematic representations of Asian heritage, we can refer to *Mulan*, a popular animated Disney film in which the protagonist, Mulan, joins the Chinese military to find who she *really* is, rather than accept the path that has been outlined for her. However, *Mulan* has drawn fire for taking the traditional Chinese poem the film is based on and changing it to be aligned with what we know to be "American" values. Differing iterations of what it means to be "American" have circulated throughout popular culture, but for youth and non-white consumers, popular media and consumer culture provide specific—and limiting—iterations of what it means to be "American" (Lee & Vaught, 2003).

When examining Disney's history with racial diversity and representation, Asian American characters have only been provided thrice. *Mulan* (1998), *Bizaardvark* through Paige and Frankie, and *Andi Mack* (2017–2019) are the only Disney productions centered around Asian or Asian American characters. These representations do not, however, focus on the experiences of Asian and Asian Americans as they move through life, nor do they give consumers access to representations of Asian and Asian American boys and men, and their experiences as well.

Historical Representations of Minorities in Media and Critical Race Theory

Addresses of minorities in U.S. popular media date back several decades. In the 1960s, the civil rights movement sparked an interest in addressing the non-existent minority character as well as discriminatory practices carried out by television producers (U.S. Commission on Civil Rights, 1977). The results of this probe found that the presence of racial minority groups in television programing to be rare, and when diversity was available, it cast characters in limiting stereotypical forms. Moreover, the findings stated that in committing to these stereotypical portrayals of minorities, both White and non–White viewer were influenced in their perceptions of racial minority groups (U.S. Commission on Civil Rights, 1977).

In a study by Maestro and Greenberg (2010) focusing on the exposure and presentation of racial minorities in prime-time television, authors identified addressing diversity in television as being a socially significant topic to "represent U.S. ethnic minorities and especially to determine what changes, if any, have occurred in the last two decades among the least represented groups" (p. 690). In addition to examining the presence of represented minorities, the work also aims to examine the available portrayals of minorities in prime-time television.

In a sample of 1996 prime time television shows, 1 percent of *all* roles in prime-time television were played by Asian American actors, which includes Chinese, Japanese, Pacific Islander and Indian representations. These eight characters, when compared to the 452 Caucasian characters (both minor and major) within the same sample provided such little insight that Maestro and Greenberg (2010) discarded attempting to analyze them further in the study (p. 695).

Refocusing this exploration into children's television more specifically, there is a limited amount of research available. However, in a 2003 study from Bang and Reece, a content analysis of 813 commercials in children's television programming revealed a slight improvement in the rate of minority presence. The American Psychological Association poses that yearly, children consume over 40,000 advertisements through various outlets. This increased exposure illuminates a validity in the exploration of how media and advertising conditions and impact the minds and perceptions of children.

(Diverse) Faces in the Online Crowd—Paige, Frankie, Vuuugle and Real Life

The series premiere, appropriately titled *First!* follows Paige and Frankie as they hit 10,000 followers on Vuuugle and are invited to begin production for their show at Vuuugle Studio's headquarters along with other popular internet personalities. In their daily lives as students, Paige and Frankie express that they often feel left out but are hopeful that their new journey at Vuuugle will give them a sense of belonging. Walking into Vuuugle's prestigious headquarters, reserved only for the online elite, Paige and Frankie are met with a sea of famous Vuuugle stars, all of whom are white. It is in this episode that we first meet "Dare Me Bro" Dirk Mann, "Perfect Perfection" star Amelia Duckworth, and Bernie. These five form the core of the *Bizaardvark* cast. Throughout the rest of *First!*, most of the background characters are white, including Vuuugle's CEO Liam.

While the episode continues to dissect how Paige and Frankie still don't feel "at home" at Vuuugle's headquarters, it has nothing to do with race, though it would be an easy concept to grasp if it did. Instead, Paige and Frankie's discomfort with their first week at Vuuugle is credited more to new-kid-on-campus discomfort, which eventually passes. *Bizaardvark* gives Disney prime opportunity to address minority and diversity topics, but instead of using the show to address these topics, Paige and Frankie are used as faces to make the show appear diverse and inclusive.

Vuuugle can be equated to online streaming site YouTube, whose top earners and channels are fairly skewed racially. *Business Insider* (2017) tracked the top 20 YouTube earners based on subscribers and ad revenue earned per view. In 2017, eleven of the top twenty YouTube earners were American-based (and white) or based in Europe. In 2018, that number moved to eight out of the top twenty earners being white. There is a large population of South America based YouTube stars like HolaSoyGerman, Fernanfloo, Vegetta777, Whinderssonnunes, and Yuya that are also positioned on the list. YouTube's top earners range from online gaming narrators to comedians to beauty vloggers, much like the stars of *Bizaardvark*. The show, however, does not reflect the diversity that is present in the online (and actual) community.

Madison Hu, Olivia Rodrigo and Representation

Paige and Frankie are a handful of diverse faces in Disney's primetime lineup for young viewers. Madison Hu participated in a recorded an interview with the Center for Asian American Media (CAAM), in which she expressed how important diversity and representation is in media today.

> Representation really does matter, no matter what kind. Not only for Asian Americans, but for other races, anyone. I just feel like representation is so important, especially for children. When I was younger, I didn't see anyone that looked like me on screen, like singers and people on the mainstream media. My immediate thought is

that I'll never be able to do that. If I had kept that mindset, I wouldn't be doing the thing that I am right now. Even if you don't want to be in the arts, just seeing yourself represented is so important. Even though I never had that, I had one character— Brenda Song in *Homecoming Warrior*.... I just want to say that representation is important. Disney Channel has *Andi Mack*, a biracial Asian American family, and *Bizaardvark*. I think it's just important to have good representation without a stereotypical light [*CAAM*, 2017].

Hu's recognition of the value of diversity in media is an important one, but not one that is actually reinforced by her character on *Bizaardvark*. Hu's character, Frankie Wong, is the daughter of a single, usually busy, doctor. The too-busy-for-family theme resonates in Bang and Reece's (2003) study, which stated that in children's commercials "Black and Asian Americans were less likely than Caucasians to be show in a home setting or in family relationships … these settings may contribute to a stereotype that…. Asian American parents are too busy at their workplace to have family time at home" (p. 62). In *Mom! Stop!* (S1E18), the *Bizaardvark* leads spend most of the episode comparing their relationship to their parents.

At the beginning of *Mom! Stop!,* viewers find Paige and Frankie in their school's cafeteria at lunch. Paige opens her lunch to find a lunch hand-packed by her mother, Gina, along with a singing greeting card that espouses a ballad of Gina's love for and pride in Paige. Frankie's lunchbox holds latex gloves, hand sanitizer, an informational card about various food hazards, and no actual food. The rest of the episode includes Gina sharing embarrassing childhood stories and photos and an eventual argument with Paige. After their argument, Paige complains to Frankie about her annoyance with her mom, when Frankie reveals that she wished her father left her notes in her lunch, and that she'd actually spent the week *trying* to get one from him, with no success. In understanding Frankie's despair in lacking an affectionate parent, Paige comes to see the value in having a mother who expresses her love.

While *Mom! Stop!* might remind viewers and commentators to appreciate their parents alongside Paige at a moral level, the episode also reinforces the previously mentioned trope of inattentive and unattached parents as being common within Asian American families, illustrated in the relationship between Frankie and her father throughout the episode. Bang and Reece's (2003) work focuses predominantly on commercials as opposed to full-length television series for children, their findings still resonate—Asian Americans are "almost never featured in family relationships," and when they are, they are even less frequently positive (p. 60).

USC Media, Diversity and Social Change Initiative published "that just 28.3% of all speaking characters were from underrepresented racial and ethnic groups—a much lower percentage than the population at large. Asian Americans were particularly invisible. At least half of movies and TV shows, including on streaming services, 'fail to portray one speaking or named Asian or Asian American on screen'" (James & Ng, 2017).

Television and media creators and producers have been claiming to orient toward a shift favoring diversity focused efforts following a #OscarsSo White campaign in in 2015. Fueled by the Oscar nominee lineup featuring all 20 award nominees for lead and supporting actors being white, prime time television shows that emphasize diversity and difference like *Blackish* and *Empire* grew in both frequency and popularity. However, television has seen few "Asian Americans in leading roles beyond ABC's *Fresh Off the Boat*, loosely based around the experiences of an Asian immigrant family in the 1980s, ABC's *Designated Survivor*, … [and] AMC's martial arts drama *Into the Badlands,* which stars Daniel Wu as a talented warrior" (James & Ng, 2017). Even in changing times, Asian American recognition is still moving at a very slow pace, and Asian actors can be portrayed through a limited number of token tropes, historically speaking.

Representation of Asian and Asian American actors in television is an important statistic to note. Popular Asian and Asian American images in media include portrayals of Asian Americans as "weak, model citizens or manipulative invaders of business in America" (Tung, 2006). Helen Zia, a Chinese-American journalist, discussed the three "fundamental stereotypes of Asian-Americans today—the gook, the geek, and the geisha" (2000). In limiting the way Asian and Asian American characters are seen on screen to racial slurs, nerds, or hyper sexualized trophy characters, television exposure from producers like the Disney Channel perpetuates the ideological premise that "racism is one of the most profoundly naturalized of existing ideologies" (Hall, 2000, p. 272).

The Emmy Awards have been recognizing outstanding actors globally since 1949, just recently commended an Asian American actress, Sandra Oh, as a nominee for the Best Leading Actress role in *Killing Eve*. Since #OscarsSo White, the governing bodies of the Oscars have pledged to double female and minority members by 2020. Historically, children's television shows are not recognized by these larger award shows, but that does not make their casting practices immune from the trends that adult television follows.

Bizaardvark's primary writers, Josh Lehrman and Kyle Stegina, are both white men. Tung (2006) discusses how the potential lack of or inaccurate representation of Asian and Asian Americans may stem from a lack of representation on the network side. In a study surrounding films from 2007 to 2017, Smith, Choueiti, and Piper (2018) found that of 1,223 film directors, only 39 were Asian directors. Of the 108 films that Walt Disney Studios released in the same seven-year period, only four were directed by an Asian or Asian American. Between the seven studios and one "other" group examined (20th Century–Fox, Paramount Pictures, Sony Pictures, Universal Pictures, Walt

Disney Studios, Warner Bros. Pictures, and Lionsgate, and other)—of 1,100 films, only 38 were led by Asian directors.

Hall (2000) discussed how ideologies surrounding race are very strongly controlled by media, describing them as "the place where these ideas [about race] are where ideas are articulated, worked on, transformed and elaborated." Television exposure has the power to become a reality to viewers, with Piehl and Ruppel (1993) noting that "attitudes, values, and behavior may be developed" at least partially by observational learning, much of which may come from television (p. 184). Throughout *Bizaardvark*, Frankie is also shown as hyper competitive and generally unemotional. *Bizaardvark* dedicates an entire episode, *Yes and No* (S2E10), in which Paige challenges Frankie to be more open to new experiences.

In *B.F.F. (Before Frankie Friend)* (S2E18), Frankie initially struggles with jealousy knowing that Paige has another close friend in her life. *Paige Is Wrong* (S2E20) also showcases Frankie's personality trait of needing to be right, as well as to win, always. This theme of jealousy, competitiveness, and narrowly focused personalities on the part of Paige and Frankie is showcased again in *The Stand-Up Stand Off* (S3E18), in which the duo go back and forth telling mean jokes about each other in pursuit of comedic value from those around them. In falling neatly into the preexisting tropes laid out "for" Frankie by popular media, *Bizaardvark* simply adds to the already limiting availability of representations by Asian or Asian American actors.

Free Labor and Commodified Identities

The commodification, or the making of something into a commercially marketable product, of identity has been discussed as a way of upholding capitalistic structures to continue to profit off what some may call uniqueness, individuality, or identity. Within the diverse main characters of *Bizaardvark*, Paige and Frankie are seen alongside their White co-stars.

Giroux (1994) theorized "diversity capitalism" as the capitalization of the ways race and diversity politics commodifies said politics to sell goods. Throughout *Bizaardvark*, Paige and Frankie spend a majority of their time conceptualizing, producing, and editing their online show, attending to the needs of Vuuugle, and working with other hosts like Amelia and Dare Me Bro on their own shows. However, at no point are viewers given indication that Paige and Frankie are paid for their efforts.

In another work, Giroux (1998) outlines the Disney corporation's "profound influence [on] children's culture and their everyday life" based on the media-produced images that permeate every aspect of our daily lives; many of which are controlled by Disney (p. 253). Further, Giroux argues media culture has become one of the primary forces "in regulating the meanings, values, and tastes … [media influence] what it means to claim an identity" (p. 254). While Disney provides non-white protagonists to consumers, the use of "diverse" characters *without* acknowledging the diverse set of experiences that come with non-white identities reduces the characters of Paige and Frankie to figureheads that "check the box" of a progressive and more inclusive media landscape, not one that manages and acknowledges the realities of being a non-white member of a predominately White population.

The almost exclusively White population is magnified in *The Summer of Us* (S3E1), in which the top Vuuuglers are selected to spend the summer months in a beach house together, creating videos and collaborating. In the episode, Paige, Frankie, and Amelia are among several selected Vuuugle creators chosen to live in the mansion for the summer. Bernie Schotz also arrives at the house, with his grandmother, an adult chaperone for the trip, in tow.

While Bernie is not a content creator and is only allowed in at first thanks to his grandmother, one of the main plots is Bernie's quest to become a content creator as well, in order to "earn" his place in the house based on merit. The majority of the episode follows Bernie's desire to escape the ties of family-connected access, while the rest of the episode centers around Paige and Frankie behaving poorly. In terms of *who* spends the summer *creating* content, on this program ostensibly about two brown girls, white male character Bernie Schotz emerges as the sole creator in the episode.

Amelia Duckworth—Family-Friendly White Savior

Amelia Duckworth appears in every single episode of *Bizaardvark*, making her an undeniably important part of the show. Though Amelia's picture is not the cover image for *Bizaardvark*, her presence throughout the storyline is vital in every episode and could be considered problematic in terms of supporting diversity. In *A Killer Robot Christmas* (S2E13), the Vuuugle crew invites a group of children to the studio for a Christmas party, without Liam, Vuuugle's CEO's approval. The group decides to have Amelia (a beauty vlogger) reprogram the computer system to block Liam from being able to see the party happening at Vuuugle. However, Bernie changes the program on accident and creates a Grinch-like anti–Christmas robot that begins to destroy the party.

Even though Paige and Frankie are painted to be the protagonists of the show, it's Amelia who saves the day. This storyline, commonly known as the white savior narrative, has been seen since popular media began. From Sandra Bullock as Leigh Anne Tuohy in *The Blind Side* to Nicole Kidman in *Lion*, the savior-role is almost exclusively reserved for white actors in popular media. While it isn't quite taking in a homeless orphan, saving a group of kids from a Christmas hating robots shooting candy canes is how *Bizaardvark* breaks down the often heavy but clear role of the white savior into something consumable for children. Amelia Duckworth, the supposedly supporting character, saves the day, while Paige and Frankie, credited throughout the show with their intelligence both in and outside of the classroom and problem-solving skills, stand by in fear.

White savior narratives limit the spaces non-white actors can enter into, as well as transfer into the ways non-white people are viewed as and treated in society as well. Language aligned with media portrayals and tropes have emerged in legislation, political rhetoric and more, creating an environment in which inter-racial relations "reinforce the images of [these] relationships as dysfunctional at best" or "dangerous transgressions at worst … rendering [people of color and cross-race relationships] invisible or to portray them as 'unnatural' border crossings" (Perry and Sutton, 2006, p. 888).

Paige and Frankie might be the clearly identified main characters of *Bizaardvark*, but there is value in noting that both Amelia and Bernie are also featured in every single episode as "supporting" characters. This frequency of appearance by both Bernie and Amelia, as well as their function within each episode as key characters, allows for the question, "Are they really *just* supporting characters?" Even further, can *Bizaardvark* be recognized as a show that projects diversity as a value when *three* of its five main characters (including Dare Me Bro) are white, along with the overwhelming majority of the supporting cast?

As noted by Alvarez (2009), "even within the narrow definition of what Asian characters can be, they are almost always trumped by their White counterparts" (p. 425). This deduction rings true as viewers examine the key role the "support" characters of Amelia, Dare Me Bro, and Bernie in not only their frequency of appearance and frequency of speaking, but also in their importance, often dominance, in the story. This is supported by the 1994 work of Darrell Hamamoto, who posed that even when Asian and Asian Americans are represented, "they exist primarily for the convenience and benefit of Euro-American [characters] … and the problems they face in daily life are not considered to be of intrinsic interest" (p. 206). Mass media productions of race typically fall into reenacting and reifying group stereotyping across race, gender, and more. For minority and marginalized groups, these representations tend to vary in both quality and quantity, whereas representations of White characters tend to "provide an abundance of positive, varied representations" for consideration (Leavitt et al., 2015).

In an analysis of the Netflix show *Orange Is the New Black (OITNB)*, Belcher (2016) outlines that the *presence* of diversity in media is simply not enough to be considered a positive contribution to the media landscape. The use of diversity countered by a "color blind" white savior or main character remains a problematic point for popular media. For *OITNB*, "refusing to whitewash its characters and their racialized struggles ... departs from current standards in the field of diversity-forward television" (p. 494). For children, this *diversity-forward* television includes Disney's *Bizaardvark*.

Although *OITNB* is not without its problematic feats, *Bizaardvark*, unlike *OITNB*, separates diverse characters from their diverse experiences and struggles, it provides an outline of the current standards for diversity in media—diversity for diversity's sake. *Bizaardvark* removes the "faces of diversity," Paige and Frankie, from their diverse identities and experiences, only to be positioned alongside an exclusively White cohort, while never addressing the potential questions of identity that may arise during different interactions within these dynamics. While Disney Channel uses Hu and Rodrigo in commercials centering around Asian American experiences and heritage, that same attention is not translated into the script of the show.

Principal Karen—A Diverse Kind of Crazy

When other characters of color happen to be presented in the show as supporting characters, *Bizaardvark* avoids casting them in the most flattering light. The U.S. Department of Education (Hill, Ottem, DeRoche, 2016) published a report analyzing the demographics of public and private school principals in the United States. The 1987–88 analysis of public schools showed that 87 percent of principals were white. Data collected until 2012 a decrease of about one percent every two years, and the data reflected public school principals being composed of white people 80 percent of United States public schools.

Principal Karen, the head of the *Bizaardvark* stars' high school, Sierra High, is played by Rachna Khatau. Khatau is an Indian American woman raised in Britain. According to the U.S. Department of Education (Hill, Ottem, DeRoche, 2016), as of 2012, less than 3 percent of the almost 90,000 public school principals were classified as a race or ethnicity other than White, Black, or Hispanic. This "other" category would include Indian, Native American, Asian, or a myriad of other racial populations. Considering that less than 3,000 administrators in America (as of 2012) identified as Indian or Indian American, Principal Karen's non-whiteness, like the non-whiteness of Pagie and Frankie, opens opportunity for representation of non-white characters existing outside of their "designated" charactature, as well as their experiences in predominately white spaces.

Unfortunately for Disney's diverse viewership, this conversation is nowhere to be found. In the episode *Clash of the Superfans* (S2E14), Principal Karen is a major character. Throughout *Bizaardvark*, Principal Karen is a known fan of Paige, Frankie, Dirk, and Amelia, but as suggested in the episode title, is raised to the level of "superfan" of *Bizaardvark*. The entire episode centers around Principal Karen and another *Bizaardvark* superfan's crazy behavior in support of the show, including showing up to a rehearsal, ignoring requests from Paige and Frankie for space, and a temporary tattoo of the *Bizaardvark* logo.

Instead of using Paige, Frankie, and Principal Karen's similarity as the non-white trio of *Bizaardvark* to address minority issues or cast a positive light on women, girls, women/girls of color, or minorities in education, the show fails to acknowledge the rare occurrence of principals being non-white, and even more rarely, Indian. Stuart Hall (2000) explains why these limiting portrayals are extremely problematic, addressing that racism and the media link directly to ideological understandings of others, because the media's main function is to (re)produce and transform ideologies. As such, Hall (2000) poses that "racism is one of the most profoundly 'naturalized' of existing ideologies" (p. 272).

The whiteness and "goodness" of Amelia Duckworth when compared to her non-white counterparts also have implications. As noted by Berger (1977) and Macdonald (1995), the construction of goodness embodied by whiteness, and its dependence on the other to reflect said goodness, is dependent on several key landmarks. Blonde hair, blue eyes, and an "ideal" body type (in American culture, a thin, fit frame) are presented as gallant and good, and distributed for the consumption of the masses not only to take in, but to use as a baseline for defining purity and superiority.

Conclusion

Disney showcases Madison Hu and Olivia Rodrigo in their minute-long clips surrounding Asian American heritage month and diversity but fails to recognize the diversity that Hu and Rodrigo bring to every single episode of *Bizaardvark*. Instead of following the conversation about difference blazed by programs like *Andi Mack*, Disney has used the diverse faces of their actors for little more than appearances. In taking diverse faces at face value, Disney and *Bizaardvark* fail to fairly and accurately represent the communities and viewer that consume their product.

In continuing to limit the ways in which Asian Americans are shown in popular media, specifically in children's media, producers like Disney add to the existing stereotypes and simplicity of consuming them without challenge. These limited narrations extend into the white savior role adopted by Amelia

Duckworth, and the dependency on most of white supporting-main characters in *Bizaardvark*. As noted by Ono and Pham (2009), "today, people sometimes think the racial landscape has shifted, even improved, but examples such as these … [make it] necessary to look at media persistently, to monitor them regularly, and to be vigilant in efforts to challenge them" (p. 13).

References

American Psychological Association. (n.d.) Report of the APA task force on advertising and children. https://www.apa.org/pubs/info/reports/advertising-children.asp.

Associated Press. (2017). Study finds Asian-American characters "tokens" on TV. NBC News. https://www.nbcnews.com/news/asian-america/study-finds-asian-american-characters-tokens-tv-n800861x.

Bang, H.K., & Reece, B.B. (2003). Minorities in children's television commercials: new, improved, and stereotyped. *Journal of Consumer Affairs*, 37(1), 42–67.

Belcher, C. (2016). There is no such thing as a post-racial prison: neoliberal multiculturalism and the white savior complex on orange is the new black. *Television & New Media*, 17(6), 491–503.

Berger, J. (1997). *Ways of seeing*. New York: Penguin.

Brenner, T. (Writer) & Rosenbaum, A. (Director). (2018). *Paige Is Wrong*. [Television Series Episode]. In J. Schubb & J. Varava (Producers), Bizaardvark. Burbank, CA: The Disney Channel.

Chang, M. (2017). Med Madison Hu of Disney's "Bizaardvark" show. Center for Asian American Media. https://caamedia.org/blog/2017/06/21/meet-madison-hu-of-disneys-bizaardvark-show/.

Fox, A., Lewis, L. (Writers) & Margolin Hahn, J. (Director). (2018) *Clash of the Superfans*. [Television Series Episode]. In J. Schubb & J. Varava (Producers), Bizaardvark. Burbank, CA: The Disney Channel.

Friedman, E., Rose, C. (Writers) & Margolin Hahn, J. (Director). (2019). *The Stand-Up Stand Off*. [Television Series Episode]. In J. Schubb & J. Varava (Producers), Bizaardvark. Burbank, CA: The Disney Channel.

Friedman, E., Rose, C. (Writers) & Rosenbaum, J. (Director). (2019). *The Summer of Us*. [Television Series Episode]. In J. Schubb & J. Varava (Producers), Bizaardvark. Burbank, CA: The Disney Channel.

Giroux, H. (1994). Consuming social change: The "United Colors of Benetton." *Cultural Critique*, 26, 5–32.

Giroux, H.A. (1998). Public pedagogy and rodent politics: Cultural studies and the challenge of Disney. *Arizona Journal of Hispanic Cultural Studies*, 253–266.

Hall, S. (2000). Racist ideologies and the media. *Media Studies: A Reader*. New York: New York University Press, pp. 271–282.

Hill, J., Ottem, R., DeRoche, J., & Owens, C. Stats in brief.

James, M., & Ng, D. (2017). In Hollywood, Asian American actors see few lead roles, and pay discrepancies when they land one. *The Los Angeles Times*. http://www.latimes.com/business/hollywood/la-fi-ct-hawaii-five-0-asian-actors-20170708-story.html.

Leavitt, P.A., Covarrubias, R., Perez, Y.A., & Fryberg, S.A. (2015). "Frozen in time": The impact of Native American media representations on identity and self-understanding. *Journal of Social Issues*, 71(1), 39–53.

Lee, S.J., & Vaught, S. (2003). " You can never be too rich or too thin": Popular and consumer culture and the Americanization of Asian American girls and young women. *Journal of Negro Education*, 457–466.

Macdonald, M. (1995). *Representing women: Myths of femininity in the popular media*. London: Edward Arnold.

Mastro, D.E., & Greenberg, B.S. (2000). The portrayal of racial minorities on prime time television. *Journal of Broadcasting & Electronic Media*, 44(4), 690–703.

McAlone, N. (2017) Most popular YouTube stars in the world—And some are making millions. *Business Insider*. https://www.businessinsider.com/most-popular-youtuber-stars-salaries-2017.

Ono, K., & Pham, V. (2009). *Asian Americans and the media*. Cambridge: Polity Press.

Perry, A. (Writer) & Countryman, R. (Director). (2017) *A Killer Robot Christmas*. [Television Series Episode]. In J. Schubb & J. Varava (Producers), Bizaardvark. Burbank, CA: The Disney Channel.

Perry, B., & Sutton, M. (2006). Seeing red over black and white: popular and media representations of inter-racial relationships as precursors to racial violence. *Canadian journal of criminology and criminal justice, 48*(6), 887–904.

Rappaport, R. (Writer) & Kendall, D. (Director). (2018) *The BFF (Before Frankie Friend)*. [Television Series Episode]. In J. Schubb & J. Varava (Producers), Bizaardvark. Burbank, CA: The Disney Channel.

Roman, M. (Writer) & Countryman, R. (Director). (2017). *Mom! Stop!* [Television Series Episode] In J. Schubb & J. Varava (Producers), Bizaardvark. Burbank, CA: The Disney Channel.

Sandell, L. (2016). Zendaya explains the real reason she came back to Disney. *Cosmopolitan*. https://www.cosmopolitan.com/entertainment/news/a59215/zendaya-july-2016/.

Smith, S., Choueiti, M., Pieper, K. (2018). Inclusion in the director's chair? Gender, race & age from directors across 1,100 films from 2007 to 2017. USC Annenberg Inclusion Initiative. Los Angeles: USC Annenberg School for Communication and Journalism.

Stegina, K., Lehrman, J. (Writers) & Countryman, R. (Director). (2017) *Yes or No*. [Television Series Episode]. In J. Schubb & J. Varava (Producers), Bizaardvark. Burbank, CA: The Disney Channel.

Tewari, N. (Ed.). (2008). *Asian american psychology: current perspectives*. Retrieved from https://ebookcentral.proquest.com.

Tung, L.L. (2006). Images of Asians and Asian Americans: The under-representation and misrepresentation of asians and asian-americans on american television. *Intercultural Communication Studies, 15*(1), 87–93.

U.S. Commission on Civil Rights. (1977). *Window dressing on the set: Women and minorities in television*. Washington, D.C.: US Government Printing Office.

Are You My Mother?

Narrative Frames in Andi Mack's Grandfamilies and Teenage Pregnancy

ANDREA B. BAKER

Tomorrow Starts Today

Disney's progressive intentions were evident from the first episode. S1E1 of *Andi Mack* opens with the revelation that Andi's older sister is, in fact, her biological mother, who until this point, has left the responsibility of raising Andi to her own mother (Andi's grandmother, Celia). For 13 years of her life, Andi had been under the impression that Celia was her mother. Thus, Disney begins to spin the tale of Andi Mack and her newly discovered family structure, including emotional tension between the three generations of Mack women, the introduction of Andi's biological father, and the opportunity for Andi and her biological parents to reunite.

In addition to the central story line, the audience is introduced to Andi's two best friends and their complex identities. Buffy is a highly competitive and outspoken girl—traits generally associated with male characters. She consistently attempts to athletically outperform everyone, especially boys, to prove that girls are equal or better than boys in the sports arena. Cyrus is of Jewish descent and struggles with the pressure of living up to societal expectations of male characteristics and behavior. Cyrus is presented as having interests and characteristics stereotypically associated with girls, such as an overdeveloped interest in fashion and a keen emotional intelligence. As the season progresses, Cyrus also reflects on his sexual orientation and struggles with his identity. In season three, Cyrus, comes out to his friend Jonah, using the phrase "I'm gay" for the first time ever on a Disney Network (Cooper, 2019)—a watershed moment in Disney history where a young character is able to articulate his gay identity.

227

Much of the popular media has given attention to Disney's decision to feature a gay character in one of its central narratives. Of course, Cyrus' story breaks barriers and is important to young children wrestling with sexuality, especially in regard to normative understandings and representation. One could argue that Cyrus' story arc has, in some ways, overshadowed the Disney network's initial marketing campaign centered around Andi's discovery that her sister was actually her mother. According to various reports, *Andi Mack* series creator Terri Minsky's key to successfully pitching *Andi Mack* was, in fact, based on the story of Jack Nicholson's real-world experience of growing up without the knowledge that his sister was actually his mother (Leahey, 2019, Barnes, 2017). Whether Minsky intended for Cyrus' story to garner more popular attention is unknown (and irrelevant, to some extent) because Cyrus' coming out scene was a truly monumental event for the Disney Channel Network. This essay, however, returns to Andi's story and Disney's portrayal of her complex family dynamics.

The Disney Channel Looks Forward

A growing body of research into live-action television sitcoms in the tween market, into which the Disney Channel started venturing during the 1990s (Zhou, 2017), suggests that the network has recently added live-action series with ethnically diverse casts such as *Stuck in the Middle* (2016–2018), *Jessie* (2011–2015), and *Bunk'd* (2015–2018), as well as feminist perspectives. Disney's *Girl Meets World* (2014–2017) was the first to explicitly articulate matters of social dynamics, power and privilege, feminism, and culture, as well as the concept of intersectionality (see Bell, Lammon and Murray in this volume). Attention to inclusivity is especially salient given American sitcoms' history of "under representing, symbolically annihilating, and/or heavily relying on stereotypes of non-dominant populations" (Zhou, 2017). The frames Disney uses to introduce contemporary issues to tweens is a deliberate attempt by the network to engage "kids" in more meaningful ways, according to a headline in the *New York Times*, "Kids Are Getting Older Quicker. And Disney Tries to Adapt" (Barnes, 2017). In the same *New York Times* article, "Gary Marsh, president of Disney Channels Worldwide, said Disney said the network was interested in '…stories that matter, that deal with more complex issues, that are emotional and resonate longer. That stick to your guts'" (Barnes, 2017). In the same interview, Marsh also candidly notes that there is a limit to how far Disney could participate in topics involving more adult issues such as sex (Barnes, 2017). Marsh's discussion with the *New York Times* indicates that the Disney Channel is keenly aware that its audience has expectations rooted in the history of the Disney brand, and although the network wants to stay relevant to the contemporary tween audience, Disney must be very cautious of the frames it chooses when dealing with certain topics. Teen pregnancy is rarely discussed and considered "a topic that's very taboo in general to discuss, especially on television" (Williams, 2017). Furthermore, grandfamilies, in which a grandparent raises a grandchild are rarely featured. That noted, *Bizaardvark*, another contemporary Disney Channel television series, features a grandmother who occupies a role as a chaperone of several tweens who live together without parents (For more on *Bizaardvark,* see Simpson in this volume). The series is a parody of a reality television about living at the headquarters of an online video channel like YouTube (in *Bizaardvark's* fictional setting, the channel is Vuuugle). It is a different concept than *Andi Mack* but also features a family structure that is not heteronormative.

This essay ultimately concludes that while Disney never takes a direct approach in addressing the issue of teen pregnancy or the grandfamily structure, the presentation of the Andi's story is only a starting point for discussion. It is an important step toward inclusivity for a major cable network and offers a new way for young people and their parents to discuss issues. On a more critical note, while Disney breaks barriers toward more inclusivity, the portrayal of the community's casual indifference does not authentically represent the real-world stories that are often heard in conjunction with teen pregnancy or grandfamily experiences and in many ways reinforces old stereotypes.

Andi's Story

As previously noted, the premiere of *Andi Mack* S1E1 opens with the revelation on Andi's 13th birthday that her super cool older sister, Bex, is in fact her mother. As Bex rifles through a memory box of old photos and trinkets from her life apart from Andi, Bex makes a confession. She pulls out a photograph of Bex in a maternity ward holding Andi in her arms. Andi asks if the woman in the picture is Bex. Bex tells her it is and then proceeds by saying, "Andi, I'm not your sister. I'm your mother" (Minsky, 2017).

And, indeed, Celia is not happy. For reasons, although ambiguous, revealed through the next two seasons, Bex left Celia to raise and care for Andi for 13 years while Bex travelled around the country attending music festivals. What Disney doesn't explicitly say but leaves the audience to infer is that Andi is the result of an unplanned teenage pregnancy. Terms, or lack thereof, in this series, are of significance.

After the secret is revealed, the entire family begins to process and cope with how they will move forward. Of course, the revelation prompted Andi to inquire about her biological father. Bex does not contact the dad, Bowie, until she is pressured by all members of the Mack family. It is mentioned that Bowie had been aware of Andi, but believed Celia and her husband to be the girl's parents. Celia and her husband had put on the farce for the entire community. Later in the season Bowie arrives on scene (S1E6) and seeks out a relationship with Andi and Bex as he slowly become more involved as a parent. By the end of the 12-episode season, Andi has moved from the comfort and security of her home life with her grandmother Celia to an apartment with Bex (and eventually Bowie) and is optimistically trying to ignite a romantic relationship between her parents, a reunification theme that continues through the following two seasons.

It is of primary interest to examine how Disney presents the concept of motherhood and family structure through its narrative frames. Who is Andi's mother and how should a mother behave? From the first episode, Andi's understanding of parental roles becomes muddled with confusion. The mother/child relationship relies heavily on the frame that suggests mothers exhibit behavior in line with certain social expectations, namely that of a caretaker and a nurturer. Celia has been acting out the role of mother for the first 13 years of Andi's life and has created a secure environment where rules and boundaries are clearly defined. Bex is presented as irresponsible and immature and exhibits rebellious teenage behavior. In the first few episodes of the series, Celia expresses a lack confidence in Bex's ability to behave as Andi's mother. Celia questions whether Andi is safe with Bex after she allows Andi to stay up all night and watch a scary movie, which causes Andi to fall asleep in class the next day and receive detention in the library, where she experiences mild panic when she is reminded of the movie (S1E3). Celia's discovery of the event leads to an argument over whether Bex is fit to be a parent. Andi finds herself in the middle of the argument expressing frustration that the two women are asking her to choose which she would like to be her mother.

> CELIA: No, of course not. We wouldn't do that [ask her to choose].
> BEX: But if we did…
> ANDI: No way! I'm not the one who created this mess. You two are the brain trust that decided that you should pretend to <u>be</u> my sister, because you don't want people to know you're really my grandmother! I'm the kid here, you're the adults. It's your job to figure this out. Let me know when you do [Dunlap, 2017].

Bex's rebellious child persona is the antithesis to Celia's overprotective mother, who worries about bike safety, breakfast options, applying sunscreen, and dating. The frames Disney chooses to present the concept of ideal mother could also be perceived as a commentary on the morality of unplanned teenage pregnancy. One can infer that unplanned teenage pregnancy ultimately causes chaos by disrupting the traditional family structure and violating social norms. In fact, Disney tackles the narrative of crossed parental roles and the confusion that deceit sows in regard to family structure after Bex is reprimanded for throwing a party for Andi in Celia's house when she was away from home on vacation and received a call from the neighborhood watch (S1E4). Bex's revelation that she is Andi's mother and her behavior thus far in the series seem contradictory and confusing to Andi. This is evidenced through the discussion that takes place between Andi and her friend Buffy (S1E5). The discussion begins with Buffy awkwardly searching for the right words when referring to Andi's mom and grandmother. Buffy comments on how cool Bex is as a mother compared to Celia. The evening before Bex had thrown a party in Celia's house while Celia and her husband were away—a classic teen house party scene.

> BUFFY: You've got Bex. She's a cool mom. She lets you have parties.
> ANDI: She makes me have parties. Don't get me wrong, it was a great party that I said we shouldn't have, and now we're in a lot of trouble for. It just feels like she's still my sister and I'm still the responsible one [McClendon, 2017].

And, again later in the same episode Andi explains the uncertainty of Bex's parenting style and her place in the family structure: "I don't know. It turns out, I like boundaries. I don't want to get out there and be bold and live life. I just want to stay in my room, and read a book" (McClendon, 2017).

Clearly Disney frames the concept of mother around themes of responsibility, restraint, and discipline. It is in these interactions that Disney underscores the traditional behavior associated with being a mother, thus addressing teen pregnancy and the implied irresponsibility.

Studies about the role of Disney mothers in feature films demonstrate that the idea of motherhood has traditionally been presented as possessing as the responsible, nurturing caregiver. In *Snow White and the Seven Dwarfs*, Snow White, who despite never having given birth portrays the ultimate American mother and woman of the Post World War II and cold war era, according to Faustino (2015). She meticulously cares for and supervises family members. Faustino (2015) also draws attention to Snow White's overwhelming desire to marry a prince and thus establish a traditional nuclear family (Faustino, 2015). Other Disney portrayals of mothers also demonstrate "the sacrificial, benevolent nature of what it means to be mother," as in *Bambi* (1942), whose mother is killed when ushering her baby to safety and protecting the fawn from the hunters. *Dumbo* (1941) also reiterates this theme when Dumbo's mother is repeatedly beaten and ultimately imprisoned trying to protect her baby, according to Faustino's analysis. This presentation of mothering, especially in light of the consistent re-releases of Disney films, contributes to the "reproduction of the traditional mothering ideology under patriarchy" (Faustino, 2015, p. 147). Furthermore, Faustino suggests, "The dreams of Disney heroines ultimately serve the male desires to have mothers for themselves and their children—while preserving the patriarchal order of power. A woman's place is in the home, loving and tending to the needs of men and children" (Faustino, 2015, p. 131).

In her analysis of *Finding Nemo* (2003), Brydon (2009) suggests that even when Disney is trying to change the narrative around parental roles, it still puts forth ideal mothering behavior. Brydon uses the illustration of Nemo's father, Marlin, who becomes responsible for his son after the mother dies. Byrdon points to Marlin's high-pitched voice and his curvy, rounded figure, suggesting that of a woman who has given birth to a child and how he "uses phrases stereotypically attributed to mothers' policing of children: 'You take one more move, mister; you are in big trouble, young man'" (Brydon, 2009, p 139). While Disney may be attempting to support and extend the concept of family structure, but motherhood is still tied to a certain framework of behavior.

What's in a Name?

Also of significance, Disney places a great deal of emphasis on role terms, especially mother and grandmother. It should be noted that in the previous conversation cited between Buffy and Andi, Andi brings up that Celia doesn't want to be called "grandma," instead preferring "CeCe." In an earlier exchange between Celia and Andi (S1E3), Celia explicitly tells Andi to call her by another name.

> ANDI: Well, what should I call you, then? Because you don't want to be called "Grandma," but you're not my mom anymore.
> CELIA: For now, why don't you just call me Celia? [Dunlap, 2017].

The importance of role clarity and terms is further driven by the tale of a major milestone in Andi's life—her first word—"Mama." The utterance is apparently directed at Celia as opposed to Bex, prompting Bex's sudden and immediate departure from Andi's life, as the audience learns in S2E4. Bex is only redeemed as a parent and thus granted the title of mother when she fosters more direct interaction and takes on guardianship for Andi over the next several episodes. The first time Andi acknowledges Bex as her mother is after Bex commissions an apartment for her and Andi to live together, apart from Celia's safe and secure home (S1E10). Bex is overwhelmed with excitement and asks Andi to keep repeating her new name.

> ANDI: This is my home, and you're my mom.
> BEX: I'm your what? My mom? You called me Mom! … That was the first time! Whoa. Say it again!! [Baker, 2017].

The intentional focus on terms is an important framing technique Disney uses in its narrative, and perhaps, according to application of Goffman's theory (1979), a method of breaking the frame of make-believe that Celia so carefully orchestrated when fabricating the family structure and playing the role of Andi's mother publicly. Goffman's theory would also suggest that this in some sense is connected to Bex's continuous childish/rebellious behavior, since she is relegated to the role of a child by Celia's persistent doubt of Bex's parental decision-making. Disney focuses on terms to reward and punish characters for their choices to deviate from traditional social order. In some sense, Disney seems to be suggesting "mother" as an ultimate term and, consequently, "grandmother" as a term of repulsion in this context; that is, the unplanned teenage pregnancy and forced grandfamily structure.

For example, in addition to the application of the term mother and Celia's request that Andi call her CeCe instead of grandma, a neighbor casts the term "grandma" as a weapon to wound Celia's pride and demonstrate that Celia's farce has been revealed. After walking out of her home one day to water the roses on her perfectly manicured front lawn, Celia runs into a neighbor, Lillian, who approaches her to seemingly discuss the flowers (S1E3).

LILLIAN: I see your older daughter is home.
CELIA: Yes, she is.
LILLIAN: Did I say older? I meant only. I hear that little cutie with the Harry Potter haircut is actually her daughter, and not your late-in-life miracle baby. I guess congratulations are in order, grandma! [Baker, 2017].

Cecelia, unable to disguise her frustration with the new label and nosy neighbor, proceeds to spray Lillian with the garden hose. It is in the focus on the terms "mother" and "grandmother" that Disney seems to be framing its commentary on the morality of teen pregnancy, and the ethical implications associated with Andi's family's decision to falsely present themselves as a traditional nuclear family in middle class suburban America. It should be mentioned that Andi's story takes place in the fictional town of Shadyside, a seemingly a white middle class suburban town on the West Coast, which is modeled after series creator Terry Minsky's hometown[1] (Owen, 2017). The factors of socioeconomic status, race, and geographic location are important underlying conditions of the community's response to how the social situation is perceived and discussed (Hayslip et al., 2019). Lillian's reaction to the news about Celia's situation could also be perceived as an attempt to bring attention to the challenges that grandparents raising their grandchildren face. In their study about "grandfamilies," Hayslip et al. (2019) examine several factors associated with grandparents raising their grandchildren, including social expectations and family reputations.

Despite their importance in their grandchildren's lives and the satisfaction associated with guiding and protecting a vulnerable child, custodial grandparents also report feeling isolated from age peers, experience a variety of physical and emotional challenges associated with caregiving, feel judged by others as failures as parents, or experience shame linked to the perceived stigma of having to raise their grandchildren [Hayslip et al., 2019, p. 152].

In addition to stigma, grandparents raising grandchildren face many challenges, including economic hardships, lack of social resources, and inability to relate to the parents of other children in the same age group as their grandchildren, among other difficulties (Hayslip et al., 2019; Dunn and Wamsley, 2018; Pilkaukas and Duniform, 2016; Hayslip and Kaminiski, 2005). Andi Mack's family seems to have been immune to most of these challenges. Is this the Disney magic? Perhaps, but regardless, Disney's focus on a grandfamily is a step toward inclusivity. The family structure in many of Disney's feature length films is traditionally married heterosexual parents with biological grandchildren, heterosexual step-parents, or single parents (Moran, 2016). Furthermore, Moran (2016) did not find any adoptive or same-sex families depicted in any of the 24 G-rated Disney feature length films in her study. Studies indicate that families in which grandparents are raising their grandchildren are "not as rare a phenomenon as is commonly believed" (Fuller-Thompson et al., 1997); an estimated six million children are being cared for by their grandparents (Hayslip et al., 2019). Media depictions of non-traditional families is of paramount importance to young children and tweens seeking to identify representations of their reality. This is especially true of the Disney brand, since its target market is kids, tweens, teens and families. In addition to acknowledging the challenges of grandparents in grandfamily situations, it is also critical to understand the challenges that unplanned teenage pregnancies create for the biological parents as well.

In their study of the portrayal of teenage pregnancy, Gugliemo and Stewart (2013) suggest that the presentation of teen parenting in reality TV shows such as MTV's *16 and Pregnant* is "often driven [by] conservative notions of morality and welfare reform and [are] couched in the language of mitigating risk for our children and young people" (p. 19, Gugliemo and Stewart, 2013). They continue on to say that the presentations of teen pregnancy reinforce "gender, race, and class stereotypes as well as heteronormative marriage" (p. 19, Gugliemo and Stewart, 2013). Disney may have consulted with the National Campaign to Prevent Teen and Unplanned Pregnancy and the National Center on Adoption and Permanency when they were in the creation phase of *Andi Mack,* but they completely omit any discussion about or related to Bex's unplanned teen pregnancy.

The audience is never told what Bex's age was when she gave birth to Andi. With the exception of the "Mama" story and memory box that carries photos of Bex in the hospital holding Andi after giving birth, Bex's experience as a teen mother and her choice to remain absent the first 13 years of Andi's life is not discussed. What is also unusual, given that Celia and her husband had been masquerading as Andi's parents, is that apparently no one in the community ever asked where their older daughter disappeared to and apparently no one in town ever saw her pregnant with Andi. Furthermore, when the rest of small-town suburban America finds out that Bex is Andi's mother, including the teachers at the school Andi attends and Bex formerly attended, as well as a girl Bex formerly babysat who is now her boss, no one says anything. The only questions about Bex's pregnancy are from Andi's friends, Cyrus and Buffy, after they see the hospital picture and assume Bex had a secret baby—until Andi reveals that Andi herself is the secret baby (S1E2). Further, there are only two comments to Andi socially in regard to the revelation that Bex is her mother. The first is an exchange between Jonah and Andi, in which Jonah's reaction is warm, receptive and awkward (at best), diplomatically speaking.

> JONAH: Hey. Your-Your mom thing.
> ANDI: You heard.
> JONAH: Yeah. That's so awesome [Minsky, 2017].

The other social mention of Andi's new family structure comes later in the same episode (S1E4), at a house party, when in a fit of jealousy, another peer creates a scene, calling attention to the absence of Andi's father. In this scene, Amber, Jonah's girlfriend, publicly asks Andy about her father as people are cheering for a dance Andi just performed for a crowd of her peers. The nonverbal behavior in the scene underscores that Amber is deliberately trying to socially shame Andi.

> AMBER: And let's not forget about Andi's new mom!
> CROWD: Bex! Bex! Bex! Bex! Bex! Bex! Bex! Bex! Bex!
> AMBER: And what about Andi's new dad? Is he here? We'd love to meet him, too [Baker, 2017].

This causes all of Andi's peers to gasp. Andi looks to Bex as if she is ready to burst in tears, then leaves the room when Bex turns all of the lights in the house off. But that's it. There is no additional narrative around unplanned teen pregnancy or its consequences. This seems to be outside of the experience many teenage mothers report. In several studies, pregnant teenagers report being socially stigmatized as irresponsible and harshly judged by their peers, as well as marginalized by the community and their peers (Guglielmo and Stewart, 2013, Fallas, 2013, Barcelos and Gubrium, 2014, Jones, et. Al, 2019, Wilson and Hunnington, 2006. Rice et. Al, 2019).

Of course, Disney does portray the relationship between Celia and Bex as problematic, thus holding to the narrative that teenage pregnancy creates chaos and challenges for the overall family and requires redemption (Barcelos and Gubrium, 2014, Fallas, 2013).

> BEX: Can we try something? What? Can we try something? Let's try to say one nice thing to each other. You just got to come up with one. I'll go first. You did a fantastic job raising my daughter. And it's hard to admit, but, probably a better job than I would've done. And I'm grateful. Very, very grateful.
> CELIA: I was going to say I like how you do your makeup. That's a compliment [Minsky, 2017].

Later in the series, Bex's relationship with Celia is transformed. After Bex finds a job, an apartment and takes care of Andi, social order is restored. Disney weaves its classical fantasy into the narrative by also attempting recreate the traditional family structure. Thus, Andi and her grandmother try tirelessly throughout the entire series to get Bex and Bowie back together, even going so far as to script a bungled and ultimately failed attempt at a marriage proposal in S1E25. Bex had intentions to ask Bowie for his hand, but then Bowie is offered an international tour position with his band. Bex attempts to call it off, but Bowie finds the engagement ring in the cake before she is able. Bex cancels wedding plans for a second time in S3E13 and crushes Andi's and Cecilia's hope at reuniting the couple legitimately. Ending the stigma is dashed again:

> ANDI: I mean, it's your decision.
> BEX: But it affects you. Obviously, you must be angry or frustrated or sad. Are you?
> ANDI: Well, what I'm feeling is not surprised. I guess that deep down, I always knew that this was never going to happen [Weber, 2019].

The fortunate news for Andi's biological family is that they are all still together and live in the same apartment. Perhaps, in Disney's world, mothers and fathers who had children as teenagers can recreate the traditionally perfect nuclear family after 13 years full of distance and lies. Of course, this can only occur once the mother reinstates her worth as a parent and the father, who is in a band that tours the country, gives up his music career and decides he wants to raise a tween in suburban America. Furthermore, no one in the community will socially marginalize the family or even broach the topic of why the grandparents created an elaborate scheme to hide their daughter's teenage pregnancy. Plausible? Perhaps. More realistically it is highly unlikely, given the research about the experiences of grandfamilies and teen moms. Regardless, Disney does extend the concept of family structure and has includes other themes in the series, especially the network's debut of the first gay middle school kid. These firsts for Disney represent progress toward more inclusive narratives and demonstrate that tomorrows start today.

NOTE

1. Minsky spent her youth in Mt. Lebanon, Pennsylvania, a suburb of Pittsburgh, Pennsylvania, which is 95.6 percent white, with a median income $89,028. 61 percent of the population has a bachelor's degree or higher, and 62 percent are married. The town has less than 5 percent unemployment and only 3.5 percent live below the poverty line (City-Data.com).

REFERENCES

Baker, P. (April 21, 2017). S1E4: Dancing in the Dark. [Television broadcast] In T. Minsky *Andi Mack*. Los Angeles: Go Dog Go.

Baker, P. (June 9, 2017). S1E10: Home Away from Home. [Television broadcast] In T. Minsky *Andi Mack*. Los Angeles: Go Dog Go.

Barcelos, C., and Gubrim, A. (2014). Reproducing stories: Strategic narrative of teen pregnancy and motherhood. *Social Problems*. 6: 446–481.

Barnes, B. (2017, March 10) Kids are getting older quicker. And Disney tries to adapt. *New York Times*. Retrieved from https://www.nytimes.com/2017/03/10/arts/television/kids-are-getting-older-quicker-and-disney-tries-to-adapt.html.

Butler, B. (2017, October 26). Disney Channel is making history with its first gay coming-out story. *Washington Post*. Retrieved from https://www.washingtonpost.com/news/arts-and entertainment/wp/2017/10/26/disney-channel-is-making-history-with-its-first-gay-coming-out-story/?utm_term=.05ffa6077254.

Coulter, N. (2012) From toddlers to teens: The colonization of childhood the Disney way. *Jeunesse: Young People, Text, and Cultures* 4(1): 146 -158.

Dunlap, E. (April 14, 2017) S1E3: Shhh!. [Television broadcast] In T. Minsky *Andi Mack*. Los Angeles: Go Dog Go.

Dunn, B., and Wamsley, B. (2018) Grandfamilies: Characteristics and needs of grandparents raising grandchildren. *Journal of Extension, 56*(5).

Fallas, J. (2013) Othering the mothering. In Guglielmo, L. (Ed.), *MTV and teen pregnancy: Critical essays on 16 and Pregnant and Teen Mom*. Lanham, MD: Rowman & Littlefield.

Faustino, Lisa. (2015). "Nearly everybody gets twitterpated": The Disney version of mothering. *Children's Literature in Education, 46*: 127–144.

Fuller-Thompson, E. Minkler, M and Driver, D (1997). A profile of grandparents raising their grandchildren in the United States. *The Gerontological Society of America, 37*(3).

Guglielmo, L., and Stewart, K. (2013). 16 and Pregnant and the Unvarnished Truth about Teen Pregnancy. In Guglielmo, L. (Ed.), *MTV and teen pregnancy: Critical essays on 16 and Pregnant and Teen Mom*. Lanham, MD: Rowman & Littlefield.

Hayslip, B., Fruhauf, C., & Dolbin-MacNab, M. (2019) Grandparents raising grandchildren: What have we leaned over the last decade? *The Gerontologist, 59*(3): e152–e163.

Hayslip, B., & Kaminski, P. (2005). Grandparents raising their grandchildren. *Marriage and Family Review, 37*: 147–169.

Holz, P. (2017). TV review. Focus on the family's plugged in. Retrieved from https://www.pluggedin.com/tv-reviews/andi-mack.

Jones, C., Whitfield, C. Seymour, J., & Hayler, M. (2019) "Other Girls" A qualitative exploration ofteenage mothers' views on teen pregnancy in contemporaries. *Sexuality and Culture*. Springer: https://doi.org/10.1007/s12119-019-09589-4.

Leahey, Lynn. (2019, June 13). Terri Minsky talks about the beginning—And the end—of Andi Mack. Cynopsis Media. http://www.cynopsis.com/cyncity/terri-minsky-talks-about-the-beginning-and-the-end-of-andi-mack/.

McClendon, R. (April 28, 2017) S1E5: It's not about you. [Television broadcast] In T. Minsky *Andi Mack*. Los Angeles, CA: Go Dog Go.

Minsky, T. (April 7, 2017). S1E1: 13. [Television broadcast] In T. Minsky *Andi Mack*. Los Angeles: Go Dog Go.

Minsky, T. (April 7, 2017). S1E2: Outside the Box. [Television broadcast] In T. Minsky *Andi Mack*. Los Angeles: Go Dog Go.

Moran, Meghan. (2016). Live-action and animated Disney films: An analysis of themes and family structures over time. (Master of Science) Resnsselear Polytechnic Institute, New York.

Owen, Rob (2017, April 6). Tuned in: Two writers with local ties debut new tv series. *Pittsburgh Post Gazette*. Retrieved from: https://www.post-gazette.com/ae/tv-radio/2017/04/07/Brian-McGreevy-The-Son-Terri-Minsky-Andi-Mack/stories/201704070054.

Pilkaukas, N., and Dunifon, R. (2016). Understanding grandfamilies: Characteristics of grandparents, nonresident parents and children. *Journal of Marriage and Family*. 8: 623–633.

Rice, W., et al. The stigma of being a young parent: Development of a measurement tool and predictors. *Journal of Child and Family Studies*, 28: 642–655.

Riley, N. (2017, March 19). Kids TV shows push cultural limits—But they're damaging kids. *New York Post*. Retrieved from https://nypost.com/2017/03/19/kids-tv-shows-push-cultural-limits-but-theyre-damaging-kids/.

Strahan, M. (2018, February 19). Andi Mack' cast dish on new season: "It makes diversity normal." ABC News Television broadcast. https://abcnews.go.com/GMA/Culture/video/andi-mack-cast-dish-season-makes-diversity-normal-53188945.

Weber, S. (March 1, 2019) S313: Mount Rushmore or Less. [Television broadcast] In T. Minsky *Andi Mack*. Los Angeles: Go Dog Go.

Williams, Tatyana. (2017, March 10) Disney Channel's Andi Mack to cover teenage pregnancy for the first time. *Affinity Magazine*. Retrieved from http://affinitymagazine.us/2017/03/10/disney-channels-andi-mack-to-cover-teenage-pregnancy-for-the-first-time/.

Wilson, H., and Huntington, A. (2006). Deviant mothers: The construction of teenage motherhood in contemporary discourse. *Journal of Social Policy*. 35: 59–76.

Wong, C. (2017, November 2) Kenya just banned a Disney show because of its gay character. *Huffington Post*. Retrieved from https://www.huffingtonpost.com/entry/andi-mack-kenya-ban_us_59fb318ee4b0b0c7fa388dcd   http://www.city-data.com/city/Mount-Lebanon-Pennsylvania.html.

Zhou, Y. (2017). Are introverts invisible? A textual analysis of how the Disney and Nickelodeon teen sitcoms reflect the extrovert ideal. (Master's thesis, Syracuse University, 2017). *ProQuest, LLC*, 10287536.

That's So Raven's Home
and *Boy Meets Girl Meets World*

Recursion, Revival and
Multi-Generational Dialogues

MICHELLE ANYA ANJIRBAG

Revival of narratives and characters in variable formats for new generations of audiences has long been part of the *modus operandi* of the Walt Disney Corporation, but it has perhaps not been done as blatantly, or arguably, as successfully, as by the Disney Channel since the late 2000s. In 2007, the Disney Channel launched its first spin-off sitcom of one of its own shows, *Cory in the House* (2007–2008) (Cory's cooking, 2007), on the back of the success of the 2003–2007 hit *That's So Raven*. *Cory in the House* allowed the channel to expand the world it created around the eponymous Raven and her adventures, and refocus it around already-beloved characters—essentially creating a new show built on an already successful group of characters, with recognizable patterns of behavior and reactions to re-engage an already-existing fan base after one of their most successful programs came to a close. A decade later sees the corporation not only fully embracing the idea of re-engagement, with several spin-offs for different programs since *Cory in the House*, but also taking a step further and re-engaging now-adult audiences, with the now-adult casts of *That's So Raven* and *Boy Meets World* (1993–2000) returning to the television screen to continue their stories in *Raven's Home* (2017–present) and *Girl Meets World* (2014–2017). Reboots of the Disney Channel's programming for tweens open spaces for cross-generational conversations on changing social dynamics for both adolescents and their families, reflecting progressions of social norms in American societies, and societal changes in both the definition of the American family and internal family dynamics. To explore this concept, this essay will first consider the contexts of tweens, nostalgia, and the cross-generational audience within the context of the Disney media structure, and then use the concepts of inter-textuality and paratextuality to consider how these concepts are invoked between *That's So Raven* and *Raven's Home*, and *Boy Meets World* and *Girl Meets World*.

The later-generation programs—*Raven's Home* and *Girl Meets World*—are in many ways narratively dependent on the earlier programs—*That's So Raven* and *Boy Meets World*—as they quite literally pick up the narratives of the former adolescent characters' adult lives, filling in what has happened to beloved characters in the interim, while simultaneously shifting the narrative focus of the show to be shared with a new set of adolescent protagonists. However, these narratives are not mere continuations of the rules, norms, and depictions of social and family life as seen in the earlier programs, and in some ways actively depart from what was "allowed" to be depicted on tel-evision for an adolescent demographic in an earlier generation of the Disney Channel. In effect, by using these connections between not only narrative arcs but also target audiences for these programs, we can arguably observe (in an albeit highly specific microcosm of media and family) how "family exerts influence on media life" and "media can shape family life" (Nathanson, 2013, p. 299). Keeping this dialogic relationship between family life and media life in mind, an analysis of the Disney Channel's programming allows a prob-ing of changing norms, changing depictions, and the changing conceptual-ization of the "tween" demographic by the corporate channel. Such an analysis might begin by examining the intertextual relationships between the contemporary-sequel programs and the original programs that narratively precede them, and the paratextual relationships between these programs and the rest of the channel. In addition to changes in thematic material, the more contemporary, updated programs (whether we think of them as spin-offs or revivals), reflect changing family dynamics, modeling different norms for intergenerational communication embedded within the program. Thus, these narratives arguably provide an example for both parents and tweens to address myriad challenges associated with the maturation of adolescents—tweens in particular—as individuals within an evolving social and cultural space.

Tweens, Family and Disney's "Politics of Nostalgia"

Tally (2005) writes about the address of families through marketing fam-ily films—films made for cross-generational appeal—specifically to tween girls (p. 322), and this idea can also be extended to the Disney Channel's programming. If we recognize, as Jeanette Steemers (2013) does, that there are three aspects to children's television culture: the institutional and industry context of production, content that is made based on age and stage organization rather than genre classification, and the child audience as an audience that evolves (p. 103), we can also recognize that the television and media viewing participated in by children happens also within the broader location of a family context (Nathanson, 2013, p. 304), and thus, another component of children's television culture becomes that cross-generational appeal. Nathanson writes that "media have the potential to bring families together as they provide opportunities for shared experiences and mutually experienced positive affect" (Nathanson, 2013, p. 302). To build that simultaneous appeal for both the tween and the adult audiences, the programs can sometimes incorporate "a kind of wink and a nod to the parents, whereas other times it may be more connected to the plot of the movie; still other times it may be trying to create a sense of nostalgia for the parents" (Tally, 2005, p. 322). The revivals of narratives from older programs vis-à-vis being incorporated into new programs meant to represent and convey a sense of continuity between generations—as seen in both the cases of *Girl Meets World* and *Raven's Home*—are arguably a step beyond that "wink and nod." Instead, they deliberately create and recreate moments of nostalgic remembrance for the older generation, reframed and recontextualized to also suit the sense of discovery for a new generation discovering their own paths to becoming older versions of themselves and their places within a larger society through these media depictions of families.

Media depictions of families especially on television, which is still the dominant medium used by children and, particularly important, shared by children with family members (Nathanson, 2013, p. 299) demonstrate the ways in which media can be seen as a vehicle in the display, dissemination, and discussion of childhood (Drotner, 2013, p. 17). As adults can and do relate to articulations about childhood across various media, media conglomerates, which are ultimately commercially driven, then employ concepts about childhood that are seen to be reflecting upon a social reality. By defining childhood as a "phase for regulated protection and transformation" where "the upbringing of the young (to adult status) becomes a key object of social interest" (Drotner, 2013, pp. 19–20), and in this context understanding "tweenhood" as an overlapping space where tweens begin to start to process and interpret dialogues of transformation for themselves in terms of who they might become (Tally, 2005, p. 316), it becomes possibly to understand family media as spaces where competing perceptions of social realities across generations can be voiced (Drotner, 2013, p. 17). Thus, media internalizes an "ongoing co-construction of mass media, childhood, and youth" where "media are at once symbolic social resources whose main characteristic is their semiotic properties. So, media are not merely conduits for the transmission of information, they are institutionally embedded meaning-making tools that connect people across time and space" (Drotner, 2013, p. 15). When considering the Disney context in particular, the reiterations of narratives familiar to an older generation but marketed simultaneously to both parents and tweens become spaces that deliberately connect two generations across time in the work of meaning-making in the present. While the process of making reboots and spin-offs to that effect by the Disney Channel is firmly rooted in the 2000s, the process of using nostalgia to draw multiple generations of audiences to the same screen is long incorporated within the Disney media strategy.

The Disney Channel has helped to shape and solidify what it means to be a tween since the mid–80s, and simultaneously, has played a role in both reflecting and shaping changing perceptions of family dynamics in America. The channel's programming adjusts to account for new social norms while showing familiar faces growing up through different stages of their own lives and embodying varied experiences. For example, fans of *Boy Meets World* who would have had to speculate on Cory and Topanga's future at the end of the show in 2000, return to characters they potentially grew up with, and witness them as adults with children, who are the new focus of *Girl Meets World*. Such a construction of narrative draws on what Richard Schickel terms the "politics of nostalgia" (Schickel, 1986, p. 157), using the revival of narratives and characters as the engine that power the channel, and creating contact points for viewers across generations. Since the inception of its family programming in the 1950s, Disney has utilized nostalgia and revival to maintain its audience base across generations, addressing both children discovering its animations and adults remembering their earlier encounters and experiences with the subject material. The original debut of the *Disneyland* program on ABC in October 1954 anticipated both this appeal to nostalgia and the greater strategy of cross-platform synergy by the Disney studio. According to Paul Wells (2002), this program

> successfully found the adult audience of 'baby boomers' who were re-familiarizing themselves with the cartoons they saw in their own childhoods (and at the zenith of Disney's public profile and popularity) and the children's audience who were seeing some of the Disney shorts for the first time in the comfort of their own home [Wells, 2002, pp. 76–77].

The program later moved across networks to NBC in 1958, and would again return "home" to ABC in the 1990s, changing names several times: becoming *Walt Disney Presents*, *Walt Disney's Wonderful World of Color*, and finally again, *The Wonderful World of Disney* in the Eisner years. In these moves and changes, we can see how the ability of the company to speak to a generationally layered audience, while also continually "modernizing" children's programming with new offerings such as *The Mickey Mouse Club* (which was also later revived for a new generation) (Watts, 1997, p. 286; Wells, 2002, p. 77; Stewart, 2006, p. 77), has been a long-held strategy of the Disney Corporation's approach to television programming. It is this strategy of revival alongside innovation that was then, in some ways, escalated in the 1990s.

Cultural conditions, including the advent of digital technologies in the mid-to-late 1990s, led to the ensuing proliferation of television services—particularly dedicated children's television channels. This led, too, to further audience fragmentation among television audiences. For Disney in particular, this included the launch of the Disney Channel UK in 1995 and the purchase of the ABC network, two moves that pushed the Disney Corporation into the position of being the second largest media corporation in the world (Potter, 2011, p. 121). Across its various channels globally, which in 2011 included 67 "'24-hour, kid-driven, family-inclusive' children's television channels" transmitted to an estimated 600 million viewers across over 100 countries, one of the most distinguishing features of the corporation's constructed relationship with its child viewers was the lack of on-channel paid advertising (Potter, 2011, p. 121). In many ways, not only does this mean that the entire channel can be read as an advertisement for the larger (consumerist) Disney ethos, where what is being sold is an image of what life might be like, it also means that viewers of the channel essentially enter a piece of the Disney universe when they begin to view a television program, and then do not leave it until they physically leave the channel. It also serves to allow for an older viewing audience to step back into a familiar, nostalgic space, which I would argue is a part of the deliberate draw of rebooting shows that are not simply a few seasons older, but have been finished for a decade or longer. As child and adolescent experiences have diversified and stratified, the strategy to continue to reach an audience with a faster turnover and shorter engagement period—the four or so years of "tweenhood"—has been maintained. To borrow a concept from both linguistics and programming, this pattern of rebooting, remixing, reviving, and/or returning to programs, narratives, and characters is a process of recursion: defining something—in this case the tween identity within the confines of the family narrative structure—by using the thing that is being defined. Tweens can see themselves in the younger characters of television programs that also focus on characters remembered by the tweens' parents now as parents themselves. Both tweens and their parents can enter a space that automatically builds roads for intergenerational communication by showing, literally, different generations of "Disney stars" communicating in familial settings, and older generations of viewers can experience a nostalgic return. The success of nostalgia-driven recursive spin-offs further bolsters that this is a successful model, and the process of recycling and remaking older properties or having them feed into new ones continues. Disney continues to define itself and its viewers through the repetition of its own creations. While the phrasing perhaps more *en vogue* in the current cultural setting might be that readers can "always go home to Hogwarts" courtesy of the brand-cultivation of J.K. Rowling, in effect, this strategy of nostalgia-fueled synergy and cross-generational content is a reflection of the Disney ethos of attempting to always bring its viewers and fans "back home" to its "magic kingdom" by one road or another.

Whether bringing the cartoon shorts originally aired in cinemas to new audiences in new contexts, or deliberately formulating children's -specific programming with all child-actors with the intent of embodying in its stars a "symbol of healthy American youth" (Watts, 1997, p. 286), the corporation uses nostalgia to solidify and maintain a multi-generational audience. Regarding the tendency of the positivity the corporation receives worldwide from a mass viewing public (regardless of negative responses from critical quarters) regarding its film corpus, Paul Wells writes that

> this may indicate that the viewing public has little interest in "authorship" and "cultural politics," and is opting to engage with and enjoy the "supernormal" world of the animated form in a *primal* rather than *interrogative* or *contextual* way. The historical or institutional issues raised by "Disney" (however defined, in this instance) have been subsumed into personal meta-narratives rather than cultural ones. Childhood experiences become adult memories, which in turn influence the next generation of childhood experiences, and so on. This continuity is based on an intrinsic trust in Disney's "form" [Wells, 2002, p. 121].

This concept of continuity and the connection between childhood experiences and adult memories, and, in fact, the very practical demographic separation between adults and tweens, becomes important when considering how tweens are positioned economically as a target demographic by media corporations. While media corporations acknowledge the influential potentials of the conceptualized tween audience, and do identify tweens as a consumer demographic of particular interest, it cannot be denied that significant economic power is still wielded by the parents of tweens, even if it is at the tweens' behest. Tweens might be in the process of asserting their own independence and self-formulation of their identities, and occupy increasingly unique social spaces with unique experiences, but they also still exist in states of dependence. Thus, it is necessary to not only speak to parents who have the ability to control, limit, or choose access to programming for tweens at different stages of their adolescence, but to speak to the conflicts inherent in navigating the various and changing power dynamics that are present as tweens age and families adapt to new normals—new schemas, even—of understanding. These schemas, or methods and cognitive structures of organizing ideas and experiences for understanding, reflect patterns and processes of learning as schemas are developed and adapted to reconcile when certain ways of understanding the world prove inadequate (Prinsloo, 2013, p. 248). In some ways, the shift to deliberately addressing a cross-generational audience on a channel that was developed to specifically address a child—then "tween"—audience reflects an evolution of the nostalgia-rooted schemas previously employed by the Disney Channel. Arguably what can be seen in the incorporation of the intergenerational audience is that the strategy is transitioning to one which is attempting, in some ways, to consolidate the previously discussed audience fragmentation. By doing so, Disney holds on to its reach and influence by continuing to transition to meet the nostalgia-fueled desires of the generation that remembers being children during the corporation's 1990s hey-day, and evolved with the channel as it in turn learned to evolve its programming, while still reaching a new audience.

Maintaining Continuity: Connecting Generations Through Recursive Programming

By reviving shows that parents themselves have seen and have their own nostalgic connection to, the Disney Channel maintains its multi-generational audience while also placing the current cultural moment in the larger context of the channel's history. By recontextualizing the contemporary moment within the structure of the channel's productions, the corporation simultaneously absorbs it—and the audience—into the larger structure of the corporation's conceptualization of its media properties. Thus, the presentation of programming allows the Disney Channel to also constantly reconceptualize and recontextualize the progression of children through various franchises as they age, from young children to tweens, and through teenagerhood, to have them then finally return as adults who remember not just a show here and there, but have a nostalgic affinity for "growing up with" The Disney Channel as a natural part of childhood and becoming an adult. As embedded in the Disney Channel in the late 2000s, the journey would possibly run from the *Fairies* franhise to then "hook them on *Kim Possible, That's So Raven*, and *Hannah Montana*, all on the Disney Channel, and then serve up *High School Musical* for older kids" (Marr, 2007). The strategy is not just about the creation of new shows based on the old, however. Disney has also engaged its television and digital platforms in a block of programming they call "Disney Replay" since 2014, where older shows are re-run with the goal of presenting tweens with something different, and simultaneously "drawing in adults who may not ordinarily access the network's digital offerings" (Umstead, 2015, p. 18). It doesn't hurt that there is a recognition that adult audiences, especially those on the older end of the 18- to 34-year-old demographic group are driven to video-on-demand platforms that allow them to "reminisce about their childhoods" and are therefore "often drawn to familiar content that resonates" with their remembrance (Umstead, 2016, p. 8). The creation of new content rooted by the old simply reflects another dimension of the overall nostalgia-driven recursion paradigm. According to Sean Coccia, executive vice president of business operations and general manager for Disney Channels Worldwide, "for Disney Channel it is not hard to reach these millennials if we deliver content that provides them with the opportunity to share an experience and time with their families…. Social media has also helped us by giving these millennial families platforms to talk about what they love and what they are seeing in the new storylines and characters" (qtd. in Umstead, 2016, p. 9).

Raven's Home is built on the success of, and remembrance of the 2000s' Disney Channel original program *That's So Raven.* Airing between 2003 and 2007, the four seasons of *That's So Raven* followed the adventures of the eponymous teen psychic, played by Raven-Symoné of previous *The Cosby Show* fame, and her friends. The show is largely considered one of the corporation's strongest franchises, being one of two shows up to that point to be headlined by a person of color (*The Famous Jett Jackson,* starring Lee Thompson Young, ran from 1998 to 2000), breaking the "65-episode rule" and becoming the first Disney series to hit the 100-episode syndication threshold of broadcast television (Alston, 2016). It incorporated the lessons learned by the network during the production of shows such as *Lizzie McGuire* and *Even Stevens,* and the skill and charisma of the eponymous actress left its own imprint on how the Disney Channel approached its later programming, as seen in shows such as *Hannah Montana* (2006–2011) and *Wizards of Waverly Place* (2007–2012). When the spin-off *Raven's Home* was announced in 2016, Raven-Symoné not only came back to the channel as an actress, but as an executive producer—the child star-turned-teen star evolving again in a new role while embracing a return to what audiences would remember. Gary Marsh, president and chief creative officer of Disney Channels World Wide, released a statement acknowledging the move as "bringing Raven home to Disney Channel once again" after "being a part of over 20 different Disney projects" across her career as an actor (Harnick, 2017). For her own part, Raven-Symoné stated her intent of attempting to address both old fans and new viewers with a family-oriented program, saying:

> I missed Disney Channel, and I wanted to return to something that was meaningful. This is a show with characters that you remember from your past. It shows what's going on in society now—we're not rich but we're two families living under one roof trying to make it work. What I love about it is the people that remember us as 15-year-olds now see us as 30-plus-year-olds—we're hoping to show how these characters have evolved [Umstead, 2017].

The idea of "evolution" is key here, as the show picks up with not only the return of Raven Baxter, but with Anneliese van der Pol reprising the role of best friend Chelsea Daniels. The premise of the show is that both women are now divorced single mothers, raising their children together—Raven's 11-year-old twins Booker and Nia, and Chelsea's 9-year-old son Levi—in the same house (Harnick, 2017). To complicate things, Raven still has the premonitions that fueled so much of the narrative of the original show, though her children don't know about her visions. To complicate things further, Booker has inherited his mom's gift without her knowledge (Pedersen, 2017). The tension between knowing and not knowing and knowing too much, as well as the process of filling in the time gap from where *That's So Raven* ended and *Raven's House* picks up, creates a cross-generational dialogue and space where families can connect in various different ways while seeing a different family structure than had been necessarily depicted on the Disney Channel in the past.

Unlike *That's So Raven*, *Boy Meets World* was not originally a Disney Channel property, running from 1993 to 2000 on ABC. Reruns aired in syndication on the Disney Channel from 2000 to 2007. The popularity of the reruns, and the online fan-base, predominantly comprised of people in their 20s and 30s, was part of the drive for Disney to revisit the characters for a different generation in the form of *Girl Meets World*, and were themselves revived ahead of the new sitcom's release (Wienman, 2013). *Boy Meets World* focused on Cory Matthews (Ben Savage), age 11, and how he learns to cope with life with his family, his history teacher, and his best friend Shawn. The show followed Cory from middle school through college across its seven seasons, and the family-centered show ended on a nostalgic note of its own with the original characters, now grown up, back in the sixth-grade classroom they started in, with the teacher who followed them through their lives offering one final piece of advice: "Dream, try, do good" (McCracken & Nelson, 2000). *Girl Meets World* picks up 14 years later from the original character's timeline. Cory and his on-screen love interest, then girlfriend, then wife, Topanga, are still married. They live in New York city with their two children, Auggie and Riley. He's a teacher, following in the footsteps of his neighbor and teacher Mr. Feeny, and she's a lawyer, as she always intended to be. While Cory and Topanga are certainly present in the revived show, the true focus of the narrative is on their daughter Riley, who is herself navigating tweenhood with her best friend Maya—a relationship that echoes that of Cory and Shawn in the earlier program. The parallels between the two programs are myriad and intentional, indicating that the there was considerable deliberation in order to attempt to address a dual audience, retain some of the "traditional family sitcom" feel of the original (Hale, 2014), and "get back to the core emotional connection that families have with each other" (Barnes, 2014) (for more in-depth discussion of *Girl Meets World*, see Bell, Lammon and Murray in this volume). What is seen from this is that, just as in *That's So Raven* and *Raven's Home*, the deliberate bricolage construction of *Girl Meets World* from *Boy Meets World*—something new from something old—is meant to consciously link the shows, marking a point of return as well as a point of departure in a new direction.

Conceiving of the relationship between *Raven's Home* and *That's So Raven*, and *Girl Meets World* and *Boy Meets World*, respectively, as forms of bricolage, brings into play the conceptualizations of these programs not as discrete entities, but intertextual and paratextual constructions that are, perhaps, best understood in relation to the preceding content, as well as within the paratextual contexts of the Disney Channel. In his work on paratexts, Gerard Genette defined intertextuality as "a relationship of copresence between two texts or among several texts … eidetically and typically as the actual presence of one text within another" (Genette 1997, pp. 1–2), and paratexts as those elements that "bind the text" (Genette 1997, p. 3), such as titles, subtitles, intertitles, prefaces, afterwords, epigraphs, etc.—the "secondary signals" (Genette 1997, p. 3) that are perhaps not themselves the "text" but add to the reader's understanding of the definition of the text itself as a work. Genette also suggested that, although it is not necessary to be aware of or understand the paratexts and hypertexts surrounding a given text, "those who know it do not read in the same way as those who do not" (Genette and Maclean, 1991, p. 266). Though Genette's conceptualization of paratexts, intertextuality, and palimpsests focused specifically on constructions within and surrounding novels, it is simple enough to transpose the idea of intertextual and hypertextual relationships as components of meaning-making for the reader/viewer to these television series. In fact, it is the hypertextual relationship that the Disney Channel relies on in these programs to draw their cross-generational audiences. It is also the hypertextual relationship that draws comparisons between what was, and what is remembered, and what is, in the "now" of the programs. These hypertextual relationships provide a unique doorway through which the Disney Channel can evolve its programming, extend the range of narrative it tells and how it represents those narratives, and, most importantly, use nostalgia as a ballast against reactions to changes in expected representations of "normal family life." As the characters continue to grow and learn, so too can viewers who have already invested in them, even as "normal" continues to evolve, as in the depictions of a "normal" family.

"Things are changing, and it's OK"—*A Different Kind of Family in* Raven's Home

The Disney Channel's depictions of family have been, generally speaking, that of a so-called nuclear family; maybe an absent mother, maybe a pet, but overall, families have a cis-gendered, straight couple with multiple children, and if there is deviation from that norm, it is rarely the focus of the show. However, *Raven's Home* marks a deliberate departure from this "traditional" family structure. Though *That's So Raven* was very much built within a traditional, nuclear family structure, *Raven's Home* represents "the family" via Raven and Chelsea as two divorced single mothers building a family together, raising their kids together. This is far from the "having-it-all" myth of empowered womanhood that plays on the conflict "between feminism and femininity" in a particular kind of post-feminist dialogue (Bickford, 2015, p. 68). Whereas *Boy Meets World*'s infamous Cory and Topanga live out the fantasy of schoolyard sweethearts who endure, Raven's relationship with high school boyfriend Devon Carter (Jonathan McDaniel) does not come to the same continuation in *Raven's Home*. While Raven and Devon did go on to get married after the first program ended, when fans come back to the story of Raven's adventures, they find out that the relationship didn't survive and Raven and Devon are divorced (Bricker, 2017). However, the relationship between the divorced parents is featured front and center, with actress Raven-Symoné telling MTV,

> we still have a good relationship, and I think that's one thing that Disney Channel is doing and working very hard to do, is showing that there's different types of divorced parents, and there's different types of relationships you can have with that. I like the relationship that Devon and Raven have right now. He's very involved in the kids' life. He's right there. He's successful in his own way. Things are changing, and it's OK [Grant, 2017].

Despite the prevalence of divorced families across the U.S., media depictions of different versions of what that can look like, specifically for children or tweens, are rare. By using already known characters, who, the last time fans saw them, were trying to make a long-distance relationship work (Grant, 2017) to step into a different narrative space, the Disney Channel uses the recursive elements of its strategy to break new ground for both new tween viewers and older fans who might be returning to the show.

The implication of "happy ever after" is very much grounded in the overarching Disney architext and transtextuality—the "entire set of general or transcendent categories" (Genette, 1997, p. 1) by which, in this case, we identify *Raven's Home* as a part of the larger Disney corporate universe and expect a certain kind of narrative to unfold. To step away from the "traditional" happily ever after where people just stay together, to one where there are different kinds of families that can still be happy, broadens the brand's image on the one hand, and on the other, takes an important step towards engaging with the realities of contemporary family life. Considering again the degree to which tween television viewing needs to be contextualized within a larger family context and can thus bring people together (Nathanson,

2013, p. 304), such depictions normalize representations of divorce or single parenthood, for both tweens and their parents. These depictions can then go on to open space for conversations about families, difference, or even the anxieties and fears that might come from moments where family life is not perfect or "happy." What becomes depicted—again, for both parents who might have been rooting for Raven and Devon (having seen themselves in that relationship in their own youth) and tweens—is that there are many ways for families to come together. In this way, *Raven's Home* reaches back into the traditions of earlier family-focused sitcoms that were written for adults as well as children, much in the way *Boy Meets World* itself was, and offers fare that contains something deeper than simply the comedy that draws new viewers in, modeling different ways families can be together, solve problems, and enjoy life.

Parents Meet Tweens—The Merging of Two "Worlds"

In some ways, *Girl Meets World* plays much more with the idea that it is a remake, and is for, perhaps, the adults reminiscing about it more than the tween audience. During its three-season run, it arguably never found the right balance between its dual audiences, the older fanbase whose dedication made the idea of a revival of the show possible, and the Disney Channel's primary target demographic of tweens. Ben Savage, who played Cory Matthews, addressed this "generational tug of war" at a *Boy Meets World* New York Comic Con 25-year reunion panel, saying, "We wanted to apply a lot of life lessons that we wrote about and talked about and give it to a new generation. They're getting a lot of the same lessons and stories that you guys got growing up with *Boy Meets World*" (Bloom, 2018). In essence, this idea of trying to address both, but openly trying to feed something from the past forward for a new generation, is threaded throughout the show. Cory and Topanga, as characters, are in many ways unchanged, and the program is in many ways driven by nostalgic recursion and wish-fulfillment. Both shows were produced by the same producers, Michael Jacobs and April Kelly. Many cast members from *Boy Meets World* have somehow remained interwoven in Cory and Topanga's lives, and those of their children. Notably, Cory's older brother appears several times, best friend Shawn returns and becomes an integral part of the new narrative, and even Harley the bully, Mr. Turner, Mr. Feeny, and Minkus remain a part of the Matthews' lives, helping Cory and Topanga to pass on life lessons to their children as they navigate their own growth. Cory's parents appear, as does his younger brother, Josh, and even both actresses who played Morgan Matthews in *Boy Meets World* appeared in the *Girl Meets World* series finale. There are flashbacks that utilize original footage, and even an appearance by young Topanga. Metatextual commentary fuels much of the humor, and the narrative is even mostly built on intertextual parallels. In *Boy Meets World,* Shawn's family is broken, and he looks to the Matthews family and several of his teachers for stability. In *Girl Meets World,* Maya's mother is similarly from an unstable background, and, over the course of the narrative, Shawn becomes a father-figure for her, along with Cory as both the best-friend's father and the history teacher. For all the similarities, however, there are still significant changes. The program has the same aesthetic feel of other Disney Channel sitcoms, and, despite so many appearances from the past, the narrative does center around Riley, Maya, and their friends, rather than the older cast. Therefore, the challenges faced by these tweens are markedly different from those faced by Cory, Shawn, and their friends, and reflect the challenges faced by contemporary tweens.

By embedding so much of the '90s program in the contemporary reboot, and embracing recursion and intertextuality, the process of meaning-making is almost arguably aimed more at the older audience that may be engaged in or approaching parenthood themselves. As Cory and Topanga navigate parenting and guiding tweens through adolescence in the digital age, parents learn new schemas (Prinsloo, 2013, p. 248) for how to address new challenges such as cell phone use, cyber bullying, and the push for more freedom and maturity, while also facing down more standard family-show fare like curfews and dating. There is also an openness in dialogue between the tweens and the adults; where in other sitcoms—including *Raven's Home*—emphasize tweens trying to solve problems alone, *Girl Meets World* embeds and normalizes a greater degree of intergenerational communication. Like *Boy Meets World* before it, *Girl Meets World* emphasizes and normalizes the idea that there are trusted, compassionate, and empathetic adults who can help solve problems and are there to keep tweens protected and safe. This is another schema being presented to tween viewers, as well as reminding parents that they can be this adult for current tweens. In essence, the intertextual, embedded intergenerational dialogues on-screen re-present new schemas for intergenerational dialogues between tweens and their families, and therefore are reflecting simultaneously old and new methods of reflecting society.

Conclusion: Intergenerational Reflections

Raven's Home and *Girl Meets World* are not the only cases of nostalgic recursion fueling new programming in the Disney Channel's line-up for teens, or even across the larger structure of Disney's mediascape. Likewise, these examples of recursion and the larger patterns of multigenerational address that might be probed across the Disney Channel's programming are not the only cross-generational facets of Disney media at large. Since the *Mickey Mouse Club*, Disney has taken a unique approach to adolescent-specific programming and representing American youth and families. Though who has been identified as able to embody that ideology since the 1950s has changed, the impetus to attempt to both define and speak to family dynamics while growing the Disney viewer-base has persisted.

In an effort to maintain their fanbase and extend the viewer base, the Disney Channel's stars jump from television programs to Disney Channel Original Movies, to other shows, and then even move to other networks incorporated under the Disney corporate umbrella. They grow with their initial audiences (because tweens, whether viewers or actors, inevitably do grow up) while introducing newer characters and stars to the next generation of viewers along the way, until, eventually, their audience outgrows the channel—except to return to it in moments of nostalgia, or with their own children in the future. Essentially, the Disney Channel maintains and transitions its viewership through its various properties by layering its stars through different programs as they age. Because of this layering, the eras of the Disney Channel become interlinked, and the intertextual and intergenerational dialogues can be read as capable of reflecting changes in society. The relationships between *That's So Raven* and *Raven's Home*, and *Boy Meets World* and *Girl Meets World*, are cogent examples of this capability, and can also be used as indications of how demographic audiences might be shifting in the eyes of the corporation. Additionally, these recursive presentations of new and changing narratives, using well-known and beloved characters, can in some ways push back at earlier preconceptions of what normal representations of families should look like, or what the power dynamics within families might look like in the face of a changing society.

Awareness of the interwoven intertextual narratives, the changes in schema, and recognition of the relationships across different Disney Channel eras becomes an intertext and paratext in and of itself, which then informs how cross-generational dialogues of the changes in this particular space might be facilitated. Beginning to look at the relationships among these four shows provides but a brief example of what might be gleaned from examining the layered, recursive, nostalgic structures that gird the programming on the Disney Channel. Further research might address these issues in terms of specific franchises, the franchises that are built on specific actors and actresses, and how these show operate in international or digital media contexts.

REFERENCES

Alston, J. (2016). *That's So Raven* changed Disney Channel in ways no one could have predicted. Retrieved from https://tv.avclub.com/that-s-so-raven-changed-disney-channel-in-ways-no-one-c-1798247263.

Barnes, B. (2014, June 25). Disney hopes new (and nostalgic) formula will draw tweens. Retrieved from https://www.nytimes.com/2014/06/26/business/media/disney-shunning-youtube-template.html.

Bickford, T. (2015). Tween intimacy and the problem of public life in children's media: "Having It All" on the Disney Channel's "Hannah Montana." *Women's Studies Quarterly, 43*(1/2), 66–82. Retrieved from http://www.jstor.org/stable/43958468.

Bloom, M. (2018, October 5). "Boy Meets World" Stars reminisce on a quarter-century legacy. Retrieved from https://www.hollywoodreporter.com/live-feed/boy-meets-world-new-york-comic-con-panel-1149849.

Bricker, T. (2017, June 2). *Raven's Home* first look is here: Watch Raven and BFF Chelsea reunite on Disney Channel. Retrieved from https://www.eonline.com/uk/news/858803/raven-s-home-first-look-is-here-watch-raven-and-bff-chelsea-reunite-on-disney-channel.

Cory's cooking. (2007, May). *Scholastic News, 75*, 13–13, T2. Retrieved from https://search-proquest-com.ezp.lib.cam.ac.uk/docview/212793776?accountid=9851.

Drotner, K. (2013). The co-construction of media and childhood. In Dafna Lemish (Ed.), *The Routledge international handbook of children, adolescents and media* (pp. 15–22). London: Routledge.

Genette, G. (1997). *Palimpsests*. Lincoln: University of Nebraska Press.

Genette, G., & Maclean, M. (1991). Introduction to the paratext. *New Literary History, 22*(2): 261–272.

Grant, S. (2017, July 19). Raven-Symoné explains how Raven and Devon's relationship has changed since *That's So Raven*. Retrieved from http://www.mtv.com/news/3024467/raven-symone-interview-devon-ravens-home/.

Hale, M. (2014). Nostalgia on the air. Retrieved from https://www.nytimes.com/2014/06/25/arts/television/girl-meets-world-and-mystery-girls-sitcoms-from-disney.html.

Harnick, C. (2017). Meet the cast of *Raven's Home*, Disney Channel's *That's So Raven* spin off. Retrieved from https://www.eonline.com/uk/news/841227/meet-the-cast-of-raven-s-home-disney-channel-s-that-s-so-raven-spinoff.

Marr, M. (2007, Nov 19). Disney reaches to the crib to extend princess magic. *Wall Street Journal* Retrieved from https://search.proquest.com/docview/399024934?accountid=9851.

McCracken, J., & Nelson, M. (2000, May 5). Episode 158 [Brave New World (part 2)]. In M. Jacobs (Executive Producer), *Boy Meets World*. USA: ABC Television.

Nathanson, A.I. (2013). Media and the family context. In Dafna Lemish (Ed.), *The Routledge international handbook of children, adolescents and media* (pp. 299–306). London: Routledge.

Pedersen, E. (2017). "Raven's Home' renewed for second season on Disney Channel. Retrieved from https://deadline.com/2017/10/ravens-home-renewed-season-2-raven-symone-disney-channel-1202185190/.

Potter, A. (2011). It's a small world after all: New media constellations and Disney's rising star—The global success of *High School Musical*. *International Journal of Cultural Studies, 15*(2), 117–130. DOI: 10.1177/1367877911416889.

Prinsloo, J. (2013). Media and learning about the social world. In Dafna Lemish (Ed.), *The Routledge international handbook of children, adolescents and media* (pp. 247–254). London: Routledge.

Schickel, R. (1986). *The Disney version: The Life, times, art and commerce of Walt Disney* (Revised and Updated). London: Pavilion Books.

Steemers, J. (2013). Children's television culture. In Dafna Lemish (Ed.), *The Routledge international handbook of children, adolescents and media* (pp. 103–110). London: Routledge.

Stewart, J.B. (2006). *DisneyWar*. London: Simon & Schuster.

Tally, P. (2005). Re-imagining girlhood: Hollywood and the tween girl film market. In Claudia Mitchell and Jacqueline Reid-Walsh (Eds.), *Seven going on seventeen: Tween studies in the culture of girlhood* (pp. 311–329). Oxford: Peter Lang.

Umstead, R.T. (2015). Disney, Nick going old school. *Multichannel News, 35*(40), pp. 18. Retrieved from https://ezp.lib.cam.ac.uk/login?url=http://search.ebscohost.com/login.aspx?direct=true&db=bsu&AN=110830286&site=ehost-live&scope=site.

Umstead, R.T. (2016). What's old is new again. (cover story). *Multichannel News, 37*(15), pp. 8–9. Retrieved from https://ezp.lib.cam.ac.uk/login?url=http://search.ebscohost.com/login.aspx?direct=true&db=bsu&AN=114587614&site=ehost-live&scope=site.

Umstead, R.T. (2017). Raven-Symoné goes home again to Disney. *Broadcasting & Cable, 147*(18), pp. 6. Retrieved from https://search.proquest.com.ezp.lib.cam.ac.uk/docview/1933858329?accountid=9851.

Watts, S. (1997). *The magic kingdom: Walt Disney and the American Way of Life*. Columbia: University of Missouri Press.

Weinman, J.J. (2013, Jan 02). Boy meets world, grows up and has a baby. *Maclean's, 126*, 71. Retrieved from https://search.proquest.com/docview/1266058980?accountid=9851.

Wells, P. (2002). *Animation and America*. New Brunswick, NJ: Rutgers University Press.

Children of Queer Bodies

Disney Channel Original Movies as Social Justice Narratives in Descendants 2

Sara Austin

Disney's most recent princess animated feature films *Brave* (2012), *Frozen* (2013), and *Moana* (2017) subvert the fairytale narrative, shifting the movies' focus from romance and marriage to the personal development of a female character and her relationship to her society. Merida, Elsa, and Moana are leaders who challenge the status quo with positive results.[1] While this change in Disney's approach to princess characters might seem sudden, Disney has been testing this model of girl-led social justice narratives in its Disney Channel Original Movies (DCOM) for two decades.[2] The relationship between Disney's feature films and DCOMs is recursive. DCOMs rely on studio success, and thus the feature films, for publicity and funding, while DCOMs allow Disney to conduct smaller test runs for how the studio approaches large social issues. Thus, DCOMs influence the tone of feature films, while feature films build the universe that DCOMs inhabit.

Since the made-for-television format allows DCOMs to be shorter, with smaller budgets and less opportunity for merchandising, these films can have a narrower appeal than feature films. This narrowing of focus and disregard for the toy market allows DCOMs to appeal to tween audiences, rather than the prepubescent focus of feature films. Unlike feature films, which require parents to take children to the movie theater, DCOMs can be accessed on television or online without parental interference. Thus, in contrast to the adventure-driven plots of feature films, DCOMs as a genre tend toward narratives of belonging, illustrating alternative ways of being and normalizing non-normative or changing bodies and queer subjectivities.

In this essay, I explore the relationship between Disney's feature films and DCOMs using *The Little Mermaid* as a case study. Unlike other fairytales, *The Little Mermaid* has a clear source text, making it possible to trace Disney's adaptation choices for both the feature films and the DCOMs, highlighting moments where the feature film, rather than the original source material, influence the DCOM adaptation *Descendants 2* (2017). Though *Descendants 2* operates in the tween universe of DCOMs, the film's relationship to its 1989 feature film predecessor and older marriage-plot-focused fairytales dooms the social justice narrative from the beginning. In this way, *Descendants 2* acts as an exemplar for DCOMs' role in the larger Disney empire. Despite their differences from feature films in terms of audience expectations and format, DCOMs are doomed to surface level solutions to the social issues they raise; solving racism, sexism, or poverty with a song and dance number in which everyone promises to get along. This limitation of DCOMs raises larger questions about Disney's cultural legacy and the company's ability to address social issues through capitalism. Using Jack Halberstam's queer failure as a metric for narrative engagement with social justice, this essay begins by reading Hans Christian Anderson's short story as a queer tween text. Next, I discuss the 1989 film's engagement with queer bodies as the movie shifts queer identity from the mermaid to the antagonist, Ursula. Finally, I focus on Uma, Ursula's daughter in *Descendants 2*, as the film's attempt to navigate the anti-queer characterization of Ursula within the social justice narrative framework of DCOMs. Uma's character arc and, I argue, inevitable failure, demonstrates the limitations of DCOMs, and Disney more broadly, to mean-ingfully engage with issues of sexuality, race, gender, and class.

Queer Failure and Queer Mermaids

In *The Queer Art of Failure,* Jack Halberstam focuses on children's films that illustrate resistance to the heterosexual binary, featuring characters who fail to grow up into the heterosexual economy. Halberstam points out that childhood is always queer, because children are not yet a part of the hetero-sexual economy and must learn to police their bodies and desires within socially acceptable bounds (Halberstam, 2011, p. 27). Halberstam touts queer failure as a desirable means of promoting community over individual success; "Under certain circumstances, failing, losing, forgetting, unmaking, undoing, unbecoming, not knowing may in fact offer more creative, more cooperative, more surprising ways of being in the world" (Halberstam, 2011, p. 2). Hal-berstam points to children's films such as *Chicken Run* for examples of this queer failure, since the main characters never grow into a self-sufficient het-erosexual adulthood, but instead rely on building community to accomplish their goals (Halberstam, 2011). DCOMs also function as narratives of queer failure, requiring tween and teen characters to separate from their parents by failing to meet parental expectations, examine the origin of social desires, and remake the status quo to fit new more inclusive models of subjectivity.[3]

Queer theory invests in breaking down binary logic and resisting normative social models, and so the critical model itself is often shifting. In the introduction to *Global Justice and Desire: Queering Economy*, Nikita Dhawan, Antke Engel, Christoph H.E. Holzhey, and Volker Woltersdorff link queer sexual desire to the political desire to be seen. They note that since desire is constantly "oscillating between lack and productivity" it may "inspire unexpected connections and transformations" (Dhawan, 2015, p. 7). Janet Jakobsen defines "queer" as an active resistance to normative social structures, suggesting that desire can be destructive as well as connective or transformative (Jakobsen, 1998, pp. 512–513). What each of these scholars notes, is that since queer desire operates outside of normative political and social structures, fulfilling, or indeed even speaking this desire, has power because it imagines a world other than the current one, in which these desires might be fulfilled. Thus, the failure to participate in the gendered discipline of bodies and desires, the failure to actively engage in a heterosexual marriage economy, and the failure to accept the political status quo are all aspects of queer failure.

Hans Christian Anderson's *Little Mermaid* (1836), is a proto-narrative of queer failure, written to express Andersen's sorrow that his friend Edward Collin did not view him as a possible romantic partner. Since Andersen kept most of his correspondence, scholars can read the passionate letters he sent to Collin describing his "womanly feelings," including lines such as "I long for you as though you were a beautiful Calabrian girl" ("Letters to and from Hans Christian Andersen, 1844–1898"). In *The Little Mermaid*, which parallels Collin and Andersen's friendship, a young mermaid (Andersen) falls in love with a prince (Collin) and wants to marry him so that she may gain an immortal soul. After the mermaid meets the prince, he admires her beauty and "loved her as he would love a little child, but it never came into his head to make her his wife" (Andersen 2018). The prince marries another woman, and the mermaid is taken up to live with the daughters of the air. Andersen's mermaid is passed over as a romantic partner not through rejection so much as invisibility. The story is clear that the prince never even considers the mermaid as a romantic option, drawing a clear parallel to Anderson's relationship with the heterosexual Collin, and the invisibility and requisite failure of both Andersen's and the mermaid's desire.

Anderson's story engages with Halberstam's queer failure as the title character is unable to achieve success as either a mermaid or a human, and so ends the story as part of a community built around empathy and service.

First, she cannot desire what her family wants, but rather follows a queer desire to be human, sacrificing her familial position to pursue a sexual and emotional relationship that her family might deem unnatural. As a mermaid, the text describes the title character as "a strange child, quiet and thoughtful" who wants to hear stories about the land, even arranging her garden to look like the sun rather than the oceanic creatures favored by her sisters (Andersen, 2018). Though the mermaid's grandmother says that mermaids "feel ourselves to be much happier and much better off than human beings" the little mermaid chooses to leave behind her family and status to become a human woman, sacrificing her voice in the process (Andersen, 2018).[4]

Second, the mermaid fails in her pursuit of the prince and does not gain heterosexual legitimacy through the marriage market. Though the prince praises the mermaid's beauty, and comments that he would "prefer" to marry her over any other woman, in the end he chooses to marry the princess his family has chosen for him. The prince believes this other woman saved his life when he was shipwrecked. Yet, the prince's love for his princess only removes the emotional impediment to a diplomatic wedding that the two kingdoms had already negotiated. Heterosexual marriage may function in the text as an expression of love, but it is also always an economic transaction first. The marriage is set as a way to secure power and trade. The mermaid is outside of the heterosexual economy not because the prince does not love her, but because there is nothing to be gained by loving her. The comments that he would prefer to marry the mermaid is made with an air of wistful imagining; the prince knows this marriage can never happen, and so it is in his best interest to desire the princess. The mermaid is marked as queer by the text not only because her body is inhuman, but because her love is impossible. She can never exist in the heterosexual economy to which she aspires.

Finally, the mermaid refuses violence as a means of saving herself, and relies on community instead. As the mermaid is about to die, her sisters approach her

with a knife: here it is, see it is very sharp. Before the sun rises you must plunge it into the heart of the prince; when the warm blood falls upon your feet they will grow together again, and form into a fish's tail, and you will be once more a mermaid, and return to us to live out your three hundred years before you die and change into the salt sea foam. Haste, then; he or you must die before sunrise. Our old grandmother moans so for you, that her white hair is falling off from sorrow, as ours fell under the witch's scissors. Kill the prince and come back [Andersen, 2018].

Again, the mermaid fails in the task her family requests; "the knife trembled in the hand of the little mermaid: then she flung it far away from her into the waves.... She cast one more lingering, half-fainting glance at the prince, and then threw herself from the ship into the sea" (Andersen, 2018). At this moment the mermaid is taken up by the daughters of the air, to become a wind spirit who can earn her way into heaven after 300 years of service to mankind by providing healthful breeze. Instead of seeing the princess as a threat to her personal gain, specifically the acquisition of a soul, the mermaid accepts her place outside of the heterosexual economy. When she refuses violence as a solution to regain her former socioeconomic place, the mermaid embodies Halberstam's appraisal of queer failure as a means of challenging the status quo. The mermaid becomes part of the spirit community, bettering both the world and her own lot by laying claim to her queer failure and refusing to participate in the established norms of her family or society.

Though Anderson's text is marketed and read as a children's story, it is perhaps more accurately categorized as tween fiction. If the main character's age is an indicator of audience, the mermaid character is fifteen years old, suggesting an appeal to teen readers. The text is also primarily concerned with questions of identity and belonging, a common trope for tween and teen literature. Though many children's stories, especially fairytales, hinge on teenage girls entering the marriage market, there are a number of contemporary fairytale adaptations for teen readers that, like Anderson's mermaid, focus on the character's inner turmoil rather than the simplistic reward the good and punish the bad storylines of tales for younger audiences. Halberstam's notion of queer failure as well as the plots of many DCOMs align with Anderson's mermaid, suggesting that the moral choice is to reject social and economic pressure in favor of community building. Yet, unlike Halberstam, Anderson's mermaid does not unmake the power structures in which she lives. Her act of defiance does not pave the way for future mermaids, nor does it encourage children to rethink heteronormative structures such as the marriage market. Anderson's story is personal. His description of the mermaid's loss and resignation may illustrate an individual embracing of queer failure, but does not go so far as to suggest the social change Halberstam thinks possible. It is only through adaptation that Anderson's work gains a clear element of social critique.

Queer Coding Ursula

Since the relationship between Andersen's mermaid and his love for Collin is well documented, it seems almost blasphemous for Disney to press his work into a heteronormative princess tale, shifting the queer identification from the heroine to the villain. In the 1989 Disney feature film, the mermaid and the prince marry and she becomes human permanently. Besides erasing all discussion of souls from the narrative, Disney makes one other major change, merging the sea witch and the rival princess into the same character, drawing the mermaid into the heterosexual economy in a way that Andersen's tale does not. It is not the mermaid's desire for the prince, but direct competition with another woman that polices her sexual behavior, both because this competition reinforces performative femininity and because it legitimizes the mermaid as a possible sexual choice for the prince.[5] In the original tale, there is no evidence that the princess from the neighboring country had any knowledge of the mermaid's love for her prince. There was no rivalry, no epic battle, no adventure. And so, Disney alters the story from a tragedy of unrequited love into a marriage plot with a villain and a hero, shifting the stage of sexual competition to more traditional fairytale ground, between a younger woman and an older bad mother-figure and erasing the mermaid's queer identification as an outsider to the heterosexual economy.

Disney feature films such as *The Little Mermaid*, *Cinderella*, and *Sleeping Beauty* do the work of teaching and policing heterosexual norms. These films regulate gendered behaviors and desires by marking bodies, especially female bodies, which exist outside of the sexual marketplace as villainous and queer.[6] Disney queer codes its villains, using stereotypical visuals and behaviors that mark them as oppositional to a heterosexual romance plot. The ugly stepsisters in *Cinderella* are portrayed as manly, especially compared to the dancer-like form and movement animators ascribe to Cinderella. The evil fairy Maleficent mocks the prince's love for Sleeping Beauty. In *The Little Mermaid*, Ursula lives in exile, in sharp contrast to the mermaid's large nuclear family. These films act as a warning, detailing the social and personal consequences to women who do not successfully participate in the heterosexual marketplace and who, consequently, are marked by the text as queer. These villainous women, the primary queer figures of the film, must be ridiculed or killed for the movie to reach its conclusion. After Cinderella's stepsisters are rejected by the prince, the audience never sees them again. Maleficent is stabbed through the heart, and Ursula through the abdomen in their respective prince's quest to save his princess.

Though scholars discuss the transformative power of queer failure, Disney undercuts this possibility of community building when queer coding villains. Dallas Baker notes that fairytale monsters are often queer bodies which transgress social and gender boundaries, and thus, must be destroyed to achieve a heteronormative happily ever after (Baker, 2010). Since many of Disney's fairytale films include a marriage plot, the stories' villains are used in this way; marked as queer and then destroyed to achieve a heterosexual romance. Queer coding villains serves two purposes. First, queer coding marks these characters as outside the heterosexual economy of dynastic marriage.[7] Second, these films suggest that all familial connections are merely a ruse for the villain to accumulate power and that queer coded characters are, in fact, incapable of love. Disney villains are estranged from family members.

If they participate in a heterosexual romance plot, it is for personal gain rather than companionship. These villains readily sacrifice both family and romantic partners in the pursuit of power. By queer coding its villains, Disney suggests that all queer bodies are incapable of empathy or love. In contrast, Anderson's original story grants its title character the transformative aspects of queer failure, allowing the young mermaid to reject violence in favor of community belonging.

Disney queer codes Ursula in order to mark her as a threating body. While Andersen's mermaid is queer because she exists outside of the heterosexual economy, Ursula is queer because she plays at femininity using the visual lexicon of drag and because she is she is a sexual threat, impersonating a human woman to fool the prince and emasculating mermen by literally withering them away into husks of themselves. Ursula is the only octopus in a world of fish-people, immediately marking her as a queer body. Additionally, her makeup is based on the drag queen Divine, marking her as queer to knowing audiences. Scholars Kerry Malla and Roderick McGillis highlight the camp and drag elements of Ursula, specifically how her song "Poor Unfortunate Souls" teaches Ariel to perform femininity. In the song, Ursula puts on makeup and talks about how human men prefer girls who do not speak. This performance is over the top, however, meant to be a parody of womanhood rather than genuine advice (Malla, 2005). Laura Sells (1995) connects Ursula to camp and suggests that as the crone figure she represents the universal feminine, a monstrous mother figure that the mermaid must separate from in order to accept the patriarchal traditions of marriage. Ursula not only serves as a queer camp figure, a sexual rival, and a villain, at the end of the film, she grows to enormous size, becoming a literal monster, as Baker suggests. Disney introduces sexual competition between the mermaid and the witch both to emphasize the potential danger of the queer coded Ursula to heterosexual women, and also to situate the mermaid firmly within the heterosexual marketplace, a departure from Anderson's text. This shift to Ursula as a sexual rival moves the role of the queer in the story from a metaphor for Andersen's love in the 1830s, to the 1980s AIDS hysteria and cultural notions of queer bodies as monstrous and threatening.[8]

Uma as Queer Descendant

In 2019, queer desire has shifted away from the explicitly sexual to encompass political and social desires for recognition, access, and equal protection under the law; a desire for the redress of oppression by changing the system. Into this social context, Disney Channel's *Descendants* (2015) brings the villain kids, a group of economically and socially oppressed children who desire to change the system. Released concordantly with Melissa de la Cruz's *Isle of the Lost* series (2015), the first *Descendants* film follows the children of Disney villains Maleficent, the Wicked Queen, Jafar, and Cruella De Ville as they move from their home on the impoverished island of villains to attend boarding school with the children of heroes and princesses in the kingdom of Auradon. As the villain kids plot to steal Fairy Godmother's wand and free their parents, they also make friends. Despite the film's focus on the villain kids and its potential to break with the marriage plots of princess movies, the main protagonist Mal, falls in love with King Benjamin (son of Belle and The Beast) and sides with him and the other Auradon students over her mother. Mal uses the wand to turn her mother into a lizard, reinforcing the heterosexual marriage plot and mashing together tropes from older Disney films by forcing the heroine to leave her family, having her fight a monstrous and power-hungry older woman, and framing the marriage plot as the teen heroine's empowering choice.

Descendants suggests that the villain kids, led by Maleficent's daughter Mal, can change upper-class perceptions of villains, leading to a more egalitarian society. Yet, the movie ends with Maleficent and the other villain parents proving that they are truly evil, and the villain kids siding with the wealthy Auradon prep students, disowning their parents and assimilating into Auradon's upper class. Mal and her friends abandon any queer desire for social change, settling for personal over political gain. *Descendants 2* (2017) revisits this premise, introducing Ursula's daughter Uma as the villain kid who refuses to assimilate. The main plot of *Descendants 2* revolves around Mal becoming comfortable with herself as both a villain kid and a future queen. When Mal and Ben fight because Mal feels overwhelmed, she goes back to the Isle of the Lost. Ben and the other villain kids follow her, but Uma captures Ben. Mal and her friends fight Uma's pirate crew, rescue Ben, and return to Auradon. All of the Auradon students go to their cotillion dance, but Ben brings Uma and says he will bring down the barrier around the Isle of the Lost as a gift to her. Mal realizes Ben is under a spell, and she and Uma fight. Uma swims away and Mal and Ben kiss.

In Uma, Disney creates a villain caught between the DCOM narrative of queer failure community building and the queer coding of older Disney feature films. In the end, princess tradition wins out and *Descendants 2* props up the status quo by allowing those in power to parrot socially liberal policy, without recognizing the systemic oppression that benefits them. Uma becomes the stock villain, opposed to Mal's princess figure, and is closely aligned with the queer coded Ursula through plot, costuming, and musical cues. While the first *Descendants* film allows villain children to assimilate into the upper classes, *Descendants 2* creates a queer coded, Black, impoverished villain who must play the role of the sexual rival and monster, only to lose in the third act so that the prince and princess can be together. In this way, Uma perfectly illustrates the limitations of DCOM's engagement with social justice issues and queer subjectivities in the larger context of the Disney universe.

The *Descendants* series combines tween movies' use of queer failure as a point of resistance to heteronormativity, and fairytales, which are more invested in policing and reinforcing cultural norms. The merging of these two genres means that *Descendants* may promise cultural change, but will ultimately fall short, re-inscribing the status quo. As a tween movie, *Descendants* focuses on the villain kids because they are outsiders, underdogs. Tween movies give young people power by letting them stand up to adults, often using individual conflicts of the movie as metaphors for larger social issues. *Descendants* empowers its characters in two ways, by making the ruler of Auradon a sixteen-year-old, and by using the fairytale trope of the bad mother as the primary antagonist. When Mal chooses to reject her mother's plan, she not only fulfills a fairytale princess role, overcoming the villain to marry a prince, she also acts as the hero in a tween movie should, separating herself from her parent's bad decisions in order to empower herself and the other young people in the movie. In choosing Ben over her mother, Mal justifies Ben's trust. The two genres of fairytale and tween movie synchronize perfectly as Mal and Ben are able to overcome the prejudices of the adults around them, gain autonomy, and fall in love, fulfilling the fairytale marriage plot.

For all of its revolutionary potential, *Descendants*, like other DCOMs is bound by the limits of Disney's existing cultural narratives and framework. Similar to the live action adaptation of *Beauty and the Beast* (2017), *Descendants* makes use of fairytale narratives as well as viewer nostalgia to sell its basic premise, transforming animated films into a live action series. To this end, the movies invest heavily in visual clues to help the audience easily connect the new characters with their famous parents and mark the villain kids as outsiders. The villain kids wear darker colors in leather and denim with lots of frayed edges and studded embellishments. Besides the darker colors and heavy fabric suggesting that the villain kids are tougher than the linen- and silk-clad Auradon Prep students, the children's clothes are also coordinated to their parents' signature outfits. Mal wears black and purple, mimicking Maleficent's robe and dragon scales. Evie wears blue and red and an abundance of red heart jewelry, recalling the colors of the Wicked Queen's robes and her request for the Huntsman to bring her Snow White's heart in a box. Carlos's clothes are black and white, like his mother Cruella's hair and the Dalmatians that she tries to turn into a coat. Uma wears a teal leather shredded minidress with fishnet underskirt and seashell embellishments. Fairy Godmother's daughter Jane wears blue flowy dresses with oversized pink bows, and Mulan's daughter Lonnie favors Chinese-inspired mini dresses.

The costuming choices not only tie the children to their parents, they also show the characters' evolution as the fabrics get lighter in both texture and color the longer the villains are at Auradon Prep, signaling their assimilation and loss of queer identity. In the cotillion scene at the end of *Descendants 2*, Mal wears a blue and yellow dress, signaling her identity as King Ben's lady rather than her mother's daughter. While Mal's costuming suggests she has completely lost her connection to the Isle, Uma's dress ties her more firmly to Ursula that even her Isle costuming. Uma's dress is a teal and gold mermaid ball gown with fishnet ruffles and embroidered seashells. The colors and silhouette make Uma look like a sea creature, a connection that the film plays on when Uma becomes an octopus creature with tentacles the same color as her gown. It is not until after Mal and Uma fight and Mal changes into a dragon, embracing both aspects of her personality, that her dress also changes to a purple and black ballgown. In this way *Descendants* and *Descendants 2* visually depicts the characters' struggles with identity.

Disney's heavy reliance on visual cues becomes an issue, however, when Mal's sexual competition for the prince is the only Black primary character in the film. The films include background characters with different representations of race, body size, and disability. However, the only Black Auradon Prep student who has a speaking role is Princess Audrey, Aurora's daughter and Prince Ben's girlfriend. In the first movie, Audrey is instantly unlikable as Mal's sexual competition, pulling Mal into the heterosexual marketplace. Not only is she rude to Mal and the other villain kids, Ben's parents suggest they think she was only dating him because she wanted to be queen. Audrey's role as sexual competition riffs on the traditional marriage plot by having the audience root against the princess, but maintains the fairytale staple of the kind-hearted heroine winning over the selfish rival. *Descendants 2* (2017) turns a one-off casting decision into a trend by bringing in China Anne McClain as Ursula's daughter Uma. Since Audrey does not appear in *Descendants 2*, Uma is the only Black primary character as well as Mal's main rival on the Isle.

In many ways Uma is a reprise of Audrey's character from the first movie, but one major difference between the two girls is that while Audrey is from Auradon, Uma represents the life that Mal left behind on the Isle. Mal's fight with Audrey involves proving that she can assimilate to Auradon, while her confrontation with Uma is about proving that she still belongs on the Isle and has not forgotten where she came from. Yet, in both instances, Mal is the White hero princess figure and audience avatar, opposed by a Black sexual rival who the movies suggest is jealous and petty. Both Audrey and Uma are played as bullies who feel threatened by Mal's presence and are mean to her to cover their own inadequacies. Most notably, both girls compete with Mal for King Ben's affections, yet Audrey and Uma only want access to power and do not really care about Ben in the same way that Mal does. Over the course of two films, the *Descendants* franchise creates two interracial relationships in which the Black woman is portrayed as power-hungry, an obstacle to be cast aside in favor of a White heroine. Since the films invest so heavily in visual cues for both world building and character motivation, this trend of Black female villains is disconcerting.

Villains, Poverty and the Deserving Poor

While Uma's connection to Ursula functions as a potential source of power and queer failure, Disney is unwilling to follow through on the critique of structural inequality that Uma represents. Both of the *Descendants* movies use villainy as a metaphor for poverty, and Uma stands in for all of the children left on the poverty-ridden Isle after Mal and the other villain kids move to Auradon. Uma's goal in the film is to challenge the system that keeps these children in poverty. Uma's introductory song "What's My Name" explains her character motivation while calling out the power structures in Auradon and the Isle. Uma entreats her fellow villain kids using nautical puns to come to her aid so that the Auradon kids cannot disrespect them any longer (*Descendants 2*). Much of the song calls for empowering villains, and Uma in particular (*Descendants 2*). The song also mocks Auradon royalty while threatening revolution (*Descendants 2*). Uma seeks to empower the remaining villain kids to remake a social structure that has marginalized them, getting rid of a royalty-based class system.

Despite these nods to an unequal class system, the movie spins Uma as jealous of Mal and suggests it is her pride that prevents Uma from accepting Ben's offer to move to Auradon, rather than a desire for real change. Uma tells Ben that when he invited Mal to the island "that's as mad as I've ever been in my life" (Ortega 2017). When Ben offers to bring Uma to Auradon, she rejects him "Me, part of your solution? Nah, I don't need you. I'm gonna get there on my own" (Ortega 2017). Ben tells Uma he just got busy being king and forgot to bring over more kids, but Uma does not want to be used by Ben to make him feel better about only allowing certain children into Auradon. He calls Uma, "an angry girl with a bad plan," and "not so different from you when you came to Auradon, Mal" (Ortega 2017). In comparing Uma to Mal, Ben tries to illustrate Uma's potential, but he also highlights the limitations of individual change. Mal was very similar to Uma, but bringing her to Auradon did not spark revolution, and so Uma has no reason to believe that her coming to Auradon would be any different. *Descendants 2* takes the premise of the first film to its natural conclusion, showing the living conditions of children still on the Isle and exploring how they might feel about Auradon. However, by drawing a parallel between poverty and villainy, Disney begins a structural critique that the film is not willing to follow through, requiring Uma to be cast aside as a queer coded stock villain.

By choosing to make villainy a metaphor, Disney illustrates the differences between charity and justice, making Uma a more empathetic character than perhaps the film intended. *Descendants 2* emphasizes that King Ben and the ruling class are the sole arbiters of which poor people are worth saving. Ben chooses the initial four villain kids because they are "the worst" and so if his experiment works with them, it can be considered a success. In the sequel, Ben invites Uma to Auradon because she is a leader, and Dizzy Tremaine is invited because Evie asks for her. The movie does not show any other children leaving the Isle. The end of *Descendants 2* suggests that Ben might choose more children to move to Auradon, but he alone chooses who is worthy and who is not. If Uma's crew is any indication, as long as Ben's approach is to invite a handful of children at a time, there will always be someone left behind. *Descendants 2*'s resolution of helping individual children instead of changing the system perpetuates a status quo that harms the children of the Isle, and so Uma's desire for structural change is not surprising. Uma's relationship with her crew suggests the possibility of Halberstam's queer failure, a remaking of the abusive system of Auradon's class structure through revolution and community. When Uma becomes an octopus monster at the end of *Descendants 2*, the hope for structural change is abandoned in favor of a system that requires poor children to prove their worth to the ruling class.

The *Descendants* films explore the relationship between the Auradon Prep students and the villain kids, specifically how children of privilege appropriate and commodify children from a different socio-economic background. Evie is a fashion designer whose history as a kid from the Isle marks her as rebellious and cool. Dizzy, who is invited to Auradon at the end of the film, designs jewelry. The Auradon kids can commodify the experience of kids from the Isle, wearing clothes and accessories made by them, or doing their hair in the same way to appropriate the villain kids' experiences. King Ben even engages in poverty tourism when he goes to the Isle to look for Mal. He dresses as a villain kid to fit in, but the song he and the others sing is all about being "cool," suggesting that he is enjoying slumming it on the Isle. This commodification of the villain kids' experiences also leaves Mal feeling isolated. She says that she feels like a fraud and the resulting anxiety leads her to run away, kickstarting the movie's plot. Though *Descendants 2* ends with Mal pledging to be herself, none of her concerns are truly resolved, suggesting that this recognition of cultural difference was just in her head all along. In this way, the franchise commodifies impoverished children's experiences for the ruling class while suggesting that the psychological damage this may cause to poor children is unimportant. DCOMs often support the real world status quo by appearing to solve complicated social issues through group song and dance numbers or big speeches at the end of the film, and *Descendants 2* provides merely one example of this larger trend.

Since the *Descendants* franchise promotes a fairytale connection between inherited wealth and moral superiority, *Descendants 2* is not prepared to deal with structural issues of systemic poverty Uma raises, and so uses her connection to Ursula as a means of dismissing them and her. Uma's recognition of structural poverty is played off as jealousy and pride. Instead of allowing Uma to champion structural change and queer failure, the final act of *Descendants 2* echoes 1989's *The Little Mermaid*, making Uma sexual competition for the prince's affection. The Auradon Prep cotillion is on a royal yacht, giving Uma access to the ocean and paralleling the wedding scene from the end of *The Little Mermaid*. After Ben is announced, Uma appears in her teal gown, connecting her to the ocean and her mother. Ben and Uma waltz to an instrumental version of "Kiss the Girl" and Ben announces that Uma will be joining the court as his lady and as his gift to her he is bringing down the barrier between Auradon and the Isle. Though Uma wants to give other children from the Isle the same advantages as the Auradon kids, the movie undercuts this message and makes her unsympathetic by cutting to her pirate crew readying to pillage Auradon.

When Uma uses a love spell on Ben and then becomes a giant octopus monster, she does so out of anger and desperation, but her association with Ursula colors this moment, relegating her to an echo of her mother. In making Uma a literal monster, *Descendants 2* is able to dismiss her as a villain without having to seriously consider her queer desire for structural change or her frustration with the other villain kids in Auradon who have also not pushed for equality. Uma has potential as a leader, but by reducing her to sexual competition for Mal, the film sidelines her revolutionary qualities and makes her seem monstrous and unreasonable. As the two girls engage in what is essentially a slap fight, Ben intervenes as the voice of reason, jumping between the girls and shouting, "We have to listen and respect each other … help me make a difference" (Ortega 2017). *Descendants 2* allows the ruling white male character to be the better champion for equality than the two girls whose lived experience led them to challenge the system in the first place. As the movie ends with Mal and Ben's kiss and a dance number about how important it is to be yourself and embrace diversity, the structural change Uma sought is abandoned for Ben's plan to bring over a few more children selected by him. Even this change relies on Evie reminding Ben of his intentions to bring in more children and providing him with a list of names. In the end, the audience is supposed to be happy for the kids who are chosen, seeing them as the deserving poor, a designation granted by a benevolent ruling class.

Social Progress and the Disney Channel
Original Movie

Disney may be willing to embrace teen movie tropes by making the children of villains the focus of the franchise, but the films are not willing to advocate structural socio-economic change. By making Uma an advocate for the children of the Isle, Disney dictates that Uma cannot possibly win in the end because her victory would not only bleed over into a real-world anti-poverty advocacy, but it would also unbalance the entire fairytale narrative. The films may play with the idea of heroes and villains by making villain kid characters such as Mal and Evie more empathetic than Princess Audrey, but the franchise is not willing to scrap this separation entirely because that would call into question the entire Disney canon. Mal may be the daughter of a villain, but at the end of the movie, she is still a Disney princess, an identification that comes with 95 years of cultural baggage.

Descendants 2 is willing to undermine Uma's desire for social justice in favor of a marriage plot, and sacrifice both Uma and Mal's experiences on the Isle to the voice of upper-class White male authority. The *Descendants* franchise presents an opportunity for Disney to rewrite the narratives of the bodies that it has marked as queer, making their narratives more empathetic and injecting some moral relativism into the hero/villain dichotomy. Yet, ultimately, the series chooses to reinforce the imagery of earlier films by marking queer bodies such as Ursula and Uma as monsters and villains and dismissing their desires in favor of marketing a new princess, Mal. Though the influence of the teen movie genre may have pushed the plot of *Descendants* toward teen agency and social change, as the characters get older and settle into prescribed fairytale roles, *Descendants 2* chooses instead to largely maintain the status quo, relying on respectability politics and incremental change.[9]

Descendants 2's approach to anti-poverty advocacy perfectly demonstrates the limitations of DCOMs, and the Disney universe more broadly, in tackling social issues through narrative. *Descendants*, like any other Disney film or television show is a product that requires the buy-in of both audience and advertisers. If Uma were to win the day, and Auradon restructured its class system, getting rid of kings and queens and admitting that those with money and power are not morally superior, that film would likely not attract advertisers or sell licensed products such as Halloween costumes and dolls. *Descendants* is, at its core a vehicle for the promotion of capitalism through expanding the Disney brand. If the film also promotes social justice or diversity, that promotion is merely a marketing technique and not the film's core purpose. Since the company is unable to offer any meaningful economic critique, DCOMs would do well to avoid discussions of class altogether, but should certainly avoid aligning morality and class standing more than their existing fairytale narratives already imply.

Though DCOMS offer space for Disney to play with social justice narratives, in order to responsibly navigate such stories, Disney should be mindful of how it aligns multiple identities such as gender, race, and class onto a single character. While diverse casting is an important metric for DCOMs, visibility alone is not enough. Disney should certainly pay more attention to casting choices to avoid depictions of Black sexuality such as Audrey and Uma. Since DCOMS exist within the larger Disney framework of queer coded villains, these films also need to be aware of how they are representing queer bodies and take care not to consistently portray these characters as stock villains and sexual rivals. Marking one character as metaphor for sexual, economic, and racial diversity places an impossible burden on that character. When Uma fails, the representative of queer bodies also fails, the film's only Black character fails, and the crusader for economic equality fails. The audience applauds this failure because Uma is the villain, standing between the audience's avatar princess Mal, and her happily ever after. By making Uma the villain, *Descendants 2* requires the audience to root against the very social justice narratives that DCOMs champion, requiring tweens to support White male authority over queer failure and community building. Thus, what appears to be a story of acceptance in which the villain kids are redeemed becomes a story about preserving the status quo and championing the moral superiority of the wealthy, perhaps making the lessons of *Descendants 2* the most socially realistic of Disney's fairytale narratives.

NOTES

1. I could argue that these social justice themed films begin with *Monsters Inc.* in 2001, but for the purposes of this essay, and the centrality of the marriage narrative, I will limit the discussion to princess movies.

2. For examples, movies such as *Zenon: Girl of the 24th Century* (1999) and *The Color of Friendship* (2000) allow teen girl characters to challenge the adults around them on large social issues such as race and gender.

3. Examples of DCOMs that do this work include the *High School Musical* (2006) franchise and *Zombies* (2018), a film in which the main character quits the cheerleading team when she falls in love with a zombie. In these films, as in the *Descendants* franchise, thwarting adult or peer expectations makes up the plot. Teen characters must learn that what their parents or friends want for them is based on an outdated social model, and not, in fact, what they want for themselves.

4. Though not related to the Lord Alfred Douglas poem "Two Loves" (1894), the mermaid's choice to give up her voice as payment to the witch may remind contemporary readers of queer desire's Victorian designation as a "love which dare not speak its name."

5. The little mermaid must compete against Ursula's deadline and interference and then against Ursula herself. Even before Ursula appears as a human, she is sexual competition for the mermaid, attempting to distract Eric long enough to run out the clock.

6. Queer coding is documented by popular sources including TV Tropes and Quail Bell Magazine, as well as academic works such as Pauline and Dion Sheridan McLeod's *Unmasking the Quillain: Queerness and Villainy in Animated Disney Films.*

7. If *The Lion King*'s Scar, *Aladdin*'s Jafar, or *Tangled*'s Mother Gothel are coded as queer, then the audience understands these characters cannot be trusted to carry on a royal line. Queer coded characters cannot hold power because they will not produce heirs and would eventually cause political turmoil.

8. Though Disney reduces Ursula to a stock queer villain in the 1989 film, the company does perform some recovery to her image in the television show *Once Upon a Time* (2015). During the story arc beginning with the episode "Poor Unfortunate Soul," the show reveals that Ursula was manipulated by her father and turned herself into a monster in order to overpower him. After repairing her relationship with her father and regaining her singing voice, Ursula is no longer a villain in the series and happily returns to the ocean.

9. Despite its dismissal of Uma and her attempts at revolution, *Descendants 2* does create a powerful and motivated character who will not be easily ignored in the third installment of the franchise. Perhaps *Descendants 3* will finally allow *The Little Mermaid* to enact a fulfillment of queer desire in the form of structural change.

REFERENCES

Allen, B. (2001, May 20). The uses of enchantment. *New York Times*.

Andersen, H.C. (2018, March 21). *The Little Mermaid*. Retrieved from Hans Christian Andersen Fairytales and Stories. http://hca.gilead.org.il/li_merma.html.

Baker, D.J. (2010). Monstrous fairytales: towards an écriture queer. *Colloquy: Text, Theory, Critique*, 79–103.

Clements, R.A. (Director). (1989). *The Little Mermaid*. [Motion Picture].

Dhawan, N.E. (2015). *Global justice and desire: Queering economy*. New York: Routledge.

Greenhill, P. (2015). "The Snow Queen": Queer coding in male directors' films. *Marvels & Tales*, 110–134.

Halberstam, J. (2011). *The queer art of failure*. Durham: Duke University Press.

Jakobsen, J.R. (1998). Queer is? Queer does? Normativity and the problem of resistance. *GLQ: A Journal of Lesbian and Gay Studies*, 511–536.

Letters to and from Hans Christian Andersen. (1844–1898). Retrieved from *The Eclectic Magazine of Foreign Literature*. http://ezproxy.lib.uconn.edu/login?url=https://search-proquest-com.ezproxy.lib.uconn.edu/docview/89751564?accountid.

Lovaas, K.E. (2006). Shifting ground (s) surveying the contested terrain of LGBT studies and queer theory. *Journal of Homosexuality*, 1–18.

Malla, K.A. (2005). Between a frock and a hard place: Camp aesthetics and children's culture. *Canadian Review of American Studies*, 1–20.

McLeod, D.S. (2016). Unmasking the quillain: queerness and villainy in animated Disney films.

Ortega, K. (Director). (2015). *Descendants*. [Motion Picture].

Ortega, K. (Director). (2017). *Descendants 2*. [Motion Picture].

Pearlman, S. (2015, March 22). Poor Unfortunate Soul. *Once Upon a Time*, season 4, episode 16: ABC.

Sells, L. (1995). Where do the mermaids stand? Voice and body in The Little Mermaid. In L.S. Elizabeth Bell, *From mouse to mermaid: The politics of film, gender, and culture* (pp. 175–192). Bloomington: Indiana University Press.

About the Contributors

Dr. Colin **Ackerman** is a research associate at the Collaborative for Academic and Social Emotional Learning (CASEL). He works on the research-practice partnership team, aiming to bridge the gap between theory and practice. His research interests include digital technology's impact on citizenship development in the K–12 classroom and popular culture as public pedagogy. He earned his doctorate in media studies from the College of Media, Communication, and Information at the University of Colorado Boulder.

Michelle Anya **Anjirbag** is a Ph.D. candidate at the University of Cambridge. She also holds degrees from the University of Connecticut and the University of Edinburgh. Her research interests include the analysis of adaptations of fairy tales and folklore, focusing on cross-period and intergenerational approaches to narrative transmission across cultures and societies. Her research focuses on depictions of diversity in Disney's fairy tale adaptations from 1989 through the present.

Dr. Janelle **Applequist** is an associate professor of advertising in the Zimmerman School of Advertising & Mass Communications at the University of South Florida. Her research interests include qualitative research methods, pharmaceutical advertising, advertising, health communication, and patient and healthcare representations via advertising.

Dr. Sara **Austin** received her Ph.D. in English from the University of Connecticut and is a visiting assistant professor at Miami University in Ohio. Her research interests focus on race, gender, and childhood identity. Her work explores monstrosity as a cultural metaphor for child identity.

Dr. Andrea B. **Baker** teaches for the Communication Department at the University of Colorado Colorado Springs, where her focus is strategic communication. Her research interests span popular media and culture as well as political communication and online forums for civic discourse. She also worked for several years in the media industry as a journalist.

Dr. Christopher E. **Bell** is an associate professor of media studies in the Department of Communication at the University of Colorado Colorado Springs. He specializes in the study of popular culture, focusing on the ways in which race, class and gender intersect in different forms of children's media. He is a TED speaker, a diversity and inclusiveness consultant for Pixar Animation Studios and WarnerMedia, a 2017 David Letterman Award–winning media scholar, and the 2017 Denver Comic Con Popular Culture Educator of the Year.

Dr. Travis R. **Bell** is an assistant professor of digital and sports media in the Zimmerman School of Advertising & Mass Communications at the University of South Florida. His research focuses on the intersection of media, race, and sport, with an emphasis on media framing and social construction.

Dr. Cary **Elza** is assistant professor of media studies at the University of Wisconsin–Stevens Point, where she teaches courses on screenwriting, film and media analysis, history, and genre. She received her Ph.D. from Northwestern. Her publications include articles and chapters on children's and teen media, science fiction and fantasy series, new media and fandom, and early animation.

Julie **Estlick** is a graduate student at University of Colorado Colorado Springs. Her research interests focus on gender studies and feminist theory.

Sloan **Gonzales** is the Program Director of the Chancellor's Leadership Class and a lecturer in the Communication Department at the University of Colorado Colorado Springs. She specializes in intercultural communication, business communication, and leadership development. Her research focuses on the role identity plays in leadership development and how we communicate inclusively.

Angela M. **Guido** is a lecturer at University of Colorado Colorado Springs with an MA in communication. She is also a social media strategist who helps small businesses develop and grow their marketing plans across multiple platforms.

Rachel **Guldin** is a doctoral candidate of media studies in the School of Journalism and Communication at the University of Oregon. Her research interests include media literacy education, critical pedagogy, popular culture, children's media, and political economy of media. She is a former elementary and middle school teacher.

Marissa **Lammon** is a doctoral student at the University of Colorado Boulder, with a specialization in the study of psychological processes in children's media.

Claudia Lisa **Moeller** studied philosophy at University San Raffaele, in Milan, Italy. Her research interests include Kierkegaard, Hamann, and the hermeneutics of television.

Hanne **Murray** is a graduate student at the University of Colorado Colorado Springs, with interest in adolescent communication with an emphasis on the development and maintenance of identity. Her work focuses on examining popular culture to discover the imposed structures that reflect and perpetuate societal expectations.

Rebecca **Rowe** is a doctoral candidate at the University of Connecticut, where she studies children's literature and media and teaches courses in composition and popular culture. Her research includes the depiction of the human body, specifically in children's media, constructions of childhood, adaptation, and the Walt Disney Company.

Dr. Allison **Schottenstein** has a Ph.D. in American history from the University of Texas at Austin. She is an adjunct assistant professor of history at the University of Cincinnati, Blue Ash. She loves American popular culture and incorporates it into all her lectures. She has written book reviews for *Pop Matters*.

Jayne M. **Simpson** is a Ph.D. student in communication at the University of Colorado Boulder, and a graduate of the University of Colorado Colorado Springs, and the University of Texas at San Antonio. Although her scholarship focuses largely on sports organizations and communication, media studies remain her first "home" in communication.

Dr. J. Richard **Stevens** is an associate professor of media studies at the University of Colorado Boulder. His research delves into the intersection of ideological formation and media message dissemination, how cultural messages are formed and passed through popular culture, how technology infrastructure affects the delivery of media messages, and how media and technology platforms shape public discourse.

Dr. Terah J. **Stewart** is an assistant professor in the College of Human Sciences at Iowa State University, where he teaches courses related to equity, justice, and inclusion in higher education and student affairs. He studies college students and their relationships to media, pop culture, socio-politics, and media consumption, in addition to critical theory, experiences of Black people in the academy, fat-body politics, student activism, critical qualitative methodology, and power conscious approaches to research.

Dr. Daniel F. **Yezbick** is a professor of English and communications at Wildwood College in St. Louis, where he also serves as intercultural education coordinator and lead english faculty. He has also lectured and published widely on media, theater, material culture, and visual rhetoric.

Index